CONSTANTINE THE EMPEROR

Constantine the Emperor

David Potter

OXFORD
UNIVERSITY PRESS

OXFORD
UNIVERSITY PRESS

Oxford University Press is a department of the University of Oxford.
It furthers the University's objective of excellence in research, scholarship,
and education by publishing worldwide.

Oxford   New York

Auckland   Cape Town   Dar es Salaam   Hong Kong   Karachi
Kuala Lumpur   Madrid   Melbourne   Mexico City   Nairobi
New Delhi   Shanghai   Taipei   Toronto

With offices in

Argentina   Austria   Brazil   Chile   Czech Republic   France   Greece
Guatemala   Hungary   Italy   Japan   Poland   Portugal   Singapore
South Korea   Switzerland   Thailand   Turkey   Ukraine   Vietnam

Oxford is a registered trademark of Oxford University Press
in the UK and certain other countries.

Published in the United States of America by
Oxford University Press
198 Madison Avenue, New York, NY 10016

Library of Congress Cataloging-in-Publication Data

Potter, D. S. (David Stone), 1957-
Constantine the Emperor / David Potter.
p. cm.
Includes bibliographical references and index.
ISBN 978-0-19-975586-8 (acid-free paper)   1. Constantine I, Emperor of Rome,
d. 337.   2. Emperors—Rome—Biography.   3. Rome—History—Constantine I, the Great,
306-337.   4. Religion and state—Rome—History.   I. Title.
DG315.P68 2012
937'.08092—dc23
[B]
2012010280

ISBN 978–0–19–975586–8

1 3 5 7 9 8 6 4 2
Printed in the United States of America
on acid-free paper

CONTENTS

Contents

PREFACE

I T IS A PLEASURE to thank those who have played a role in making this book possible. First, that means, as always, my family, both here in Ann Arbor and in Norfolk, Connecticut, where this book began to take shape. Then too my colleagues in the Department of Classical Studies at the University of Michigan, whose congenial and collegial company makes it a pleasure to go to work, and whose willingness to alleviate my ignorance or question my certainty is perpetually engaging. I owe a great debt to the students at Michigan in whose suitably skeptical company I have been exploring the texts that form the basis for this book for many years. Finally, I owe special thanks to Lester Monts, Senior Vice Provost for Academic Affairs at the University of Michigan, whose generous support made it possible to undertake the work in Rome that was crucial to the completion of this book, and to Bill Martin, who has, over the years, shown me what it means to run a large and complex organization without losing sight of crucial values (something of which, I think, Constantine would approve). Pete Oas helped this book take shape on many genial mornings over coffee in the welcoming confines of the Expresso Royale on Plymouth Road in Ann Arbor; Maud Gleason was, as ever, a source of important advice, given her vast command of the intricacies of medical literature; Robert Lister and my colleague Ellen Muehlberger provided guidance in matters of the faith; and Laura McCullagh showed me how to think about Helena. It is also a pleasure to thank Professor Christopher Smith for sharing the hospitality of the British School at Rome, and Professor Greg Woolf for his generous assistance in helping me find my way around. It is also a pleasure to thank Dr. Andrew Meadows of the American Numismatic Society for his help with numismatic material. Harriet Fertig and Jessica Stephens offered a great deal of help at a late stage; the book is better for their careful reading and frank advice. Samantha Lash, Jonathan McLaughlin, and Tiggy Talarico provided a great deal of important help with the final proofs, for which I am also extremely grateful.

Stefan Vranka at Oxford University Press suggested this project to me and has provided excellent advice throughout. Most important, in helping me follow that advice, has been the absolutely fantastic editorial work undertaken by Sue Phillpott. Her efficiency and judgment are outstanding; without her work this book would be very different. I am also very grateful to two leading Constantinian scholars of our time, Hal Drake and Noel Lenski, for sharing their work with me in advance of publication. Molly Morrison has managed the production of this book with impressive efficiency.

Finally, it is a great pleasure to dedicate this book to two very dear friends who have helped me navigate the ancient and modern worlds for the last three decades. This book then is dedicated to Robin Lane Fox and John Matthews.

ABBREVIATIONS

Act. Ab.	*Passio sanctorum Dativi, Saturnini presbyteri et alio-rum.* (*Acts of the Abitinean Martyrs*)
Gesta con. Carth.	*Gesta Collationis Carthaginiensis cum Donatistis,* AD 411 (*Acts of the Council of Carthage with the Donatists in 411*)
Amm.	Ammianus Marcellinus, Latin historian, 4th century AD
Apul. *Met.*	Apuleius of Madaura, Latin prose writer, 2nd century AD, *Metamorphoses,* or *The Golden Ass*
Aristid. *Or.*	Aelius Aristides, Greek orator, 2nd century AD, *Orations*
Artem. *On.*	Artemidorus Daldianus, author of a work on dream interpretation, 2nd century AD, *Onirocriticus* (*The Interpretation of Dreams*)
Ath.	Athanasius, bishop of Alexandria, 4th century AD
Apol. Contra Ar.	*Apologia contra Arianos* (*Defense against the Arians*)
Epist. ad *ep. Aeg. et Lib.*	*Epistula ad episcopos Aegypti et Libyae* (*Encyclical Letter to the Bishops of Egypt and Libya*)
Hist. Ar.	*Historia Arianorum ad Monachos* (*History of the Arians for the Monks*)
De synod.	*De Synodis* (*Concerning the Councils of the Church*)
Aug.	Augustine of Hippo, bishop and writer, AD 354–430
Ad Donat.	*Ad Donatistas post collationem* (*Against the Donatist party after the Council*)
Breviculus	*Breviculus collationis cum Donatistis* (*Summary of the Council with the Donatists*)

C. Cresc.	*Contra Cresconium (Against Cresconius)*
C. Parm.	*Contra epistulam Parmeniani (Against the Letter of Parmenian)*
C. litt. Petil.	*Contra litteras Petiliani (Against the Letters of Petilianus)*
Ep.	*Epistulae (Letters)*
Aur. Vict., *De Caes.*	Aurelius Victor, Latin historian, 4th century CE, *De Caesaribus (Concerning the Emperors)*
[Aur. Vict.] *Epit.*	Pseudo Aurelius Victor, Latin historian, 4th century CE, *Epitome De Caesaribus (Short History Concerning the Emperors)*
Chron. Pasc.	*Chronicon Paschale (Easter Chronicle)*, chronicle of world history from Creation to ca. AD 630
Const. *Orat.*	Constantine, emperor AD 306–337, *Oratio ad Sanctos (Speech to the Assembly of the Holy)*
Cyp. *Ep.*	Cyprian, bishop of Carthage, AD 249–258, *Epistulae (Letters)*
Dio	Cassius Dio, Greek historian of Rome, ca. 164–after AD 229
Epiph. *Pan.*	Epiphanius of Salamis, Christian writer 4th–5th centuries AD, *Panarion (Medicine Chest)*
Eunap. *VP*	Eunapius of Sardis, Greek sophist and historian, 4th century CE, *Vitae Philosopharum (Lives of the Philosophers)*
Eunap.	Eunapius, *History*, ed. Blockley
Euseb.	Eusebius of Caesarea, bishop and scholar, ca. AD 260–339
HE	*Historia Ecclesiastica (Ecclesiastical History)*
LC	*De Laudibus Constantini (In Praise of Constantine)*
MP	*Martyrs of Palestine*
VC	*Vita Constantini (Life of Constantine)*
Eutrop. *Brev.*	Eutropius, Latin historian, 4th century AD, *Breviarium ab urbe condita (Brief History of Rome from its Foundation)*
Festus, *Brev.*	Festus, Latin historian, 4th century AD, *Breviarium (Brief History)*

Firm Mat. *Math.*	Firmicius Maternus, 4th-century AD writer in astrology and religion, *Mathesis*
Fronto, *Ant.*	M. Cornelius Fronto, orator and tutor of Marcus Aurelius, ca. 95–ca. 166 CE, *Letters to Antoninus Pius*
GL	*Grammatici Latini*
HA	*Historia Augusta*, anon. history of Rome, 4th or 5th century CE
Aurelian	*Life of Aurelian*
Cari, Carini et Num.	*Lives of Carus, Carinus and Numerian*
Herod.	Herodian, Greek historian of Rome, 3rd century AD, *History of the Empire from the Time of Marcus*
Jord. *Get.*	Jordanes, historian of the 6th century AD, *Getica* (*History of the Goths*)
Jos. *BJ*	Josephus, 1st century AD, *Bellum Judaicum* (*Jewish War*)
Jul.	Julian "the Apostate," Emperor 361–363 CE
Caes.	*Caesares*
Or.	*Orations*
Lact.	Lactantius, Christian apologist, ca. AD 240–ca. AD 320,
DMP	*de Mortibus Persecutorum* (*Concerning the Deaths of the Persecutors*)
DI	*Insitutes Divinae* (*Divine Institutes*)
Lib. *Or.*	Libanius, Greek rhetorician, AD 314–ca. AD 393, *Orations*
Lk	*The Gospel According to Luke*
Luc.	Lucian of Samosata, Greek prose writer, b. c. 120 AD
Alex.	*Alexander the False Prophet*
Nigr.	*Nigrinus*
M. *Theod.*	*Martyrdom of Saint Theodotus of Ancyra*
Mal.	John Malalas, Greek chronographer, ca. AD 490–570s, *Chronographia* (*Chronicle*)
Marc. Aurel. *Med.*	Marcus Aurelius, Roman emperor AD 161–180, *Meditations*
Opt. *Tract.*	Optatus of Milevis, *Against the Donatists*
Or.	*Origo Constantini imperatoris* (*Descent of the Emperor Constantine*)

Or. *C. Cels.*	Origen, Alexandrian priest and scholar, probably AD 184/5–254/5, *Contra Celsum* (*Against Celsus*)
Oros. *Contra Pagan.*	Orosius, Christian Roman historian of the 5th century AD, *Historia Contra Paganos* (*History against the Pagans*)
P. Ath.	*Passion of Athenogenes*
Pan.	*Latin Panegyrics*
Pet. Patr.	Petrus Patricius, *Historiae* (*Histories,* ed. Müller *FGH*)
Philostr.	Philostratus of Athens, Greek sophist and writer, d. c. AD 244–249
VA	*Vita Apollonii* (*In honor of Apollonius of Tyana*)
VS	*Vitae Sophistarum* (*Lives of the Sophists*)
Phil. *HE*	Philostorgius, Christian writer 5th century AD, *Historia Ecclesiastica* (*Ecclesiastical History*)
Plin. *HN*	Pliny the Elder, Roman politician and scholar, AD 23/4–79, *Historia Naturalis* (*Natural History*)
Plin. *Ep.*	Pliny the Younger, Roman politician, ca. AD 61–ca. AD 12, *Epistulae* (*Letters*)
Procop. *Aed.*	Procopius, Greek historian, 6th century AD, *De Aedificiis* (*Concerning Buildings*)
Socr. *HE*	Socrates of Constantinople, Greek historian, 5th century AD, *Historia Ecclesiastica* (*Ecclesiastical History*)
Soz. *HE*	Sozomen, Greek historian, 5th century AD, *Historia Ecclesiastica* (*Ecclesiastical History*)
Suet. *Jul.*	Suetonius, Latin biographer, ca. AD 70–ca. AD 130, *Life of Julius Caesar*
T. Theos.	*Theosophiae Tubingensis* (*Tübingen Theosophy*)
Tac. *Agr.*	Tacitus, Roman historian, ca. AD 56–after ca. AD 118, *Agricola*
Theod. *HE*	Theodoret, Christian historian 5th century AD, *Historia Ecclesiastica* (*Ecclesiastical History*)
Theoph. *Chron.*	Theophanes, *Chronographia* (chronicle of world history from AD 284–813)
Zon.	Johannes Zonaras, Byzantine historian, 12th century AD, *Epitome of the Histories from the Creation to 1118*

Zos.	Zosimus, Greek historian, late 5th–6th century AD, *New History*

Documentary and Legal Texts

D.	*Digesta* (*The Digest*, massive survey of Roman juristic writing from the time of Justinian, 6th century AD)
CIL	*Corpus Inscriptionum Latinarum*
CJ	*Codex Justinianus*
CTh	*Codex Theodosianus*
Coll.	*Collatio Legum Mosaicarum et Romanarum* (*Comparison of the Laws of Moses and the Romans*)
Consult.	*Consultatio* (*Consultation*; advice from a jurist to an advocate)
Frag. Vat.	*Fragmenta Vaticana* (*Vatican Fragments*; quotations of Roman legal texts preserved in a Vatican manuscript)
IGBR	*Inscriptiones Graecae in Bulgaria Repertae*
ILS	*Inscriptiones Latinae Selectae*
IRT	*Inscriptions of Roman Tripolitania*
PE	*Price edict* ed. Lauffer
P. Bon.	*Papyri Bononienses*, ed. O. Montevecchi. Milan 1953
P. Oslo	*Papyri Osloenses*. Oslo.
P. Oxy.	*The Oxyrhynchus Papyri*
P. Panop. Beatty	*Papyri from Panopolis in the Chester Beatty Library Dublin*, ed. T.C. Skeat. Dublin 1964
PSI	*Papiri greci e latini.* (Pubblicazioni della Società Italiana per la ricerca dei papiri greci e latini in Egitto)
P. Ryl.	*Catalogue of the Greek and Latin Papyri in the John Rylands Library, Manchester.*
Select Papyri	*Select Papyri* (The Loeb Classical Library).
TAM	*Tituli Asiae Minoris*

Reference Works

FGH	*Fragmenta Graecorum Historicorum* (ed. Müller)
FGrH	*Die Fragmente der grieschischen Historiker* (ed. Jacoby)

PIR²	*Prosopographia Imperii Romani* (2nd edition)
PLRE	*The Prosopography of the Later Roman Empire*

Journals

AJA	*American Journal of Archaeology*
AJP	*American Journal of Philology*
AS	*Anatolian Studies*
AugStud	*Augustinian Studies*
BICS	*Bulletin of the Institute of Classical Studies*
BMCR	*Bryn Mawr Classical Review*
BZ	*Byzantinische Zeitschrift*
HTR	*Harvard Theological Review*
GRBS	*Greek, Roman and Byzantine Studies*
JEH	*Journal of Ecclesiastical History*
JLA	*Journal of Late Antiquity*
JQR	*Jewish Quarterly Review*
JRS	*Journal of Roman Studies*
JTS	*Journal of Theological Studies*
MAAR	*Memoirs of the American Academy in Rome*
MEFRA	*Mélanges de l'École Française de Rome*
PBSR	*Papers of the British School at Rome*
RhM	*Rheinisches Museum für Philologie*
ZPE	*Zeitschrift für Papyrologie und Epigraphik*

MAP OF THE ROMAN EMPIRE

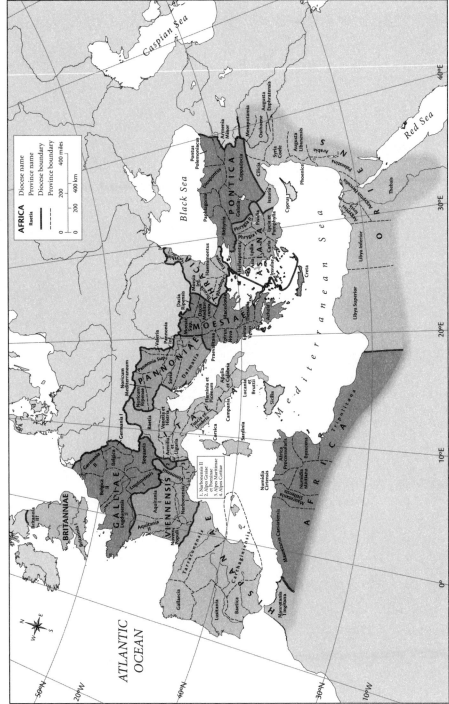

INTRODUCTION

THE ROMAN EMPEROR CONSTANTINE changed the world. For many mil-
lions of people across this planet, an institution that he introduced and
promoted has become a central part of their lives; they use or hear words that he
approved. In the twenty-first century, Constantine is best known as the Roman
emperor who converted to Christianity and in so doing made it possible for
Christianity to become a world religion. Without Constantine, Christianity
probably would not occupy the place that it does today. Without him it is unlikely
that Christianity would have emerged from the mass of conflicting, if often quite
similar, belief systems coexisting in the empire into which he was born. Even if
there are fewer practicing Christians than there were a couple of generations
ago, the immense impact of Christian thought upon the behaviors and thinking
of the many generations who came after Constantine makes it very difficult to
imagine a world without it. When he was born around AD 282, it would have
been far easier to imagine a world in which Christianity had a marginal place.

Constantine's father Constantius was a member of the Tetrarchy (gang of
four) otherwise known as the college of four emperors assembled by the emperor
Diocletian, in whose court Constantine spent his late teens and early twenties.
Diocletian would remain one of the crucial influences in Constantine's life. His
attitude toward the older man was ambivalent: often he reacted against things
he had seen Diocletian do, but almost as often, he adapted Diocletian's practices for his own purposes; much of his later career was shaped by Diocletian's
strongly held opinion that sons should not succeed their fathers into the "imperial college."

Diocletian retired as emperor in 305, and Constantius died in office in 306.
As the result of a coup launched by Constantine and Constantius' generals on

the day that Constantius died, Constantine became emperor. Initially ruler of just a part of the empire—Britain, France, and Spain—he gradually took over the whole of it through a series of civil wars. The first, in 312, ended with his takeover of Italy and Africa after defeating his brother-in-law, Maxentius, at the battle of the Milvian Bridge on the Tiber outside Rome. It was in the course of this campaign that Constantine became a Christian. At the time that I am writing, the 1700th anniversary of this event is rapidly approaching.

The next round of civil wars ended in 324 when he defeated Licinius (also his brother-in-law), who had once ruled the vast arc of lands running from modern Croatia to Egypt. In the wake of this victory he founded Constantinople, modern Istanbul, on the site of the ancient city of Byzantium. For the next thirteen years with the assistance of a group of experienced officials he ran the whole empire, virtually recreating the collective government of Diocletian.

Constantine lived his entire life within the imperial court, which he saw as the central institution of Roman life. He believed that the emperor's job was to defend the empire from external foes while creating a more just and ordered society for his subjects; he can often be seen acting on those principles. At the same time, his powerful personality led him to commit acts of violence against those closest to him. A deeply complex man of seemingly boundless energy, Constantine was remembered in later generations not only as the first Christian emperor, but as the emperor who shaped the future course of the Roman world.

In the modern world, Constantine tends to be seen as a somewhat less complex character. Although many people may not be aware of Constantine's role in creating the Nicene Creed that they might recite on a Sunday morning, or associate him with the words "We believe in One God, the Father Almighty, maker of Heaven and Earth," those are his words and they do reflect his belief in God. Otherwise we may encounter him in many places throughout Europe and the Middle East. We meet him at the great arch that stands in the heart of modern Rome commemorating his victory over Maxentius at the battle of the Milvian Bridge. So too we can still see churches built on his orders in Rome—San Giovanni on the Lateran and Santa Croce in Gerusalemme—and in its vicinity. In the Pio Clementine Vatican Museum we may view the sarcophagus that was once designed to hold his body (it actually held the body of his mother Helena, in its original location in the mausoleum hard by the modern church of Santi Marcellino e Pietro ad Duas Lauros). In Turkey we might recall that Istanbul was for many centuries Constantinople. If we go to York in England we will see his statue outside the cathedral, which may have been built atop the very building that served as his headquarters on the day he became emperor. Wonderfully displayed in the Cleveland Museum of Art is a magnificent gold pendant that was part of a massive decoration that Constantine probably handed to one of his most senior officials.[1] If we visit Trier we can see the remains of the palace that he occupied for a half dozen years before he went to Rome, and in Jerusalem we can still visit the Church of the Holy Sepulcher, on the site of the church he ordered to be built. In many museums we will see the image of Constantine staring at the sign of a cross in the sky, inscribed with the words "In this Sign Conquer." It is by far the most popular story of how he came to be a Christian, and so it is his Christianity that dominates our picture of the man today.

While our tendency to see the significance of Constantine's life in terms of his confessional choice is reasonable, this was not always the way Constantine himself would have seen it. For him, the conversion of his empire to Christianity was at first neither a primary goal nor a foreseeable outcome. He approved if his subjects joined him in his faith, but they were far more important to him *as subjects*. Constantine's aim was first and foremost to wield more power than anyone else in the world and the exercise of that power was his paramount concern. He understood that power needed to be negotiated, that people needed to be convinced rather than commanded, that they needed to accept his leadership, that they could not be shifted too far from where their moral compass pointed.

The assertions that I make here depend upon a particular reading of the sources for Constantine's reign, and those sources are sufficiently diverse to allow a variety of interpretations in the centuries that separate his life from ours. In general, these either focus on his religious life or on his administrative habits. All of these sources are to some degree problematic, either because the narrative they offer—when they offer a narrative at all—is highly colored by partisan passion, or because they give us snapshots of the emperor in action that need to be viewed against a complex background: a background that itself must be constructed from documents of many sorts, from works of art, from buildings, from information gleaned about careers that are often incompletely known, and from study of the way people at various levels interacted with each other.

The story that follows falls into eight parts. In the first three I describe the world into which Constantine was born and the influences to which he reacted. In the subsequent sections, I tell his story through the sources as they were written rather than reading backward from the end of his life, seeking to show how he governed and to identify the people with whom he worked most closely. By placing Constantine within the institutions of the Roman state at the time that he was born, and looking at the circumstances that shaped those institutions in the decades before he was born, I hope to reveal a man who did indeed change the world and who did so in ways that may not have been quite those that he intended.

I

IMPERIAL RESURRECTION

1.

THE CRISIS OF AD 260

I N THE EARLY SUMMER of AD 260, Sapor, the emperor of Persia, stepped on the back of Publius Licinius Valerianus, formerly emperor of Rome, to mount his horse. Or so it was alleged. What is beyond doubt is that Valerian, as he is more commonly known these days, had fallen captive to Sapor outside the city of Edessa in southwestern Turkey. A persistent rumor claimed that Valerian had been betrayed by his senior subordinates. That too may be true.

The empire at the time of Valerian's capture stretched from Britain in the west to the Euphrates and the Jordanian desert in the east. Hadrian's wall defined the empire's northern boundary in Britain, while the Rhine and Danube were essentially the northern frontier from the North Sea to the Black Sea with one significant salient north of the Danube in the region of modern Romania. The Sahara defined the southern limit of the empire's North African provinces, and the island fortress of Elephantine, just north of the Nile's first cataract, was the boundary in Egypt. Although the peoples of the empire were as diverse in those years as are the residents of these regions in the twenty-first century, two languages enabled communication across these vast territories: Latin in the west—the area including England, Wales, France, Spain, Italy, southern Germany, Austria, Hungary, Croatia, Serbia, Romania, Morocco, Tunisia, Algeria, and Egypt—and Greek in the east—roughly modern Albania, Greece, Bulgaria, Turkey, Syria, Lebanon, Israel, Jordan, and Egypt. Across their borders, the Romans faced generally hostile populations, of whom the most significant were the Franks and Alemanni, confederations of the Germanic peoples north of the Rhine, and, along the Danube, confederations of other Germanic peoples, of whom the most powerful would be the Goths. Sapor's Persian state comprised modern Iran and Iraq and some territory now incorporated into the Central

FIGURE 1.1

The triumph of Sapor. Sapor I of Persia is celebrated in this relief at the sacred site of Naqsh-e Rustam in modern Iran for his victories over three Roman emperors, one of whom, Valerian, kneels before him. Source: Jenn Finn.

Asian Republics. To govern his lands and keep the empire's enemies at bay, an emperor depended upon an aura of invincibility and the loyalty of senior officials who agreed to subordinate their ambitions to his own.

The consequences of Valerian's capture were dire (see figure 1.1).[1] But it is also the case that if the empire had not been shaken to its core in 260, the major actors in this book—Diocletian and his colleagues, then Constantine and his contemporaries—would most likely never have had the opportunity to prove their mettle. The Roman Empire of Valerian was still a deeply conservative institution in which power resided with members of families that had long histories in government. Diocletian and Constantine may not even have come from families with long histories as Roman citizens much less as aristocrats.

In the months after Valerian's capture, the Roman Empire split into roughly three parts. France, southern Germany, Spain, and Britain declared fealty to the commanding general on the Rhine, who had risen in revolt and murdered the surviving son of Gallienus, the son of Valerian who had shared power with his father. In the east, those subordinates suspected of betraying Valerian swiftly set up a regime to challenge Gallienus while at the same time offering some resistance to Sapor's armies as they ravaged the cities of southern Turkey. The

Persian assault enhanced the damage done eight years before when Sapor had destroyed another Roman army and sacked Antioch in Syria, the principal city of the region. In the wake of the sack of Antioch a gentleman of Emesa (the modern Homs in Syria) named Uranius Antoninus had raised a force to resist the Persians, calling upon the local god, Elagabal (another character who will play a large part in the story that follows), who resided in the form of a meteorite in the city's principal temple. Uranius Antoninus is mainly known to us now through a few lines in a contemporary oracle, and from the garbled account of a later historian, as well as from coins minted on his behalf. From these scant remains we may glean that he had some success, and his career exemplifies the point that powerful local forces could be gathered to support—or resist—those of an emperor.

Far better known to us is Odaenathus, lord of Palmyra, the great trading city in the Syrian desert, who rose up to fight the Persians in 260. He rallied the forces of his city, long enriched by the caravan trade, and proved a fierce foe to the Persians, inflicting severe defeats upon them as they withdrew from Roman territory; he continued to attack them as his new Roman ally, one Macrianus, attempted to enforce his claim to the throne of the empire for his sons by invading the territory of Gallienus in 262.

Gallienus had survived the Gallic rebellion, the disgrace of his father's capture, and two revolts in the Balkans, this too in the year 260. He made short work of Macrianus, and, when Odaenathus disposed of his former allies' surviving supporters in the east, Gallienus recognized him as the chief administrative authority in the region. Odaenathus appears to have been delighted, placing his new Roman title of *corrector* on par with the title he awarded himself after further victories over the Persians at a ceremony outside Antioch: that title was King of Kings, which was also the traditional title of the king of Persia. By the end of that summer the Roman Empire was blessed with an emperor based in Rome, an emperor in Trier in Germany, and a King of Kings in Palmyra serving as *corrector* of the east.[2]

Divided government was nothing new to the Roman Empire, which could be governed by a single person only under extraordinary circumstances. It was Augustus who had founded the imperial system within which Gallienus worked, and after his victory over Antony and Cleopatra in 30 BC, he had ruled as the leader of a coterie whom he had gathered to himself during the civil wars that began with the murder of Julius Caesar in 44 BC. As his principal compatriots died off, Augustus had shaped a system of succession whereby each generation would produce several heirs designate. At his death in AD 14 his adopted son Tiberius, who had been his effective co-ruler for several years, succeeded him. Other arrangements followed, often depending on particular circumstances. At times, groups of favorites could be identified as playing the role of a cabinet that managed most of the day-to-day affairs; at others, as in the time of Marcus Aurelius (AD 161–180), a specific co-emperor was named.

Collective government meant that it was possible for children to hold the titular position of emperor—Nero (AD 54–68), for instance, was only seventeen when he took the throne, and several of the emperors in the decades before Valerian's reign had been even younger. When he seized the throne after a brief civil war in AD 253, Valerian had associated Gallienus with himself as co-emperor and Gallienus' sons had served as deputy emperors until their untimely deaths around the year 260. Moreover it was not without precedent for an emperor to be on dreadful terms with a co-claimant. Septimius Severus, who took the throne in 193, had first shared power with a rival for several years before destroying him in a bloody civil war.

What made Gallienus' position unusual was not that he was associated with other significant authority figures, but rather, the state of his army. The Roman army that existed before 250 had been organized into units of heavy infantrymen (legions), numbering roughly 5,000 men when near full strength; they were supported by independent units—called cohorts comprising infantry or combined infantry and cavalry, and *alae*, or wings, if of cavalry alone. The army was recruited from across the empire, though with a tendency to favor troops from border regions or from military families. To be a soldier was a very fine thing. They were well paid, honored as partners in government, and often free to supplement their incomes by extracting "protection money" from civilians, or simply making off with their property. Since the time of Augustus they had enjoyed significant privileges upon retirement: chiefly immunity from taxation for themselves and their families and exemption from the public services that were required of most people of standing within a community. Soldiers, with their generous benefits, were men of some standing.

The immunities they enjoyed were a feature of the way rank was expressed in the Roman world. In theory, every man (women were not supposed to participate in the males' spheres of public life, and they were never allowed to vote even in Classical states that were theoretically democratic) had duties to fulfill in accordance with his status in society. This was a principle of great antiquity both at Rome and in the Greek city-states, whose constitutions and concepts of citizenship were in some ways similar, and it exercised a profound influence over social organization throughout the empire. According to this theory, those at the bottom of the social scale were either slaves or manual laborers, or tenant farmers paying rent to the people whose land they farmed. As more humble folk (*humiliores*) they could not hold office and in most places could not vote; if they were charged with a crime they could be tortured into confessing their guilt during their trial and were subject to far harsher legal penalties than their betters. In addition there were free peasants, also regarded as among the humble, as were most shopkeepers and small-business owners.

People everywhere were assessed for taxation both on their persons and on any land that they worked (for tenant farmers taxes were included in their rent); they were also taxed on certain financial transactions. For people who owned enough land not to have to work, or for businessmen who employed others, the setup was different. Such people might be known as "respectable sorts" (*honestiores*) if they were members of the local curial class—the class that could hold office and serve on the city council. Eligibility for membership of a group like this was not set by any specific criteria: as one man put it in words that were as true when he uttered them in the sixth century as they would have been in the fourth, "A man who was great at Gaza would be of the middling sort at Caesarea, a peasant at Antioch and poor in Constantinople."

Whatever their actual wealth, members of the curial classes, in addition to being taxed, were expected to pay for the public services needed to keep their community running. Some of these jobs were prestigious and rated as "honors"—for instance, the public priesthoods, especially the priesthood of the local version of the imperial cult, and administrative positions such as, in Latin, *duumvir*, one member of a board of two men who served as joint mayors, or *curator*, also, essentially, a mayor. Other jobs were grubby such as street cleaning and keeping the sewers in order; or dangerous such as the role of police chief; or unpleasant like making sure that people did not cheat each other in the marketplace; expensive such as funding games, or immensely time-consuming such as serving as a tutor for orphaned children, a task that involved managing the property of these children and making basic legal decisions on their behalf. Such services were seen as "gifts" to the people of the community and were known as *munera* (sing. *munus*) in Latin and *philanthropeia* in Greek.

The performance of these jobs was essential for maintaining the structures of urban life, and they were divided into three categories. Tasks classified as "personal" were those that people were supposed to perform "by mental application and bodily labor" without financial damage to themselves; "patrimonial" services required expenditure drawn from one's property; "mixed" duties were plainly the most irritating category, since such tasks were both expensive and time-consuming.[3] Those who performed tasks directly related to the government of the empire or to the advancement of civilization (a basic purpose of Roman imperial government, at least in theory) tended to be immune from civic *munera*. As time passed, the urge to acquire immunity from such duties became a routine feature of civic life. Germane to obtaining this immunity was the ability to land a position in the imperial rather than the civic administration—called, significantly, *militiae*, once a term that meant variously "abroad," or "military service," and by the time of Gallienus, any sort of "government service." Once in that service, whether as soldier or as bureaucrat, the ability to secure immunities depended on one's rank and branch of service. For a soldier serving in the emperor's guard the basic term of service was sixteen years, in the legions it was twenty, and in the auxiliary forces twenty-five. As the length of service suggests, the ideal Roman army was rather middle aged, with the average age for a soldier around twenty-eight (assuming that the typical recruit was eighteen). The age structure of the army reflected a sense that what made the army good was hard training and length of service.

Gallienus' biggest problem was that there were not all that many soldiers left at his disposal who would be in line to acquire the cherished immunities: the heavy losses of recent years meant that the Roman preference for legions filled with experienced soldiers was unrealizable. About a third of the Roman army had passed under the control of the rival empire in Gaul. About a quarter of the army, the part that had been stationed on the eastern frontier, was dead, in Persian captivity, serving with Odaenathus, or somewhat suspect for having served under Macrianus. That left Gallienus dependent on the imperial guard, stationed in Italy, and the troops of the Balkan army. It was the alliance that began to develop in these years between leaders of the Balkan armies, including men who might not have expected to rise to the highest commands in the Roman state, and of the traditional governing class—wealthy members of the imperial Senate from Italy, Africa, and the eastern provinces, people who traditionally held provincial governorships and other high offices—that would shape the future of the Roman empire. After Gallienus there would not be another Roman emperor from an Italian aristocratic family until the fifth century AD.[4]

We can't now know to what extent Gallienus or those around him were aware that fundamental changes would be necessary if the imperial regime was to survive, but fundamental change began to occur in the 250s and 260s, and one of the most significant contexts in which it occurred was religion.

Decius (reigned 249–251) and Valerian had both taken rather extreme positions about the relationship between the empire and the gods, possibly in response to the perception, fueled by repeated military failure, that something was very wrong in that respect. In Decius' case the immediate background was a civil war, which he had won, after a series of military actions the results of which had been at best ambivalent, and concerns stirred by his predecessor's celebration of Rome's 1000th birthday (there were those who thought that the arrival of a new millennium might portend catastrophic change). So it was, shortly after becoming emperor in 249, that Decius had issued an edict (a general order) commanding all Roman citizens and members of their families to sacrifice and then to obtain a certificate stating that they had done so by a specific date—probably a certain number of days after the edict was received by the local authorities responsible for drawing up the certificates and managing the actual sacrifices. Certificates surviving on papyri were clearly produced by official scribes to be signed by people as they made their sacrifices and by those who came with them to witness the act. The thinking behind the decree, whose implementation depended on the record-keeping apparatus of the tax system, seems to have been somewhat similar to that of an edict of Caracalla (ruled from 211 to 216) in which citizenship was granted to most inhabitants of the empire so that they could share in his joy at having been spared from "terrible danger"—a euphemism generated by his hatred for his younger brother whom he had had murdered in the arms of their mother. In both cases the people of the empire would join their ruler in celebrating what he saw as an important success and in correcting the errors of the past.

There is no obvious reason for thinking that the edict was motivated by a desire to eradicate the very small number who believed they formed a community distinct from believers in the traditional gods and whose consciences would prevent them from sacrificing. Records of the execution of Christians, the group in question, at this time suggest that they would be allowed to go about their business if they performed the sacrifice, and that many Christians did just this.[5] In some communities, though, terrible conflict arose about how best to respond to the imperial order, as arguments for conscientious resistance were countered by the argument that if persecution came from the Devil, it was best avoided.

Valerian presented a much more serious problem than Decius had. He appears already to have been hostile to Christians when he seized the throne in 253, and four years later he issued an edict that attempted to force them to conform to the religion of Rome. His main concern seems to have been obedience, for when he ordered the arrest of prominent Christians, he also allowed them, if they sacrificed, to be set free. Exile or imprisonment were the punishments for failure to conform. At the same time, he banned meetings of Christian congregations and deprived them of the use of their cemeteries. His order went beyond Decius' edict on sacrifices in singling Christians out, but not so far as the numerous bans on cults that had been imposed throughout Roman history in that it did not order the cult's demise; people were clearly puzzled.

The Senate accordingly asked Valerian what they should do with people who had been imprisoned for noncompliance. Valerian's response was brutal. Leading Christian men who persisted in their practice (he notes that there were senators among their number) were to have their property confiscated, and if they afterwards persevered in their beliefs, they would be executed. Christian women of high standing, too, would have their property confiscated, and members of the palace bureaucracy were to be sent to the mines as slaves. The edict remained in force until Valerian's capture by Sapor, and one of the first acts of the Christian community at Rome when the news of his fate arrived was to elect a new bishop.

In 262 Gallienus officially reversed his father's policy, issuing an edict of his own whereby Christians were guaranteed freedom to worship as they wished and restoring confiscated property.[6] For the next forty years emperors would treat Christianity as a religion like any other legal religion in their empire.

A second change concerned the shape of the army. At some point—certainly before the mid-260s—a new cavalry force came into being that appears to have been designed as an elite central reserve. The men associated with the command of this unit in our admittedly rather pathetic sources for the period all come from outside the traditional aristocracy. At the same time, the customary dominance of the legion—hitherto commanded by members of the Senate—as the primary tactical force began to erode. Again the process is unclear, but what we do know is that soldiers cease to be depicted wearing the heavy metal armor of earlier centuries in favor of leather armor, and they appear to have adopted spears or lances as their primary weapon in place of the heavy javelins and short swords of earlier eras. Indeed, all the soldiers of this new model army look much more like members of auxiliary units in the old army, which were smaller and capable of more varied tactical deployment than were the legions.

Thus in the handling of both religion and the military, the reign of Gallienus reflects significant change from the previous decades. The devaluation of the legion seems also to have had a significant effect on the nature of the imperial government, as commands that were once prized by members of the Senate were downgraded or even eliminated. According to later tradition this resulted from an edict issued by Gallienus, but in fact it reflected shifts in the way the empire was governed that were accelerated in the wake of Valerian's demise.

In the centuries between Augustus and the accession of Gallienus, a system of imperial government developed in which administrative function and social class had been closely aligned. Unlike local government where eligibility for office was locally determined, imperial government insisted on precise wealth qualifications. To be a member of the Senate, a person needed to have property valued at a minimum of 1,200,000 *sesterces*, a sum that at the end of the first century AD would produce an income roughly seventy-two times that of a soldier in the legions, and the vast majority of senators had property well in excess of the minimum. Then one needed to make a good impression on people and—unless one was spectacularly well connected—hold minor administrative or military positions in one's early twenties. A young man who shone in this department could acquire his first senatorial office in his mid-twenties and thereafter a fairly regular series of positions would give him experience in military, financial, and judicial affairs. If he continued to succeed at this stage he could expect to hold a praetorship in his mid to late thirties (there were sixteen praetors each year compared to the twenty-five quaestorships, the post of fiscal adjutant that was the entry-level position for the Senate). After that he would take up a series of posts, which would likely include the command of a legion and the governorship of a province.

Success in military command and provincial administration, the respect of colleagues, and a certain amount of diplomatic skill in dealing with the imperial court could result in promotion to consulship, once the chief office of state. By the third century there might typically be eight consuls in any given year, holding office in pairs for three-month periods. The first pair, which might well include the emperor and an heir apparent or an especially favored individual who was being honored with a second consulship, was the "ordinary" consulship, in that the consuls in this group gave their name to the year. The other pairs were known as "suffect" or replacement consuls. After holding a consulship a man would be in line for a major provincial governorship, possibly including command of a substantial army, and various other important jobs. The culmination of a career like this might be the urban prefecture, a post that gained in importance during the third century as its holder was responsible for the civil administration of Rome, and emperors were very often out of the city. The reason for this was simply that the emperors of the time were expected to take personal charge of major military campaigns—hence Valerian wasting away in captivity.

The second branch of government had its origins in the fiscal administration of provinces where the Roman state owned land, and in the administration of the vast estates held by the emperor in what was known as the *patrimonium*, the inalienable property that passed from one ruler to the next. Augustus had tried to keep the administration of his property separate from that of state properties, but even by the time of Nero (AD 54–68), this had become impractical and the management of revenue-producing properties had fallen under the control of the palace. The agents of the palace were either freed slaves or equestrians, men from families with property worth at least 800,000 sesterces (though many would in fact have senatorial-size estates). The name of the order derived from ancient practice according to which the rich served as the cavalry (*equites*) in the early Roman army; it was a custom that rapidly fell into disuse when the Romans encountered enemies who fielded competent cavalry.

In the first century there was no hard-and-fast rule determining what sort of person would be in charge of a province, though estate management was largely the business of freedmen. The most famous procurator of all time—Pontius Pilate—was an equestrian, while another well-known procurator, Felix, was a freedman. Both governed Judea. In the later first and the second century, a more predictable system came into being through which people were regularly reviewed for promotion or reassignment and the top positions were held exclusively by equestrians. These positions were graded by salary at 60,000, 100,000, and 200,000 sesterces. Someone at the bottom of the scale was making more than a typical centurion in the legions, whose base pay in the second century was around 36,000 sesterces, but less than a chief centurion, who could rake in more than 100,000 sesterces a year.

Notwithstanding the modern images of a Roman centurion as a hardy chap promoted from the ranks, the typical centurion was a rich man who might pass from a military to a civilian post, but not expect to compete with members of the senatorial order unless he had risen to one of the most important roles in the state such as governor of Egypt, prefect of the grain supply, or commander of the emperor's guard—the praetorian prefect. By the third century this last post was often a sort of prime minister; the one who held it might be an experienced jurist, since a mass of legal correspondence passed before his eyes; and two became emperor after an imperial assassination—in one case the prefect almost certainly had a role in engineering the killing, and in the other, he was accused of doing so.

During the regime of Valerian and Gallienus, the upper echelon was filled with members of the senatorial order, most of them from the wealthy areas of North Africa, Italy, and the Aegean rim. The prominence of Italy was inevitable given that no matter where they were from, senators were required to maintain estates there. The prominence of North Africa was partly a reflection of that region's wealth and partly because the Severan dynasty, which had ended in 235, derived from Lepcis Magna (in modern Libya). Valerian's own family was from Etruria, and his wife was the daughter of a man who had been consul in 207 and the sister of the first individual to be named prefect of Rome by Valerian.[7]

By the time of Gallienus' assassination in 268, his regime looked very different. At that point he was engaged in the siege of Milan; ensconced against him there was Aureolus (his former general and formerly commander of the

FIGURE 1.2
Emperors of the mid third century. Shown here are Valerian (a), Gallienus (b),
Claudius (c), and Aurelian (d). Source: Courtesy of Author.

cavalry corps that had been created a few years before as a mobile reserve). The
praetorian prefect, who in one version of the story was the prime mover of the
conspiracy against Gallienus, was Marcus Aurelius Heraclianus—a significant
name, for the vast majority of Romans who took the *praenomen* (first name)
Marcus and the *nomen* (family name) Aurelius did so because their ancestors had received citizenship as a result of Caracalla's edict of 212. We know
that Heraclianus had a brother named Marcus Aurelius Apollinarius because
another general, Traianus Mucianus, erected statues to them in his hometown
in the Balkans.[8] Another man with the significant post-212 nomenclature was
Marcus Aurelius Claudius (Claudius II), described in one of our sources as a
man "who, after the emperors, appeared to govern the empire."[9] According to
one account of the assassination, other participants in the plot were Marcus
Aurelius Marcianus, an important general; Marcus Aurelius Aurelianus
(Aurelian, like Claudius, a future emperor); and the commander of a Balkan

cavalry unit named Cecropius—it is he who allegedly struck the fatal blow. Another important member of the general staff was a man named Pompeianus the Frank, whose name is highly suggestive of a place of origin outside the empire near the vicinity of the mouth of the Rhine where the Franks then lived.[10]

The multiple accounts of the death of Gallienus look as if they were shaped by the politics of the next few decades, as Claudius would later be elevated to virtual sanctity (which he does not seem to deserve) while Aurelian, who would himself be murdered as the result of a plot that closely resembles one that figures in one of the stories about Gallienus' demise, would be remembered as something of a thug. This too seems unreasonable, for it was Aurelian who, when he reunited the Roman Empire, was loath to slaughter his enemies.

Whatever the truth, the two things we know for certain are that Gallienus was killed in the summer of 268 and that the army chose Claudius to succeed him. Aureolus, who seems to have tried to surrender to his former colleagues, died in battle at Milan when his overtures were rejected.

Claudius was now confronted with a series of problems—not least, confusion in the east, where Odaenathus had been assassinated that spring and there had been a massive raid by tribes ordinarily resident north of the Danube. Then, in Gaul in 269, the regime had been thrown into chaos following the death of its leader in a military mutiny. During the two years or so that remained to Claudius, he managed to defeat the raiders in the Balkans, botch an opportunity to end the regime in Gaul, and alienate the Palmyrenes. In light of what might seem a rather mediocre record, it is perhaps not surprising that when he died in the summer of 270 as a Palmyrene army was invading Egypt he had not been able to secure agreement that the throne would go to his brother, who lasted about two weeks before falling victim to an army under Aurelian.[11]

2.

THE RENEWAL OF THE

ROMAN EMPIRE

A MUCH LATER WRITER, looking back on the last decades of the third century, would write of the emperors who came from central Europe as if they were a coherent group, a school of generals nurtured by Aurelian and his successor Probus. However, the record from 268 to 280 suggests, whatever people might think later, that these officers did not all see themselves as part of a unified group. Rather, each new emperor had to find a way to forge his own governing coalition that reached well outside the group of generals with whom he had associated before taking the throne. If one wished to rule the empire, it was best not to rock the boat too much when taking on the job. Both Claudius and Aurelian shared power, initially, with members of the old aristocracy.[1]

The situation confronting Aurelian was grave—Claudius had won a big battle in the Balkans, but heavy raids continued to pummel the empire from north of the border; one even penetrated Italy. Aurelian's strength of character and ability to dominate a situation emerge perhaps most clearly during his first year on the throne: even though he lost a battle to these raiders he does not seem to have faced a serious attempt to unseat him. By the beginning of 272 he had taken sufficient control of the military situation to be able to imagine confronting the Palmyrenes. Just how serious a threat these people posed to his regime at this point is open to question. Zenobia, Odaenathus' widow and the dominant force behind the throne of her young son, Vabalathus, did not claim the title of emperor for her boy and retained in office many of the officials who controlled Egypt under Claudius. She seems to have created general stability— for instance, a legal case could proceed without interruption; similarly, we may presume that there was no disruption in the annual Egyptian grain shipments that were crucial for the survival of the city of Rome.

Enough evidence survives concerning Aurelian's war with Palmyra—there is good reason to think that Constantius, Constantine's father, served in this war— to give us some impression of the complexity of the operation. Aurelian was not simply a superb general; he was also a man with a keen sense of the political and psychological aspects of warfare. At a strategic level, perhaps the most notable aspect of the campaign was Aurelian's ability to coordinate the reconquest of Egypt with his advance through Asia Minor. Both operations seem to have met with minimal resistance, and diplomacy was a significant feature of the advance. This lesson was not lost on Constantius, and it was a lesson that would be passed on to Constantine, for whom willingness to find a place in his own regime for former enemies was an important quality as he rose to power.

That Aurelian favored diplomacy over fighting might also have been advertised through the work of a contemporary at Athens, Publius Herennius Dexippus. He wrote a history of the wars between Rome and the peoples north of the Danube that includes two great set-pieces in which Aurelian demonstrated that he shared in a Greco-Roman heritage that gave him the strength to resist aggressive barbarians. In the campaign against Palmyra, diplomacy may also have played an important role as the Palmyrene armies offered no serious resistance before Aurelian reached Antioch. Other aspects of surviving narratives stress the favor of the gods shown to Aurelian, manifest through the failure of oracles to support the Palmyrenes as well as in battlefield miracles that helped the Romans. The most important of these allegedly occurred in the final battle outside Emesa, when the Roman line seemed about to give way only to be refreshed by a divine apparition. Upon entering the city's main temple, Aurelian recognized its god as the one who had saved his army.[2]

The saving god could only have been Elagabal, but Aurelian presented him to the world as a typical Greco-Roman divinity in human form. He now revealed this god to the world as the Invincible Sun (Sol Invictus) and ordered a massive temple to be constructed in his honor at Rome. The celebration of his cult was accompanied by the creation of a new priesthood into which senior members of the Senate could be (and were) recruited as a sign of imperial favor.

Aurelian's successful creation of a new cult around Elagabal is especially significant in light of the god's previous, less fortunate, history in the capital.

The cult image of Elagabal—a meteorite—had been brought to Rome when his teenage priest had become emperor in the wake of a civil war in AD 217. The young ruler, who is conventionally referred to as Elagabalus, after his god, constructed a massive temple for his god and insisted on celebrating the god's original rites, which included orgiastic dancing around the cult image. Members of the Roman aristocracy regarded these rites as distasteful. In this form the cult of Elagabal lasted in Rome only until 222, when the Praetorian Guard murdered the emperor Elagabalus, who had by then offended wide cross-sections of the Roman establishment. It was at this point that Elagabal was sent home to his temple in Emesa. The new and "improved" form of the god introduced by Aurelian was far more palatable and successful.[3] Aurelian's version of Elagabal as Invincible Sun would prove immensely important for both Constantius and Constantine. Constantius, who may well have been at the battle of Emesa, appears to have been devoted to the god, and Aurelian's example showed Constantine that it would be possible to make a previously unpalatable divinity acceptable in the imperial pantheon—especially if that god was connected with a notable victory.

While Aurelian pressed the claims of his miraculous victory, he seems to have done little to upset the status quo in Syria on his arrival there and similarly in Egypt. When members of the local Christian community of Antioch came to him claiming that the presiding bishop, one Paul of Samosata, was a supporter of the Palmyrene regime, he refused to take on the case and referred the matter to Christian bishops in Italy for a decision. Zenobia was brought to Rome where she was allowed to live out her days in polite society; meanwhile, a local intellectual named Callinicus of Petra who had dedicated a history of Egypt to her as "a new Cleopatra" seems to have been permitted to redeem himself for this faux pas by composing a work on the "Restoration" of the Roman Empire.[4]

In writing on the restoration of the Empire, Callinicus was picking up a theme that had been in the air for a while. Before leaving Rome, Aurelian had begun to construct a massive circuit wall. While there are many reasons to build a wall, not the least being to create an administrative boundary and control the flow of population, there was no obvious reason that wall-building should suddenly have been a concern at Rome; nor was defense an obvious need. The city had not been approached by a foreign enemy since the third century BC; not even the raiders with whom Aurelian had dealt in northern Italy had posed a threat, and it is unlikely that he would have advertised that he was doubtful whether he could defend his capital. But city walls had long had meanings and purposes that were not purely practical. For a provincial city, an encircling wall indicated importance. But for Rome, whose standing was unimpeachable, walls perhaps had a different meaning. In the rhetoric of the second and third centuries AD, the Roman Empire was a fortress of civilization surrounded by walls that kept the forces of barbarism at bay. Now, as the emperor set out to restore the meta-phoric walls to their former extent and grandeur, the city's new physical circuit could be a symbol of renewal and confidence in the future.[5]

The initial settlement with Palmyra appears to have been so generous that some failed to understand that they had in fact lost. Leading members of Palmyrene society rebelled as soon as Aurelian headed home and approached the governor of Syria, offering him the throne. He demurred and notified Aurelian, who returned and destroyed the city. In 274 the loyal governor shared the consulship with Aurelian; the consul of the previous year, who had been chief of the watch (a senior equestrian position) under Gallienus was also the praetorian prefect. His consular colleague was a Marcus Claudius Tacitus, who may have been Italian but whose lack of obvious connection with any major aristocratic family makes it likely that he too had played a role in Aurelian's campaign of "restoring the empire." Although there was still room at the top for members of the Senate, these appointments by Aurelian, along with keep-ing an ordinary consulship for himself in four of the six years of his reign, reflect his desire to reward supporters, which is hardly surprising in a time of civil war.[6]

The empire that Aurelian "restored" would not be the same empire that had existed before 260. Before setting out on the eastern campaign, the emperor had decided that the region of Dacia, north of the Danube, could no longer be defended by walls, symbolic or otherwise, and ordered the abolition of the provinces there. In so doing he evidently inconvenienced the family of a man who might then have been serving in his army, one Maximianus Galerius (another future emperor). More problematic was a decision Aurelian made after his victory in Gaul to "renew" the silver currency of the empire, which had long subsisted on the notional equivalence of twenty-five silver coins—*denarii*—to one gold coin (*aureus*), no matter how low the actual silver content of a denarius might be (by this time it was virtually negligible).[7]

The problem with imperial finance was one that every regime throughout history has had to contend with: namely, that there was an imbalance between income and expenditure. The largest items in the imperial budget were the army and the cost of the subsidized food supply for the population of Rome, a mainstay of government since the time of Augustus. The cost and organization of Rome's food supply was closely entwined with the overall economy of the empire as the surplus produced by the agricultural lands in Africa and Egypt was siphoned off to Rome through a complex but efficient delivery system. The one emperor who had tried to cut costs by limiting distributions had fallen victim to a revolt in AD 238, a point presumably lost on no one, and it is perhaps significant that despite his financial difficulties, Aurelian saw fit to supplement Rome's food supply with distributions of pork (a staple of the central Italian diet).

The army was another matter, though here too freedom of maneuver was limited. In the first two centuries AD the proportion of the empire's population under arms had declined as the size of the army had not kept pace with the increase in the population as a whole; but the cost of maintaining the army had continued to occupy a relatively steady proportion of the budget (about 40 percent at the best estimate). Septimius Severus (reigned AD 193–211) shattered this equilibrium when he doubled legionary pay and increased the size of the army by 10 percent, the latter move necessitated by the acquisition of new territory in the east. His successor, Caracalla, made things much worse with a further increase in salaries, which proved impossible to undo. Caracalla's successor alienated his army when he tried to roll back the increase by introducing differential pay scales for soldiers serving at the time of his accession and new recruits, which opened the door for the rebellion at Emesa, which resulted in his death and Elagabal's first arrival at Rome. In the time of Philip (the former praetorian prefect who became emperor when his predecessor was murdered after a failed invasion of Persia in 244), there is evidence of an attempt to enhance revenue collection that seems not to have worked. One papyrus contains an appeal for the "divine intelligence of Decius" (reigned AD 249–251) to fix the fiscal problem said to have begun with Severus (the solution was not forthcoming). A secondary problem by the time of Aurelian as the process of "renewal" took place, was concern in some parts of the empire for the legitimacy of the coinage in circulation. In Gaul especially the coinage in circulation for the previous fifteen years had been created by a regime that was officially illegitimate, while in Egypt, in the early 260s a governor had had to order bankers to accept coins with the image of the emperors on them—not something the bankers were keen to do, presumably given that the images were those of two usurpers.[8]

Although Aurelian was trying to tackle a real problem, his solution was too extreme. The result was the collapse of confidence in the imperial coinage, rampant inflation, and the destruction of the accumulated reserves used as endowments across the empire. A monetary system that had been reasonably stable for centuries was thereby overthrown, and efforts to restore confidence in it would be a source of constant stress over the next several decades.

Aurelian had reunited the empire, but he had not united the general staff behind his vision. In the late summer of 275 a cabal of officers murdered him near Perinthus, close to the city of Byzantium. It would not have been lost on Constantius—or other officers whose careers were now moving forward—that even the most successful Roman emperor in the past half century could not guarantee his personal safety or control the succession.

The succession turned out to be very complicated. A story was told much later about how the general staff deferred to the Senate in the selection of a new emperor, which, after an interregnum of some six months appointed a new ruler; this story has tended to overshadow a far more dramatic sequence of events. It appears that the assassins thought they would be able to determine the succession; but when they failed they fled to Syria, where they seized control of the province from an unpopular governor whom they also murdered. Strikingly, coinage continued to be minted in the name of Salonina, Aurelian's wife, who seems to have maintained some sort of control over the situation while the army selected Claudius Tacitus as the next emperor.[9] Those who supported Tacitus did so on the assumption that he would avenge Aurelian. The assassins, however, proved bolder than could have been expected, penetrating Tacitus' encampment in central Turkey and killing him. A brief civil war ensued between the army's new candidate, Marcus Aurelius Probus, and Tacitus' brother. Probus won, and then invited the assassins to a banquet where he murdered them.[10]

Probus' subsequent reign was chaotic. Several military revolts took place in Gaul, there was a war between two Egyptian cities, and a major operation was needed to suppress warlordism in southern Turkey. Probus himself fell victim to a rebellion orchestrated by his own praetorian prefect, Marcus Aurelius Carus, in 282.

Notably absent from the narrative of these years is any reference to the Persians. Sapor had died in 270, and the revolutionary and religious fervor that had ignited his regime (as it had that of his father)—the desire to serve the god Ahura Mazda and stamp out his enemies—faded as the regime faced severe internal problems. Marcus Aurelius Carus proposed to take advantage of these weaknesses by launching an invasion of Persian territory, which he did during the summer of 283. The Persian defense appears to have been utterly uncoordinated and the Roman army may have captured Ctesiphon, the capital of the Persian Empire. At that point Carus died, probably of unnatural causes as he is said to have been struck by lightning. His younger son Numerian was made co-emperor with his older brother Carinus, who had remained in the west, and the Roman army withdrew to its own territory. What happened next remains both profoundly important and profoundly obscure.[11]

Numerian appears to have survived his father by only a few months. We find him responding to a petition at Emesa on April 5, 284. His response is a detailed discussion of what should happen if a person whose property has been administered for him during his youth wishes to sue his guardians once he has attained majority; it addresses a significant point of law and is surely the work of the legal staff that traveled with every emperor. On 20 November the army proclaimed a new emperor at Nicomedia in northwestern Turkey (modern Izmit). Somehow and somewhere between these points Numerian had died. Tradition (admittedly highly serviceable to the reputation of the new emperor) held that Numerian's father-in-law, the praetorian prefect Aper, had him murdered and concealed his death: this he achieved by transporting the body in a closed litter, explaining it away by pretending that Numerian was suffering from an eye ailment that necessitated keeping out of the light. The fact of death was only admitted when the body began to produce olfactory evidence of decomposition.

At this point it seems to have been generally agreed that the army was not going to serve the co-emperor Carinus and would need a new emperor of its own. So the general staff met and announced to the army that the new ruler would be Gaius Valerius Diocles, until then a relatively junior officer in command of a guard unit. According to tradition, Diocles' first act was to swear to the army that he had not murdered Numerian; his second was to draw his sword and skewer Aper, who was standing nearby on the platform from which he was addressing the soldiers. The last part of the story, at least, may be open to some doubt since the most hostile contemporary witness—Lactantius—does not mention it, and it seems unlikely that he would omit a tale implying that the emperor he despised began his reign in a fit of homicidal fury.[12]

Even without Aper's dramatic end, there are signs that the situation in Nicomedia was getting complicated. Diocletian—as Diocles, highly conscious of the symbolic power of nomenclature, soon called himself so that he would seem more "aristocratic"—was not obvious emperor material. His family originated at Doclea in the Balkans, though it is likely that he grew up near Split, where he would later construct a large retirement palace for himself. Although stories about his being the son of a scribe or a freedman of a powerful senatorial clan are either impossible to prove or inherently improbable, they may reflect the perception that Diocletian was the tool of the aristocracy. He would share the consulship in the year of his accession with the illustrious aristocrat Pomponius Bassus, who must have been with the army in order to figure as Diocletian's colleague in the first place.[13]

News of the eastern army's selection of a new emperor was greeted in the west with a rebellion against Carinus, who may have been as deeply dislikable as later tradition makes him out to have been. Carinus crushed this revolt as he made his way east, and according to one tradition was murdered by an officer whose wife he had raped. This account reads like a confused version of another story about Carinus' death: namely, that he was killed by the aggrieved officer in the battle he fought against Diocletian at Margus in the Balkans just as his army was on the point of victory. According to another version, Carinus fled to the west after losing to Diocletian and was killed in Italy.

There can be little doubt that Diocletian's triumph was achieved amid a welter of betrayal and deceit, and that good traitors knew how to cover up their actions. Still, it is telling that his consular colleague in 285 was a man who had begun the year as Carinus' colleague and praetorian prefect, Titus Claudius Aurelius Aristobulus, who would go on to be prefect of Rome in 295–296.

There is also a story, possibly not totally fictional, that Constantius, then serving as governor of Dalmatia, on learning that Carinus planned to kill him, changed sides to aid Diocletian. The reason for supposing Constantius was in the Balkans at this time is that Constantine, the subject of this story, had recently been born at Naissus, the modern Nis in Serbia—the date is probably February 27, 282. Constantine's mother, Helena, whom later tradition variously describes as a woman of very low standing (or the daughter of a British king), most likely belonged to a respectable family from Drepanum in Bithynia, a district of what is now northwestern Turkey.[14] The city believed to be her home would be renamed Helenopolis in her honor, probably by her son when he became emperor. We cannot now know how or where Helena met her husband, but we can be reasonably certain that Constantius' actions in 284–285 drew favorable attention from members of the victorious faction, for he was soon moving in exalted circles. What better way to secure the potential of a brilliant career for his young son?

II

DIOCLETIAN

———————————————

3.

THE NEW EMPEROR

DIOCLETIAN HAD WON THE WAR. He could now rejoice in the sole possession of a post whose previous eight incumbents (counting only those who could claim control of Rome) had been murdered, some after only a few days or weeks in power. Meanwhile raiders beset the Rhine and Balkan frontiers, local warlords could still be tempted to carve out mini-empires for themselves within their provinces, and there seems to have been no settlement of outstanding disputes with the fortuitously feuding claimants to the Persian throne. It would only be a matter of time, though, before a new King of Kings emerged in the east with full authority over his rivals.

There is no indication that by the beginning of 285 Diocletian had devised a road map for the future—beyond the need to eliminate Carinus. With victory won, the problem of governing began. While the emperor plainly had some powerful supporters within the upper echelons of the governing class, he had no relative upon whom he could depend for assistance in ruling the empire. Furthermore, the great and powerful who supported him had just betrayed his predecessor. Faced with the challenge of enforcing his authority on multiple fronts and the plain fact that many to whom he might turn for aid had been in senior positions for longer than he had, he took the novel step of promoting to the rank of deputy emperor, or Caesar, a man who was not a blood relation and who had occupied, as far as we know, no major post in the civil or military hierarchy.

The individual he chose was from the area around Sirmium on the Danube. All we know for certain about his background is that in a speech given in his honor a few years later, a Gallic rhetorician named Mamertinus would say that he had served as a soldier since his youth, and that he had traversed the

(a)   (b)

FIGURE 3.1
The new emperors: Diocletian and Maximian. Source: Courtesy of Author.

Danubian lands and the entire expanse of the Euphrates. This presumably meant that he had served in Carus' expedition, which we might reasonably expect anyway. The chosen man's name was Maximianus—or Maximian as he is now more often called. He would play the role of Hercules, the great defender of civilization, to Diocletian's Jupiter (see figure 3.1). The names were well chosen, as might be expected of a man who seemed already quite sensitive to the nuances of nomenclature, for Jupiter and Hercules were also gods intimately related to the foundation of Rome. So it was appropriate that their earthly avatars should play the leading role in the "restoration of the empire," Aurelian's claim to having done something of the sort being downplayed both at this point and in the future.[1]

Maximian's appointment took place at Milan. Diocletian may have moved on from there to Rome, a city which he is otherwise known certainly to have visited on only one other occasion in keeping with the practice of his recent predecessors who had spent most of their time elsewhere, before returning to the Balkans. The appointment was accompanied by some marital musical chairs among members of the inner circle. Maximian now married Eutropia, a woman from Syria who had previously been the wife of Afranius Hannibalianus. Afranius, the descendant of a noble family of senatorial stock from Asia Minor, had eschewed a senatorial career so as to rise to the top of the equestrian ladder and had been praetorian prefect for a number of years. He would still be in post when he was accorded an ordinary consulship with his colleague as praetorian prefect, Julius Asclepiodotus (another easterner) in 292, and would subsequently hold the prefecture of Rome. It is these appointments along with the evident support that Diocletian had garnered from Pomponius Bassus and Aristobulus that reveal the vague outlines of a governing group characterized by Balkan generals on the throne and traditional aristocrats, in these years with a distinctively eastern tinge, occupying the prominent positions around them.

Maximian's first job as Caesar was to ensure the loyalty of Gaul where imperial authority remained weak. The first group he had to contend with would be described a few years later as rebellious peasants—most likely a considerable distortion of the truth. Their leaders took upon themselves the trappings of imperial power, much as Uranius Antoninus and Odaenathus had done in the east and as had a variety of other characters throughout the empire. In fact, it is now unclear whether wearing imperial-style clothing or minting coins in one's own image represented a claim to actual imperial power or was merely a means of asserting local importance by taking upon oneself the trappings associated with power.

Whatever the truth may be, Maximian defeated the Gauls, then moved on to the Rhine where he had to deal with a wide variety of raiders, and it was at the end of 286 that Diocletian recognized his achievement by raising him to the rank of co-emperor, or Augustus. Years later, in the speech that has already told us something of Maximian's background and his campaigns, Mamertinus refers to a further round of marital politics. Here Maximian is told that he has been joined by marriage to a man holding the leading position in his entourage. What is meant by "leading position" is unclear—it need not be the praetorian prefecture since at this point the emperor did not have a "personal prefect" as he would later, and it is more likely to refer to a military command. But we can be reasonably certain that the person in question was none other than Constantius, who at about this time married Maximian's stepdaughter, Theodora. What we also know is that Constantius had won some notable distinction as an independent commander, capturing a king of the Alemanni, a tribal coalition in southeastern Germany, and that he had conducted some sort of operation across the Danube.[2]

Although the new marriage left the young Constantine in his father's house, the transition could not have been an easy one for a seven-year-old boy. Constantine's constant stress in later years on his place as rightful heir is a sign of just how profound the impact upon him had been. So too it is clear that his relationship with his mother remained profoundly important: it was she who would emerge at his side many years hence in the worst domestic crisis of his reign—a crisis that arose in part from his passionate relationships with the women in his life. Helena was probably in her late twenties when she was dumped by Constantius, and there was not much of a life left open to her at the time—former imperial consorts were not abundant in Roman history and the condition had often been fatal in the past. We can now only guess at her courage and determination as she made a new life for herself. We may sense in the later record the role that she played in protecting her son, giving him refuge when the world seemed to have turned against him, reassurance that he was still loved. Constantine would later help every one of his subjects understand just how important she was to his life, and the monuments to Helena after her death help us remember that debt to this day. It is hard to imagine that she would not enjoy the laughter of children playing outside what was once her palace in the park on Rome's Viale Carlo Felice—or that her son would have changed the world if she had not given him the strength to face the uncertainty of his future.

4.

EMPERORS AND SUBJECTS

THE RHETORICIAN MAMERTINUS PROVIDES us with a great deal of information about the theory, practice, and challenges of governing the empire in the 280s. Some of what he has to say would scarcely have been news a century before, but other comments point to the evolution of a fresh concept of government. There may have been nothing new in the notion that to be an emperor was to stand on "a lofty pinnacle of human affairs." But this emperor has a different perspective as he surveys both land and sea to discover which governors are administering his particular form of justice, which generals are successful; he receives correspondence from everywhere, and to everywhere dispatches his instructions.[1] He distinguishes between a governor, here called (as would later become typical) a *iudex* or judge, and a general (a *dux* or leader), and in so doing introduces a radical change in the governing philosophy of an empire in which, for centuries, military glory had been a defining feature of the ruling aristocracy as a whole and in which a provincial governor had expected to command whatever forces his province possessed. We do not know exactly how or when the change took place, though Mamertinus' language suggests that this was already the accepted division of authority. If it was not—and there is no obvious reason to think that it was—a development of the new regime, it is most likely a practice that began to be institutionalized in the years after 260.[2]

Less problematic is the relationship between the two emperors: they are partners in power, each doing what he needs to do to make Rome strong. There is no clear subordination of one to the other—while there can be no doubt that Diocletian is senior, Maximian is a partner rather than a servant. Maximian had hitherto been concentrating his activity in Gaul, while Diocletian had been to the east and back, where "the kingdoms of the Persians had recently surrendered to him." The "surrender" appears to have consisted of an embassy from King Bahram II guaranteeing the existing frontier, possibly agreeing to a formal peace treaty: this, given the recent Roman assault on Bahram's homeland, might be regarded as something of a diplomatic coup for Diocletian as well as a sign of the chaos that continued to beset the Persian kingdom. This state of affairs included not simply the struggle between Bahram and his brother, Hormisdas, but also a period of intense religious fanaticism.

Kartir, chief of the Zoroastrian priesthood, with Bahram's support, was seeking to stamp out other religions throughout the Persian Empire. This equation between religious and imperial authority was far removed from the Roman understanding of civic cult, or even that of the organized worship of the emperors through the imperial cult (a structure that served an important role in propagating imperial propaganda). The desire to impose religious conformity had not even been a feature of Valerian's persecution, or of Decius' edict of 250 on sacrifices. Valerian had been interested only in getting Christians to do what he told them to do, not in forcing everyone to worship in the same way, while Decius had been content that everyone just show up to sacrifice once. Aurelian's patronage of Sol Invictus, Invincible Sun, had served to promote a divine favor, channeled through himself, that was manifestly *not* open to others. Nonetheless, a desire for a more specific alignment between an improved religious message and imperial power can be read into the equation of Diocletian and Maximian with Jupiter and Hercules. In both Persia and the Roman Empire we sense the government's growing ambition to centralize its authority on the institutions of imperial rule and to enhance its overall message.[3]

Diocletian spoke to his subjects more often and more generally than had emperors since the mid-first century AD. Although all emperors might dispatch very long missives to their subjects, before the period we are investigating here the bulk of the evidence for communication of an overtly ideological tone (as opposed to the ideology implicit in pretty much any imperial communication) relates to the first, Julio-Claudian, dynasty that ended with Nero's suicide in AD 68. There are no documents like Augustus' monumental autobiography, or the lengthy decree settling the crisis that shook the Roman state with the death of an imperial heir apparent in AD 19–20, surviving from later eras. What we do possess from the later first to the mid-third century are many imperial responses to specific requests for favors, for permission for a given group to

assert certain rights, for the resolution of a dispute with neighbors, for recognition of services, for redress of grievances, or for the resolution of internal crises—the longest surviving document of Marcus Aurelius (reigned AD
161–180) is a letter to Athens about a series of disputes among citizens.

Some documents, even if ostensibly sparked by parochial concerns, might
also impose new regulations for the empire as a whole, as does a text of the
late 170s relating to a request from people about to be saddled with the cost of
gladiatorial shows for the imperial cult; they asked the emperor to rescind what
was effectively a sales tax on the gladiators whom they would have to purchase.
Marcus Aurelius takes advantage of this request to impose an empire-wide
price-fixing scheme. It is a sophisticated plan, allowing for different prices for
gladiators in places of greater and lesser wealth and providing the mechanism
for setting prices in line with local norms where people were not rich enough
to afford really good gladiators.

Marcus' action with respect to the gladiators is evocative of the way that one
of his predecessors, Hadrian (reigned AD 117–138), used complaints and queries
from a number of places to enunciate empire-wide policies relating to public
entertainment. In one case, questions had arisen about how to schedule games
so that athletes could get to them. To deal with the problem the emperor summons people who have issues to see him at Naples: at the same time he takes the
opportunity to issue a new calendar of games. As with Marcus, it is likely that
his response goes well beyond any individual request, showing how an astute
emperor might make use of the process of "petition and response" to initiate
change. In another letter Hadrian responds to some petitions about specific
issues that have arisen at various games in such a way as to create a virtual char-
ter of rights for traveling entertainers. In both cases the emperor could have
issued an edict telling people what to do. Instead, he chose to adopt a mode
conforming to their image of an emperor needing to respond to the complaints
of subjects rather than seeming to rock the imperial boat.

Over these centuries the message that people tended to get was that the
emperor embodied a group of virtues that essentially defined his job. These
were courage (*virtus*), fairness (*aequitas*), duty (*pietas*), foresight (*providentia*),
and generosity (*liberalitas*). Of these qualities the first was most obviously manifest in war while generosity was shown though lavish entertainments, building
projects, distributions of food (usually limited to Rome), and help for those in

need. Duty, in the sense of pietas was the duty that one had toward the gods and in maintaining proper relationship with other humans, while foresight increasingly took on an aspect of a nearly divine ability to see into the future. Justice was done every day through the answering of petitions.[4]

Diocletian and those around him were fully conscious that the age-old system of petition and response was not simply a passive tool of government. A few years after Mamertinus' speech two major projects were set in motion that would effectively codify Roman legal practice largely on the basis of responses to petitions, or rescripts. The leading actors in this movement were three jurists, Gregorius, Charisius, and Hermogenianus, all of them with established careers before Diocletian's arrival on the scene. Gregorius had risen, under Carinus, to the immensely important position of *magister libellorum* (master of petitions), which gave him oversight of responses that the imperial court issued to the literally thousands of petitions with which it was inundated in the course of a year. Charisius may have been with Maximian on the day that Mamertinus spoke. He was the emperor's *magister libellorum* in 286–287 and held the same position under Diocletian in 290–291. Hermogenianus was *magister libellorum* for Diocletian in 295–298, after which he became praetorian prefect, a post that he would keep until 302. While Gregorius and Hermogenianus were responsible for massive new guides to Roman law, Charisius was the author of an important work setting out the way government was supposed to operate; his writings include books on civic *munera*, witnesses, and the duties of the praetorian prefect.[5]

The labor of Diocletian's leading lawyers differed from the legal compilations writing of what is now seen as the "classical period" of Roman jurisprudence in the second and early third centuries AD, which tended to involve extensive commentary on the praetor's edict. The importance of the praetor's edict stemmed from much earlier Roman practice in which the *praetor urbanus*, the senior magistrate at Rome who was in charge of the court system, issued a statement—his edict—of the way the civil law would be administered in his year of office. These edicts of necessity tended to be repetitive, but it was not until the AD 130s, in Hadrian's reign, that a permanent form was promulgated. This "Perpetual Edict" had four parts and a series of appendices. The first section dictated the procedure for bringing an action, the second and third sections laid out measures for which actions or other forms of intervention would

(a)   (b)

(c)   (d)

FIGURE 4.1

The new college of emperors: Diocletian (a), Maximian (b), Constantius (c), and Galerius (d). Note not only the close resemblance that the four emperors bear to each other, but also the change in the images of Diocletian and Maximian from those used earlier in the realm (see fig. 3.1).

Source: Courtesy of Author.

be granted (e.g., the appointment of guardians for minor children or, in the case of a pregnant widow whose child would have a claim on the deceased father's estate, appropriate supervision of the pregnancy and birth). The fourth section dealt with the way that judgments would be executed. Commentaries on the praetor's edict tended to include a great deal of input from individual jurists, quotations from the work of jurists of whom they approved, plus the occasional opinion of an emperor who could be shown to have had the wisdom to agree with a given jurist's views.

Gregorius and Hermogenianus produced codes that, although organized along the lines of the praetor's edict, illustrated points of law through quotations from rescripts. Although rescripts were largely composed by jurists they went out under the name of the emperor rather than of a lawyer. The effect of the new codes was to assert that the operation of the law was founded upon actual precedent and the actions of imperial officials. The idea that a code of conduct could be defined by a collection of responses to petitions as in the case of Hadrian's handling of entertainers and games, had not previously formed a central tenet of legal procedure. One reason for this was that emperors tended to contradict each other: Hadrian in his letter implicitly reverses a decision by his immediate predecessor. In the codes, careful editing removed overt contradiction, and the principle was established that in cases where contradiction *was* observed the most recent rescript would be the authoritative one. Gregorius' code, which drew on rescripts from AD 196 to 291 was completed in 292, while Hermogenianus' Code, based on rescripts from 293–294 appeared in 295.

The dates upon which the great works were issued are significant. The year 293 saw a major shift in the structure of government.[6] In 293 the empire acquired two more junior emperors.

In the course of his speech of 289, Mamertinus noted a problem that still loomed on the horizon: a "pirate" who threatened the empire's Atlantic frontier.[7] The "pirate" was one Carausius, previously commander of the garrison on the Rhine, who had proclaimed himself emperor at the end of 286 or the beginning of 287, allegedly to protect himself from the charge of peculation. At the time of Mamertinus' speech, Carausius had just been driven from his bases in Gaul, and it was expected that he would be similarly ousted from his final refuge in Britain during the coming year. That did not happen as a storm seems to have deposited Maximian's fleet on the rocks. In the wake of this disaster, Carausius regained a foothold on the mainland from which he was driven only with difficulty. In 293 his regime still retained its presence on the mainland, but Maximian was in no position to deliver the final blow. For that he chose Constantius, whom he elevated to the rank of Caesar. A few weeks later, Diocletian did the same for Maximianus Galerius, to whom he married his daughter Valeria.

Exactly what prompted the appointment of Caesars at this particular time or the selection of the one in the west ahead of the one in the east we cannot know. The outcome was that Constantius would always be regarded as having precedence over Galerius, just as Diocletian always had precedence over Maximian. In any event, the war with Carausius was the most important crisis at hand, and Constantius was already an imperial son-in-law. The decision to use him for what could be a risky operation may have reflected a simple recognition that the stability of the realm required that the Augusti stay out of the line of fire in situations where failure would be seriously embarrassing. Constantius, through an adroit combination of military might and diplomatic guile would, after a few years, accomplish the reconquest of Britain. Likewise several years hence Galerius would prove his own very considerable mettle on the battlefield, when he took on a command that might have had fatal consequences for the regime if Diocletian had needed to play an active role.

One result of the expansion of government was that there were now four imperial courts rather than two, and it is perhaps not accidental that the new codes provide coherent guidance about how the imperial courts could interact with their subjects. The legal records of this period suggest that the expansion of the administration to include the two Caesars was the result of a deliberate plan rather than an expedient reaction to a crisis (as some scholars have supposed). The codes also give us a view of the purpose of government, for although some of their documents are memoranda to imperial officials, the vast bulk are responses to people who fall well outside the ranks of the imperial aristocracy. These people are soldiers and members of curial classes at all levels, men of the middling sort, women (about a quarter of those addressed), and even some slaves and freed persons. In a very real sense the individuals who appear in these documents are the emperor's "public," the people to whom he addressed himself, and as such the codes mirror an important development in the definition of what it was to be Roman.

Definitions of Romanness, which tended to be both a cultural and a legal phenomenon, had never been straightforward—and if these definitions had been it is unlikely that a man like Constantius, whose family had no ethnic connection with the Romans of earlier times, could have become an emperor.

There was really no way that definitions of Romanness could be simple or consistent; the imperial elite depended for its power on people who were widely dispersed, who largely spoke no Latin, whose lives were shaped by radical differences in climate, history, and class. In one sense, to be Roman meant pursuing a way of life that the elite Romans found acceptable and useful. It might mean learning Latin, it might mean acquiring a taste for aspects of central-Italian life—more often involving wine rather than the pork products in which Romans delighted. Or it might simply mean bloody-minded and brave service in the army. In a famous passage in the sixth book of the *Aeneid*,

Virgil has the specter of Anchises comment that while others might excel at the arts, it was the job of the Roman to rule people with *imperium*, to humble the proud and spare the weak. The sentiments appealed sufficiently to the emperor Augustus that he alludes to them in the autobiography that he assembled in the last year of his life. At other times he had sought to resist the extension of Roman citizenship through its most obvious means, the freeing of slaves, by limiting the number of slaves that any one person could free and by creating a class of semi-citizenship modeled on the existing concept of partial citizenship known as Latin Rights: such rights enabled a person to receive the protections of full citizenship against arbitrary treatment by magistrates, but not to vote. In the provinces, citizenship tended to be limited at this point to the rich, who could hold high office in places that had been granted municipal rights involving a Roman-style civic constitution and the award of citizenship to those at the top.

In a speech that he gave to the Senate, Claudius I (reigned AD 41 to 54) suggested that Roman citizenship could be infinitely extensible as people became more civilized. One popular alternative means of acquiring citizenship was bribery, and Claudius' wife Messalina, who also attracted scandal in more notorious ways, was allegedly at the center of a palace ring that peddled the franchise to the provinces. This scam is immortalized in the *Acts of the Apostles* when the Apostle Paul tells a centurion who is intent upon flogging him for fomenting public unrest that he can't do that because he, Paul, is a citizen. When the centurion asks how Paul acquired that status, he is impressed to discover that he inherited it; he confesses that he paid a lot of money for his own citizenship. And it appears to have been during Claudius' reign that men retiring from military service were granted formal discharge diplomas on bronze tablets, copies of which were also installed on a temple at Rome, guaranteeing their citizen rights. From the time of Augustus onward there is some evidence to suggest that no one checked very carefully on the citizenship status of men who had been recruited into the legions—you had to be a citizen to be a legionary, and in some cases it is clear that people became citizens immediately upon enlisting.

Another way to become a citizen was to have a powerful friend. The younger Pliny, whose extensive (and carefully edited, by him) correspondence survives, sought citizenship from the early second-century emperor Trajan for the numerous relatives of his doctor, on the grounds that the doctor had saved Pliny in a recent illness. Several decades later Cornelius Fronto, then tutor to the future emperor Marcus Aurelius, sought the franchise for his friend Appian of Alexandria, on the grounds that he was a jolly good chap. This must have seemed more important than the fact that Appian had worked for the imperial treasury and was the author of a major history of the rise of the Roman Empire.[8]

These cases illustrate various ways in which the "legal" definition of citizenship could be applied. The most fundamental discussion of cultural Romanness appears in the biography, composed at the end of the first century by Tacitus, the greatest historian of the Roman world, of his father-in-law, the general Agricola, who served for many years as governor of Britain:

> Since people who are scattered and crude are, from that, inclined to war, while the peaceful are inclined to quiet through pleasures, Agricola began privately to encourage, and publicly to give assistance so that they built temples, marketplaces and houses, by praising the eager and criticizing the slow so that rivalry for honor replaced compulsion. He educated the children of chieftains in the liberal arts and preferred the natural intelligence of Britons to the industry of the Gauls, so that those who had previously refused to learn Latin desired eloquence. In this way there developed an affection for our way of life and the toga was commonplace, and gradually there was a decline to the tools of the vices: porticoes, baths, and the elegance of dining. That which was called civilization amongst the ignorant was part of submission.[9]

A crucial aspect of what Tacitus observed was that adaptation to Roman ways might make the empire easier to govern, but those who voluntarily took up aspects of Roman life did not automatically achieve the legal status of Romans. Indeed, during the first and second centuries, the socio-urban architecture of the empire became a series of local variations on general themes of Greco-Roman urban life, with Greek styles tending to predominate as the model in the eastern part of the empire, and Italic styles in the west. Places like Trier retained the signs of their origins as the winter encampments of Roman legions, with street systems laid out on the pattern of a camp, while a city like Ephesus retained a decidedly Greek feel even though its main marketplace was entered via a triumphal arch that had been erected by a pair of wealthy freed slaves formerly belonging to Agrippa, Augustus' right-hand man. Ephesus would have a stadium, for instance, and a theater, but it would not have an amphitheater, the quintessential western venue for gladiatorial combats and beast hunts, although they were extremely popular there. Trier had a large amphitheater that was built through the city's defensive wall. Byzantium, a very ancient Greek city at this point, had a very Roman circus, but that was because the place had played a major role in supporting a losing cause during the civil wars of Severus' time and he had rebuilt it incorporating some Roman attractions.

The cultural dynamic of theme and variation would continue throughout the empire, even though questions about who should be a citizen largely ended when Caracalla's grant of the franchise in AD 212 made Roman citizens of the vast majority of people, whether they would ever have dreamed of wearing a toga or could speak a word of Greek or Latin. The main consequence of Caracalla's action, as it appears in Diocletian's codes, was to enhance the importance of status definitions based on immunity from public services.[10]

The Diocletianic codes thus came into being at a point when Roman society was in flux, when there were new priorities and perhaps all the more need to interact with government, which now played a greater role in defining people's relationships with each other. It is therefore not surprising that the people we encounter in the codes have a wide range of problems with which they were seeking the emperor's help through a rescript. Although given legal authority as a precedent when included in the code, a rescript did not have quite the same standing when simply issued to the individual. Essentially it stated that if the situation was as the petitioner described, a magistrate should decide the case in his favor. Inevitably it was possible for both sides in a legal action to obtain favorable rulings that would then have to be adjudicated by the presiding magistrate. The sheer volume of work that went into answering the masses of petitions that flowed into an imperial palace was such that it was quite possible that the staff would not notice that they were issuing rulings that might be contradictory.

Among the 942 people that we meet through petitions preserved from the Codex Hermogenianus are Lucius Cornelius, Macedonius, Platonianus, and Zoilus, all of whom received rescripts on December 16, 294, at Nicomedia, the city that was rapidly emerging as Diocletian's preferred residence. Lucius Cornelius, who has a difficulty with a debt, is told that if his creditor will not accept the payment of what he owes after he has made any offsetting payments, he can bring an action. Zoilus' problem is that a man who was indebted to him has assigned the payment of the debt to a third party who owes him money. It appears that the third party is unwilling to pay and Zoilus is told to sue him. Macedonius' problem, involving pledges of property to repay debts, occupied the lawyers a good deal during this year (there are sixteen surviving rescripts on the subject from 293 to 294). Macedonius seems to have acquired some property in payment, then finds that a third party is trying to claim it on the grounds that it is actually his, possibly after having renounced possession at some earlier point. Macedonius is reassured that if the third party, who is twenty years old, has earlier given up claim to the property, he has no business claiming it back.

Platonianus' case is particularly interesting. He appears to have gone blind and, because of this, someone has tried to remove him from his seat on the town council, possibly claiming that a blind man is incapable of participating in public life. The ruling is that blindness is different from loss of civil rights for disgraceful conduct, which would indeed have necessitated giving up his seat. The decision that disability should not prevent an otherwise qualified individual from participating in public life is in line with a ruling the previous year stating that illiteracy didn't disqualify a person from being on the town council. Similarly it was ruled that "persons afflicted with public disgrace (*infamia*) may hold no offices that would have been given them if they were of intact dignity, but they may have no excuse from curial or civic *munera* and it is necessary for them to pay customary levies for public defense."[11] Clearly the authorities were concerned that some people might try to avoid tiresome responsibilities by getting themselves into trouble.

The matters decided on 16 December, while no doubt important to those concerned, were relatively routine to the lawyers. Their responses appear to have been brief (they certainly are as they have come down to us). The requests do not seem to have offended their sensitivities; and neither, for instance, did a freedman named Lucillus, clearly a person of some means, who tried to use his status to excuse himself from civic *munera* only to be told quite matter-of-factly that "the condition of being a freedman cannot provide an excuse from *munera* or offices in the city in which the freedman is resident." The tone of the response could, however, be very much harsher as a man named Polymnestor found when he claimed that his profession as a philosopher merited a grant of immunity from service on a city council. He was told in no uncertain terms: "Your profession and your desire disagree with each other, for although you claim to be a philosopher, you are overcome with the blindness of avarice and you only wish to evade the burdens that are linked to your patrimony. Because you have tried this in vain you will be able to teach others by your example."[12] Similarly, someone on the legal staff was plainly appalled by Bithus, who had tried to sell his wife as a prostitute and was complaining that he had not been paid:

> You say that you put your wife up for sale: you therefore understand that
> your petition contains confession of your being a pimp and there is no place
> for an action on the secured amount because of the shameful reason for
> taking the payment. Although the shameful action was engaged in by both
> sides and the action would cease with payment of the claim, nevertheless,
> since it arose from a stipulation made against good morals it is shown that
> the action must be denied through the intervening authority of the law.[13]

Bithus' wife was clearly in a dreadful situation, like many others who figure among the petitioners here. For instance, a man named Olympius is so poor that he had sold his son into slavery; in another case a woman named Aurelia Euodia, forbidden by law to act for her underage son, seeks redress because she feels that he was forced to sell property at what she regards as an unfair price. Then, another woman is told that it is for the provincial governor to decide whether the offense committed against her is awful enough for her, as a woman, to bring suit, while a woman named Dionysia is told that "it is established that it is a male responsibility to undertake the defense of another and that is beyond the female sex."[14]

To be effective as well as authoritative, rescripts asserting moral positions such as denying the ability of women to act as tutors or expressing disgust at the appalling behavior of Bithus, needed to be locatable within the broader moral compass of the Roman people. Much of our evidence for the orientation of this compass comes from collections of proverbs, fables, and wise sayings. These varied sources of wisdom suggest that there were some general patterns of behavior that many people might agree were right or, on the other hand, worrisome (even if that sense might not stop a man negotiating with a person who was pimping his wife). In the realm of "wise sayings" or "gnomic literature," it might well be possible to find support for the belief that women should stay at home or that they were dangerous to deal with. Even though Roman law gave them control of property, and although well-to-do women could be highly visible in civic life and female entertainers could be phenomenally successful, there remained a very strong negative view against women, reinforced with batteries of misogynistic quotation from the literature—centuries old by the time of Diocletian—that were still central to school curricula. These "wise sayings" imply that women's role is to ensure the biological security of their society and if they aren't having babies they aren't doing their job. This view is less pronounced in fables and proverbs, which may reflect the tastes of less exalted members of society who were less concerned with these issues, but it remains true that the animals of Aesop's fables tend to be male, that the slave experience chronicled in the anonymous *Life of Aesop* is exclusively that of male slaves, and viewpoints that might be identified as specifically feminine are missing.[15]

In a world of limited literacy—and the Roman Empire was one in which full command of letters was restricted to the few—storytelling was an essential way of passing on received wisdom, and handbooks were widely used to shape all manner of communication. Although most people would need some knowledge of letters, since they had to deal with a government obsessed with documentation, few had much more literacy than being able to make sense of their tax records. Even if they had, they still might have preferred to use the services of a professional writer who could turn their words into the kind of language that an imperial official was accustomed to and would know how to make use of standard letters to shape a client's concerns. The dependence on "writing professionals" can also explain why people could be in reasonably responsible positions—for example, eligible for civic *munera*—and yet claim to be illiterate, or "slow writers."[16]

A great deal of communication in the Roman Empire seems to have followed a conventional pattern, suggesting that there was a premium on sounding like everyone else. And similarly with much of the thinking that prevails in both popular and educational literature, this is invaluable in offering some sense of what people thought was right and wrong and what constituted their basic concerns. Many stories and sayings focus on power relationships: how slaves could deal with their masters, how the poor could deal with the rich, what the obligations of those with money were to those less fortunate. Envy, for instance, was something judged best avoided, a lesson that may initially have been lost on the young boy who had to copy out eleven times "Do not be eager to be rich lest envy cause you misfortune." The poor could take comfort—if it can be described as such—in the fact that they have not far to fall whereas the wealthy should beware that the higher they stand the more vulnerable they are to the caprices of fate.[17]

Friendship is always important, but that too is something one must be careful about: one's friends should be like oneself—it's no good to make friends with people who are very different from yourself, as anyone knows who is familiar with the story of the bull who goes to dinner with the lion, only to flee when he discovers that he's the main course.[18] Likewise you have to be cautious about whom you laugh at, because if you laugh at a joke in the presence of the person who is the object of that joke, he will hate you: "Untimely laughter leads to weeping."[19] Anger is always a bad thing—the rich, especially, have to be wary since their anger can threaten serious harm to those around them. The story of Hadrian hitting his secretary and blinding him in one eye is a case in point. The emperor suffered great remorse, asking the man what he could do in recompense, to which the secretary replied that he could not return his eye. Indeed, wisdom could well be equated with caution and one needed to be aware that the gods were watching. One should be able to identify disgraceful conduct and should always seek to do the honorable, or so the literature suggests.[20] There is a fascinating collection of oracular texts, predictions obtained either by casting knucklebones or by selecting a letter that correlates with a divine saying. The seekers of these oracles trusted in a traditional religion based on faith in the gods' beneficences and believed implicitly that the gods took care of people.[21] They also inclined to the view that the gods helped those who helped themselves.

The language of Mamertinus, and of others whose words survive from this period, echo the feelings of popular literature in describing the deeds of Maximian and Diocletian, especially in presenting them as striving tirelessly to do right and defend the state. Distant as the two emperors must seem, they had to be in touch with the values of the society they led. This was a lesson that Constantine would learn as he was growing up, and it is one that he would never forget. In his years of power, Constantine will often seem to be responding to precisely the sorts of concerns that are raised in the literature of popular morality.

5.

A NEW LOOK

THOSE WHO ENCOUNTERED THE emperors through the legal system as described in the last chapter represent a tiny minority. Emperors had long since come to rely on more widespread forms of communication to get their messages across, though the different media used suggest greater and lesser degrees of imperial interest in communicating with the people.

One of the most significant audiences for Diocletian and Maximian comprised their own officials and the people who lived near to them in what was an ever-expanding number of imperial palaces. Less than fifteen years before Diocletian's accession, Aurelian had exalted the importance of Rome with his new circuit wall and the establishment of Sol Invictus' cult in the city, though he was very rarely resident there himself. Probus and Carus, two other recent predecessors of Diocletian, spent most of their time in the provinces. There were provincial cities that possessed all the appurtenances needed by an imperial entourage for a long stay—Alexandria was such a city, as was Antioch, which was a crucial base for wars with Persia; and Sirmium (now Sremska Mitrovica near Belgrade in Serbia) had had an imperial palace since the days when Marcus Aurelius stayed there for long periods. Trier may have been the primary base for the Gallic emperors, or it might have been Cologne. All of these were already places of importance whether an emperor resided there or not.

Diocletian took a radical step when he decided to build an imperial palace at Nicomedia, the site of his accession, making the city another headquarters along with Alexandria, Antioch, and Sirmium. Soon afterward, new palaces appeared at Trier and Lugdunum (Lyons) in Gaul, an imperial complex of some sort was built at Cordoba, and in Italy a new capital district emerged in the north with palaces at Aquileia and Milan, which had become an important base for the defense of Italy in the reign of Gallienus. Then, during the 290s, Serdica (the modern city of Sofia in Bulgaria) joined Thessalonica and Sirmium as the site of a palace. Lactantius, foe that he was of Diocletian's regime, gives us an idea of such projects: "Here there were basilicas, here a circus, here a mint, an arms factory, a house for his [Diocletian's] wife, one for his daughter...thus he always raved, seeking to make Nicomedia the equal to Rome."[1]

What Lactantius observed was true of all new imperial capitals: as centers of administration they needed facilities such as mints, and they also needed spaces for emperors to meet the different ranks who lived in their palaces. As a general rule, emperors met the common people at the frequent public games. So it is not surprising that Trier, which already had a large amphitheater before Maximian and Constantius established their presence in the city, found the building expanded; and Sirmium, Thessalonica, and Nicomedia all acquired new circuses. The spectacles at the amphitheater might be specially themed to enable the audience to relive a recent imperial triumph—for instance, Titus had long ago staged throughout the empire the execution of Jewish prisoners of war after the capture of Jerusalem in AD 70; and in the reign of Trajan, at least one Gallic city staged the death of Decebalus, king of the Dacians whom Trajan had conquered. These were moments in which the people could relish the power of their emperor and celebrate with him their mutual salvation. Other buildings that tend to crop up in imperial capitals are large bathhouses, which expressed a ruler's readiness to provide high-quality care for his people, and the massive basilicas that Lactantius so deplored where justice could be administered.

The importance attached to bathing is perhaps best seen in the huge bathhouse that Maximian would begin to construct at Rome in the name of Diocletian after his defeat of tribal raiders in North Africa. The building was probably begun in 299 (the year Theodora would give birth to a daughter named Fausta who would grow up to be Constantine's second wife) when Maximian was actually in the city. The finished monument would stand not simply as a symbol of victory and a testament to imperial largesse, but also as an incontrovertible statement of imperial stability, as its dedicatory inscription commemorates Diocletian and Maximian, retired by the time the building was finished in 305, and their successors.[2]

If the common person—the sort who might come seeking a rescript—was typical of those who frequented the theater or the bathhouse, the audience in a basilica was rather different. The great hall of a basilica would focus attention on the person of the emperor at the far end; the people who filled the hall on ceremonial occasions would be members of the court or local dignitaries. These encounters would be the occasions when panegyrics would be delivered, and the speaker's words would be complemented by the hall's rich trappings that might include memorials to victories such as paintings illustrating the phases of a recent campaign.

Such paintings appear to have been for many years an important element of imperial communication. They featured initially in the triumphal processions that celebrated victories in the years before Augustus, the most famous being perhaps the one carried at a triumph of Julius Caesar in 46 BC depicting a victory in northern Turkey and bearing the caption *veni, vidi, vici*: "I came, I saw, I conquered." Celebratory painting became increasingly widespread in later centuries. One third-century emperor put on displays at Rome to commemorate his victories on the Rhine and the Danube; another seems to have circulated pictures giving his version of the murder of his predecessor in an attempt thereby to prove he had had nothing to do with it. About a century after the promotion of Galerius and Constantius, one writer complains that a recent display focused on the hand of the Christian God in chasing off the barbarians rather than on scenes of imperial courage, and there are signs elsewhere of people reacting to similar images.

In the case of palatial art, some paintings might represent specific events, while others might take as their subject more general themes such as the submission of barbarian peoples to Rome. Paintings of this kind on display at the imperial palace in Milan when Attila arrived there so outraged the Hun that he commissioned a new painting showing the Romans submitting to him. And artistic themes didn't have to be specifically military. Maps were popular items. Not all of them were in palaces, but the palace at Trier may have been home to the very large map that is the prototype of our most extensive surviving map showing the Roman world as a collection of cities linked by the imperial road system.[3]

Although very large crowds might see their ruler at the games, there is no reason to think that the general public got close to the ruler at ceremonial events in the great basilica. Crowds stayed outside during imperial visits, while only individuals of importance would be in a position to hear the emperor

FIGURE 5.1
This image of the tetrarchs, now built into the Cathedral of St. Mark's at Venice, once stood in
Constantinople, where it was most likely also a transplant. It is a forceful statement of the theoretical
unity among the four members of the college and especially between the Augusti with their respective
Caesars. Source: © Shutterstock.

speak. About the time of Diocletian, the court ceremonials began to get more
elaborate and the emperor sought, more than many of his predecessors had,
to be seen as different from those who served him. Diocletian limited the use
of purple cloth to himself and his three colleagues; he wore a gold crown and
spectacular jewels.[4] Constantine, himself visible at many of these events after
he joined the court, seems to have adopted Diocletian's sense of spectacle with
relish and would show an adept sense of public theater at later points in his
life.

Whatever people saw when they witnessed an emperor's coming, it was
also important that those who could not see him be given a clear image so
they could imagine how he looked. For the first few years of their joint reign,
Diocletian and Maximian had been portrayed in the style of their immediate predecessors but as of 290, they took on a new appearance, a bit more

substantial than before. There was a further change in 293 when the silver coin-age was reformed so that all four rulers—Diocletian, Maximian, Constantius, and Galerius—appear with full-featured, heavy-set busts, and with very little to distinguish one from the other (fig. 4.1).[5] In addition, the people might now be treated to novel depictions of their emperors. The most famous in existence are in the Vatican Museum and in St. Mark's Cathedral in Venice: carved out of porphyry, these feature bearded emperors hugging each other (fig. 5.1). Perhaps inspired by this, some citizens began to cut their hair short and grow their own "imperial beards"; others would take home small images or have a lamp in the house with an imperial bust on it.[6] Reactions such as these offer some indica-tion of a polyvalent discourse going on about power, and signify that some imperial subjects, at least, were willing to take seriously the claim that they were living in a brave new world. As of 296 many would still need a good deal more convincing.

6.

PERSIA AND THE CAESARS

IN 293, even as Constantius and Galerius were taking up their new posts, Narses, the son of Sapor, the former king of Persia, rose up from his base in Persian-controlled Armenia and overthrew other claimants to the throne. Diocletian appears to have congratulated him on his victory—but this was scarcely enough to keep the peace indefinitely: three years later Narses attacked the Roman Empire.

The year 296 was a good one in which to launch an assault. In the west, Constantius was preparing for the final invasion of Britain. He would accomplish the destruction of the breakaway regime, now led by Allectus, who appears to have replaced Carausius, the "pirate" we met in chapter 4, after his defeat in 293. At the same time, a revolt had broken out in Spain, which attracted the personal attention of Maximian; he would then move to the Rhine in case the tribes north of the river should take advantage of Constantius' departure for Britain to raid across the border. Trouble may once again have been brewing in Egypt where there had been a revolt three years before, related, it seems, to the reprise of open war between two communities that had also fought each other under the emperor Probus during the 270s. Galerius had dealt well enough with that revolt, but the rebellion that broke out in 297, which threatened the stability of the region as a whole was more serious. It involved some imperial officials proclaiming themselves emperor—a situation clearly requiring the attention of Diocletian.[1] The Egyptian revolt meant that Galerius was on his own in dealing with the initial Persian attack.

Galerius' most serious problem as Narses advanced along what was probably the route his father had taken in 260 was that he did not have enough men to resist the full force of the Persian army; and with campaigns raging in three other theaters there were no significant reserves at hand.[2] Lacking enough men to resist efficiently, the outcome of the initial campaign was variously described as a disaster stemming from Galerius' imbecility or a hard-fought series of ultimately unsuccessful battles. According to one tradition, in a review of the troops at the end of the campaign Diocletian forced Galerius to follow his chariot, which (if true) may have signified to the soldiers that their commanders were apologizing, demonstrating their determination to do a better job. It is possible that this most hostile account is not the most accurate, though, for the Persians seem not to have passed beyond the Euphrates, perhaps indicating that the Roman failures were not catastrophic. In 298 the war shifted to the Armenian highlands and here, where the cavalry that were the strength of the Persian army were less effective, Galerius scored a massive success. One story has him displaying considerable courage by scouting enemy positions in person. Narses' army was routed and his harem captured. The Roman forces seem then to have crossed the Tigris, at which point the Persians allegedly decided to negotiate.[3]

The fate of Valerian appears to have been very much in the air in the lead-up to the campaign. Lactantius says that Diocletian used Galerius in command because he feared that if he didn't he would follow Valerian into footstool-dom; although the account may be false, Romans of Diocletian's time largely believed the story of the indignity to which Sapor subjected Valerian. In a later account we are told that the Persian ambassador opened the negotiations with a reminder to the Romans that their two empires were the world's great powers, and that it behooved neither to seek the destruction of the other. When he added that the Romans should be mindful of the changing fortunes of the world and not seek to press their advantage too far, Galerius blew up, pointing out, "Indeed you observed the rule of victory towards Valerian in a fine way, when you deceived him through stratagems and took him, and did not release him until his extreme old age and dishonorable death. Then after his death, by some loathsome art you preserved his skin and brought an immortal outrage to the mortal body."

The outcome of the Roman victory was perhaps more modest than might have been expected, given the rhetoric of revenge on the Roman side. The principal Roman demand was that Persia surrender control of five regions on the east bank of the Tigris in the area leading north into Armenia, which, having been dominated by the Persians in recent years, was now securely relocated in the Roman camp. The rulers of all these lands were expected to act in Rome's interests. The other demand was that trade be controlled through the city of Nisibis at the eastern edge of the Roman province of Mesopotamia. This move effectively recognized shifts in trading patterns arising after the destruction of Palmyra in the 270s. That city had controlled trade from India, through lower Mesopotamia and across the desert to Syria. It appears that Narses got his harem back.[4]

The new model Roman army had proved its worth. Its main tactical units included more cavalry, some light horse for scouting and harassing enemy units or pursuing the defeated, plus other heavily armored units on the model of the extremely effective Persian heavy cavalry, and smaller, more lightly armed infantry units. The typical Roman infantryman was now protected by a large shield, a bronze helmet and a leather chest-protector in place of the chain mail or segmented iron of earlier periods, and he preferred a lance to the javelins and short swords fundamental to former legionary tactics. Impressive as the triumph had been, it is striking that in the wake of the great victory, Diocletian avoided any move that would have required him to enlarge the army, which would have happened if he had chosen to garrison new territories taken from Persia. The vastly increased number of units that appear in the record from this time forward represent not a significant increase in the overall manpower of the military, but simply a different manner of deployment, just as the much smaller forts that come into being at this point along the Rhine and Danube reflect a tendency to deploy fewer troops on the frontier and more in positions from which they could react to rumor of invasion passed along from the forward defenses.[5]

It is in the wake of the twin triumphs over Persia and Allectus that we get complementary glimpses of the two Caesars, one in the words of a panegyric delivered immediately after the reconquest of Britain, the other in the spectacular sculptural decoration of Galerius' palace at Thessalonica. In the words of an orator or at the hands of a sculptor, the messages are remarkably consistent, drawing attention to the linkage between the rhetorical and plastic arts in shaping the outward image of the imperial college.

The speech to Constantius opens, as so often, with a confession of the orator's inadequacy for his task—this one is a retired imperial official who could recall his subject's successes as a general in the early years of Maximian's reign—and with a reminder that Constantius is there in the hall with them. Constantius, the speaker goes on, experienced a divine rebirth when he was selected as Caesar; his promotion in the spring chimed in with the rebirth of the world. The reason that the emperors needed two new Caesars was simply that the world was too big to be run by two men; there were too many places needing to be visited too often. Appointing two new emperors solved the problem and brought the imperial college into accord with nature: just as there were four elements and four seasons, so it was right that there be four emperors.[6]

Having explored the cosmic significance of Constantius' elevation as he sees it, the speaker assesses his accomplishments in the context of those of his co-emperors: the victories over Sarmatians, the defeat of the Egyptian rebellion of 293, and the campaigns against Carausius. Constantius' arrival (*adventus*) is presented as the beginning of victory—stress on the glory of the emperor's advent is commonplace in a panegyric—with the capture of Gesoriacum (Boulogne), then more victories at the mouth of the Rhine. The speaker conjures up images of the barbarians surrendering themselves to Rome, giving up their lands to farm in Roman territory. In this narrative the history of the previous decades collapses, so that it would seem that the new regime succeeds directly from that of Gallienus, a tendency that illuminates perhaps the contemporary interest in Valerian, Gallienus' father and co-emperor. At this point the rhetorical flood hides the complexity of what Constantius was trying to do. As Philip II with his grand armada in 1588, or, more recently, Napoleon and Hitler discovered to their cost, England is not an easy place to invade in the face of determined resistance.

Constantius had every reason to fear determined resistance. The enemy fleet intact, there was a substantial army on the island—and Constantius was limited in the number of men he could bring with him. Logistical factors—the most important being the size of the available ports—restricted the number of men that Constantius could bring to about 20,000, which was probably a smaller army than that of his enemies. And those enemies had proven themselves dangerous adversaries in the past, by land and sea.

To overcome the obstacle facing him, Constantius had to be able to win the war waged in the shadowy land of spies. He had to be able to keep his intended landing place secret from the enemy; he needed to know where the enemy fleet would be, where their troop formations could be found. He would need to know what roads to take when he landed, and he would need to try and keep the enemy from destroying the province if it looked like they were going to lose.

Advance planning was everything, and Constantius planned brilliantly. He slipped past Allectus' fleet to land his army in the south of England; he crushed his enemies on the road to London and occupied the city without a fight. It is tempting to see the massive hoard of nearly 4,000 coins plainly buried in the context of Constantius' invasion that was discovered near Rogiet in Wales in 1998 and the one found in 2011 at Faye Minter in Suffolk with 627 coins of Allectus and Carausius as signs of the confusion and fear that his arrival brought to his foes. Constantine, now in his early teens, would most likely have been in Trier as news of his father's victory arrived; he would also have been of an age to understand what he had done and how he had done it. Did his father also tell him of the old days with Aurelian, who had shown that the best way to end a civil war was with a careful mixture of diplomacy and violence?[7]

The panegyric on Constantius places his accomplishments within the spectrum of idealized imperial behavior—the courage of the emperor; the humiliation of foreign foes, and especially of their leaders; the successful transfer of populations and the unity of the new regime with the natural world. These were themes that could be taken up in art as well as in words, and it is through art that we may perceive the way that Galerius was now being seen.

Our evidence for Galerius comes from the piers of two arches belonging to what was once an octagonal structure leading into a palace (see figure 6.1). Carved on four of the inside walls nearer the palace itself are images referring to Galerius' campaign and on the outer panels more general images of imperial power. Proceeding from the outside in, the first inner panels depict specific events, then farther out are others illustrating the broader concept of victory in the east—the overall impression suggesting that Galerius' triumph was but one episode in an ongoing tale of conquest. On the first of the campaign-specific piers are three panels: one showing a cavalry charge, another the capture of Narses' harem, the third the Roman advance across the Tigris. The fourth panel depicts animals in such a way as to suggest that even the natural world is an enthusiastic witness to the glory of Rome. The neighboring panels show the final battle, the submission of the barbarians and the imperial

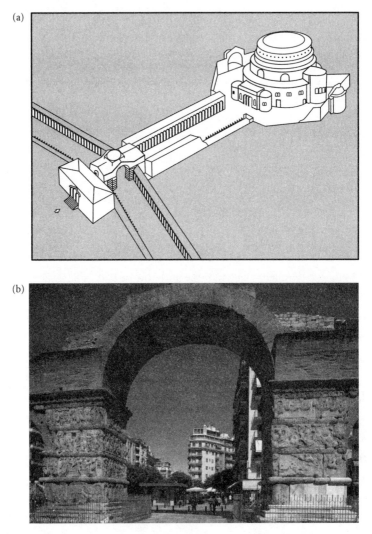

FIGURE 6.1

Arch of Galerius in Thessalonica was once the entrance to his palace as seen in the reconstruction in (a). As a visitor entered the palace, he or she would literally be surrounded with images of imperial victory and the ideology of the regime including the relationship between the emperors and the gods and the all-encompassing reach of imperial power. Source: © Shutterstock.

adventus ceremony, then more animals. Opposite are depictions of another imperial *adventus*, personal combat between Galerius and Narses, who, as he is unhorsed, looks rather like a Roman general, the Augusti on their thrones flanked by the Caesars (Diocletian appears somewhat larger than Maximian) and a procession of Victory goddesses.[8]

The image of Galerius' fight with Narses is striking not simply as confirmation that Roman generals were expected to lead from the front but also because it echoes Sasanian art in which the king is depicted in personal contact with the enemy—one surviving example shows Sapor unhorsing Valerian (see figure 6.2). On the outside panels of the first pier we find the emperor dispensing mercy, personifications of Persian cities, and more animal processions, while on the outer side of the second pier are portrayals of the abstract qualities of victory in the east, the virtue of the emperor, and a triumphal procession. Roma, the divine manifestation of Rome, is accompanied by victory goddesses, one of them carrying a commemorative shield, then more animals. Roma represents here the idea of the Roman Empire rather than the city itself: where the image of Roma does represent the city she is shown in the company of other great cities—a forceful statement on the part of Diocletian and his colleagues that the center of the empire was no longer that one city in Italy that had been the formal seat of their predecessors' power.[9]

It is perhaps difficult to overemphasize the importance of the year 298 for imperial morale. Finally, after years of internal strife and uncertainty as to whether Rome could successfully deal with the full force of the Persian Empire, the questions had been satisfactorily answered. The last internal rebels, in Egypt and Britain, were dead, and Persia had been badly beaten. The new regime had justified its own pretensions and ousted Aurelian as the reputed restorer of the Roman world. Aurelian was not alone, of course, in having his role redefined: beyond the language of panegyric there is no more significant illustration of the importance of the regime's historical revisionism, and increasing sense of superiority than Arcadius Charisius' history of the praetorian prefecture.

In Charisius' account, praetorian prefects were appointed in place of masters of horse who had been assistants to people holding the office of *Dictator*, the all-powerful magistracy of the Roman Republic whose role Julius Caesar had transformed in the last years of his life (49–44 BC) into the foundation of his power as head of the Roman state. The result was that

when the government of the Roman state was transferred to permanent emperors, praetorian prefects were chosen on the model of masters of horse by the emperors, and greater power was given to them for the improvement of public discipline. From these swaddling clothes the

61

(a)

(b)

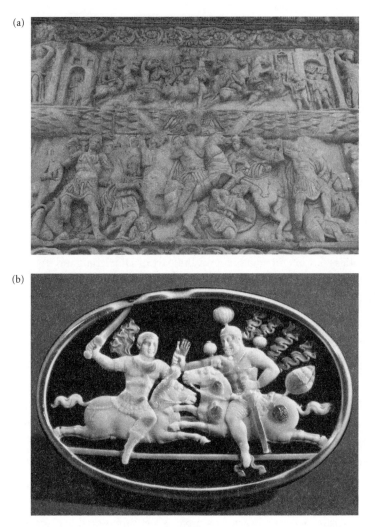

FIGURE 6.2

The victory of Galerius over Narses is represented by this scene in which Galerius is shown unhorsing the Persian king. The image here is evocative of Sasanian imagery represented, for instance, on the great Cameo showing Sapor's capture of Valerian and represents the assertion that Rome had now reversed the verdict of 260. Source: Mike Leese. Photo (Cameo): Bibliotheque Nationale, Paris. Erich Lessing/ Art Resource, NY.

authority of the prefects has deservedly expanded so greatly that it is not possible to appeal from the praetorian prefects. Although there had previously been an open question whether, in law, an appeal was possible from the praetorian prefect, and there existed examples of those who had appealed, the right of appeal was later rescinded by an imperial statement read out in public. The emperor believed that those men who had been brought on account of their singular industry and demonstrated faith and seriousness of character to the magnificence of this office would decide no differently in their wisdom and light of their dignity than he himself would decide.[10]

In fact, the office of praetorian prefect had nothing whatsoever to do with the earlier master of horse, and to say that it had is no more than an antiquarian fantasy intended to prove that contemporary institutions had existed since the earliest time. There's nothing new in that, but what is novel is the idea that the emperor would state that, at least in the context of the legal system, an official should be a clone of himself. Given this understanding of his role, the prefect, at least in theory, was responsible for the integrity of the empire's day-to-day administration—the meaning of "public discipline" in this passage—and this too resonates with the spirit of the new codes whereby his lawyers represent the emperor himself in setting guidelines by which people should deal with their problems. The self-righteous self-confidence implicit in Charisius' statement would become an ever more pronounced feature of Diocletian's regime in the years after the Persian war.

As Diocletian's regime entered a new phase, so too did Constantine enter a new phase of his life. We can't be sure when it was, but already by 297 he may well have left his father's court and moved to Diocletian's. In one of the few autobiographical statements that survive from his own pen, he would later say that in his youth he had seen both Babylon and Memphis. It may be that the reference to Memphis means he was with Diocletian when he suppressed the Egyptian rebellion, though there would be another opportunity to visit there with him a few years later; the reference to Babylon should mean that he saw something of the last phase of the war against Persia.

Constantine was now in his mid to late teens, an age when young Romans of good family left home for places of higher education, and at home the palace was filling up with the offspring of his father's marriage to Theodora. In the end they would have six children: the sons were Flavius Dalmatius, Julius Constantius, and Hannibalianus; the daughters are known to us as Constantia, Anastasia, and Eutropia (Anastasia, an overtly Christian name commemorating the resurrection, is unlikely to have been the name of an emperor's daughter at birth).[11] Constantia, the oldest of the girls, would be of marriageable age by 313, and Eutropia may have been the youngest.[12] Anastasia was felt to be marriageable in 316. The fact that none were married before their father's death in 306—and, indeed, for some time after that—suggests rather strongly that their births fall between 295 and 306, or in the case of Constantia and Anastasia between 295 and 300. Although Constantine's relationships with his stepbrothers and sisters would prove important in later life, the chance to leave his infant siblings and seemingly perpetually pregnant stepmother behind may have been something of a relief.

When he reached court, Constantine would have continued his education in Greek and Latin when not accompanying Diocletian on campaign. He may have had a private tutor (if so, that person is unknown to us), but, on the rare occasions when the court was resident at Diocletian's preferred capital of Nicomedia, he may have sought out the city's leading professor of Latin. This man was of North African extraction with a broad knowledge of Latin letters, especially of the classical period—he knew Virgil very well, as would any well-educated person of the time, and was deeply interested in what he perceived to be the imminent end of the world. This man was Lactantius.

∽ III ∽

CONSTANTINE AND DIOCLETIAN

———————————

7.

THE COURT OF DIOCLETIAN

T HE YEARS THAT CONSTANTINE spent at Diocletian's court saw radical efforts by Diocletian and Galerius to reform the empire—efforts that were largely unfruitful. Did observing this futility that would unfold in the years after the great triumph over Persia have an impact on Constantine? We cannot know for certain, but we do know that when his turn came to rule the Roman world he did not attempt to emulate Diocletian. Perhaps by then he had learned the limits of imperial power. He would certainly learn a great deal about how government worked, about how to deal with the people who worked in large institutions and about the art of war. He would show a precious mastery of all these areas when he took power for himself in his mid-twenties. He would also fall in love.

Late imperial courts were more than the massive building complexes where emperors and subjects could communicate with each other. They were vibrant communities in their own right, bringing together diverse individuals and agendas of all sorts. They were also mobile, and although Lactantius claimed that Diocletian was trying to build up Nicomedia as a new Rome, the emperor was rarely there during the years that Constantine was at court. Constantine tells us that he saw Memphis and Babylon in his youth, so he must have joined the court where it was most often located in those days: on the road. Diocletian was in Egypt from 297 to 298, in Syria to support Galerius' operations against Narses by February 299, and residing most often at Antioch, though he would go as far east as Nisibis, a powerful fortress just to the east of the Tigris to complete the peace negotiations with Persia. Last attested at Antioch in July of 301, the court appears to have headed off again later that summer for Egypt, where it remained until 302. It was back at Antioch by the autumn of 302 and in Nicomedia from the end of 302 through March 303, at which point Diocletian and his entourage made the long, slow journey to Italy. Although he would fall desperately ill in Rome in December of 303, he again took to the road, making his way back to Nicomedia. It was there that he would end his reign on May 1, 305.[1]

To be a courtier of Diocletian was to be a traveler, and while some cities were equipped with the infrastructure of palaces and all that went with them, court life was not the same as palace life. Court life involved participation in a hierarchically organized community that could function as the effective government of a great empire at whatever point it might stop for the night.

The court, or *comitatus*, of Diocletian included people ranging from transport personnel, soldiers, cooks, and domestics of all sorts to the great ministers of state and those who served them.[2] The military escort appears, in Diocletian's time and in his particular entourage, to have consisted of recently raised units of the imperial guard, both infantry and cavalry, including horse archers and heavily armored cavalrymen.[3] This escort amounted to about 3,000 men, enough to provide security but not enough for a decisive military intervention. There would also have been a corps of young "officers in training" or *protectores* (guardians), in whose company Constantine would have moved. When the bureaucrats and servants are added into the equation, it appears that the traveling court numbered some 6,000 persons.

At the time Constantine arrived, two of the leading ministers were Hermogenianus, the author of the great code of the 290s and now praetorian prefect, and Sicorius Probus, who apparently had overall charge of foreign affairs. Also present would have been whoever held Hermogenianus' old job overseeing responses to petitions, as well as the man in charge of the emperor's official correspondence and two finance ministers. One of these financial officials, *rationalis rei summi* (accountant of the highest account), controlled the mines, the mints, and the collection of taxes in cash, while the other, the *magister rei privatae* (master of the private account), ensured that money continued to flow in from the rents of the vast properties that passed from one emperor to the next, and that all property that should come to the emperor—such as property for whom no owner could be found, or in the form of gifts—was duly received by him. There would also have been the *praepositus* and his staff. The *praepositus*, or "stationed official," worked in very close proximity to the emperor, minding his bedchamber and wardrobe. He would have been a eunuch, possibly from abroad since castration was technically illegal in the Roman Empire, even though the ban was not necessarily enforced. Law tended to give way to utility in the Roman world and doctors were familiar with modes of transforming a healthy male into a eunuch. According to one expert:

> Since we are at times compelled to castrate against our will by persons of high rank, we will briefly describe the method of doing it. There are two ways to do it, by compression and by incision. The operation by compression is performed this way: children of young age are placed in a vessel of hot water, then, when the body warms, in the bath, the testicles are squeezed with the fingers until they disappear, and, being dissolved, can no longer be felt. The method by incision is as follows: let the person to be castrated be seated upon a bench, and, with the fingers of the left hand grasp the scrotum with the testicles and stretch them, making two straight incisions with the scalpel, one for each testicle. When the testicles appear they should be cut around and cut out leaving only the very thin bond of connection between the vessels in their natural state. This method is preferred to compression.[4]

Recompense for service at court was not especially lavish, something that may have made payments in kind (usually enough to feed an official's entire staff and possibly with enough left over to sell if he wished) and exemptions from civic *munera* especially important to those who served. Our evidence on this point is not ample, but what there is seems significant: namely, that the remuneration of one senior official was set at 300,000 sesterces. The figure as a salary for a senior palace official had not changed in more than a century and was thus worth vastly less than it had been before the high inflation during Aurelian's reign.[5] The inelasticity of salaries in the face of inflation may have made the early fourth century a time when imperial service was not dominated by people much wealthier than those who served on the town councils of major cities, and it is interesting that a later reminiscence expresses approval that Diocletian encouraged a "better class" of official and eliminated those of bad character.[6]

Although close proximity to the emperor at private moments—and to the empress, who might travel with the court—made palace eunuchs potentially very powerful, by reason of their physical condition, they were not usually included in the most important meetings of the emperor's inner circle, or *consistatorium*, so called because the members of this group would be standing (*consistentes*) throughout the proceedings. The fact that at a meeting of the consistatory, one person—the emperor—would sit while the others stood reflects an important aspect of the hierarchy within the palace and indicates how the various functions were defined according to their proximity to Diocletian. On a typical day, most people's station in life would dictate their activity: cooks would cook, soldiers would drill, the financial staff would deal with their accounts, the legal staff would answer petitions. The emperor had no direct role in these activities, and it is unlikely that Diocletian was consulted about the private rescripts that went out in his name since they were not conclusive. He would have been directly involved, though, in cases where a matter could be settled once and for all. In such a situation he would consult with the most senior staff and hear embassies from important places. A passage has survived in the later Codes showing Diocletian doing just this. It concerns an embassy from Antioch. We are told that when certain leading men of that city had been brought into his presence—presumably intending to claim that certain categories of courtier should not receive immunities from public service—a man named Sabinus (probably an Antiochene, as he seems to have spoken in Greek) made a comment to which Diocletian responded (in Latin): "Freedom from personal and civic *munera* has been granted by us to certain ranks, these are those who have served as protectors and *praepositi*. They are therefore not to be called to personal or civic *munera*."[7]

The response to this embassy does not show Diocletian's manners at their best. He is abrupt, and the point he is making is that his government communicates in Latin (in previous centuries emperors had responded to their Greek-speaking subjects in Greek). On the other hand, it is worth noting that he is speaking in his own right, and to ambassadors who have been allowed to speak to him directly.

The incident demonstrates that manners at court were complicated, and that our ability to understand just how people might have interacted is often complicated by the later reflections of individuals accusing Diocletian of having introduced outrageous new habits that set the emperor apart from his subjects. Such perceptions say a good deal more about the way Diocletian was remembered than about how he actually behaved, but it is undeniable that changes in court ceremonial did take place, especially practices concerning entrances into major cities, which became far more elaborate so as to induce a new sense of awe. The question however remains: just how unprecedented were these apparent changes and what impact did they have on the daily business of government?

It appears that Diocletian's interactions with his senior staff could be relatively informal. Lactantius certainly presents Galerius as speaking quite frankly to Diocletian; and at one meeting with Maximian, where only the two of them were present, Diocletian spoke very straightforwardly. Members of the emperor's innermost circle were expected to know things that others did not, and it is very likely that their exchanges were unobstructed by the intense formalism that was rapidly becoming standard in other areas of court life. A further sign of a distinction being made between those on the inside track and others are texts that identify certain very high-ranking people—praetorian prefects and the heads of the major bureaus of government—as consistatory companions (*comites consistoriani*).

Although members of the inner circle might speak their minds to the emperor, it does appear that membership in such a circle was far more limited than in earlier eras when emperors might invite members of the elite to weekend retreats or join important subjects for dinner. The ordinary person was now kept at a greater distance and forms of address that in earlier centuries might have appeared extreme or ridiculous—the satirist Lucian makes fun of people who see themselves as "more lordly than the others, expect worship to be paid them not from a distance in accord with Persian custom" who expect people to kiss their hands or breast—were now typical. Diocletian formalized behavior of the sort disdained by Lucian as a way of enhancing the impression of his magnificence, allowing only people of importance to be seen approaching him so that they could kiss the hem of the purple clothing that was now to be worn only by a member of the imperial college. How often was this ceremony performed with the traveling court? That remains unknowable, but it was not likely a feature of daily life. Such formal ceremonies are presented in the sources as something special and quite possibly were enacted only when the emperor entered a major city; they would also have the effect of showing off the important people in his train to those with whom they were staying.[8]

The young Constantine was a noticeable figure at court—Bishop Eusebius later claimed that he remembered seeing him pass through when he was with Diocletian, and Constantine's memories of Diocletian appear to have been very powerful. So too were his feelings about the lives of his courtiers; later in life he would be solicitous of their well-being, and in his dealings with his senior officials he appears to have been quite open. Like Diocletian, he would often display signs of a powerful temper, but—and this seems to have been unlike Diocletian—he also seems to have been capable of backing down or changing his view of a person.[9]

Other, less spectacular behaviors associated with emperors were, no doubt, more common in the daily life of the court. These included the process of moving from place to place—although not every stopping point would be of sufficient importance to merit a formal entrance ceremony—as well as making public sacrifices to the gods, and going on hunting trips. We can obtain a unique insight into the impact of the court's arrival in a new place from a collection of letters written by the official in charge of the city of Panopolis, the modern city of Akhmin, in southern Egypt in AD 298 about the time that Constantine joined the court, and it may well be that this correspondence preserves the earliest official documentation connected with Constantine's career in the imperial service. Diocletian had passed by earlier on his way to deal with tribes beyond Egypt's southern border, and, it seems, to see how the area was settling down after a revolt.

We may get some sense of how Constantine and other members of the court may have traveled the Nile in this year from the memoirs of Richard Pococke, an Englishman who journeyed down the Nile in 1737 and who describes for us "the great ships" with two masts, covered in matting supported "by means of poles set upright with others tied across the top, under which awning the passengers sit by day or repose by night." Since Pococke was in a small boat and disguised for his own safety as a Copt, he seems envious of the leisure in which others could travel. In the late summer, when Constantine would have been on the Nile, the temperatures would have been in the nineties and any shade would no doubt have been welcome. What we cannot know is whether, in the vicinity of Panopolis, Constantine would have met the ancestor of the cult of the healing snake who in Pococke's time was believed to be a former sheik, whom "God, out of a particular regard" transformed into "a serpent, which never dies, but is endowed with the power of healing diseases and conferring favor on its votaries." Pococke suspected that the cult had roots in much more distant antiquity than his informants could have known.[10]

The person who provides a sense of what it was like to have the court come to town in Diocletian's time was Panopolis' *strategos*, whose name was probably Apolinarius. The title *strategos*, the Greek word for general, had been used for local administrators in Egypt ever since the arrival of Ptolemy I, Alexander the Great's general who had taken Egypt over after Alexander's death in 323 BC. Ptolemy and his heirs had superimposed a Greek administrative system on the existing Egyptian structures, and it is this that lends the massive documentation surviving on papyri its particular flavor. Here we find practices dating from the time of the pharaohs before Ptolemy mingled with the latest in Roman administrative wisdom; and Greek mingling with what was now becoming the standard form of written and spoken Egyptian: Coptic, a language descended from that of the common folk who had served the pharaohs and survives to this day in Egypt's Christian communities. The *strategos*, despite his military-sounding title, was not at all a soldierly figure, although he was responsible for the maintenance of public order in his town. When not dealing with miscreants, the *strategos* (who inevitably came from a neighboring district) had the difficult task of mediating between the needs of the people he was overseeing and the demands of the imperial government—a classic mid-level functionary trapped between the often idealized vision of the way things worked that existed in the minds of his superiors and the stubborn irascibility of the people he was supposed to manage.[11]

From the correspondence (known from a long papyrus roll) which opens on September 11, 298, it is clear that preparations for the court's arrival have been going on for some time and that Aurelius Isidorus, the procurator of the province—Lower Thebaid—in which Panopolis was located, was getting increasingly anxious. It would be he who would presumably have to answer to officials at court if things didn't go well. In late July or early September the *strategos* had written to local officials about the need to appoint people who would ensure that food and other necessities were provided. A second letter refers to a communication from Aurelius Isidorus about the provision of ships needed to transport necessities for "the arrival of our lord the ever-victorious emperor Diocletian senior Augustus." The third letter appears to deal with the difficulties of getting people to heed Isidorus' instructions. This letter, which the long-suffering official appears to have signed using a date in the Egyptian month of Thoth, refers to unpaid taxes from some point in May "to the nones of August (August 5) in the consulship of Faustus and Gallus," suggesting that Isidorus was getting his orders from higher up in the administrative chain, where people naturally used Roman dates, not Egyptian.[12]

Life appears to have become even more fraught for the *strategos* between the 11th and the 15th of Thoth as the town authorities evidently do not share the sense of urgency that is exercising him and Isidorus. Moreover, people connected with the court are starting to show up in the area. On September 13 the *strategos,* no doubt getting rather desperate, writes to a person of some local consequence (possibly the leader of the town council at Panopolis): "with regard to the supply of the *annona* [tax revenues collected in kind rather than cash] which have been ordered to be stored in various places in connection with the fortunate arrival of our Lord the emperor Diocletian the Senior Augustus, I have written you both once and a second time so that you will select receivers and overseers of provisions for the most noble soldiers who will be entering our city," and still nothing is done. On the 19th the situation seems ever more dire. Finally on the 23rd it appears that people are at last beginning to cooperate.

The *strategos,* himself a new appointee, is trying to organize all this against the background of the recent suppression of a revolt by Domitius Domitianus probably connected with Diocletian's order to reorganize the provincial tax system, and some of the ambivalence about Diocletian's arrival, as expressed, perhaps, in the locals' slowness in responding to the *strategos'* requests may be connected with this. However, there is little or no evidence in any of the correspondence for anyone doing anything that can be directly associated with the revolt except possibly the issuing of the note about arrears in taxation earlier that year, and a note elsewhere about arrears for the previous year. Some officials, including Aurelius Isidorus, had been in office before the rebellion—we know this because he transmitted an edict concerning the tax increase that may have sparked the revolt—and he may have kept his job during it. Similarly, the leaders in the towns through which Diocletian would be passing had not obviously resisted the rebellion, nor, for that matter, had the troops, whose units are receiving full pay in documents datable to 300 and seem to be getting their full pay in 298 as well. In the 270s, Aurelian and the Palmyrenes had both set high standards of nonintervention in local affairs, and Diocletian was following suit.[13] The *strategos'* communication, taken as a whole, illustrates a crucial point that Constantine seems to have assimilated thoroughly by the time he left Diocletian's court—that power at every level was something that needed to be negotiated.

The court's journey to Panopolis, while stressful for everyone, enabled the center of imperial power to shift for several months to southern Egypt, and as a diplomatic act this may have helped facilitate the reintegration of the area into the empire.

The food that was being collected to supply the court as it passed through the Panopolis area was nothing special—largely local produce, which at this point meant wheat with which to bake bread. For Egyptians, bread was a staple. Their diet would also include a wide range of vegetables—lentils, beans, asparagus, turnips, cabbage, chickpeas—as well as fruits, fish, cheese, and various meats such as chicken, mutton, goat, and pork in various forms (including sausages). Menus for two dinners that would not have appealed to the local jet-set to be held in the Egyptian city of Oxyrhynchus read: "For dinner on the 5th: a Canopic cake, liver. For dinner on the 6th: 10 oysters, 1 lettuce, 2 small loaves, 1 fatted bird from water, 2 wings…" The diet that we recover from these documents is evocative of the Christmas feast to which Pococke says he was treated by the Coptic community in Akhmon/Panopolis, "chiefly consisting of rich soups, ragoos, pigeons and fowls stuffed with rice and roasted lamb."[14]

While the basic diet seems, from these menus and other similar items, to be astonishingly consistent through the ages, at about this time there was one change of great cultural significance, arguably one of the more radical in Egyptian history: wine replaced beer as the alcohol of choice among the population as a whole.[15] For the soldiers, who were also supplied by the *strategos*, their diet was most likely similar to that of the rest of the people, though the quantity of meat (especially pork) that would have been available for them to consume was a good deal greater. The farther up the court ladder one progressed, the chances are that the quantity and variety of meat consumed increased proportionally. This may have been linked with the hunting expeditions that were one of the great passions of aristocratic Roman life, and a pleasure long associated with the notion that the ruler needed to protect his subjects from dangerous predatory animals (especially the feral swine that are often presented as public enemy number one in the natural world).[16]

Hunting, in the aristocratic context, appears to have been organized along the lines of a major military operation. Two of the spectacular mosaics in the Roman villa at Piazza Armerina in Sicily—mosaics created in the lifetime of Diocletian and Constantine—portray massive hunts and give us an insight into an activity that may also be alluded to in the processions of animals adorning the Arch of Galerius mentioned earlier. The grander of the hunting mosaics is to be found in the "transverse corridor" that runs for sixty-five meters between the villa's audience hall and the inner courtyard, known as the peristyle court because it is surrounded by colonnades. The corridor terminates at either end in a rounded apse, the northern one offering a mosaic showing the female personification of Africa; the southern one shows the female personification of Armenia or India (the mosaic is too badly damaged to allow certainty).[17]

The composition that runs between the two apses is also of interest to us. It falls into three parts. At the northern end, hunters (who are obviously soldiers) are trapping African animals in a variety of ways. The central panels show animals being transported to what is plainly intended to be Italy, while the southern end has images of animals captured from elsewhere. There is good reason to think that the soldiers shown as engaged in the hunt are closely connected with Maximian, while the owner of the house, who must have been an important court official, probably figures in the transportation scenes. There are occasional scenes that show humans killing or being killed by animals, but the principal message from these mosaics is about the collection of animals for Rome, and especially, Rome's control over the natural world, from the west coast of Africa to the farthest eastern boundary.[18]

The second, much smaller mosaic, located in a nearby room, is more conventional, dividing the action into four registers. In the top register huntsmen are heading out to hunt rabbits; the second panel centers on a sacrifice scene, with more scenes of rabbit hunting. The third register shows falconers on one side and a horseman spearing a rabbit on the other; the bottom register depicts people chasing gazelles into a net, while on the other side hunters engage with a boar. Here the most powerful message that comes across to the viewer may be the socially unifying aspect of the hunt—the humble rabbit hunter is engaged in the same operation as the master of the house, each in his proper role. The hunt in this sense is the peacetime extension of military service.[19]

The personifications in the apses of the great hunting mosaic at Piazza Armerina and the depiction of the man sacrificing in the lesser one serve to underscore the important notion that humans are acting on a stage laid out before the eyes of the gods. So it was that one of the emperor's most important functions was to consult with them before undertaking any deed of importance. The usual way of doing this might be through animal sacrifice or by consulting an oracle.

All animal sacrifice, especially public animal sacrifice at which the emperor presided, was a very formal event at which a god was invited to demonstrate approval for the action of humans by agreeing to share a meal with them. The ideology informing these sacrifices, as depicted, for instance, on the triumphal arch of Trajan at Beneventum, focused on the role of the emperor in ensuring that the relationship with the gods remained intact. Here he stands in front of a group of garlanded officials, presumably fellow priests—the emperor always held a number of priesthoods, including that of *pontifex maximus*, or chief priest of the college that was charged with overseeing religious ceremonies— the whole representing the commingling of civil and religious roles that had been typical of Greco-Roman culture for at least a millennium by the time

FIGURE 7.1
Diocletian sacrificing as seen on the arch of Galerius. Source: Mike Leese.

Diocletian took the throne (see figure 7.1). These officials would have marched in the procession ahead of the attendants who accompanied the sacrificial beast to the altar. The emperor is pouring an offering (wine) from a small dish on to a small altar. A young boy stands next to him, holding a box containing incense that the emperor will offer once he has emptied the dish of wine. The eyes of all the priests are on the ruler, symbolizing the belief that the person making the sacrifice will (or should) determine whether the gods will be happy. Before the sacrifice actually began the emperor would have offered up a prayer to the gods, a rite clearly described by the Elder Pliny:

> It does not accomplish anything to sacrifice victims without a prayer, and it is not the right way to consult the gods. Furthermore, there is one form of words for asking an omen, another for averting one and another for commendation. We see that our highest magistrates address the gods with fixed prayers; that to prevent a word being left out or spoken in the wrong place, one person reads it out first from a script, another person is posted to keep watch, a third is given the responsibility to see that silence is maintained; and that a piper plays so that nothing but the prayer is heard.

Once the prayer was said and the burnt offering made, servants, usually slaves belonging to the state, would prepare the animal (on the Beneventum relief, it is a bull); although Romans of a certain class might hunt animals in the wild it was not thought fitting for them to engage in the menial task of butchering. This was done after the animal had had a piece of hair snipped from its fore-lock in the expectation that it would seem to nod its head—its agreement to being eaten was seen as useful—before being stunned with a hammer. Its throat would then be cut.

Once the animal was slaughtered, it would be cut open so that its innards could be inspected. If there was anything out of the ordinary to be seen, the sacrifice would be called off or the process repeated until it became clear that the gods were in fact well disposed. At this point it seems likely that a sacrifice at which Diocletian was present would include the official inspection of the entrails by a priest, or *haruspex* (pl. *haruspices*) trained in the art of divination from animal guts (and other natural phenomena). Then the innards would be placed on the altar, to be burned as the god's part of the meal. As soon as the animal could be butchered and cooked, the emperor and his priestly colleagues would settle down for their share of the food.[20]

All religious systems have active and passive aspects—the active involving the search for new revelation, the passive the repeating of actions that would seem to ensure the continuing goodwill of the gods. Sacrifice was a crucial moment at which the active and passive features of a cult came together. The ritual leading up to the sacrifice tended to be carefully choreographed so that it conformed to earlier, successful sacrifices, but the moment of sacrifice was the turning point. The process might be interrupted by some natural phenomenon or unexpected noise, or the innards of the beast could be found to be not quite as they should; it was invariably a moment of tension, and when an emperor was the sacrificer, it was also a moment when his authority was open to question—most important, were the gods still on his side? Only the success of the sacrifice could reaffirm the truth. A consequence of this implicit tension was that Diocletian exploded, or so Lactantius says, on a day in 302 when a sacrifice failed:

> Since he was, being fearful, an avid investigator of the future, he was sacrificing herds of animals and seeking the future from their entrails. Then certain attendants who were knowledgeable in the Lord put the immortal sign on their foreheads as they were standing by the fire, with this done the rites were ruined through the flight of the demons.[21]

Pagan belief was founded on the principle that the gods could be seen to intervene in human affairs through the predictions that they gave, either through approving sacrifices or through their oracles. People could go to see places where the gods were said to have been active—there was a site near Troy where what seems to have been a massive fossil was identified as the body of a giant killed in a primordial battle at the dawn of Jupiter's reign over the gods, and Troy itself was chock-full of mementos thought to be linked with the Trojan war. In fact, any major city in the eastern part of the empire was filled with inscriptions commemorating predictions of the gods that had come true or enjoining rites upon the people of the city. Aurelian's exaltation of Invincible Sun, when he claimed that the god had revealed his favor for Rome in the course of the final battle at Emesa, was a classic example of the active aspect of worship. According to Christian doctrine, which did not deny the possibility of miraculous events favoring its pagan neighbors, these wonders were not the result of a god's action—there being only one god, in their view, and he was not interested in helping people who did not worship him—but rather the work of demons who delighted in confusing mortals with their wiles. These demons were important to Christians in other ways as well, for one of the things that true believers were good at doing was uncovering the false actions and the actual harm that demons could do.[22]

Having set the scene at the sacrifice, Lactantius goes on to say that the *haruspices* did not see the expected signs and insisted that the sacrifice be repeated. Still the signs were bad, and the head *haruspex*, Tagis, finally told Diocletian that there were bad people around whose presence offended the gods. Diocletian was outraged and ordered that everyone in the palace was to sacrifice—if they refused they should be flogged—and that military commanders should make sure that all their soldiers sacrificed as well.[23]

The story as Lactantius tells it is not without its problems. The name of the chief *haruspex*, Tagis, is Etruscan, and the name is somewhat generic for *haruspices*, looking to the region now known as Tuscany where this priestly art was born. Diocletian's subsequent order was a traditional "Christian test," used for centuries to find out whether someone accused of being a Christian actually *was* a Christian, based on the theory that no committed Christian would offer a sacrifice. This was the issue that had fractured Christian communities after Decius' edict on sacrifices in 250. But by this point, Christianity having been legal for nearly forty years (hence the presence of Christians in the palace staff), it had plainly not been an issue recently. One might also wonder at the logic of Lactantius' tale, implying as it does that Diocletian's sacrifices ordinarily went off without a hitch, and by implication that the Christians in the palace did not see attendance at sacrifices as necessarily problematic.

The acts of a church council held a few years later in Spain include provisions for those who had held a duumvirate (essentially the position of co-mayor), holders of priesthoods of the imperial cults and of local priesthoods. If, for instance, a man holding a priesthood of the imperial cult (which he could be required to take on as a civic *munus*) offered sacrifice after having been baptized, the bishops ruled that he should not even receive the last rites; while a person who holds a priesthood of the imperial cult and sponsors a *munus*—in this case the word "gift" means a spectacle including beast hunts, gladiators, and quite often the execution of condemned criminals in horrific ways—but did *not* sacrifice would receive last rites after doing penance. A catechumen (a probationary member of the Christian community) could be baptized within three years of having held his priesthood. A duumvir could not receive communion during his year in office, while ex-priests, even if they continued to wear the wreaths they had worn in office could be admitted to communion within two years of holding office so long as they did not sacrifice.

From these rulings it is clear that Christian leaders were trying to reconcile their faith with the practical necessities of living in a pagan society and with the obligations of the church's wealthier members to their wider communities. Another ruling, that people who were killed attacking statues of the pagan gods could not be entered onto the list of martyrs, was plainly intended to dissuade Christians from provoking the pagan community, stressing that those who brought trouble down upon themselves deserved no honor.[24]

The decision concerning martyrdom was a profoundly controversial one, for some members of the Christian community believed that they should minimize dealings with the secular world and would most likely have been appalled by the rulings regarding Christians who held pagan priesthoods. The scene that Lactantius paints at court illustrates precisely the sort of trouble that extremists could cause for their fellows, and while he spins the story against Diocletian, he elsewhere admits that people should not seek martyrdom. It seems likely that some incident at this time led to the expulsion of some Christians from imperial service—this much is confirmed by another contemporary witness, Bishop Eusebius of Caesarea—but it is not clear that an event like the one described by Lactantius, colorful though it might be, was actually the cause. Eusebius seems to have thought that a senior officer named Veturius talked Diocletian into taking action against the Christians.[25]

In sum, what Lactantius really tells us is no more than that sacrifice was an important court ritual and that in 302, Diocletian decided to expel from imperial service Christians who failed a sacrifice test. In fact, the year 302 seems to be an important turning point in Diocletian's reign, for it is at this time that his regime becomes far more interventionist than hitherto.[26]

8.

IMPERIAL EDICTS AND

MORAL CRUSADES

A S WE HAVE SEEN, the traditional forms of communication between emperors and subjects, barring an imperial appearance in their midst, were rescripts and letters responding to particular local complaints. General orders or edicts were rare: the most famous of all edicts in Roman history, the decree that "went out from Caesar Augustus that all the world should be taxed," in the Gospel of Luke, was not an edict at all but rather an order for a provincial census to take place in areas administered by Quirinius, governor of Syria, in AD 6. Quirinius' census formed the basis for the tax regime in Syria for centuries to come, and, as in so many areas of Roman administration at this period, nothing really changed. Orders seeking to innovate were relatively rare. It was mainly a question of making existing practices work better—Diocletian issued a number of such orders in the 290s. Their format was barely different from those of earlier orders. They would be addressed to "all provincials" opening with a preface explaining why the emperor was taking the action he was followed by a series of instructions—for instance, as in the case of Decius' edict on sacrifices, telling people how they should go about carrying them out.[1]

The reason edicts were relatively rare is probably that Roman emperors realized they were unlikely to be effective, and because the emperors had a viable, if somewhat clumsy, method of getting their message out through the system of petition and response. The reason that orders delivered this latter way were more likely to be effective than edicts was simply that responses were addressing issues raised at the local level, while edicts expressed concerns arising from the more remote confines of the court. Also, court issues might have less resonance than rescripts, unless the order was for something that people would like (such as ways to become a Roman citizen) because the remit and standing of local administrators like the *strategos* at Panopolis differed profoundly from those of, for instance, the procurator of the private account in the province of Lower Thebaid.

Imperial administrators, who tended to come from outside the province, were on a ladder of promotion supported by generous exemptions from civic and personal *munera*, while local administrators were often performing their administrative tasks to satisfy their obligations regarding civic or personal *munera*. This being the case, if the imperial government was looking for results, persuasion was often a good deal more effective than command. In practical terms, government officials, aside from those managing imperial estates, tended to intervene at the local level only if there had been some spectacular demonstration of local ineptitude, usually involving fiscal mismanagement, the administration of justice in serious cases, and the collection of taxes. In two of these three areas, the role of the imperial administrator was more often that of a referee—albeit a referee who could torture or execute people who annoyed him—than that of a hands-on manager. Radical change, even in the area of taxation, was difficult to implement since the urge for efficiency could be met with passive resistance at the local level, as illustrated by the events around Panopolis in 298. Diocletian's response to revolt, as it appears in the records of the *strategos*, ignores the fact that the people he was visiting and the soldiers whose pay records fill a great deal of the *strategos*' dossier had all recently been supporting a man who had defied Diocletian's authority.

Diocletian's conduct in Egypt shows that he recognized the limitations of imperial power, and the first group of edicts he issued were all linked to reforms in the legal system during the early 290s. Several of his actions over the next decade suggest strongly that he, or those around him, decided to experiment with ways of expanding the reach of the court into the lives of the average Roman. The issues that most concerned the emperor were fiscal and moral reform.

Diocletian's view that one ought to be a good person to be a Roman emerges with painful clarity in an edict that he issued in 295 on the subject of close-kin marriage. The issue would seem at first glance to be a simple one: essentially, that people should not marry their siblings or children, or their grandmothers (mentioned as a possibility). This was a standard feature of Roman law. The problem was that close-kin marriage was relatively common in some parts of the empire; this was especially true in Egypt, where the law was now declaring as un-Roman something that people who had become Roman citizens after Caracalla's edict had been doing for centuries. The edict, in declaring such unions null, at least granted amnesty to those who entered into them before the edict's promulgation. In the strikingly self-righteous preamble the emperor states:

> Since to our pious and devout minds those things which were chastely and morally established by Roman laws seem especially worthy of reverence and worthy of devout preservation for all times, we do not think that we should ignore those things done by some persons nefariously and incestuously in the past, and since they are either to be restrained or punished, the discipline of our times encourages us to rise up. There is no doubt but that the immortal gods themselves, favorable as always to the Roman name, will be pleased in the future if we see to it that all those who live under our rule shall be observed by us to live pious, religious, quiet and chaste lives in all matters.

The further purpose of this edict, it is stated, is to ensure that the good reputation of those seeking marriage be protected and that any children be free from taint (he had recently issued a rescript banning children born of incestuous relationships from holding imperial administrative posts, though not civic *munera*). The edict notes correctly that marriages between close kin were always forbidden by ancient Roman law, people ought to remember that they live under Roman laws and institutions, that the present ruling contains nothing new and that the Roman Empire only gained its present greatness by safeguarding all its laws and the sanctity of religion. To marry injudiciously would be an act of ignorance and barbarity.

The nature of the document, the fact that it went out to all corners of the empire, makes it extraordinarily improbable that Diocletian did not approve its wording, even if he did not personally draft it. It must surely represent both his feelings about the issue and the role of the gods in the Roman world (which might help explain why he became so angry when a sacrifice went awry).[2]

A document like this would be received by an assembly of the local people who would listen, heads bowed and bared, as it was read out. Ordinarily a letter would accompany it from the provincial governor explaining what the emperor was saying (a redundant exercise, but useful to us because sometimes due to the vagaries of document preservation, the governor's letter survives when the edict doesn't).

The point of any edict was to activate the local bureaucracy to obey the order of the emperor. In the case of the one on close-kin marriage, the relevant officials would be those who worked on the census, keeping detailed records of every household through the house-to-house survey that became the basis for one of the main imperial taxes—the capitation tax, levied in various ways upon humans and animals. It is possible, as we shall see when considering some local officials enforcing a later edict, that such men might not consider the object of imperial displeasure to be as criminal as the emperor himself might think. The process of arousing local authorities to action was often complex, which might well be why in Decius' edict on sacrifices a clause was inserted saying that the order would have to be carried out by a certain date. In another instance, the edict ordering a new assessment of tax liabilities throughout the empire, it appears to have taken an exceptionally long time, even when there were no rebellions to contend with, to actually complete the required surveys. For the tax edict of 297 we have documents from the archive of the long-suffering Aurelius Isidorus chasing down declarations of olive groves in 298, 299, and 300. In Syria can be seen a series of inscriptions relating to the activities of census-takers in the countryside who were evidently charged with determining village-by-village liabilities. Here, the necessarily thorough surveys of village territory could open up entirely new areas for corruption: another probable reference to the impact of the taxation edict in Isidorus' dossier points to collusion between local leaders and officials charged with conducting the survey.[3]

The language of a letter that Diocletian would write a few years later to the governor of Egypt is in many ways similar to that of the edict on close-kin marriage of 295. This time the object of imperial wrath is a religious group devoted to the teachings of the mid-third-century Persian visionary, Mani. Mani's career provides a remarkable example of the way a missionary faith could spread during that era, and the attraction that new ideas about the divine might have even for eminent persons. Odaenathus' widow Zenobia, for instance, is said to have met with his missionaries, and Sapor himself appears to have been interested in what Mani had to say. It was Bahram II's brother, Hormisdas, dominated as he appears to have been by Kartir, the leading light of the Zoroastrian revival that accompanied the rise of the Sasanians, who would execute Mani as a heretic. The teachings of Mani, who appears to have been very widely read in the religions of the period, combined elements of Christianity with Zoroastrianism along with his own powerful imagination to describe the eternal struggle between the forces of Light and Dark. While he was in Alexandria, Diocletian had learned from Julianus, the governor of Africa, that a new sect, which Julianus seems to have researched very carefully, had arisen "from the Persian race which is opposed to us," and was challenging received doctrine. Diocletian was appalled that anyone should seek to challenge the wisdom received from the ancients: "The immortal gods are disposed to order and arrange matters through their foresight so that those things that are good and true are approved and fixed by the wisdom and constant deliberation of many good, eminent, and the very wisest men." He had heard that the Manicheans had disturbed people's calm and upset whole communities. Furthermore he feared lest (as, he felt, often happened) "there should be an attempt, through the execrable customs and savage laws of the Persians, to infect with their malevolent poisons, men of a more innocent nature, the temperate and tranquil Roman people, as well as our entire empire." Julianus was therefore ordered to arrest all the Manicheans he could find and burn them, along with their books—though if he should find any in the imperial service, he should instead send these individuals to the mines.

To carry out the order, Julianus would have to rely on local authorities, and since Diocletian probably relied on him as his source of information on this point, he most likely thought that Julianus' own province was the only place that Manicheans were to be found. In any event, the Manichean community survived whatever savagery Julianus unleashed upon them to play a powerful role in the intellectual development, later in the fourth century, of the future St. Augustine; and in Egypt, they set up communities off the beaten track in places like Medinet-Madi and Kellis, in which precious Manichean libraries were discovered in the twentieth century.[4]

If moral reform was one pole of Diocletian's moral compass—and it seems that it was—another was administrative efficiency as defined by fiscal reform

and improved management. A change in census procedure in 297 was one feature of an ongoing reformation of the provincial administration that saw the
progressive division of the large provinces of the earlier empire into smaller
units. In some cases the change made use of earlier internal divisions within
provinces; these tended to be subdivided into smaller districts whose financial
affairs were overseen by local procurators who had reported directly to the
emperor and were outside the orbit of the governor.[5] Elsewhere, new provinces—Lower Thebaid is one—were created as the emperor thought best.

In addition to his growing concern about personal morality, Diocletian
seems to have been bothered by the pathetic status of the imperial coinage
and aware that there might be substantial regional variation in the prices of
basic goods and services; this was only to be expected given the breadth of the
Roman Empire, where major ecological differences could not fail to result in
widely varying economies.

The first problem Diocletian set out to solve was galloping inflation. Everyday
transactions now required massive quantities of the bronze coinage that was
the basic medium of exchange. Evidence for reform survives in the coins of the
period, which are minted to a new, much heavier standard, and an inscription
from Aphrodisias in western Turkey. The inscription comprises an edict and an
explanatory letter to or from the local governor: the sum total of the information they offer tells us that the imperial coinage was to be retariffed at double its
face value. Debts contracted to the *fiscus* (the treasury) or to private individuals before September 1, 301, were to be repaid according to the old standards,
while those contracted on or after that date were to be paid according to the
new regulations.[6]

It is unlikely that the edict on coinage was conceived in a vacuum: it was
probably intended as a prelude to one of the most interventionist acts ever
attempted by an ancient government. This was the Edict on Maximum Prices,
issued between November 20 and December 10 of 301. Taken together, the
edicts look like a prescription for a new fiscal order based on what Diocletian
conceived as a fair dispensation across the entire empire. But whereas the edict
on coinage appears to have been a reasonable response to the problem of inflation, the price edict was not. It is perhaps significant that Lactantius, in the
course of lambasting Diocletian for all manner of woes suffered by the Romans,
mentions the price edict, but not the coinage reform.[7] Both edicts also involved

physical actions that people could not miss. In the case of the coinage edict it meant that people would be carrying around the new, heavier coins. In the case of the edict on prices it meant that there might be a massive new monument erected in their town, or that the wall of a public building might be covered in writing so people could see what things should cost (see figure 8.1). Both are powerful symbolic acts reflecting the new confidence that government had in its own virtue, a confidence seemingly born of success on the battlefield.

The connection between external victory and internal order, at least in the mind of Diocletian, is very evident at the start of the edict:

> The memory of the wars that we have fought successfully rightly gives thanks to the Fortuna of our *Res publica*, together with the immortal gods, for the tranquil state of the world placed in the embrace of the most profound peace, and for the goods of peace, on account of that which was striven for with great sweat; decent public opinion as well as Roman

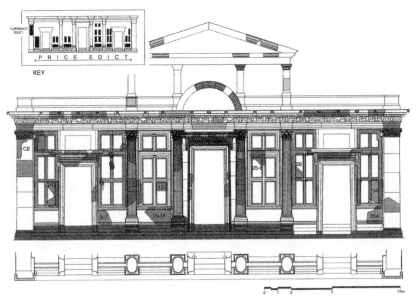

FIGURE 8.1

The Edict on Maximum Prices was a massive document whose inscribed form was a demonstration of the ambition of government. This reconstruction shows how the decree was exhibited in the city of Aphrodisias (western Turkey). Source: Phil Stinson. With permission from the Aphrodisias Excavations, New York University.

majesty and dignity demand that it be stabilized faithfully and ordained decently so that we who, by the benign favor of the gods, have stifled the seething ravages of barbarian nations in previous years by the slaughter of those nations, will surround the peace founded for eternity with the proper foundations of justice.[8]

The justification for the edict derives from the "excesses perpetrated by persons of unlimited and frenzied avarice" that were not checked by self-restraint, from the action of individuals who "have no thought for the common need."[9] The emperors are acting in accord with their subjects, who can no longer ignore what is happening; hence "we hasten to apply these remedies long demanded by the situation, satisfied that no one can complain that our intervention against evil-doers is untimely or unnecessary, trivial or unimportant." In so doing they "exhort the loyalty of all, so that the regulation for the common good may be observed with willing obedience and due scruple."[10] Moreover, the particular victims of high prices are the very agents through whose efforts the security of the state has been won—the soldiers.

In practical terms, the Edict on Maximum Prices was an act of economic lunacy. Price controls had long been part of civic life, and it may be that Diocletian did not realize that a policy that might have short-term benefits in times of food shortage could not be translated to an empire-wide level with any hope of success.[11] In simplest possible terms, the edict ignored the law of supply and demand, the fact that prices were set by the availability of goods, and that the cost of goods was affected by the cost of transport. It could be objected that the prices in the edict—which were set for an enormous range of goods and services—were intended as maximums and thus that the numbers appearing in the edict are in fact unrealistically high for many parts of the empire. But this doesn't seem to be so.

The driving force behind the edict was a desire to set maximum prices for the goods and services listed, but the state too would have to pay those prices, and it is inconceivable that the *fiscus* would willingly overcharge itself across the length and breadth of the empire. In fact, except for the price of wheat, which does appear to be set near a maximum rate of one hundred denarii per *modius* (the customary wheat measure, about two gallons), prices generally appear to have been below the going rate in Egypt at the time the edict was issued.[12] Moreover, while the edict includes differential prices for some goods in different stages of production, as well as transport costs, it does not appear to recognize that those transport costs needed to be added to production costs in the computation of a fair price. This omission cannot be taken as evidence that every community in the empire was essentially self-supporting, for in the computation of transport costs the edict demonstrates awareness that every kind of transport needed to be factored into the structure of the economy. What happened was simply that it factored these costs in inadequately, and this may well reflect the way the court paid for things. It is quite likely that someone at court would pay 1,200 denarii for a hundred pounds of pork sausage and then 25 denarii to a camel driver to move it to where it was needed. One of the problems faced by the procurator of Upper Thebaid in 298 was that he had to arrange both to collect the food for the imperial visit and, separately, to make sure that it got moved to the right place.

A further problem with the edict was the mechanism of enforcement. Earlier edicts could rely on the structures of the existing imperial institutions—the mints, the financial organizations including the banks that changed money, and the officials who made lists of people for the capitation tax. In this case, those responsible for enforcing the edict would have been local market officials (this task was yet another personal *munus*). These were individuals who had minimal connection with the organs of imperial government and, if Lactantius is to be believed, showed minimal competence in handling the situation so that prices skyrocketed, blood was shed, and goods were ultimately driven off the market.[13]

Despite Lactantius' vehemence, the impact of the prices law cannot be traced in any other source no matter how hostile to Diocletian (it is not even mentioned by Eusebius). This might suggest that the edict was repealed within a short time of being issued, possibly because it was seen to be a massive failure. Another possibility is that people very soon started to ignore it. The inscriptions containing the tariffs survive from more than forty places, and if the edict had been repealed, it is likely that the stones containing it would have been destroyed. Lactantius states that "the law dissolved through its own necessity," which could support either repeal or irrelevance.[14] It is notable that these inscriptions come only from a part of the empire where Galerius too was active, so it would seem plausible that the sudden interest in the widespread inscription of a Latin edict had something to do with his own tastes and his own notion of what it was to be Roman, for this edict too reflects something of the imperial sense of appropriate Romanness. The surviving record of Latin inscription from these years is abnormally weighted away from the western emperors in favor of the eastern—Diocletian, Galerius, and their successors.

Does the prevalence of inscribed versions of an imperial edict in one part of the empire as opposed to another reflect the way that an edict was actually enforced? It is quite possible that there was a connection and there is certainly some reason to think that the next of Diocletian's edicts was unevenly enforced throughout the empire. This edict, aimed at forcing Christians to conform to what Diocletian felt to be the norms of Roman life, was issued in February 303 after the emperor had arrived at Nicomedia and settled into his palace after many years on the road. It is not at all clear why he should suddenly have decided to pursue the Christians, who were by this time an established group within the empire and could not readily be associated with "barbarian habits." Lactantius' suggestion that the edict stemmed from the incident of the failed sacrifice in 302 seems unlikely given the length of time separating the two, though other incidents involving Christians refusing to sacrifice might have aggravated the situation.[15] But Lactantius' suggestion that Galerius played a role in the decision to go after the Christians does seem believable as he would show himself to be an implacable foe of the Christian community right up until the last year of his life. According to this version, Galerius saw the persecution as a way of arranging the succession in his own interests, and, despite Lactantius' obvious prejudice, there might well be an element of truth in what he says: the events of the next couple of years worked entirely to Galerius' advantage. It was his aim not to be disadvantaged if Diocletian should predecease Maximian. He may well have had a particularly strong dislike for Christians and have sensed that Constantius was, if anything, well disposed to them.[16] By supporting Diocletian's new antipathy, he could convince the aging emperor that his own interests needed to be protected if the system of the tetrarchy was to endure. Still, Diocletian may have hesitated; both Lactantius and Constantine himself, who was at court at the time, report that he made no decision about what to do until he had consulted the oracle of Apollo at Didyma (a famous oracular site on the west coast of Turkey). The final decision rested with Diocletian alone, and when he made his decision he stressed that people who did not worship the gods as he thought right were offending the very beings whose good favor had restored the state.[17]

What we do know is that the edict was promulgated at Nicomedia on February 24, 303, then in Palestine by March, and that local officials in North Africa were trying to enforce it in a somewhat desultory way in mid-May.[18] The terms of the edict were that churches should be destroyed and Christian scriptures should be burned; that Christians in the imperial service were to lose their rank, or, if they were freedmen, be reduced to slavery; and that all were to be deprived of the right to answer legal actions against them or to file complaints against people who assaulted them. The last two provisions are of particular interest in that they constituted an open invitation for the people of the empire to join with the emperors in "purifying" Roman society of what Diocletian took to be the evil of Christianity. In this way the edict colluded in the assumption of central government that Roman citizens shared with the court a basic interest in defending society against those regarded as malefactors.[19]

Events were to move very fast in the next twelve months. Shortly after the promulgation of the edict, a fire broke out in the palace at Nicomedia that would be blamed on the Christians, resulting in numerous executions; and rebellions occurred in Commagene and Syria (though this last had nothing to do with religion as it was a military mutiny involving the local aristocracy). Constantine later recalled that Diocletian had been terrified by the fire, which he said had been caused by a lightning strike. He does not mention another event, one that seems to have infuriated Diocletian: this concerned a Christian who tore down a copy of the edict and abused the emperors as barbarians. This person was incinerated by imperial command. A second edict ordered the arrest of Christian leaders.[20]

The flow of the edicts down the chain of command is illustrated by a declaration made by a lector to a local financial official at Oxyrhynchus, showing us how a local official would transmit a report of what was in a church to senior officials in charge of imperial finance. Concluding with the statement that he has done his duty "in accordance with what was written by our most illustrious prefect Clodius Culcianus, I also swear by the genius of our lords the emperors Diocletian and Maximian, the Augusti, and Constantius and Galerius, the most noble Caesars, that these things are so and that I have falsified nothing, or may I be liable to the divine oath."[21]

Despite formal involvement of senior imperial officials who received the report, the final responsibility for making sure that edicts were observed lay with the local authorities. The lector is making his declaration to them because they are responsible for ensuring that he delivers church property to a person who plainly knows him. In the record of the persecuting activities of Munatius Felix, the *flamen perpetuus* and *curator* of Cirta (a major city in what is now Algeria) on May 19, 303, we see the official, who knows several leading Christians by sight, scouring the town for someone who may have a copy of the scriptures that he can confiscate, a quest that speeds up after he arrests a couple of more recalcitrant types. In the end, Munatius seems a most unwilling persecutor, taking it on trust that whatever is handed over to him is a book of scripture.[22] Our evidence for his actions, the written record of his search, adduced years later during the investigation of a controversy within the Christian Church arising out of the persecution, shows many signs of having been composed to prove to his superiors that he was taking their instructions seriously. Here we may see the typical local bureaucrat going about his business:

> When Diocletian for the eighth time and Maximian for the seventh time were consuls, 14 days before the calends of June (19 May), from the records of Munatius Felix the perpetual priest of the imperial cult [*flamen*] and *curator* of the colony of Cirta. When he arrived at the house in which the Christians met, Felix the perpetual priest of the imperial cult and *curator* said to Paul the bishop: bring out the writings of the law, and anything else you have here, as it is written so that you will be able to obey the order.
>
> Paul the bishop said: the readers have the scriptures, but we will give you what we have.
>
> Felix...said: Point out the readers or send for them.
>
> Paul the bishop said: you know who they are.
>
> Felix...said: I don't know them.
>
> Paul the bishop said: the public records office knows them, the clerks Edusius and Junius.[23]

In the face of this sort of marginally vigorous action, one North African bishop wrote that Christians should simply hand over the works of heretics instead of scripture so that the authorities would have something to burn and they should make no effort to provoke them.

The question of how to respond to the edict would create horrendous problems within the Christian community. Many people followed the example of Bishop Paul in Cirta who appears to have been no more than marginally uncooperative with the authorities, while others objected strongly; and in some places the persecuting authorities were more vigorous than in others. One of the latter areas was Egypt, where the prefect Culcianus—mentioned in the text from Oxyrhynchus—appears to have been a relentless enemy of the Christian community. A contemporary pagan grammarian who lived in Alexandria may be expressing his disgust at Culcianus' activities in a poem in which he wrote that it was not surprising that the murderer flourished since Zeus would have killed his own father (any reference to Zeus in this way must have made an audience think of Diocletian's adoption of the title Jovius, as Jove/Jupiter was the Roman version of the Greek Zeus). More often, it appears that officials were reluctant to push the persecution to the limits of their authority. In the eight years after the first edict was issued, records in the Balkan provinces where Galerius—arguably the most hostile of the original members of the imperial college—resided most often, forty-two executions are attested, while in Palestine, also home to some active enemies of the church (as well as to a large Christian community), there were seven executions under the original edict and perhaps as many as 200 in later years.[24]

The death toll in the great persecution, although insignificant by the standards of twentieth-century bigotry, is a very poor guide to the total impact of the edict on the Christian community, whose members were subjected to constant harassment from their neighbors and whose relationships with each other were profoundly altered. The psychological impact of the edicts was intense on those who were uprooted or whose lives were ruined and on those who felt they must keep their community together. At the root of the discussions and quarrels that would continue for decades was whether one should resist, and by defying the authorities risk bringing destruction upon one's fellows, or find ways to accommodate the authorities while continuing to practice one's faith. The question was especially acute for those in positions of leadership whose authority might be ruined in the eyes of one or the other faction for years to come.

Within a year of the second edict, in preparation for the celebration of the twentieth anniversary of Diocletian's accession—and now of Maximian's, as by historical sleight of hand his regnal years had been equated with Diocletian's—a third edict proclaimed a general amnesty, though it seems that there was a qualification in the case of the Christian clergy who were required to sacrifice (in some cases their jailers were willing to say that they had sacrificed when they had not and seem not to have been eager to continue their incarceration).[25]

The "great persecution" ended some eighteen months after it had begun; in some parts of the empire its repercussions would continue to haunt the church for more than a century. Lost in these dates is the question of what Constantine thought and did as the edicts were issued. Later he would react against this sort of government, but what did he think and how did he act in 303? He was a visible member of the court; many years later he would feel the need to reintroduce himself at length to the Christian community at Nicomedia.[26] Did he then have a guilty conscience, a memory of things that he had not done, people he had not protected? He would also later say that he recognized in himself things that were in need of improvement; did some of these things involve a display of moral courage?

Perhaps matters of conscience were not so important to him in 303; he was a new father, a member of the court, and loyal servant of the state. It was a good idea then to follow orders and go with the flow. More than twenty years later, when he was ruler of the world, the events of these years were still fresh in his mind. He would never forget, and there is no reason to think that he was proud of the man he had been in 303.

9.

MINERVINA

Then with a pose of genial wantonness she adopted the charming pose of Venus tread-ing the ocean waves. She even for a moment covered her hairless parts with her rosy little hand, a deliberate gesture rather than a modest concealment. "Engage," she said, "and do so bravely. I shall not yield before you, nor turn my back on you. Direct your aim frontally, if you are a man, and at close quarters. Let your onslaught be fierce; kill before you die. Our battle this day allows no respite." As she spoke she mounted the bed, and eased herself slowly down on top of me. She bounced up and down repeatedly, manoeuvring her back in supple movements, and gorged me with the delights of this rhythmical intercourse. Eventually our spirits palled as our bodies lost their zest; we col-lapsed simultaneously in a state of exhaustion as we breathlessly embraced each other. Engaged in these and similar grapplings we remained awake almost until dawn. From time to time we refreshed our weary bodies with wine, which fired our sexual urges and renewed our pleasure.

IN THIS SCENE and others like it, Apuleius explores the theme of passion in his magnificent novel, known variously as the *Metamorphoses* or *The Golden Ass*, a tale of magic, lust, adventure, fractured relationships, class antagonism, and finally divine revelation. As one of the great works of the previous century, it is probable that Constantine knew it, or some other version of the tale of Lucius, a young man whose curiosity led him into a relationship (glimpsed above) with the maid of a witch in whose house he was staying. This maid accidentally (or so he believes) changes him into an ass. Then follow many picaresque adventures. Finally, in an amphitheater where he is scheduled to have sex with a woman condemned to death for murder, by consuming roses he is transformed back into a man. Years later, when Constantine was emperor, there would be images from *The Golden Ass* and, it seems, a portrait of Apuleius himself painted on the ceiling of a reception room that may have been used by Fausta, who was then his wife.[1]

One of Apuleius' themes is the effect of sexual passion on the judgment of a man, a feature of the seemingly endless discourse of sexuality in the ancient world: wide ranging and amply illustrated whatever the source.

For some, the ideal relationship between a man and a woman was one in which the woman was completely subordinate to her partner, and sometimes many years younger. Expectations of marriage and of sexuality varied immensely: according to medical theory, men who had sex too often risked discharging too much seed and thereby weakening their own masculine essence; others who enjoyed sex thought that they needed to control their urges, as a moral test; other men didn't care one way or the other. Theoretical discussions of what women thought and wanted are based entirely on the male perspective running the gamut from fascination with rampant nymphomania to the desire to be persuaded that the woman of their dreams was a virgin on her wedding night. When it came to marriage, some people, the younger Pliny for instance, married girls to who were in their early teens and wrote of them more as daughters than partners. Pliny's tastes are well known because his letters have survived, but there is good reason to think that his predilections may have struck his contemporaries as odd. Men did tend to marry women who were younger than they were, but—at least in first marriages—not a great deal younger. Outside of the aristocracy, it seems likely that most Romans in their mid-twenties sought wives in their late teens. Aristocrats married a bit younger—in their late teens— to women who were close to them in age. In this respect Constantine appears to have followed suit.[2]

We know very little about Minervina, the woman he would marry. We don't know for certain where she was from though it was quite possibly Antioch. Constantine would later be called a "wife-loving adolescent," which should mean that he married before the age of twenty. And, as a member of the court, he would have been in Syria from 299 to 301 making Antioch a not unlikely place for him to have found a wife—to which we can add that city was wealthy and well stocked with families linked to the court. Although later tradition would assert that Minervina was a prostitute, this claim is no more soundly based than the similar tradition about his mother Helena.[3] Crispus, the child born of the relationship between Minervina and Constantine, was legitimate;

furthermore, Constantine chose to assert Crispus' legitimacy at the time of his second marriage in 307, at which point, if the matter had been in doubt, it would have been profoundly awkward to do so. Also for the child to be of readily asserted legitimacy, there could not have been a large status gap between mother and father.

So Minervina was probably in her late teens when she and Constantine married, and it is more likely than not that her parents were members of the imperial aristocracy. No doubt they were delighted at the union between their family and that of the distant but glorious Caesar in the west. Constantius must also have given his blessing to the union since Constantine, as a young Roman with a living father, was technically *in potestate* (in the power) of the head of the family, the *paterfamilias*. Being *in potestate,* Constantine was unable to marry or undertake any other significant activity without his father's permission.

Crispus was probably born in 303. Minervina was not at court in 307, which makes it very likely that she died in or shortly after the birth of her son.[4] For Minervina, as for any other young women in the ancient world and in the developing world today, where the death rate in childbirth is roughly one in sixteen, childbirth was a fearful experience—which may explain why demographic evidence from Egypt during our period suggests that life expectancy for women could be slightly lower than for men. In the case of Minervina, assuming they had married when Constantine was in his late teens, the relatively late appearance of Crispus suggests that there may have been some unsuccessful pregnancies earlier in the marriage. For upper-class women like Minervina, who should have lived in somewhat healthier conditions than most, the primary causes of death were obstetrical hemorrhage and (in the case of first pregnancies) eclampsia. It is probable, then, that Constantine's first wife bled to death in the aftermath of their son's birth. Crispus' well-being was entrusted to a wet nurse, the usual practice with an upper-class baby, whether his mother lived or died.

Constantine's marriage may have been a brilliant match for Minervina and her family, but less so for Constantine: Galerius had a daughter who was of marriageable age and the fact that she was not Constantine' chosen bride indicates that, in Galerius' view, Constantine was unlikely to become emperor. That this decision would have been made around 299–300 bears significantly on the way Diocletian saw his reign ending, for it must have been clear, even by

300, that abdication was a strong possibility. By this time, the palace he would occupy in his declining years—still on view at Split in Croatia—was beginning to take shape, if not already built.

Did it matter to Constantine that he now seemed most unlikely to be emperor? It seems far more likely that in these years he was more interested in Minervina, and he would have known full well what the marriage meant. With Minervina's death his world changed; in the next few years he would take enormous risks and show the sort of immense ambition lacking at the time of his marriage—or a cannier sense of the political world. And there would always be Crispus, whom he loved, whom he would never send from court, and whom he would raise to the rank of Caesar before something went terribly and fatally wrong with their relationship some twenty years after Diocletian's long-awaited abdication.

10.

THE SUCCESSION

D IOCLETIAN HAD DECIDED TO open the celebration of his twentieth
year in power, or *vicennalia*, in November of 303 at Rome. It would
be the first time in a decade that he would meet with Maximian in person.
The encounter would be a moment of symbolic significance, as the two
self-proclaimed saviors of the Roman world appeared together before the
people of the city which, although no longer an imperial capital, was still very
much felt to be the heart of the empire. And so it might also have been a suit-
able place, deep inside the territory of Maximian, for Diocletian to stage one
last demonstration of his superior authority. He had come to Rome not only to
celebrate the anniversary but also to gain Maximian's agreement to a definitive
plan for the succession.

It had been clear for some time that Diocletian did not intend to die in
office—that was the point of the retirement palace being built in Split and
explained the absence of a tomb in a capital like Nicomedia (Roman emperors had a tendency, when they could, to make elaborate preparations for their
burial). It was even admitted by a source hostile to the abdication scheme that
Diocletian and Maximian had both planned on retirement.[1]

Despite strong claims Lactantius would put forward at a later date that
Constantine was seen by all as an obvious candidate for Caesar, there is no
evidence that this was ever in prospect. Lactantius' assertions do not appear
in other pro-Constantinian sources, including a series of top-level speeches
delivered during the next decade. Moreover, the fact Constantius was married
to Theodora, Maximian's step-daughter, and Galerius to Diocletian's daughter
Valeria, and that Galerius' own daughters were married to Maxentius, the elder
son of Maximian, and to a soldier named Maximinus all more than suggest that

marriage was a marker for potential promotion. Constantine was outside the charmed circle.

Although Galerius did not force the removal of Constantine from the line of succession, there is reason to believe that he pressured Diocletian into arranging the retirement of the Augusti in the wake of the *vicennalia* celebration.[2] It was on this occasion that Maximian and Diocletian confirmed the agreement at a meeting in the temple of Capitoline Jupiter, quite possibly setting May 1, 305, as the date so that Maximian could enjoy a final blaze of glory when he presided over the *ludi saeculares*; scheduled for 304, these would commemorate the one-thousandth anniversary of the foundation of Rome according to the calculation used by Septimius Severus. While there is some corroboration for the idea that abdication had long been in view, there is more to suggest a sudden change in the way it would work. It is striking that, as mentioned earlier, the count of Maximian's regnal years was changed in 303 so that they suddenly equaled those of Diocletian. There would have been no point in the change except to disguise the fact that he had held power for one year less than his colleague.

Also striking is other evidence, from coins, suggesting that important decisions were being made in the east without prior consultation with the west. The mint at Trier, for instance, produced coins in 303 for Diocletian announcing the fulfilment of vows taken the previous decade, and also prospective vows for the next one. The mint at Nicomedia issued no such coins, suggesting that the mint master there had gotten the word well in advance of his counterpart at Trier that there would be no thirtieth year.[3]

The crucial evidence that something dubious was going on both in the timing of the abdication and the choice of successors lies in the events of the next few years. While we can't know whether the new Caesars to succeed Constantius and Galerius, Severus and Maximinus Daia, were selected in 303, we can be quite sure that neither of the successors was close to Maximian and Constantius. Both were friends of Galerius; and while one, Maximinus, was Galerius' son-in-law, neither had yet occupied a top-level appointment.[4] We also know that Constantius was no friend to the new arrangement. There were some immediate and major changes in the empire's administrative structure after the abdications that reflect the tension of the times.

We have little information about the period between December 20, 303, when Diocletian left Rome for the last time, evidently suffering from a serious illness, and May 1, 305. Probably after spending some time at Ravenna he returned to the Danube, where he took command in Galerius' company of a campaign against a Germanic tribe called the Carpi. He reached Nicomedia by August 28 that year and appears to have remained near his capital after that. Maximian apparently left Rome almost immediately after Diocletian did and went to Sirmium, where Lactantius claims he had a stormy meeting with Galerius.[5]

When May 1, 305, dawned, Constantius and Maximian were ensconced at Milan, while Galerius and Diocletian were at Nicomedia. In both places, the same drama was to unfold, one that had no parallel in earlier Roman history. Diocletian went out to a high platform built on the spot where he had, twenty-one years before, addressed the army and received its acclamation as emperor. The place was well marked with a high column upon which there was a statue of Jupiter. He would have been resplendent in his purple robes and jewels as he sat in the cart that bore him to the site. All around him would have been members of the court, soldiers invited from throughout the empire to witness the event. When members of the platform party had taken their places—Constantine was a member of this group—the senior emperor came forward to speak. He was old, so he said, he was tired, he wished to rest from his labors and so he would now pass power to others. The new Caesars, Severus and Maximinus, were announced though Severus was far away that day, in Milan, where he was participating in a similar ceremony with Maximian and Constantius. The chief actor in Nicomedia was Galerius, who brought Maximinus forward to face Diocletian. Diocletian removed the purple cloak from around his shoulders. He placed it on Maximinus. In so doing he ceased to be emperor. One can only imagine what it was to witness this—tens of thousands must have held their breath while the act took place. Then they would have exploded into acclamations of the new Augustus, Galerius, and the new Caesar. The man who had recently been the most powerful human anyone there had ever seen walked off the platform, remounted his cart, and was carried back to Nicomedia. Shortly thereafter he set out for Split, to enjoy a life of ease in his new palace.[6]

Never before had a man at the height of his power voluntarily laid that power aside, exploiting the very symbols that he had made those of the imperial office. There is perhaps no more powerful expression of the surprise that gripped the empire when news of the two abdications spread than the text of an inscription from North Africa honoring "our Lords Diocletian and Maximian the senior

Augusti, and our Lords Constantius and Maximianus (Galerius) the invincible Augusti and Severus and Maximinus the most noble Caesars."[7] With the ceremony of May 1, Diocletian and Maximian had ceased to be lords of anyone or anywhere.

Diocletian chose his troops as the audience for his abdication, for he hoped it would be the army that would guarantee the new order. At Milan, Maximian took off his purple cloak and handed it to Severus, while proclaiming Constantius Augustus.[8]

Diocletian's hopes for the army would prove ill founded: it would soon become clear that, so far from uniting behind the college of Caesars, it would prefer to distribute its loyalties between them.

Constantine's impression of that day would emerge over time. He would never build a retirement palace. He preferred to die in office. Retirement was one act of Diocletian's he could never hope to match.

FATHERS AND SONS

11.

THE NEW REGIME

SEVERUS STEPPED DOWN FROM the platform where he had received the purple cloak, now his, and descended into a morass from which it would have taken a very wise man a long time to escape. He would have neither the opportunity nor the wisdom to do so, and Galerius would soon be making his success virtually impossible. Confounding the situation, Galerius' staff appears to have comprised very different people than those who were important in the west. We do not have for this group the mass of information provided by the record of the prefects of Rome for Maximian's allies, but it is perhaps significant that the few names we do have are either men from the Balkans or likely easterners; they are people like Valerius Licinianus Licinius, a close associate who had been with Galerius in the Persian war; Pompeius Probus, who would become his praetorian prefect; and Tatius Andronicus.[1] For all that the new regime presented itself to the public as the continuation of the old (see figure 11.1), there were tensions now that were far more pronounced than in the past.

As Maximian removed himself from center stage to the villa near Rome that he had selected for his retirement, it became increasingly clear that the years before his abdication had witnessed some subtle changes in the makeup of the senatorial power set at Rome. The previous mixture of eastern and western officials that appeared in the consular and prefectorial lists of the city of Rome—the people for whom we have the best evidence—had given way to a group that was largely Italian.

We know of seven prefects between 299 and 306—a new one was to be appointed annually. Only one of these men came from a family whose main base of operations was outside of Italy or North Africa. This was Lucius Aelius Aelianus Dionysius who held the post in 301–302. Another who figures in these

(a)   (b)

(c)   (d)

FIGURE 11.1
The new college: Constantius (a), Galerius (b), Maximinus Daia (c), and Severus (d). Sources: (a–c) courtesy of the author; (d) courtesy of the American Numismatic Society.

years is one Marcus Junius Caesonius Nicomachus Anicius Faustus Paulinus, urban prefect in 299–300; he was the scion of two of the most powerful families of the era, the Caesonii and the Ancicii, whose blood was arguably bluer than the waters of the Aegean. A dedication he made to the invincible god Hercules, probably in the 280s, attests his early adherence to the court of Maximian. His successor was Pompeius Appius Faustinus, whose devotion to the cause of Maximian was also demonstrated by a dedication to the invincible god Hercules when he was urban praetor; a few years later he served as corrector of Campania in southern Italy. That post appears to have been a senatorial sinecure, since it involved administering an area where many of this class had their vacation homes. While there, Pompeius had erected a dedicatory inscription to Constantius. In his year as prefect of the city, Aelianus' successor, Nummius Tuscus, dedicated a statue to "our greatest lords in war and peace, Marcus Aurelius Maximianus Pius Felix eternal Augustus and Flavius Valerius Constantius the most noble Caesar having been preserved with honor increased by their piety and clemency." Junius Tiberianus, who took office in 303, had been governor of Asia after holding a consulship under Probus in 281; he was the son of the urban prefect of 291 and so would have had close ties with the urban elite. The prefect for 304–305 was Aradius Rufinus, from a Roman family, and for 305–306 it was Titus Flavius Postumius Titianus, who advertised his descent from Roman cultural figures of the past century, was a priest of the Divine Sun (Aurelian's god), and held sundry Italian sinecures. Gaius Annius Anullinus, the prefect for the next year, was cut from the same cloth and a close relative of his was serving as praetorian prefect.[2]

As a man whose career had been hitherto military and, it seems, largely based in the Balkans, Severus had no obvious or easy connection with this group, although Constantius, as the other western emperor and son-in-law of Maximian, did. Whatever motivated these families—and the bare records of their careers do not allow us extensive insights into their minds—they would retain their influence in the coming years and gain in stature as power shifted away from Nicomedia and the Balkans to a dynasty based in the west.

Galerius only exacerbated Severus' incompatibility with his new colleagues. And strained relations with Constantius made the rather loose association between emperors and regions impossible to maintain. Constantius was the senior Augustus, but under a system that seems to have come almost immediately into effect, the government was divided between the new rulers.

In the new system, the empire was divided into twelve dioceses, or groups of provinces, under the control of civilian officials who reported directly to a designated praetorian prefect. In Diocletian's last years these officials were known as *vicarii*, or *agens vicem prefectorum praetorio* (acting in place of the praetorian prefects.)[3] The title implies that the praetorian prefects had been given general oversight of the civil administration of the provinces, but—and this is important—they were given this authority as a group, just as Diocletian and his colleagues held their authority as a group. In 306, an official previously described as "acting in place of the praetorian prefects" appears as "acting in place of the praetorian prefect" (*agens vicem prefecti praetorio*).[4] The change from plural to singular suggests that specific prefects now had particular authority in one portion of the empire, and that they were seen as serving a particular member of the imperial college. This change is also reflected in the language of Eusebius, for example, who could speak of Constantine's "father's portion" and of "those who governed the other parts" meaning Galerius and his colleagues.[5]

The most important practical effect of this change was that Galerius could issue an order for Italy and expect it to be obeyed without consulting Constantius, and so he did. He began his reign with a lengthy edict about the evils of corrupt officials and people who brought false accusations. At the same time he issued an order to include Italy within the general imperial census, thereby eliminating the exemption from head and land taxes that its inhabitants had enjoyed since the beginning of the imperial system, and, indeed, for more than a century before that. Lactantius' claim that responsibility for this decision rested squarely upon the shoulders of Galerius is likely to be correct, for the inclusion of Italy in the census represents the reversal of the policy that Maximian and Constantius had been comfortable with. It is also probably true, as our source maintains, that the actual registration fell as a terrible burden upon all and sundry. Furthermore, a measure of this sort was bound to infringe on the long-held prerogatives of precisely the people who filled the senior offices of state around Severus and must further have undermined his authority, making him look like little more than the agent for the Danubian regime.[6]

Constantius' response to Galerius—if it may indeed be seen as a response—changed the life of Constantine and the course of European history. What Constantius did was to send Galerius a letter demanding that Constantine leave Sirmium, where he was then residing at Galerius' court, and come to Trier. It was later alleged, possibly with some truth, that Constantius feared for his son's safety—he does look like something of a potential hostage, and Maximian's son, Maxentius, who had been at Nicomedia, was now living outside of Rome, making the asymmetry of the young's men's positions all the more striking.

If the events of the late summer of 305 may be seen as a response to Galerius' opening salvoes of imperial self-aggrandizement it is because the order to begin the registration of Italy for the census, like the edict on false accusations, seems to have been enacted almost immediately: while the edict on accusation was hardly as offensive as the census order, the penalties it imposed on people who bore false witness in legal cases resembles very much the moralizing style of Diocletian's later legislation. There is thus a veiled implication that Galerius is the new Diocletian. This may also be a factor in the issuing of a new persecution edict against the Christians, which was enforced in lands that Galerius and Maximinus controlled. It was never enforced in regions that Constantius ruled directly.[7]

Constantine's move to the west in this atmosphere of increasing tension was a major political event, and took place within months of the abdications of Diocletian and Maximian. The earliest that we can place Constantine at his father's side is January of 306, in the context of a campaign in Britain that had recently begun. The decision to bring him to Trier (or Britain) is unlikely to have been greeted with unalloyed joy by all members of the family. The arrival of the twenty-something prince would have trumped whatever hopes the teenage sons of his stepmother Theodora might have entertained. Moreover it may have been obvious, by now, that Constantius himself was not in the best of health.[8]

The story of Constantine's return to his father looks in part to his need for legitimacy after July 25, 306, when, without consulting Galerius, he took his recently deceased father's throne for himself. But the story looks as well to other tales of princely derring-do that helped establish an emperor's public persona. Galerius, after all, had scouted Narses' camp in person. Constantius had had to be hoisted out of the way of a band of raging Alemanni to the top of a city wall. Later that same day, he reemerged with reinforcements and destroyed his foe despite being wounded. Constantine's problem was that Galerius kept trying to kill him.

At first we are told that Galerius would expose Constantine to dreadful dangers, sending him on dangerous missions against the barbarians north of the Danube. Then, when he could keep him at court no longer, he planned to murder him on his way home—in the earliest version of the story Severus is allotted this task—but Constantine outwitted him. Getting wind of Galerius' evil plan, he rode like the wind through the night, pausing only to kill the post horses that might aid the pursuers he knew were behind him. So it was that he came to his father at Gesoriacum (Boulogne) as he was setting sail for Britain. In a somewhat later version of the story, he would barely reach Constantius before he died, and in yet another, he escaped by taking advantage of Galerius' drinking habits. The old man got so drunk the night that Constantine fled the palace that he forgot to order the assassination. It was only when he woke up from his stupor—about noon the next day—that he found that Constantine had flown the coop.[9]

The various versions of the story all serve a purpose—to question the legitimacy of Galerius, to impugn the character of Severus, to conceal the amount of time that Constantine had with his father before his death (the less time, the less likely it could be that his proclamation was the result of an extensive conspiracy as opposed to the spontaneous act of soldiers, as the event was presented), and to make Constantine appear decisive, clever, and brave.

In reality, Constantine's return was very likely a great deal less dramatic. Minervina had died, but their son Crispus, now aged about three, would have been with Constantine. The boy would have whatever tutor had been engaged to look after him and the necessary servants. The party probably did cause a certain amount of disruption en route since an imperial prince could scarcely have traveled without a military escort as well. It does seem that Constantine joined his father when he was about to sail.

We have no information about the subsequent campaign in Britain, but it would seem that the proclamation of victory before January 6, 306, was premature. Constantius' presence in York in July suggests that operations in the north were ongoing through the summer. Still, even if victory was elusive, the operations gave Constantine a chance to forge links with members of his father's senior staff and to prove his ability. Few of those men could have had expectations of further advancement if Constantius died and Severus, as would have been the case, succeeded him. On the other hand, for well-placed and well-paid officials, open rebellion was a dangerous course, and it is perhaps testimony to Constantine's ability to impress his elders that on July 25, 306, the senior staff was willing to stage-manage his acclamation by the army when they learned of Constantius' death. One account says that the praetorian prefect was sufficiently taken by Constantine to become the moving force behind the conspiracy to put him on the throne.

A speech delivered in 310 would assert that Constantine was so horrified at the prospect of becoming emperor that he leapt on his horse and would have ridden away if the troops had not stopped him. However, this story alludes to one of the oldest aspects of imperial ceremony, namely, that Rome's rulers had for centuries pretended that they were amazed, surprised, or worried at the prospect of taking power, so we can safely assume that the scene had been well rehearsed. All the same, the language of what is an immensely skilled presentation weaves together various themes to do with imperial recognition in such a way as to justify an act of open rebellion as a response to the will of the people:

> Great Gods, with what good fortune did you bless Constantius Pius even in death. The emperor, about to make the journey to heaven, saw that person whom he was leaving as heir. As soon as he was removed from the earth, the entire army agreed on you, all minds and eyes marked you out, and, although you would have referred the issue about what to do about the highest matters of state to the older emperors, the soldiers anticipated in their eagerness what they would approve with their judgment.[10]

A true emperor must never seek power for himself—rather, he must be revealed by the gods. Thus popular acclamation was a divinely inspired act, meaning that Galerius' promotion of Maximinus in 305 could be seen as a usurpation. The reference to the older emperors (in this case, Galerius) gives us no pointer to the complex history of the months following July 25, 306.

At first, it seems, Constantine was acclaimed as Caesar. It was at this point that he sent Galerius a portrait of himself to announce that he was assuming a role in the administration of the empire. The confusion in the sources over the next few weeks or months reflects the speed with which Constantine moved to

(a)   (b)

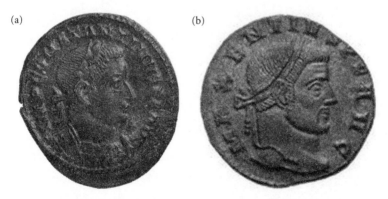

FIGURE 11.2
The rebels of 306: Constantine (a) and Maxentius (b). Sources: (a) courtesy of the American Numismatic Society; (b) courtesy of the author.

secure his position. Coins acknowledging Severus as Augustus that preexist any coinage for Constantine were minted at Trier. Given the distance between York and Trier, the rapid arrival of Constantine, with substantial forces to support him, perhaps even before Severus had had time to react to the news, must have surprised everyone. Then, too, troops must have been dispatched to the south of France to secure the passes over the Alps. These events make two things clear. One is that the Gallic regime clearly was deeply loyal to Constantine and his father, more than it had ever been to Diocletian. The second is that Constantine was capable of rapid and decisive action.[11]

Galerius was not happy, but he preferred to negotiate rather than fight, accepting Constantine as Caesar. How long would this settlement last? Events were moving so fast that it might prove impossible to stick for long with any decision. What would Galerius do?[12]

12.

MAXENTIUS AND FAUSTA

IT IS ALLEGED THAT MAXENTIUS, Maximian's son, could not bear to remain a private citizen in the wake of Constantine's seizure of power. This is possible, but a person cannot seize a throne by himself, especially a person who has had minimal command experience and who is barely twenty years old. Just as the acclamation of Constantine was a collective action by Constantius' senior staff, so too the proclamation of Maxentius was the act of a government faction heartily sick of Severus. The choice of Maxentius, at least initially, may have seemed an admirable compromise: it would be easier for Maximian, whose return to the political scene could readily be anticipated, to negotiate, should he choose to do so, whether with Constantine or with Galerius if he did not appear to be trying to reclaim his old position. By doing so, he briefly acquired a semblance of superiority to both his son and Constantius.

The praetorian guard, a shadow of its former king-making self now that emperors were no longer resident in Rome, was to be the primary tool for engineering Severus' downfall. According to Lactantius, it was disgruntled soldiers of the guard, angry that Galerius was planning to eliminate their camp, who decided to acclaim Maxentius as Augustus. In another version of the events, the active agents in the conspiracy against Severus were two tribunes of the guard named Marcellinus and Marcellus along with Lucianus, who happened to be the official in charge of pork distributions—it was he who started the revolt by murdering the *vicarius* (deputy) of the urban prefect, a man named Abellius. It was only then that the praetorian prefect Anullinus, a relative of the Anullinus who would continue as urban prefect after the revolt, was won over to the anti-Severan cause. The role of both Anullini is most likely as important here as the praetorian prefect of Constantius may have been in Britain.[1]

The revolt that put Maxentius on the throne may well have been a sign of Galerius' diplomatic failure in the months after his accession; his aggressive assertion of authority—showing no evident concern for the interests of the people who had been running the western empire for the last several decades—was an act of managerial incompetence. His assumption that Severus would be able to stifle the revolt on his own revealed a similar lack of judgment, based as it was on the belief that soldiers who had served under Maximian for years would be willing to march against their former commander. So it was that Galerius refused to negotiate with Maxentius—who did not immediately take an imperial title for himself, being content with the title "leader of the youth," a position routinely filled in the past by heirs apparent. It soon became clear that Galerius had misunderstood the nature of the opposition. Maximian formally emerged from retirement to support the rebellion. Severus' army deserted him outside Rome and he surrendered to Maxentius at Ravenna, to which city he had fled after the failure of his assault. Galerius' failure to intervene at this point constitutes yet another failure on his part to understand the emotions of those he wished to rule.

It is against the background of these dramatic events in Italy at the end of 306, and in anticipation that Galerius would invade the peninsula in the near future, that Maxentius and Maximian turned to Gaul. Maximian's youngest daughter Fausta, now aged about eight, would be the key to an alliance with Constantine. The wedding took place after a failed attempt to draw Diocletian out of retirement to settle the crisis in September of 307.[2] The speech that has come down to us from the day of the event reveals just how hard it would be for Constantine to establish a role of his own in the world of giants in which he now found himself. It is clear that, in the eyes of the speaker, Maximian completely overshadowed his son-in-law that day. At the same time, elements of the speech open a window onto the concerns of Constantine's own mind.

That part of the afore-mentioned speech concerning Constantius' death must have come from within Constantine's palace: significantly we are told that the sun himself carried Constantius off to the heavens, from where he watched and listened to the proceedings in a nearly visible chariot. In these lines we see the first indication of the interest that Constantine would take in divinities associated with light. The sun god alluded to here must be, as his appearance on numerous issues of contemporary Constantinian coinage reveals, Invincible Sun (Sol Invictus), the god of Aurelian.

Also revealing is the discrepancy between two passages on Constantine's marital career. In one, the speaker asserts that a picture in the palace at Aquileia showing a boy receiving a helmet as a betrothal gift from a young girl presages the current marriage (even though it must have been painted years before Fausta's birth around 299). In the other passage, Constantine is praised for his commitment to his earlier marriage saying, "At the very beginning of your youth you formed a marital disposition and admitted nothing of wandering pleasures or the delights conceded to youth into this sacred breast—a new marvel, a young man devoted to his wife!" The implicit reference is not simply to the legitimacy of his marriage to Minervina, but also to the legitimacy of his son. Did Constantine care that people should think him loyal to his family? Or did he see in his first son's experience something of his own situation as the product of a first marriage who might have to give way to the demands of a second marriage—and a marriage, no less, to the same family?[3]

A final aspect of Constantine on display here is one that people ignored at their peril: that he could be an implacable foe. Addressing him, the speaker notes that Constantine had excelled at massacring the Franks, even executing two of their kings by throwing them to the beasts at the amphitheater in Trier.[4] The incident would continue to be raised years after it was relevant, which signals the importance that Constantine attached to it. It is likely that the kings' capture occurred in the context of a significant victory—Constantine's first great success, perhaps—while the gruesome deaths of the two men, a rare event as defeated German kings tend to end up in Roman service, showed that Constantine would act without mercy when he deemed it necessary.

From the very first moment of his reign he showed himself to be a superb soldier, which meant not simply that he was brave, but that he possessed the arts of command, the mastery of the detail needed to conduct a successful military operation. It meant that he understood issues of supply and how to organize a column on the march, that he could identify an enemy's strengths and weaknesses, that he was able to convince his soldiers—many of whom were a good deal older and more experienced than himself—that he was someone to whom they could entrust their lives. Constantine could deliver an army to the battlefield in a state of fighting readiness, and he had the necessary sense of timing to carry out a successful assault and ensure the enemy's defeat. Perhaps above all else, he knew how to work with his staff and how to get the best out of them. Finally, the executions of the two kings showed that Constantine understood that displays of pain and suffering for public pleasure were a fact of life in the Roman Empire; they were a valid way for an emperor to connect with his people. And he saw no reason to avoid such spectacles.

In 307 Constantine had much to look forward to: he was gaining in reputation and his efforts at diplomacy had borne fruit in his marriage to Fausta, a crucial statement that a member of the old guard would take him seriously— but he needed to be careful. This old guard still mattered: the wedding day speaker greets the rulers as "Maximian perpetual Augustus and Constantine, rising emperor." To some, including this speaker, Constantine was not so much a ruler in his own right as the natural extension of Constantius, repeating the pattern of his father's marriage to secure his own power. It is a sign of his wisdom, the speaker goes on, that he realizes that imperial power is best acquired not through right of succession, but as a due reward for merit in the style of his illustrious predecessor (something that Constantine would utterly reject within a few years). Maximian, the speaker says, had long foreseen the match (a point connected with the odd discussion of the painting in the palace at Aquileia). And, in a less than subtle jab at Galerius, he suggests that while others make gifts of wealth or office, Maximian is unique in combining the gift of marriage with that of the highest power: "you with a greater soul than others give both what your piety holds most dear and what your fortune holds most significant."[5]

Maximian is the one who gave Constantine his name—from the god who was the founder of his family, who proved himself the descendant of Hercules not through adulation but through deeds. Then follows the standard panegyric summary of Maximian's career: his restoration of imperial power in Gaul, his crossing of the Rhine—just like Mamertinus, the speaker claims that Maximian was the first person to do so—the repeated expeditions against the Germans in the company of "his brother" Diocletian, and victories in North Africa.[6]

Maximian did not retire through sloth or idleness, the eulogy continues, but according with a plan long since made in the spirit of fraternal piety with Diocletian: if he were to retire so too must Maximian—the two must be partners for their entire lives. The consequences of their devotion were dire. When Maximian left, the state collapsed as if its foundations had been pulled from under it, the land shook and almost toppled, Rome included, but then: "Rome itself acted out of the majesty of its name and showed that it could even command an emperor; she took back her armies and restored them to you when you had brought forth the authority of a private emperor for settling souls."[7]

Maximian's return marks a return to order. The orator sees him once again on the pinnacle of command, blessed with a son who is like him in visage, spirit, and power, and this line will be enriched by the progeny of Constantine. As a way of interpreting the new relationship, it appears that, at least briefly, Maximian was adopted into Constantine's line as his "grandfather."[8]

For all the bluster of the wedding panegyric, Maximian's power still depended upon the support of the aristocratic faction that had sickened of Galerius and Severus. Maxentius is nowhere mentioned in the speech. Did this mean that he was no more than a pawn in a game Maximian sought to dominate? Despite the union of Constantine and Fausta, it seems that the relationship between Gaul and Italy was far from settled and there was no guarantee that the next generation of emperors would enjoy the same bond of friendship that Maximian and Diocletian had supposedly had. Constantine was extremely cautious about committing himself: he had taken what he needed from the alliance—namely, further support for the legitimacy of his position, without giving any pledge of military help in return. Furthermore, Maximian's position may not have been nearly so strong as the orator made it appear, and it was about to worsen.

Shortly after the wedding, Galerius invaded Italy, advancing as far as Rome. But it soon became clear that he lacked the resources to lay siege to the city that Aurelian had so well fortified back in the 270s. There may be some irony here, in that Maximian was protected while Galerius was undone by the legacy of a ruler whose achievements both had been happy to bury. Galerius first tried to negotiate, sending two of his most trusted officials, Licinius and Probus, to speak with Maxentius, talking as if the exchange were between father-in-law and son-in-law—which sounds like a Galerian take on the language of the speaker at Constantine's wedding.[9] When this approach failed, Galerius had to withdraw and his army, by now short of supplies, began to fall apart, looting as it went.

The outcome of the campaign as it petered out in the autumn of 307 could scarcely be regarded as glorious for either side, and it may be that some in Rome, whose estates had been left unprotected and vandalized, began to wonder whether Maximian had begun to lose his touch. The difficulties were compounded by Maxentius' decision, seemingly taken on his own authority, to order Severus' execution. Maximian meanwhile was becoming ever more irascible, and his relationship with Maxentius as well as with those who had supported him was growing problematic. Maxentius most likely took the view that the regime needed to concentrate its resources on self-protection whereas Maximian dreamed of playing on a grander stage. In April of 308 the tension between father and son reached the boiling point. Maximian evidently decided that he could only achieve his ambition if Maxentius were to leave the field. According to Lactantius, he summoned a public meeting at Rome and tried to blame the present troubles on his son, seized the purple cloak from his shoulders, and cast him from the platform. Maximian's political theater backfired when the crowd rose up in Maxentius' support, and Maximian had to flee to the court of Constantine, who appears to have welcomed his father-in-law with open arms.[10]

The situation in 308 was complicated by Diocletian's decision to emerge from retirement and take up the consulship, a sign that he intended to lend Galerius his active support. Diocletian still had an authority that no one else could claim and an ability to help others see where their best advantage might lie. Constantine, familiar as he was with Diocletian's ways of doing business, appears to have recognized a chance to secure his own position without reference to the damaged authority of his father-in-law. Galerius realized that his Caesar, Maximinus, could not be moved from the east and that a replacement would be needed for Severus. Maximian, the man most obviously in need of a new reason to exist, proved an admirable go-between. He met with Galerius and Diocletian at Carnuntum on the Danube to make sure that Constantine was included in any new imperial order, and on November 11, 308, that new order was duly announced. On that day, in the presence of Diocletian and Maximian, Galerius announced a replacement for Severus, who would hold the rank of Augustus, which Severus had held at the time of his death. The new Augustus was Galerius' long-time friend and associate, Licinius. At the same time, the imperial college recognized Constantine as Caesar so that he, along with Maximinus, would assume the title "son of the Augusti."

Diocletian returned to his palace at Split, where he allegedly devoted his time to the cultivation of cabbages. For his part, Maximian retired to Gaul where it appears that he once again formally waived any claim to the throne and, it is alleged, swore an oath to Constantine that he would remain in retirement.[11] If the council of Carnuntum represents a final diplomatic triumph for Diocletian in securing the regime of Galerius, still his favored associate, it also represents a victory for Constantine. By seizing the best option available to him, even though the weakness of his own claim to power was obvious to all, he secured his own position without having to make any major concession.

The audience for this display of dynastic reordering was primarily the same that had witnessed the rather similar performance at Constantine's wedding: imperial officialdom. It is unfortunate that we have no direct evidence for what was said at Carnuntum, though the verbal acrobatics performed to convince officials who gathered there that all was well, and that all had been well of late—surely essential to such a speech—would no doubt have been impressive. But could any speech counter all the nasty gossip that was flying about? We may discern with Lactantius' help something of what this was. Lactantius was not alone in suggesting that Diocletian came from a poor background— possibly a servile one—and it is unlikely that he was the only person to suggest that Galerius' wife Valeria and her offspring displayed the signs of their savage barbarian heritage. It was someone else who spread the tale that Constantine's mother Helena was a whore, and others still would have things to say about Maxentius' personal habits (not very flattering).

The events at Carnuntum may well have given rise to further stories about Galerius' intentions even though by this time it was plain that he was intending to retire and that his retirement palace was taking shape at Romuliana (modern-day Gamzigrad in Serbia). One story in particular, plainly intended to justify Constantine's action and cast aspersions on Galerius' claim to be defending Diocletian's legacy, focused on Galerius' desire to seize power from Constantius. Galerius' plan was to force Constantius' resignation by uniting with the two Caesars against him, and he had always intended to replace him with his old friend Licinius, whom he wished to reward for his years of friendship. Then, when he had ruled for twenty years as Augustus, Galerius would abdicate, leaving the rank of junior Caesar open for his own son, Candidianus, who would then be twenty-nine years old. It is a story that dates itself, as none of this would be relevant before 308 when Licinius became Augustus, and none of it would be all that relevant after 312, when Licinius would marry Constantine's half-sister, Constantia.[12]

Like all good propaganda, some aspects of the story were grounded in observable reality: for instance, Galerius did promote Licinius to the rank of Augustus over the head of Maximinus.[13] But one crucial feature, Galerius' hope for his son, reads too much like Constantine's own claim to the throne in 306. Still it was now more necessary than ever to make the case that Galerius had cheated first, that Constantine not be perceived as the first person to break Diocletian's "rule" of 305 that sons should not succeed their fathers in power. But, according to the stories now flying about, Galerius already intended to break that rule, and this may be connected with other stories about the grooming of Constantine to take up the position of senior Caesar, only to be replaced through the machinations of Galerius. Such a story reiterated the point that "Diocletian's rule" was no rule at all.

13.

THE END OF MAXIMIAN

Maximian's importance went into a steady decline after Carnuntum; he disappears from coins by the end of 308 while in some places the "Divine Constantius" begins to appear. It is hard to imagine that he did not now bear some resentment toward both his son and son-in-law. Two years after the settlement at Carnuntum he would once again try to seize the throne, this time from Constantine. He would not survive the attempt.[1]

Even as the events unfolded at Carnuntum, Maxentius, now styling himself Augustus, was faced with a serious revolt in Africa. It was in the spring of 308 that Lucius Domitius Alexander, who had been serving as *vicarius* of the African provinces since 303 or earlier, proclaimed himself emperor, in fact, co-emperor with Constantine—the two appear on a North African inscription as "the emperors our Lords, Lucius Domitius Alexander and Flavius Constantine Augustus." It is not possible to know whether he approached Constantine for support as his own forces advanced far enough north to take control of Sardinia, but the official nature of the inscription—it is a milestone—makes it extremely likely that he did. Given that Alexander effectively took control of Rome's food supply, he might expect a ferocious response from Maxentius, which duly took place. Domitius was killed in 309 during an invasion led by Volusianus, who was Maxentius' praetorian prefect.[2]

Constantine's refusal to intervene while Maxentius diverted major forces to North Africa reveals another aspect of Constantine's character: the ability to engage in the rational assessment of risk. An invasion of Italy at this point, while no doubt a simpler military operation than the one he would launch in 312, was also less likely to yield total victory given that Maxentius was in North Africa; and Constantine would simply be exchanging with Maxentius the opportunity to rule a starving city while trying to find the fleet required to oust his rival from Africa in what would be in a worst-case scenario an amphibious operation.

The fact that Maxentius was able to carry out a successful invasion of Africa and end the revolt is a sign that he had some genuine military talent around him. Instead of intervening in these events, Constantine continued to do what he always did—that is, to campaign against peoples along the Rhine that year, and at the start of 310 he built a large bridge over that river, an act presented as symbolic of his domination over the tribes on the far side. In the spring he was called away from those operations to meet what would remain one of the oddest crises of his career, this one generated by Maximian.

When he formally retired for the second time, swearing that it would be for good, Maximian did not drop entirely from sight. Lactantius has him play the role of an adviser; an earlier account suggests that he may simply have been resident in Arles, as on his retirement from public life he was given splendid gifts, the freedom of a private citizen, and the wealth of an emperor.[3] Then, as Constantine marched into Germany, Maximian suddenly appeared at Arles in a purple cloak, symbolizing his claim to imperial authority. He then wrote letters to the armies asking their support and promised gifts to those who would come to his aid.[4] When he learned of his father-in-law's action, Constantine returned immediately to his own territory while Maximian fled to Marseilles, where, according to the speaker of the panegyric delivered shortly after the event, the city surrendered while Constantine was delaying the assault. As for Maximian, the speaker says, "I do not believe that, when he came forth into the light, he would have accepted the offer of life, which was offered, but rather he ran into an unavoidable fate and one that would bring an unjust end to many men, he brought a voluntary death to himself."[5]

This earliest version of the story with Maximian committing suicide before he could meet Constantine face to face was unsatisfactory. It was later asserted that the old emperor was returned to the palace where he attempted, with Fausta's help, to murder his son-in-law. Fausta revealed the plot and, according to the most detailed version—Lactantius'—a eunuch took Constantine's place in his bed. When Maximian murdered the eunuch, Constantine revealed himself with his guards, offering Maximian the choice of how he would die. He hanged himself.[6]

The existence of the second story is presumably explained by the fact that no sane person believed the first, and that Constantine looked bad for having killed his father-in-law. Fausta's involvement in the second story not only represents Maximian's further repudiation by his own daughter but also suggests that Constantine was a man of preternaturally merciful disposition.

The two stories reveal several aspects of the young emperor's character that have so far been merely glimpsed. Despite what he might have wished people to believe, Constantine was not by nature a merciful man—Maximian had done nothing to deserve his mercy anyway, and we have no reason to think that he received anything from Constantine other than a death sentence as soon as Marseilles surrendered. Another thing that emerges from these stories is that Constantine had anything but a tin ear. He sensed that the original explanation for Maximian's death sat badly with people, so he allowed a new one to be circulated—and possibly more than one since there are hints of an earlier version of the story involving Fausta. Finally, we sense in Constantine a man conscious of his position and image, expecting others to defer to him, to await his instructions; this is nicely illustrated when, at one point in his speech, the panegyrist of 310 waits for Constantine to give him a lead: "I am still in doubt as to what I am to say and expect advice from the nod of your divinity."

The orator who described the circumstances of Maximian's revolt had more to talk about than that sad event. In Constantine's presence he revealed some new and important facts about his ruler. First was a new family tree:

> I will begin first with the divinity of your origin, which perhaps most people at this point do not know, but which those who love you most do know. There is an ancestral connection that links you with that Divine Claudius [II], who was the first man to reform the ruined and shattered discipline of the Roman empire, and annihilate the vast forces of the Goths bursting from the jaws of the Black Sea and the mouth of the Danube. Would that he had been a longer restorer of the human race and a less rapid companion of the gods. Although that most fortunate day that was recently celebrated with appropriate worship is held to be the birthday of your power [July 25], since it first clad you in the garb you now wear, nonetheless the fortune of power descends to you from that founder of your line. That ancient prerogative of the imperial house advanced your father himself, so that

you stand in the highest position and above the destinies of human affairs
the third ruler after two rulers from your own family.[7]

What is perhaps most striking about the notion of Claudius as Constantine's
ancestor is that it contains an implicit response to Diocletian's talk of restoration, debunking claims that he and his colleagues were the first to achieve this.
Unlike Aurelian, the actual restorer of the unified empire, Claudius had not
become a controversial figure in Diocletian's time. He was remembered for a
big win over the Goths near the city of Naissus where Constantine had been
born, and that seems to have been it. Claudius was, however, close enough in
time as Aurelian's immediate predecessor that to exalt his victory in the heart
of modern Serbia was to imply that the Balkan frontier, where Diocletian
and Galerius spent so much of their time, had been secured well in advance
of their reign. Constantius was emperor because he can now be proclaimed
the descendant of an emperor, and Constantine is emperor because he is the
son of Constantius: "You entered into that sacred palace not as a candidate
for imperial power, but as one designated for it, and immediately the ancestral gods saw in you a legitimate successor. There could be no doubt but the
inheritance would seek that person whom the fates gave to the emperor as
his first son."[8] Here the speaker looks to the comments made around 307 that
Maximian had been the "author" of Constantine's power; and the broader
claims of Diocletian and his colleagues to authority granted them by the gods
and by the goodwill of the provincials are rejected outright. As the panegyrist
observed: "No chance agreement of men, nor some unexpected consequence
of favor, made you emperor."[9] Clearly the conference at Carnuntum is what is
being alluded to here, just as mention of candidature refers both to the torrent
of earlier proclamations of the emperors' good relations with their subjects
and the favor of the gods who had granted them victory. Through the invented
link with Claudius, Constantine now asserts the sole principle of inheritance
as grounds for holding power.

After Constantine had dealt with Marseilles and Maximian, he heard that
the Franks had launched yet another raid across the Rhine. On the way to deal
with the invaders he stopped at a shrine of Apollo, possibly around Grand in
what is today the region of Lorraine in northern France. There the god himself
appeared to the emperor, so the panegyrist says:

I believe, Constantine, that you saw your Apollo accompanied by Victory offering you laurel crowns each of which forecast thirty years. This is the number of years that ought to be owed to you beyond Pylian old age [the reference is to Nestor the aged hero in Homer's *Iliad*]. And—why should I say "I think"—you saw yourself and recognized yourself in the appearance of him to whom the divine songs of the Bard granted the rule of the whole world.[10]

In a genre that is scarcely given to originality of expression, this scene is remarkable, and there can be little doubt that the source of information about this epiphany was the sole witness to the event, Constantine himself, but there may be some question as to whether the author of our panegyric was the first person to receive the news. The explicitly visual aspect of the description— that Constantine should have recognized his own features in those of the god, the image of the god carrying a Victory (a popular theme in contemporary art)—and the assertion ("why should I say 'I think'") suggest that he and the others listening to the panegyric could see it all for themselves in a picture of

FIGURE 13.1
The basilica of Trier was a place where Constantine would meet his subjects on ceremonial occasions.
The panegyric of 310 was quite likely delivered in this space. Source: Berthold Werner.

the event. Finally, the allusion to Virgil's Fourth Eclogue in the "divine songs of the Bard," a poem regarded as prophetic by some in its treatment of the birth of a child who would bring peace to the earth, and the suggestion of ruling the entire empire seem a highly personal statement of intent.[11] A shrine of any divinity had multiple meanings, both local and universal, and if indeed the orator was tempted to remind Constantine of his connection with a local shrine, this would in no way contradict the universal message he attributes to the vision.[12] The fact that accounts of such visions are not the stock-in-trade of panegyrists should mean that this one feels there is something unusual about Constantine's link with the god. Others around him may have been having similar thoughts. It is now that his mints begin to celebrate Constantius' god Sol Invictus, Invincible Sun, who might readily be identified with Apollo no matter what the nature of the Apollo at the shrine that Constantine visited.[13]

The narrative of the vision is significant not just because it points to a divinely authorized campaign to take control of the whole empire, but also for what it reveals about Constantine. There was no need to advertise imperial access to divine guidance and support; these were readily attributed by the public to any emperor. Here there is something more, just as there was to have been in Aurelian's proclamation forty years earlier that Sol Invictus had saved the day outside Emesa. There the god had turned the tide in battle. Here the god seems to be guiding the emperor down a very particular path. Did Constantine believe it was now his turn to be favored?

He had survived in the court of his remarried father and had survived in the courts of Diocletian and Galerius; he had already proclaimed his wondrous salvation from Galerius' plots and had managed to hold on to his throne in the face of sundry other threats. Constantine would scarcely be the only person in the ancient world to sense, or hope, that he had a divine friend. Constantine had survived against extraordinary odds—and now he could rejoice in the conviction that he was doing the will of his own god. And it was this god's will that he should rule the world.

V

THE ROAD TO ROME

14.

THE GATHERING STORM

MAXENTIUS HAD NOT BEEN IDLE. Evidently aware that his regime depended upon both the goodwill of the senatorial aristocracy and the people of Rome, he had done his best in the years since his father's expulsion to stabilize his relationship with each group. His entourage abounded with old-school aristocrats, but he also did much to embellish the city of Rome itself, for the good of all.

Among the senior nobles who stood by Maxentius was Anullinus, who occupied, along with his brother, important positions in the year of Severus' overthrow. In August of 307, Attius Insteius Tertullus succeeded Anullinus as prefect of the city and seems to have played an important role in Galerius' defeat; as we learn from the base of a statue erected by a mercantile association:

> The association of the wholesale merchants, freed from fear and peril, erects this bronze statue for the distinguished man, exceeding the industry of all previous prefects, Attius Insteius Tertullus, quaestor, praetor as a candidate of the emperor, consul, official in charge of the building of the wall and gates [?], prefect of the city of Rome, because of the care that he took so that the fortune of those who were afflicted with great want, the stress of their misery and incomparable dread when they were in open danger, was restored and tended, growing strong again with their earlier potency restored, received eternal strength, because of his outstanding deeds and singular generosity.[1]

Nothing (aside from his name) is known of Tertullus' successor, Statius Rufinus. But the next in line for the prefecture, Aurelius Hermogenes, was the descendant of an eastern family that had come to Rome in the time of the emperor Elagabalus (reigned 218–222), and, unusually for men holding such a high position at this time, had served as governor of Asia. His family may also have retained estates in central Turkey that Galerius probably confiscated— the estates were home to famous horses used by the imperial government later in the century. The prefect who took office on October 28, 310, was Gaius Ceionius Rufius Volusianus, a member of a great aristocratic clan who had himself already rendered Maxentius important service. He would prove to be a man of great political flexibility.[2]

From outside the aristocratic circle, Maxentius drew in one Rauricius Pompeianus, whose name betrays no affiliation with any aristocratic family.[3] He would be praetorian prefect in 312. At the same time, the North African victory is a sign that Maxentius' army was highly functional and that Maxentius had achieved some hold over the general population, dealing with the threats of mass starvation that resulted from the outbreak of a rebellion in the area that produced most of the grain needed to feed Rome.[4]

Maxentius' building projects in the heart of Rome were extensive and designed to drive home a major point: while Diocletian, his colleagues, and heirs might like to think that the center of power was wherever they happened to be, he had no doubt that Rome was the center of the world. He carried out a visible revamping of the imperial palace overlooking the circus maximus, setting his own additions atop those of the Severan dynasty; renovated the great Severan bathhouse on the southeast side of the Palatine; built a new bathhouse of his own; repaired and enhanced Aurelian's wall. One of his most stunning achievements was the massive basilica in the Roman Forum that may have become the headquarters of the urban prefect, demonstrating the importance that he attached to the office and its holders—also the purpose of the so-called Temple of Romulus at the entrance to the Temple of Peace.[5]

The first of Maxentius' major projects had been to repair the Hadrianic temple of Venus and Rome, damaged by a fire in 307, which harked back to the myth of the city's foundation. In the version best known through Virgil's *Aeneid*, Aeneas, who established the line of kings from which Rome was founded, is the son of the goddess Venus. As an indication that this was not an act of ideological expediency Maxentius had named his son, born before 306, Romulus, after the legendary first king of Rome.[6] Romulus was the son of Mars, and it was in the Forum that Maxentius dedicated a statue group representing Mars with Romulus and his brother, Remus, and bearing the inscription "Our lord the emperor Maxentius Pius Fortunate Invincible Augustus dedicates this to Mars the Invincible Father and to the founders of his eternal city."[7] In the Licinian Gardens, where Gallienus once had a residence, he built a ten-sided domed hall and next to it a massive apsed hall; and, somewhere near the modern church of St. John Lateran, he erected yet another house for himself. Two other projects, one a huge statue set up in the basilica, the other a triumphal arch between the Colosseum and the Palatine, possibly intended to celebrate the victory over Domitius Alexander (if not Galerius or, now, both), are most famous in the forms in which Constantine repurposed them.

Outside Rome, along the via Appia, Maxentius updated an existing villa to serve as a suburban palace, complete with its own circus. It was in this villa in 309 that he would bury his son Romulus in a tomb that stood in a similar relationship to the circus as the *ara maxima* ("Great Altar") did to the Colosseum. The *ara maxima* celebrated the visit of Hercules to Rome and his destruction of a dreadful monster, before the foundation of the city.[8]

Maxentius' assertion of his Roman identity took on a distinctly hostile tone toward Constantine in the wake of Maximian's death in 310. Maxentius had no cause to celebrate his father after having driven him to Gaul, but as soon as Galerius died in 311, Maxentius' mint at Ostia began to produce coins commemorating "the deified father Maximian," "the deified kinsman Constantius," "the divine father-in-law Maximian (that is Galerius)" (referring to his own marriage to Galerius' daughter), as well as the "deified Romulus." The implication is obvious—that Maxentius was part of the ruling house but that Constantine, who had not appeared on a coin minted in the lands of Maxentius since 308, was not. On another matter of some significance, Maxentius had ended the official persecution of Christians in his lands at about the time he had sent his father to Gaul. By doing so he drew a sharp distinction between himself and Galerius, whose persecution edict remained in effect from the time of his accession.[9]

For Galerius, his imperial colleague Maximinus, and, one presumes, Severus, Christian persecution had a decidedly ideological aspect. In the years after Severus' death in 307, persecution continued, albeit sporadically in the east—and more vividly in Maximinus' lands than elsewhere—but Galerius seems to have gradually come to realize that the symbolic power of the victim-ization was becoming counterproductive as the empire divided between the "anti-Christian" east and the "tolerant" west. Furthermore, it was fairly obvious that Licinius and Maximinus hated each other, and that civil war would likely follow Galerius' death. In that event, Licinius would need to make a deal with either Constantine or Maxentius to avoid the threat of war on two fronts.

By the spring of 311 Galerius also knew he was dying. Although we don't know what killed him—there is no reason to think that Lactantius' grisly account of his death, with vermin in his guts and emitting an odor of corrup-tion that befouled an entire province, is necessarily true—but the fact that his death was not sudden is reflected in the language of the edict of toleration he issued in the months before he died. He would not admit that he was wrong to have persecuted the Christians; they showed self-indulgent idiocy when "they did not follow the practices of the ancients, which their own ancestors had, perhaps, instituted, but according to their own will and as it pleased them, made laws for themselves that they observed." Still—despite death and impris-onment—Christians had persisted in their beliefs. It was then purely a result of his habitual practice that he "decided to extend our most speedy indulgence to these people as well, so that Christians may once more establish their own meeting places, so long as they do not act in a disorderly way."[10]

In ending the persecution, Galerius is asserting that ancestral tradition is identical with the well-being of his subjects, that the purpose of persecution edicts is to ensure that tradition be preserved, thereby protecting the average person from the menace of aberrant behavior. Now that they are released from fear of persecution, Christians may join with everyone else in praying for his health. Even if they persist in their ill-advised nonconformity, they will at least be praying for the right things. And it could certainly never be suggested that he had done something wrong: his logic is intact even as he allows the Christians to carry on being foolish.

Constantine and Maxentius had long since strengthened their relations with the Christian Church. Members of the church in Rome had called Maxentius in to settle disputes in their community arising from the issue of proper behavior during the persecutions. Constantine was in touch with a bishop from Cordoba in Spain named Ossius, as well as with the leaders of the Christian communi-ties at Trier and Cologne. This one point of contact could not, however, make up for other differences, and the death of Galerius would set off a round of diplomatic negotiations. It was Licinius who was in most danger: his appointment as Augustus had been directed against Maxentius every bit as much as it had been resented by Maximinus, who had spent the year 310 engaged in a border war with the Persians, perhaps in an effort to prove his credentials to the army in the likely event of war as soon as Galerius died. We don't know if it was Licinius who initiated negotiations with Constantine in 311 or the early part of 312, but a level of agreement was clearly reached.[11] The terms, insofar as they can be reconstructed from later events, appear to have involved some sort of military demonstration by Licinius that would tie down some of Maxentius' forces in northeastern Italy, followed by a pledge of support by Constantine for what would be Licinius' subsequent war against Maximinus.

These negotiations telegraphed an invasion of Italy from Gaul. As Constantine contemplated the imminent outbreak of war with Maxentius in the spring of 312, he was clearly worried. Maxentius had defeated Severus and Galerius, who was a formidable soldier. He had ousted his father, and he had defeated Domitius Alexander. He had a good, experienced army, controlled a series of fortified cities in northern Italy, and had been working on the already impressive defenses of Rome. Constantine knew that emperors needed the aid of the gods to succeed, but who would his god be? He also knew that no god was more at odds with the ideology of Diocletian and Galerius than the god of the Christians. Was this significant? We can sense the trouble in Constantine's mind, and we get an inkling of the new messages he was sending out with the aid of a speech delivered in the summer of 311 at the city of Autun in central France.[12]

Autun was the capital of the Gallic tribe of the Aedui, and, as the panegyrist reminds the emperor—who appears to have been present to hear his composition—the Aedui had a long history of loyalty to Rome. Such was that loyalty, in fact, that they had rebelled against the Gallic regime in 269, hoping that the emperor Claudius II or his military commanders would come to their rescue. That had not happened, and Autun had been sacked.[13] In 306, as the consequence of the tax reassessment carried out under Constantius, the city had been assessed as having 32,000 *capita* (heads) as the basis for calculating the "head" or capitation tax the city would pay each year. In Roman taxation theory, an adult male counted as one head, while women and children ordinarily counted as a fraction of a head, as did animals. The tax would be collected by the town council, which was responsible for making sure that each person paid up for the *capita* at which he or she had been assessed. If there was a short-fall, the tax officials would be responsible for making it up out of their own funds (something that made this a *munus* to be avoided in case there should be any question of the accuracy of the assessment or if some disaster should have decreased the population between assessments). Constantine reduced the assessment to 25,000 about the time of his visit.[14]

The author of this speech, unlike those of other speeches that have so far offered us insight into Constantine's mind, makes it clear that he is speaking for the people of Autun rather than for the court. Thus, while he has clearly a mastery of the basic outlines of the new order—Constantine's descent from Claudius in particular—his observations are nonetheless those of an outsider making use of odd snippets that he heard, such as the notion that Constantine is interested in the goddess known as Mens Divina, the divinity, Divine Mind: he notes that "things sent from heaven come swiftly to earth, for thus does that Divine Mind which governs the entire earth create immediately what it conceives."[15] The emperor has come to Autun, he says, with him "who is the ally and comrade of his majesty," probably a reference to that divinity whom Constantine had met the previous year—possibly in the guise of Sol Invictus the Companion who appears on contemporary coins.[16] The most important point that this outsider had taken away from what he has heard is that in nei-ther case does the chosen god belong to Diocletian's pantheon.

15.

THE BATTLE OF THE MILVIAN BRIDGE

T O INVADE ITALY WAS no simple task. Maxentius had the advantage of
well-developed defenses, and Constantine's force would be limited both
by the need to defend the Rhine frontier while he was away and by considerations of logistics. To supply armies larger than 40,000 men seems to have been
beyond the capacity of the ancient military art, and Constantine had before
him the example of Galerius' failure, which had begun with the collapse of
the army's supply lines. For the campaign to be successful, he would need to
strike hard at northern Italy, compelling the enemy forces to give battle in the
open, overwhelming them before they could withdraw behind strong defenses.
Only if he was successful in this operation would he be able to march his army
to Rome without calling on extensive reinforcements that would denude the
Rhine frontier or make his own columns too big to supply. He would then have
to capture one of the most impressively fortified cities in the world.[1] No wonder
he appears to have been spending a good deal of time in prayer.

There were three ways that an army could advance from Gaul into Italy,
and to each there were advantages as well as disadvantages, as any student
of the civil war of AD 69 would know. On January 1 of that year, Vitellius,
the governor of what was then Lower Germany—so called even though in
our reckoning it was the northernmost of the two Roman provinces on
the Rhine because it was farther from the sources of the river—had been
proclaimed emperor by his troops. By early March, Vitellius' generals had
managed two crossings of the Alps with a total of some 40,000 men, uniting
on the plain of the Po valley near the city of Cremona. Here they defeated
the armies of the rival emperor, Otho, who saw that he would be unlikely to
do better by prolonging the combat and committed suicide. The victorious

armies of the spring were defeated in the early autumn by forces emerging from the Balkans, fighting in the interests of Vespasian, who had been proclaimed emperor in Judea in early July.

The armies of Vitellius had used two of the main passages over the Alps; one crossed the Petit St. Bernard pass between Mont Blanc and the Graian Alps, and the other crossed the Maritime Alps. The southern route involved an easier passage of the mountains, but an army and its supply line on this route were open to attack from the sea, which is precisely what happened to Vitellius' men. An army coming through the Petit St. Bernard, a steep if short passage for an army to negotiate, risked getting trapped before the walls of Eporedia, the modern city of Ivrea, which had been founded around 100 BC to control the pass. If one could count on incompetence or treason—a crucial factor in AD 69, when the unit garrisoning the area had declared for Vitellius—this might not be a risk. But AD 69 had been a time of considerable chaos: Otho seized the throne only on January 15, having arranged the murder of his predecessor Galba; Galba had taken the throne a few months earlier after the suicide of Nero.

In 312 the situation was different. Maxentius' main forces were already in northern Italy, albeit concentrated around the imperial capitals at Milan and Aquileia, but still close enough to be able to resist anything but the swiftest and best-disguised advance from Gaul.[2] Faced with a potential holdup at Eporedia as well as a rival who had at his disposal the major naval bases of the Mediterranean, Constantine chose a third route, this one across the Alps near Mt. Cénis. The first garrisoned city that he would hit was the modern Segusio. According to reports that formed the official tradition for later generations regarding the campaign, Segusio refused to surrender but fell to an immediate assault as Constantine's men scaled the walls and set fire to the gates.[3] The operation appears to have been well planned, and it created an immediate problem for Maxentius' commanders: Turin was the next city in Constantine's path.

Turin was a major city. Could it simply be abandoned? Could it be reinforced before Constantine arrived? Neither operation was plausible because the biggest formations of Maxentius' northern armies were still around Milan, and the abandonment of a major city would have a serious psychological impact. The effects of the destruction of Segusio were no doubt already felt, as the citizens of Turin would have been aware that, in the event of a siege, their fates would be tied to that of the garrison. Constantine could have had no doubt about the stress he was causing.[4]

The dilemma facing the commander at Turin reflects Constantine's own understanding that war, especially civil war, was a political as well as a military process: if significant units of Maxentius' army were seen to be defeated or retreating before him, it could undermine the loyalty of others. The element of surprise was the one thing that Constantine might, with luck, be able to control since it would have been difficult for Maxentius' commander, Rauricius Pompeianus, to know exactly where Constantine might be appearing in Italy. The approaches to both the pass at Mt. Cénis and the Petit St. Bernard began at Lyons. If Constantine could keep his intentions secret, he would have an advantage given that the enemies' spies couldn't move much faster than he could.

In the planning of this campaign, two immensely important aspects of Constantine's character emerge—both the capacity to look into the mind of a potential opponent so as to understand the constraints under which the opponent operated, and a fundamental ability to command the enormous amount of detail necessary for launching a successful operation.

The earliest account of the battle outside Turin claims that the battle was won by a charge of Constantine's heavily armored cavalry, which, massed in a wedge formation, overthrew the front of their enemies and turned their army in rout. Such cavalry had come into Roman service in the time of Aurelian, who first introduced cavalry units whose riders wore tall helmets, covering their bodies with chain mail riding heavily armored horses to supplement the existing heavy cavalry units whose lance-wielding men wore chain mail coats covering only their torsos and rode unarmored horses in battle. Such super-heavy cavalry had long been used by some tribes north of the Danube and in Persian armies, and they could be very effective against unformed infantry or more lightly armed cavalry units, or units whose flanks had been turned. They were not especially useful against formed infantry as their horses would not charge home against massed spearmen, and their effectiveness was limited in bad weather (the heavily burdened horses tended to bog down in mud) or on hot days when heat exhaustion would set in rapidly. When opposing armies both had such units they tended to cancel each other out. Indeed, on another source for the campaign—the arch erected at Rome to commemorate Constantine's victory— heavily armored cavalry are notably absent from depictions of Constantine's side (they do show up in Maxentius' army, but as drowning men in the Tiber). Constantine's heroes are more lightly armed horse and infantrymen, and rightly so. In a battle between two technologically equivalent armies—as would have been the battle of Turin—victory went to the side with the better soldiers (see figure 15.1). As these men moved into battle, wielding their spears and long swords, experience mattered. An enormous advantage was held by men who had stood their ground when a comrade had gone down with a Frankish axe in his skull, who knew that they could rely on their neighbors as they fought the brutal one-on-one battles to their front that would determine their fate. The longer a battle went on, as the wall of bodies between two units grew, as exhaustion threatened, the better the chances of the veteran. It was less likely

(a)

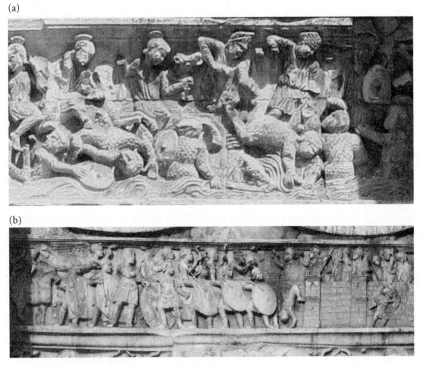

(b)

FIGURE 15.1

The army of Constantine. Note the stress here on Constantine's infantry and the winged Victory that accompanies them in the bottom picture, showing the capture of Verona, while the top picture shows the battle of the Milvian bridge where, interestingly, the only mailed cavalry are on Maxentius' side and they are being driven into the river by Constantine's more lightly armed horsemen.
Source: Courtesy of the author.

that men would start looking to the rear—units always broke from the rear as people began to slip away rather than take their turn in the front rank—in a unit whose men had fought together, whose men were familiar with the dreadful sounds and odors of combat. The day at Turin went most likely to Constantine's veteran infantry, men who had fought in the yearly battles with the Franks and Alemanni, and took from those encounters the experience that gave them a decided advantage against the men of Maxentius.[5] In the end Maxentius' men broke; Turin surrendered and was spared a sack—something perhaps easier to arrange since the army had been fed a city a few days earlier.

The battle of Turin was the critical turning point in the Italian campaign. The surviving forces in the north pulled back in the direction of Verona, leaving open the road to Milan, which followed Turin in surrendering without a fight. To have so easily won control of an important imperial capital was a victory of symbolic significance and led other cities in the area to pledge Constantine their loyalty. Staying a few days at Milan, which enabled his soldiers to rest while he stabilized his control, Constantine then set out in pursuit of Pompeianus and the surviving Maxentian forces.[6] Pompeianus, who seems to have just suffered a preliminary defeat at Brixia (Brescia), first chose to defend Verona; but soon, possibly fearing treason, he tried to break up the siege line with a sally in force—duly repulsed by Constantine—even though Pompeianus made his escape in the course of the battle with a view to commanding the reinforcements coming to raise the siege.

The final battle of the northern campaign would thus be fought outside Verona, where Pompeianus failed to break the siege and his army fled, much of it subsequently going over to Constantine. Constantine then occupied Aquileia on the northwest coast of the Adriatic, the site of the palace that allegedly had his youthful image on display. The later version of the last battle has Constantine doing his best imitation of Galerius during the Persian war, setting off on a scouting mission with no more than a couple of comrades before the two sides engaged. The story of Galerius' scout may be no more based in fact than this one, but both served to emphasize the role of the emperor in every phase of a military operation. Insofar as the anecdote about Galerius may have been well established, the invention of this story illustrates the constant battle that Constantine felt he had to wage against the memory of the old regime.[7]

Constantine's victories in the Po valley made it impossible for Maxentius to rely on the defenses of Rome, and with a substantial portion of his original army now destroyed it is unlikely that he could muster a force much greater (if any greater at all) than that of Constantine. Treason may well have been in the air—many of Maxentius' associates would rapidly find places in the highest echelons of Constantine's regime, which suggests that negotiations may have been opened between their houses and his camp as he moved south. Lactantius says there were demonstrations in the circus at which the crowd proclaimed Constantine's invincibility, while the panegyrist of 313 says that the divine spirit and eternal majesty of the city robbed Maxentius of his senses (these may be two ways of saying the same thing, since Lactantius is ignorant of a very great deal that happened during the campaign).[8] As Constantine approached Rome, Maxentius appears to have ordered the Sibylline books to be consulted—these were rather remote descendants of the collection that had guided important aspects of Roman religious practice for many centuries.

On October 28, Maxentius reappointed Anullinus as prefect of the city (evidently as a good luck gesture), the position he had held on the day Maxentius seized power. He then rode to war, though probably with little confidence as he stowed away the symbols of his imperial power in wooden boxes under a shrine near the Palatine. There they would remain until December 2006 when Italian archaeologists uncovered them. They contain, wrapped in linen and silk (probably), three lances, four javelins (Maxentius' hunting gear?), a base into which standards could be placed, three glass and chalcedony spheres, and a scepter. When he hid these objects, Maxentius was no doubt aware that there was a good chance he was not coming back.

Although the battle of the Milvian Bridge is often seen nowadays as the culmination of Constantine's career, the moment at which he became a Christian as the result of having seen the vision of a cross in the sky inscribed with the words "in this sign, conquer," and as a victory of faith over tyranny, none of these perspectives has much to do with what actually happened—and not even Eusebius claims that the vision was immediately before the battle, where it ends up in very many more recent depictions of the conflict. Constantine had begun the spiritual journey that would result in his conversion well in advance of the battle—before crossing the Alps if our reading of the obscure reference to Divine Mind in the panegyric delivered in 311 is any indication. Maxentius

FIGURE 15.2

Constantine's victory. Despite the poor state of preservation it is possible to pick out Constantine, who is the second figure on the left, and the shape of a winged figure leading him onward (this would be a Victory), while the figure wearing the large crown is the city goddess Roma.
Source: Courtesy of the author.

himself was hardly a persecutor, and the battle does not seem to have been particularly hard fought. Constantine arrived outside Rome riding a wave of success; Maxentius commanded an army whose men knew that they were probably overmatched. It could not have helped morale any that he drew them up with the river to their back as if making a statement that they could fight or die—not really an effective line to take with men who would have been well aware that Constantine was not in the habit of massacring his prisoners.

When the armies were drawn up, Constantine's men appear to have displayed a new symbol that combined the Greek letter *Chi* (pronounced with a strong "ch") with the letter *rho* (our "r"); this could be interpreted either as a reference to the name of Christ or to the word *chrestos* ("good luck"). Lactantius says that this was because Constantine had announced that he had a dream that had instructed him to place this symbol of the "Highest God" on their shields. In so doing he looked to a long tradition in which Roman generals had revealed such visions to their men on the day of battle. Not even Lactantius suggests that this was a specifically Christian sign on the day, even though it would later figure on the Labarum, Constantine's personal standard, and become a symbol of imperial Christianity. On October 28 it was a device to raise the morale of the men before they attacked.[9]

Attack they did, and, as at Turin, his infantry appears to have won the day. His cavalry chased the remnants of Maxentius' forces into and across the river. Maxentius himself was evidently seen to fall from the bridge into the river, or that is what the panegyrist of 313 would have us believe: "the Tiber devoured that man, sucked into a whirlpool, as he was vainly trying to escape with his horse and impressive armor up the far bank."[10] On the arch that was dedicated at Rome in 315, the left-hand side of the panel depicting the battle shows Constantine on the bank looking over at Maxentius who is falling from the bridge into the river as the goddess Victory, standing beside the goddess Roma, beckons to him from the far bank—two of three female figures who play an immensely important role in the original story telling how Constantine found the confidence to launch the invasion of Italy.

16.

FREEDOM OF WORSHIP

CONSTANTINE DIDN'T STAY LONG in Rome. He made a ceremonial entry into the city, at the end of which he did not sacrifice to Capitoline Jupiter. (This decision could be taken simply as a feature of Constantine's ongoing rejection of the trappings of the old regime; why should he sacrifice to a god associated so closely with Diocletian?) Then he set about forging a new regime in which those who had served Maxentius would have a place. For a start, he decided to retain Anullinus as prefect of the city for the next month before replacing him with Aradius Rufinus, who would hold the office until December 313; at this point he would be replaced by Caeonius Rufius Volusianus, who would be prefect until August 315. These appointments might also be emblematic of the problems Maxentius faced before marching from Rome on October 28. But while the sixth-century historian Zosimus says that Constantine executed a few of Maxentius' friends, it doesn't seem that those friends came from the aristocratic Roman families that had once supported him. One other thing that Constantine did before leaving town was to order the restitution of property confiscated from the Christian Church during the persecution: Maxentius may have ended the persecution, but he had not gone as far as to do that.[1]

With arrangements made for the administration of Maxentius' territory, Constantine went to meet his co-emperor Licinius at Milan, arriving there by March.[2] The two men cemented their alliance with Licinius' marriage to Constantia, Constantine's oldest half-sister. It is tempting to imagine that Constantine introduced his prospective brother-in-law to the knowledge of the Highest God revealed on the campaign just passed, but the announcements of support by non-Galerian and Diocletianic divinities that would be a feature of Licinius' self-representation in the next year perhaps needed no special encouragement given that Maximinus was himself a die-hard devotee of the old way of doing things.[3] Constantine would most likely have pointed out to Licinius that his half-sister was now a Christian. He might also have discussed with him the possibility of drawing up a restitution edict because if Licinius defeated Maximinus, such an edict would offer a splendid way of declaring the power of the "Highest God" who would by then have guided them both to victory.

The agreement that Constantine made with Licinius in Milan was of great importance for solidifying their relationship both with each other and with the past. They could assert the role of a new god in aiding them to victory, and do so in terms that both rejected the associations with specific gods that had characterized the old regime, and asserted their own equality in the good relationship that each had with the "Highest God." In more specific terms, they could reject the bigotry inherent in defining a good Roman as someone who was not a good Christian. It was an act that underscored very well established aspects of Maximinus' regime: Maximinus had made persecution one of the centerpieces of his rule in the months after Galerius' death. In so doing he had enunciated his own special relationship with the traditional gods.

The new high priest of persecution was Theotecnus; a member of the city council at Antioch in Syria, he had erected a statue of Zeus Philios (Zeus the friendly) that appears to have given oracles. It is not clear how this worked, though Eusebius' assertion that Theotecnus "put on a display of this marvel through which he gave oracles, even to the emperor," makes it quite possible that he had rigged the statue to do something. It was not unknown, for instance, for people to drill a hole through the back of a statue and insert a speaking pipe (a crane's windpipe worked well) so that the statue would seem to speak. Theotecnus' activities inspired civic officials throughout the east, who on the advice of provincial governors sent messages to Maximinus asking him to initiate a persecution. At the same time, it appears that someone in the court forged the *Acts of Pilate*, which contained a denunciation of the Christians. The title of this composition suggests that it resembled a particular form of Christian text, an account of a martyrdom based on a putative transcript of the encounter between a magistrate and a prospective martyr—here the conversation would be between Pilate and the Savior himself. It would quite likely have revolved around sorcery—pagans tended to suggest that Jesus was no more than a commonplace magician—and the question of Jesus' mortality.[4]

Maximinus did not now issue an edict ordering persecution. Rather, his favorable responses to petitions, worded very similarly to the message of Theotecnus' god requesting that Christians be expelled from civic territory, triggered a series of local persecutions. Three of these petitions have survived, one directly through Eusebius' history of the church, and two on inscriptions from Asia Minor. These inscriptions along with other documents also reveal that in 312 Maximinus was still wary of provoking open war with Licinius; he recognized the claim of the two western Augusti to be consuls for the year.[5]

Local initiatives in persecution made 312 a very difficult year for many Christian communities. In Alexandria, Bishop Peter was arrested and executed. At Ancyra (Ankara in modern Turkey), where Theotecnus had been sent as governor, seven virgins, leaders of a deviant Christian community, were arrested and drowned. After recovering their bodies in the middle of the night, another member of that community publicly launched a verbal assault upon Theotecnus himself, which resulted in his equally public incineration. At Pedecthoe in Armenia, anonymous letters attacking the emperor's policy led to the arrest and execution of a man named Athenogenes. Marcus Julius Eugenius, an official on the staff of Diogenes, governor of Pisidia, was tortured repeatedly but survived to become bishop of Laodicea.

There was still, though, no all-encompassing edict, and as the year drew to a close, Maximinus appears to have realized that he needed to step back. He refused to allow the people of Nicomedia to expel the Christians from their community, and by the end of the year he had issued an edict of toleration.[6]

Maximinus' edict did nothing to ease his relationship with the western Augusti, and it was now clear to him that if he were to have any chance of survival he would need to strike first. In the spring of 313 he sent an army across the Hellespont. Licinius met Maximinus at Adrianople, and on the day of the battle announced to his army that he had had a dream in which a divine messenger told him to pray to the Supreme God. That morning of April 30 he wrote out the prayer, apparently received verbatim from the angel—an event scarcely unparalleled in the history of ancient visions—and had it distributed to his men. The prayer, which the soldiers were ordered to utter three times, ran thus:

Supreme God, we pray to you, Holy God, we pray to you. We commend all justice to you. We commend our safety to you. We commend our empire to you. Through you we live, through you we emerge victorious and fortunate. Highest, Holy God, hear our prayers. We lift up our arms to you. Hear us, Holy, Highest God.[7]

As Licinius' troops prayed, looking to the future, Maximinus seems to have been looking to the past since the very next day would be the anniversary of his proclamation as Caesar. After the mass prayer, the two emperors met briefly to see whether they could resolve their differences. When that failed, battle was joined. Licinius won an outright victory, and Maximinus fled to the east, pausing briefly at Nicomedia to gather up his family. He planned to make a final stand at Tarsus but failed to defend the narrow passes from the Anatolian plateau into the Cilician plain. Then at the approach of Licinius' army, he committed suicide.[8]

On his way east, Maximinus had issued a final edict stating that everyone knew that "we take unceasing thought for the good of our provincials, and desire to grant them such things as are best calculated to secure the advantage of all." In the course of these calculations he had realized that while Diocletian and Galerius "our fathers" had ordered the abolition of Christian assemblies, this had coincidentally resulted in "many extortions and robberies...practiced by the officials, and that this increased as time went on to the detriment of our provincials." He therefore ordered the persecution to stop.[9] Although Maximinus isn't stating here that it was wrong to persecute Christians for being Christians, he is saying that it was unfortunate that local officials had let things get so out of hand that they had persecuted the wrong people. It is thus in the interests of *non*-Christians that he orders the end of persecution and the restoration of church property (presumably on the assumption that some of it was wrongly confiscated). And it is somewhat ironic that, using the language of Diocletian and Galerius, Maximinus the devout pagan was the emperor who brought the persecution of the Christian Church to an end.

Although Maximinus' edict obviated the need for immediate action on the part of Licinius, a statement on the place of the church plainly offered a vehicle through which the new regime could distance itself from the past. So it was that on June 13, 313, Licinius issued his own restoration edict at Nicomedia, declaring that it represented the gist of his discussions with Constantine at Milan the previous year.[10] It is this document, repetitive and enormously long, that stands in the Christian tradition as the official beginning of a new era in the relationship between church and state. From the ideological viewpoint, it was precisely that, for it expresses a message of inclusion that goes far beyond the edicts of Galerius and Maximinus. While these two emperors had promised that they would no longer persecute the Christians for the good of the state as a whole, in this edict Licinius and Constantine state that the Christians are protected by the Highest God, who has aided them in their victories. All who worshipped the gods were therefore to be treated equally. It is a stunning assertion by a Roman emperor that freedom of thought is a good thing, and it remains such even though neither Licinius nor Constantine would always follow through on this point.[11]

We have two copies of this document, one in Latin in Lactantius' *On the Deaths of the Persecutors*, which presumably tracks the original very closely, and a Greek translation in Eusebius' *History of the Church;* they differ from each other in a few points of detail, but those differences are no greater than we would expect in texts of a document that was copied by many different hands as it was distributed about the empire and to which governors would add their own preambles.[12] What is most significant is that the document, once wrongly known as the Edict of Milan (there was never any such thing) and attributed to Constantine, is the product of a pagan emperor who had decided that Constantine's approach to the "Christian question" was correct. Although the "Edict of Milan" is really a letter of Licinius to the governors of the eastern provinces, it still represents a sea change in the direction of imperial policy. Christianity is no longer to be shunted aside as "un-Roman" or the practice of eccentrics. As was the case with Aurelian's cult of the Invincible Sun, Christianity is now associated with the very substance that holds the empire together: the ideology of imperial victory.[13]

17.

THE CONVERSION OF CONSTANTINE

CONSTANTINE'S MEETING WITH LICINIUS at Milan marked the end of one phase of a spiritual journey that had begun for him, it seems, in 311. It had then gathered speed in the course of the Italian campaign when Lactantius said he was inspired by a dream to have his soldiers paint a new symbol of divine favor upon their shields before the battle of the Milvian Bridge. It was much later that Eusebius said Constantine had been moved to become a Christian because of the vision of the cross in the sky, which Eusebius says he had seen in southern France.[1]

The visions reported by Lactantius and Eusebius are not the only visions that are reported in Constantine's career, and other reports are a good deal closer in time to 312 than are those of the two Christians. It is striking, for instance, that the panegyrist of 313 should write:

> What god, what so present majesty, encouraged you so that with almost all your companions and generals not only silently muttering, but even openly fearful, to sense through yourself that the time had come for the liberation of the city against the warnings of the *haruspices* [diviners]. You do indeed have some secret understanding with that Divine Mind (*Mens Divina*), which has delegated our concerns to lesser gods and deigns to reveal itself to you alone.[2]

Mens Divina first appears in relation to Constantine in the panegyric of 311 and we may suppose the divinity started to become prominent at that time. The one that Constantine advertised meeting in 310 took the form of Apollo, who was decidedly male. *Mens Divina*, in Latin, is feminine and the scarce representations of her in the imperial tradition show her as female (divinities who are grammatically feminine and represent abstract qualities are also personally female). If the panegyrist was referring to a painting of this encounter, it would have shown Constantine face-to-face with a woman just as the Arch of Constantine shows him being welcomed to Rome by the female Roma and her companion Victoria, goddess of victory. Just as important is the setting: as in the vision of Apollo, Constantine is alone with the god, just as he is alone in Lactantius' understanding of the encounter and Licinius is alone with God's messenger.

The interpretation and presentation of dreams were significant aspects of imperial communication. Artemidorus, the author of a major work on the interpretation of dreams in the second century AD has this to say about "public" or "cosmic" dreams:

> A man will not dream about things about which he has not thought. People do not see dreams about private things about which they have not thought. It is impossible for a person who is small to receive something outside of his power, to have a vision of great affairs, being powerless. It is contrary to reason since dreams are private and come true only for the dreamer unless he is a king, magistrate or of the great. These men have reflected about public affairs and may receive dreams about them, not as private men entrusted with small matters, but as rulers who are concerned about matters for the common good.[3]

Some dreams—many of them known through the career of Septimius Severus, who advertised the premonitions that made him think he might become emperor—needed to be understood through analogy. In Severus' case, for instance, we are told that one day when he entered the Senate he dreamed that he had been suckled by a she-wolf as Romulus had been. In another dream water flowed from his hand as if from a spring—a good sign in an Artemidoran system of interpretation where clear flowing water could indicate power because streams do as they wish. In a third, when he was a governor, he dreamed that the Roman world saluted him and then later that he gazed down upon the earth from high above, laying his fingers everywhere as if on the strings of an instrument so that they all "sang together." Finally, he dreamed that he replaced

Pertinax (his predecessor as emperor) on a horse, a dream that was commemorated by a statue at Rome. In fact, the dreams of Severus represent not only his destiny but also his technical command of what was known in those days as dream interpretation, something that he combined with a well-advertised knowledge of astrology. He was well aware that dreams have to be described by the person who has them, and that he would be all the more impressive if his dream narratives made sense to professionals in the field.[4]

Severus, of course, was not the only dreamer or visionary to rule Rome in the century or so before Constantine, and his interest in the subject may have mediated earlier traditions into forms that his third-century successors could appreciate—one reason that imperial miracles all tend to seem a bit similar. One of the striking moments in the reign of Marcus Aurelius (161–180), who seems to have mentioned his dreams only in private, was the astonishing act of some divinity who intervened to save the day: in response to Marcus' prayers, this god relieved a Roman army, cut off and suffering from thirst, from the hordes of barbarians who surrounded it by striking at a distance, smiting the barbarians with a terrible deluge.[5] Marcus' miracle, picked up by Severus, was later resuscitated by Probus. In addition to the story of Aurelian's recognizing the god who saved his army at Emesa, that emperor's entire campaign in the east was punctuated with signs of divine interest. One was a hostile prediction at a shrine in Lycia (southern Turkey) and an unfortunate series of events at the temple of Aphrodite at Aphaca near Baalbek in modern Lebanon. Such interventions were only natural since, as Artemidorus wrote, divine signs whether positive or negative should accompany important changes in the world order.[6]

Artemidorus also notes that the most important dreams were ones in which a man saw an actual god. Such experiences, narrated at various times and in various ways, all stress the extraordinary power of the moment for the dreamer. In one striking case, that of a doctor named Thessalus who claimed to have been taught an ancient form of healing by a god,

> When the third day had come, setting out at dawn, I came to the high priest. He had prepared a pure chamber and everything else for the vision. I, because of the great eagerness of my soul, without the knowledge of the high priest, had brought a papyrus and a pen to write down, if the opportunity arose, whatever was said. The high priest asked me if I wished to speak with

the soul of a dead man or with a god. I said "Asclepius" [the Greek god of healing], and that it would be the culmination of his kindnesses if he allowed me to speak with the god, one on one. He promised this to me without pleasure, as his expression showed. Calling me into the room, and ordering me to sit facing the throne upon which the god would sit, and summoning the god through secret names, he left, closing the door. I was sitting there, shaking in body and soul because of the astonishment of the vision, for no human words are able to describe either the sight or the beauty of his adornment. Taking my right hand he began to speak, "O blessed Thessalus, today a god has honored you, and when they learn what you have done, men will give you honor as if you were a god; ask me therefore about the matters for which you have come and I will answer all your questions." On my side, I heard him with difficulty—I was astonished and my mind was entranced by the beauty of the god—nonetheless I asked him if I had erred in the prescriptions of Nectanebo, to which the god responded that King Nectanebo, an immensely wise man and one embellished with all virtues, had not received from a divine voice anything that you want to learn.[7]

In another case, this one described by a Greek intellectual of the second century AD, Aelius Aristides, we are told:

Athena appeared to me not long after that, holding her aegis [shield] and her beauty, size and whole form were that of the Athena of Pheidias in Athens. There was a scent from the aegis that was sweet, and it was like wax, and it was amazing and beautiful and great. She appeared to me alone, standing in front of me so that I could see her as well as possible. I showed her to the people who were standing with me—they were two of my friends and my foster sister—and I called out and named her Athena, saying that she was in front of me and that she spoke to me and I pointed to the aegis. They did not know what to do, but were at a loss and feared that I had become delirious until they saw that my strength was being restored and heard words that I heard from the goddess.[8]

Encounters of the sort described by Thessalus and Aristides are just the kind that Constantine allowed it to be known that he was experiencing. Moreover, they are more powerful, more intense than Aurelian's moments of recognition or the dreams in which Severus put his faith. Constantine claims not to be a practitioner of the technical arts of dream interpretation, but to be the sort of person who could enter the presence of a god. The divinity who gave him the confidence to invade Italy was present before him. Speaking a few years after the event to a meeting of bishops, he writes:

> The eternal and incomprehensible religious piety of our God will not allow the human condition to wander uselessly for long in the shadows, nor does it allow the hateful desires of certain men to prevail for long so that he should not allow them to be saved, opening a path with his shining beams of light to turn them to the rule of justice. I have learned this through many examples and I measure these things through myself. For there were of old things in me that seemed to be lacking in justice, nor did I think that the heavenly power could see those secrets that I bore within my breast. Verily what should have been allotted to these things? Plainly one abundant with all evils. But the all-powerful God who sits in the watchpost of heaven gave me what I did not deserve; truly I cannot say, nor can those things be enumerated which heavenly benevolence granted to me its servant.[9]

What did this god reveal to him and what did the god look like? The first question is perhaps easier to answer than the second. God revealed to Constantine how to leave behind the error of his ways and thus succeed in the future. This vision is not the one Lactantius mentions before the battle of the Milvian Bridge that resulted in the new embellishment of the army's shields, but one that showed Constantine a new way—surely the one that the panegyrist of 313 placed before the decision to invade Italy. The truth of this vision was proven to Constantine by his victory, but even then he could not reveal to those assembled listeners that what he saw was not Mens Divina, but rather the Christian god, a god of light who could see into his very heart. Indeed, the light imagery that he uses links with the imagery of shadow that precedes it; but the reference to "the watchpost of heaven" may imply that the god he met was in heaven (and glowing or giving off shafts of light that could be interpreted metaphorically).

Constantine's story implies that the revelation that God awarded him in person, saving him from the errors and moral dilemmas that had troubled him, was not one that could be discussed in great detail (as the single reference to Mens Divina in the panegyric of 311 and the absence of specificity in the panegyric of 313 may indicate). Mens Divina may have been sufficiently abstract a concept to allow multiple interpretations. What we can be sure of, though, is that it was one thing for an emperor to be kind to Christians, but quite another to publicly acclaim the power of their god before the world. It's unfortunate that we hear nothing from those Christians who were closest to Constantine at the time. But four bishops, at least, were with his army by the time it reached Rome: three from Gaul, a fourth from Spain. The presence of these bishops—Maternus from Cologne, Reticius from Autun, Marinus from Arles, and Ossius of Cordoba—suggests both that Constantine may have added them to his retinue as he moved south from Trier, and that his decisive revelation occurred before he opened the campaign, as the panegyrist says.[10]

As time passed, the conversion narrative would change, as Constantine himself would change and become ever more confident in his new God. At first, this new God was a new facet to a spiritual life that did not require the abandonment of other gods, or even strict adherence to Christian doctrine. Constantine felt apparently that he could recognize the God of the Christians as powerful without subjecting himself to the discipline of the church—something, it is worth noting, he would never do. Still, the private moment would someday become public, and when it did, a new element would be added to the story.

It is this process of change that is reflected in the tortured prose of the most famous of all the conversion narratives for the modern world: the one that appears after Constantine's death in Bishop Eusebius' biography that included the tale of the cross in the sky. Eusebius grafted this story onto another account suggesting a mental journey that Constantine undertook as he sought the god who would help him in the struggle against Maxentius. The fact that Eusebius says Constantine told him the tale "much later" is, sadly, a poor guarantor of anything, as he uses exactly the same language to describe miraculous events in a later campaign that could have been learned only through Constantine himself, given that there was a shortage of other witnesses at the time.[11]

Eusebius' account begins in the twenty-seventh chapter of the biography's first book: when he was thinking about the invasion of Italy, Constantine reflected that those who had placed their faith in many gods had failed, while Constantius (albeit never an invader of Italy) "had, throughout his whole life,

honored the god who was the savior and protector of his kingship and the pro-
vider of every good thing." Constantine therefore "decided that it was necessary
to honor only his ancestral god."[12] What Eusebius does not point out is that the
"ancestral god" was none other than Sol Invictus, as the panegyrist of 307 had
already observed: "Surely you see and hear these things, Divine Constantius,
whom Sun himself took up in an almost visible chariot to heaven while he was
seeking his nearby sunrise."[13]

The god of Constantine's father, Constantius, was a god of light who could
guide him forward, but, as Constantine suggests in his letter to the bishops at
Arles, the god that he may have known as Sol Invictus was also "our God," the
God of the Christians. In chapter twenty-seven, he already knows who God is,
but in the next he seems not so sure, for Eusebius comments: "He then invoked
this god in prayers, asking and begging him to show him who he was and to
stretch out his right hand to assist him in his plans. As he was praying and
making earnest entreaties there appeared to the emperor a most astonishing
divine sign."[14]

The question that springs to Constantine's mind at this point is a standard
oracular one: the individual approaches a god to ask him who he is as a way
of getting information about proper cult observance. The most famous, which
occurs several times in slightly different forms, involves people who know per-
fectly well that the god they are consulting is Apollo.[15] The vision of the cross
in the sky, which Eusebius says was witnessed by the entire army, is simply
delivering to Constantine a sign that will win him a battle: the answer to his
question is that the god he is looking for is the god who gives visions in the sky
and promises victory. Constantine doesn't fully understand what this means
so he is granted a dream in which Christ tells him how to make the battle
standard; the emperor explains the heavenly vision to his followers and tells
them to make the battle standard that is described. Then, oddly, Eusebius says
that Constantine did not know who the god was who gave him the sign in the
sky, so he asked others in the hope they might be able to tell him what he had
seen. They then assure him that he had seen the Christian God.[16] At this point
Eusebius has reinterpreted the dream: in this version it has inspired a conversion that he says has already taken place. In so doing he restates the original
question, making it clear once and for all that Constantine does indeed already
know which god is at issue here.

These many confusions are tell-tale signs that stories of somewhat different origins are being conflated, and it is all the more striking that in his earlier *History of the Church*, one draft of which was completed in 313 (and the last one shortly after 324), Eusebius seems not to have heard of the moment of conversion—indeed, as he admits, he only learned the story of the cross in the sky from Constantine himself "much later." How much later is unknowable, though it does seem that Eusebius refers to it in 336 when he delivered a speech in honor of Constantine. Had he just learned it then? The reference is not well developed and is linked with another story that he says he learned well after the events in question from Constantine himself.[17]

In his ignorance at the time, Eusebius is no different from Lactantius, who, at the end of his *Concerning the Deaths of the Persecutors*, reveals himself to be delighted that vengeance was wreaked upon the persecutors, but he is not so delighted that the emperors are now Christian. For Lactantius the victorious emperors are assisted by the Christian god and are friendly to Christians, but he stops short of saying that either one *is* a Christian. His understanding here is in line with that of others, for very few could have known what Constantine had learned from his contact with Divine Mind that gave him the confidence needed to win the battle. Years after the event, the author of a panegyric delivered at Rome would offer a long paean to the mysterious divine force that guided Constantine—and again in language that bespeaks an inward-looking experience:

> God the arbiter of all things looks upon us from on high, and although human minds bear deep recesses for their thoughts, divinity will nonetheless wend its way in and explore the whole; nor is it possible, since the divine will imparts to us the breath which we draw, when we are nourished by so many good things, that he will hide himself away from the cares of the earth and does not judge between the lives of those whose good he governs. That force, that majesty that distinguishes right and wrong, which weighs, tests and examines all the actions of those who are deserving, that divinity protected your piety, that divinity broke the madness of that tyrant, that conscience aided your invincible army, burning with chests full of so many victories with such strength as much as a god is able and your love ought to provide, so that the splendid army overturned the frightful

battle lines, the unknown strength of men and steel, so that you were able to consume in fortunate combat whatever the long cogitation of crime was able to devise.[18]

The moment of divine inspiration as described here differs from another vision, the apparition of a heavenly host, which was the talk of "all the Gauls," appearing "even though heavenly things are not accustomed to come before the eyes of mortals."[19] Constantius sent these heavenly warriors, it was said, and would turn the tide in Constantine's favor during the battle at the Milvian Bridge as they fought (albeit invisibly) at his side (where they had been earlier in the campaign is not made clear).[20] The visions of 312 reflect earlier stories, showing that the dramatic events of the original campaign remained open to improvement. The variations stemmed, of course, from the fact that there was never one authorized, consistent public version of the story for the simple reason that Constantine's original vision was not a public event. His encounter with his new God, like other imperial visions, was a profoundly important moment for the emperor. The details would be communicated to others only on a need-to-know basis.

Constantine was aware of the way gods communicated with emperors: they did so in person, with no one else present, or they made their presence known to the emperor in their dedicated temple—as when Aurelian recognized that Elagabal had helped him in his fight with Zenobia. It was to Constantine and Constantine alone that Apollo appeared in the vision of 310. Aelius Aristides' encounter with Athena showed that a person could see a god who was invisible to those around him. Constantine first revealed his own experience to other Christians, and it was also to his new co-religionists that he revealed the nature of his personal journey toward the new faith and the enlightenment that his new God offered. As for what he saw in his vision, there may be a reflection of it in the language of the letter to the Christians at Arles—for his God was "in the watchpost of heaven." To this extent the vision revealed a heavenly God drawing Constantine to his new faith; but at least for now, it was a heaven that had appeared only in the recesses of his own mind. The process whereby the god of his vision became the Christian God was not going to be immediate.

The question "who is God" could be answered in terms of identifying one divinity with another. In 312, Constantine's god was both the Sun and the

Christian God. It may not have been hard to make this leap, for in some Christian communities the sun god was already equated with Christ. And it is with solar imagery that he is depicted in two third-century paintings in the Roman catacombs, as well as on a sculptural depiction of the story of Jonah, which was understood by some Christians to be an allegory for the Resurrection. Other Christians had noted that some of their fellows understood the rising and setting of the sun as a metaphor for the resurrection, and some others saw the sun as their god, facing the rising sun when they prayed. Lactantius himself would observe that "the east is attached to God because he is the source of light and the illuminator of the world and he makes us rise toward eternal life."[21] Was it knowledge of this kind of equation that enabled Constantine to see that the God his father had followed, the God who had received his father into the heavens, was actually the God whom the Christians revered, the God whom Galerius and Diocletian despised? Was it this knowledge that enabled him to answer in a new way the question of who God was?

As Constantine pondered his future, certain things may gradually have fallen into place to convince him that as the man who would cast away the world of Diocletian he would be doing it as the agent of the God who most obviously was not part of that emperor's vision of the world. For Constantine, conversion was not the result of a sudden momentous revelation, but a journey over time and in his own mind.

VI

WAR AND PEACE

———————————

18.

REWORKING PAST AND FUTURE

CONSTANTINE REMAINED FOR ABOUT a month in northern Italy after the marriage of Licinius and Constantia, then left for Gaul, reaching Trier by the end of May. Here, probably in August, he listened to the panegyric describing his campaign of the previous year. He would remain in the area, except possibly for a trip to Britain in 313 until the early summer of 315, campaigning against the tribes north of the Rhine. About midsummer of that year he returned to Italy, staying in Rome for a couple of months, perhaps celebrating there the dedication of the great arch commemorating his triumph over Maxentius.

The remodeling of Rome from an architectural ode to the ambitions of the departed dynast to a monument for the triumphant liberator and the very act of liberation was rapid and effective. The Rome that one sees today is redolent of Constantine's victory—the only readily available image of Maxentius is of the drowning man on the arch. The twenty-first-century recovery of Maxentius' imperial regalia shows too that Constantine appears to have had no interest in the physical appurtenances of his predecessor. Similarly, he had no need of Maxentius' guard; all of his special guard units were cashiered, and the city was left without the Praetorian Guard for the first time since the reign of Augustus.

The project of revamping Rome's physical environment fell into three parts. One was the assimilation of major Maxentian monuments in the city center for use by the new regime; a second was the redefinition of buildings and spaces previously dedicated to Maxentius' service away from the city center; the third was the triumphal edifice known down the centuries as the Arch of Constantine. Responsibility for the first and third of these projects resided with the Senate, while Constantine himself looked after the second.

Some of the Constantinian changes to the Maxentian original were minimal. It appears that all that was added to the Basilica Nova—a project technically under senatorial control—was an apse at the north end (necessary for structural reasons). Other changes were more substantial. It was evidently Constantine who decided that the original rectilinear façade of the Temple of Romulus needed to go in favor of the current curved face. We do not know what he did with the temple of Venus and Roma—only a few of its columns remain today—but it may be significant that one of his earliest major structural undertakings at Rome was the renovation of one of the city's oldest temples.[1]

As for his new projects, the most significant at this point was the large church he built over the site of the camp of Maxentius' horse guards on the Caelian hill. The location was convenient for a number of other properties that had fallen into his hands, including one that was known as early as 313 as the House of Fausta, a grand structure capable of accommodating (as it would) an entire church council. This site, which would later be closely associated with Helena as the Sessorium, before becoming—after her death—the Church of Santa Croce in Gerusalemme was associated with an entertainment complex including both an amphitheater and a circus, the outlines of which still extend along the Viale Carla Felice-Viale Castrense. Would Fausta and Helena greet their subjects in these places? The circus, perhaps significantly, extends almost to the new church that emerged in the same area, known at first as the Basilica Constantiniana, now as the Church of San Giovanni in Laterano. The bishop of Rome made it his residence. Would Helena meet him at the circus, and did her proximity to the bishop here give her the experience she needed to undertake a mission to the east in the last year of her life? San Giovanni stood directly atop the *praetorium* (command center) of the old camp, celebrating Constantine's god and the victory he had brought him over his enemies. A second grand church, planted above the guards' burial ground on the Via Labicana served a similar purpose.[2] One church that he did not build, however, despite claims that were made later, was St. Peter's on the Vatican. The ancestor of the modern basilica was built during the reign of his son, Constans.[3]

The transformation of Maxentius' buildings and the construction of new churches were symbolic statements of victory. But it was especially and spectacularly on the arch that rose in the valley of the Colosseum that the story of that victory would be told. The location of the arch was significant. It straddled

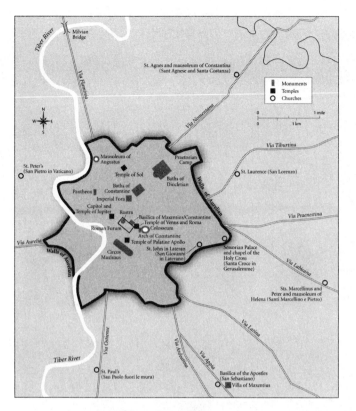

FIGURE 18.1
Plan of Constantinian Rome. After A. Tayfun Öner.

the by then traditional (if recently underutilized) triumphal route along the Via Sacra and framed the colossal statue of the Sun God, first erected by Nero (once displaying that emperor's own features, later that of the sun god, and most recently redesigned with those of Maxentius' son Romulus). The choice of site had been Maxentius' and the project may have been intended to commemorate the victory in North Africa or, more probably, the repulse of Galerius. As it stands today, the arch represents the linkage of Constantine with earlier tradition and with the divine. In Constantine's time, as you made your way up the Via Sacra from the south, you would see ahead the smiling visage of the Colossus, the head newly sculpted in Constantine's image, emerging over the top of the arch and gazing down at the fixture that stood on top of the arch—a bronze statue of the emperor in a four-horse chariot. When you got closer, the Colossus would be fully visible through the central gateway.[4]

(a)

(b)

FIGURE 18.2

The arch of Constantine. As we see it now we miss the full effect that would have been provided, as this reconstruction shows, by its orientation with the great Colossus, which honored the Sun God. Source: ©Shutterstock. Reconstruction is after Marlowe (2006).

Aside from the addition of the Colossus, one of the most stunning aspects of the new arch is the reuse of sculpture from earlier periods. This practice looks back to a tradition begun under Diocletian, whose own triumphal arch, on the Via Lata, had made use of sculpture from the Julio-Claudian era; and

Maxentius too had used earlier material for the tomb of his son. The arch transcends those earlier experiments, however, in the complexity of the message it creates and in the remodeling of the heads of earlier emperors to represent Constantine, Licinius, and, in one case it seems, Constantius.[5]

The arch presents three sculptural elements arranged in three registers. The top one comprises ten tableaux, four on the north and south faces, one each on the east and west, and set behind eight statues of defeated barbarians that once embellished a monument of Trajan. These tableaux are all taken from monuments of Marcus Aurelius and depict imperial rites and functions. On the south side the images are of the emperor "giving" a king to a barbarian people, his speech to his army, the performance of a ritual before military standards, and a display of barbarian prisoners. The north side depicts the emperor's arrival and departure from Rome, a triumphal procession and the distribution of bounty to his people. The east and west sides show victories over barbarians. The arch's dedicatory inscription is the central element on the north and south side.

On the central register are another four images on each side, this time taken from a monument of Hadrian. The south face shows a hunt with the emperor and his companions standing outside a gate, then sacrificing to the god of the woods, hunting a bear, and finally sacrificing to Diana, goddess of the chase. On the north side are scenes of a boar hunt, a sacrifice to Apollo, a dead lion, and a sacrifice to Hercules. The two top registers then set the actions of an emperor in their historical context, emphasizing the emperor's courage, piety, and generosity using images closely evocative of court rituals. The third register depicts Constantine's victory. The south face below the scenes of imperial departure shows the capture of Verona, and on the other side of the entrance, the victory at the Milvian Bridge with Constantine advancing in the company of Roma and Victoria past the drowning form of his rival. On the north side there are scenes of Constantine's arrival in Rome; on the east side he speaks to the people of the city and on the west he distributes coins to people who approach him.

The story of the conquest continues on both the east and west faces, with a frieze showing the departure of the army from Milan beneath the setting moon, and on the east the sun rising above the triumphal entry into Rome. It is the east side that conveys the arch's message most clearly, for here Constantine stands front and center, surrounded by his court, and at either end of the *rostra* (the great speaker's platform in the heart of the Roman Forum) are shown the statues of Hadrian and Marcus that adorned it. Behind Constantine are the four columns erected in honor of Diocletian and his colleagues in 303, flanking a statue of Jupiter. The triumphal arch of Septimius Severus is visible off to the left. What we see here is the sculptural representation of Constantine's message: the influence of Diocletian is clear, but the empire that he had labored to restore was not, in the end, of his own devising, but rather that of the Antonine age.[6] Similarly, the gods depicted on the arch—the Sun and Moon, Apollo, Diana, and Silvanus—are all divinities who had little place in Diocletian's regime; the allusion to Hercules with, it seems, Constantius offering sacrifice to him in the company of Constantine is a reference to family history. Other imperial heads were recarved in the images of Constantine and Licinius who were, at this point, still honored jointly as the liberators of the state from the foulest tyrants and the restorers of public security.[7]

While the visual imagery of the arch links Constantine with the great emperors of the second century, the inscription recalls Augustus the first emperor:

> The Senate and People of Rome dedicated this arch, decorated with images of his triumph, to the Emperor Caesar Flavius Constantine Greatest Augustus, pious and fortunate, because, at the prompting of the divinity, by the greatness of his mind, he, with his army, avenged the State upon the tyrant and his whole faction at the same instant with just arms.

The words are carefully chosen, for the phrase *instinctu divinitatis* ("at the prompting of the divinity") uses strictly traditional language to describe the moment of inspiration; a Christian formulation would most likely have *inspiratione divinitatis* ("with the inspiration of the divinity"). This is appropriate to the illustration, for it is indeed a female divinity—in this case, Roma—who escorts Constantine into the city and draws Maxentius to his doom.[8] This tallies with the version of the story in the panegyric of 313, but it is not the only allusion in these lines. Anyone who grew up in Rome would have regularly passed by the bronze tablets inscribed with the emperor Augustus' summary of his accomplishments, placed in front of his Mausoleum on the bank of the Tiber; the opening line of that text was "At the age of nineteen I assembled an army upon my own advice and at my own expense, through which I brought forth the state [*in libertatem vindicavi*], oppressed by the domination of a faction into freedom." The reference to the "faction of the tyrant" on the arch's inscription might reasonably remind those who read it of the connection between Constantine and Augustus who had likewise rescued Rome from the tyranny of a faction to a new age. The victory with "just arms" was thus not a victory in a civil war, but in the struggle against tyranny, which transcended other forms of conflict.[9]

By 315, Rome had taken on a new form, and one that was distinctively Constantine's. His victory needed to be seen as a victory for the god of Constantine, but not necessarily as a victory for the Christian god. This god could be perceived in very traditional forms or in untraditional ones. Past and present could coexist; for whatever his religion, Constantine was also emperor, and as emperor he ruled in the finest tradition of the past. Moreover, he was also very much a distant emperor in these years. Trier remained his base of operations—something that may have made relations with the senior Roman aristocrats somewhat easier since they retained some freedom of action while he was away. And it was important to keep them happy, for even as the arch celebrating the last war was taking shape, a new war was brewing.

In the summer of 316, Constantine began a slow progress down the valley of the Rhône, celebrating at Arles on August 7 the birth of his and Fausta's first son, whose name would also be Constantine. The emperor would then be at Verona in September and in Serdica in December, and would remain in the Balkans thereafter, with but one brief journey to Italy in 318. His primary bases of operation in those years would be at Sirmium and Serdica.

The transfer of the nucleus of government from Gaul to the Balkans was the direct result of the collapse of his relationship with Licinius. This breakdown was connected with the fecundity of Fausta, who, throughout these years, was Constantine's inseparable companion (see also figure 27.1). It also had to do with the fact that Licinius' wife Constantia became pregnant within a year of her husband's victory over Maximinus, giving birth to their first (and only) son in 315. Constantine immediately sought to exclude his nephew (called Licinius) from the succession by naming his brother-in-law Bassianus, the husband of his half-sister Anastasia, as Caesar with authority over Italy. Bassianus' appeal may have been strengthened by his powerful connections, including his own brother, at Licinius' court. Meanwhile there is some evidence to suggest tension within the ruling aristocracy in Rome, for in 315 Ceionius Rufius Volusianus ended his urban prefecture and was driven into exile by enemies within the ranks of the Senate. His fall coincided with the exile of the poet Optatianus. Both would later return in glory, which is more than could be said for Bassianus, whose influence waned as Fausta's pregnancy waxed.[10]

Bassianus became the first victim of the conflict between the two imperial colleagues when Constantine accused him of conspiracy and had him executed.[11] He then demanded that Licinius hand over Bassianus' brother as an accessory to the alleged offense. Licinius, who had been on the eastern frontier—where he had alienated the people of Antioch, a city closely associated with Maximinus, by refusing to provide them with gifts—refused and set off westward. He then ordered the statues and images of Constantine destroyed at the city of Emona, an act that constituted nothing less than a declaration of war. The fact that battle was joined on October 8, 316, at Cibalae (now Vinkovci in Croatia, near Sirmium on the western end of Licinius' domain) shows that he was heading for Constantine's territory even as Constantine was heading toward his.[12]

In the months that followed, Constantine displayed both the ability that had brought him victory over Maxentius and a new overconfidence that nearly caused his destruction. We can know little about the battle of Cibalae except that Constantine was the aggressor, as had been his wont in the Italian campaign, in a battle that raged from dawn until dusk. It appears that he was visibly in command of the right wing, which finally drove back Licinius' left wing, at which point Licinius fled and his army collapsed—or so the story goes.[13] Licinius withdrew to Thrace at the eastern end of the Balkans, allegedly breaking bridges behind him to slow Constantine's pursuit, then rallied his forces, appointing an experienced officer named Valens as his co-emperor.[14] Battle was now joined at Adrianople, the vital crossroads city that was so often the scene of deadly conflict, and here again Constantine was victorious in a hard-fought battle. The tide turned in his favor when a previously detached unit showed up behind Licinius' lines. It is a tribute to Licinius' abilities that he was able to keep his army together, then to take advantage of Constantine's natural aggression. From what we can tell, he probably anticipated that Constantine would press on after him toward the Hellespont, and in what remains one of the epic acts of deception in Roman military history, he now broke contact with his rival and instead of retreating east, he moved around to the west, placing his army across Constantine's lines of communication at Augusta Traiana, the modern Stara Zagora in Bulgaria.[15]

Although the strategic advantage now lay with Licinius, he chose to nego-tiate, which may be a sign of the fear that Constantine's unbroken string of battlefield successes instilled in him. So too may be the fact that the final terms were highly advantageous to Constantine. According to the treaty, finalized at Serdica on March 1, 317, Licinius ceded his European territories, except for Thrace, to Constantine, and agreed to execute Valens. The new Caesars con-firming the principle of biological succession were appointed: Constantine's sons Crispus and Constantine II, along with Licinius' young son, Licinius II.[16] It was thus inevitable that the descendants of Constantius would dominate the next generation.

The continuing importance of Constantius is evident in the panegyric com-posed by a Roman named Nazarius in 321. Although Nazarius ostensibly treats only the campaign of 312, his stress on Constantine's sons, now Caesars, and on the role of Constantius in sending divine aid for the invasion of Italy enhances the sense of dynastic continuity. At the same time the panegyrist seems to track more closely the tale of Constantine's relationship with Licinius than his rela-tionship with Maxentius.[17] Constantine, so Nazarius says, offered Maxentius an alliance, but Maxentius fled until it was no longer in virtue's power to remain at peace; then how could anyone have been so foolish? How could anyone have shown more restraint than Constantine in dealing with someone of so different a kind?[18] The insane tyrant of 312 has been folded into a disappointing relative who would need to be chastised.

The fact that Maxentius should be portrayed as the arch-bogeyman of recent years is all the more striking in light of the exaltation of his sister. Fausta now had coins minted with her image on them, and is styled Augusta as, most recently, had been done in the case of Galerius' wife, who was Diocletian's daughter. In 318–319 the mint at Thessalonica issued coins honoring both Fausta and Constantine's mother Helena, as "the most noble woman." In both cases, the reverses depict a laurel wreath surrounding an eight-pointed star, which has been plausibly linked with a series of consecration coins commemorating Maximian, Constantius, and Claudius II. The appearance of the two women on the coinage may thus be linked with Constantine's claims to legitimacy through both his father and the resurrected memory of his father-in-law.[19]

As the stress on dynastic stability increased, the chances for peace were slowly evaporating.

19.

GOVERNING THE EMPIRE

THE YEAR AFTER THE defeat of Maxentius, it becomes possible to observe Constantine in the business of actually governing his empire. The earliest surviving constitution in the Theodosian Code, the vital repository of imperial administrative documents that was composed a century after Constantine's death, is extracted from an edict issued on January 18, 313; the subject—the abuse of the poor by the rich—is one that would often occupy Constantine. Here he says: "Since the registrars of municipalities, acting with the connivance of the rich, transfer the burden of providing sustenance for soldiers to those who are less fortunate, we order that whosoever should prove that he was subjected to an additional burden will be subject only to his original assessment."[1] In another extract from the same edict, he is quoted as threatening to punish people who make false accusations—a statement that reiterates the earlier Galerian edict on accusations, which is attributed by the editors of the codes to Constantine, quite possibly because it was he who confirmed that it would remain in force.[2]

The fact that these are extracts from the same edict makes it quite likely that Constantine was responding to complaints he had been receiving in the wake of his march on Rome, and doing so in a way to demonstrate to his new subjects that he intended to be responsive to their concerns. Constantine believed strongly that in a properly functioning society, people should not try to escape the responsibilities that come with their status; and furthermore that they should be secure in the status to which they were born unless they had done something wrong. So it was that in 314, writing to Volusianus (the urban prefect who would be exiled at the end of this, his second term in office), he goes on at length on the subject of status declaring that if a person has been enslaved "under the tyrant" he should be set free, and anyone who tries to keep that person in bondage should be punished since "It is our pleasure that those people who knowingly lie about free persons who wrongly sustain the necessity of slavery should be subject to peril."[3] In addition, those who have incurred *infamia* (disgrace) as a result of their criminal activity should find that the "gates of dignity do not lie open to them."[4] The language is evocative of the stress on religious freedom in the edict that Licinius issued after the defeat of Maximinus. Here we see the fusion of ideology with practical action, which is something that will routinely reappear in Constantine's administrative record.[5]

Other legislation of this period casts a good deal of light on the problems besetting the new regime as seemingly—to us—abstruse issues of administration turn out to reflect much larger issues. One of these, for instance was how to integrate people who had served under Maxentius into Constantine's administration. A very revealing rescript from March advises a treasury official named Aemilius that when his rescripts contain the phrase "integral status," with reference to a house that he has given to someone, that means "as we have written before" that it should include "slaves, beasts, crops and the rights thereunto pertaining."[6] Aemilius' ignorance of what Constantine meant by a basic term suggests that it might have meant something else under Maxentius. In another case Constantine is writing about the social status of *navicularii* (ship captains); at the heart of the questions he received on this point from the official in charge of Rome's grain supply is whether one's obligations as a ship captain were more important than one's other obligations. Basically the answer is (with occasional qualifications) that the obligations of being a ship captain come first. This is hardly surprising because if the captains aren't sailing, Rome starves.

Elsewhere we find evidence of something that would be an abiding concern—the efficiency of the court system. On April 15, 314, Aelianus, the governor of Africa, received a letter from the emperor telling him that he ought not "in accordance with an earlier law" allow people to appeal a preliminary ruling, since that sort of appeal threatened to clog up the court system, but that he should allow appeals only after the whole case had been heard. If someone showed up at his court appealing such a ruling, he should fine him for making an incorrect appeal, then hear what he had to say. The earlier law to which Constantine referred was a ruling that reached Volusianus at Rome on February 25. The emperor would repeat these same instructions in a letter to

Aelianus' successor, Petronius Probianus, a man from Verona probably related to Petronius Annianus, Volusianus' consular colleague in that year (he would be prefect of the city in 329–331).[7] The fact that Aelianus, Volusianus, and Petronius, all experienced officials, should be hearing from Constantine on the same point within a couple of months of each other suggests that he was indeed introducing a new rule. On September 13, 315, he posted an edict stating, "No rescript that is contrary to the law is to have force, no matter how it may have been requested. Judges must rather follow what the public laws command."[8] The rather brusque tone suggests some frustration and the difficulty in getting people to change deeply ingrained habits

Perhaps the most revealing aspect of Constantine's work in these years comes from a series of letters dealing with the penal code. In these letters it becomes clear that Constantine took a very conservative approach to governing and that he had no problem dealing with the traditional—largely pagan—aristocracy that dominated the officeholding class. One of these men was Aco Catullinus, the staunchly pagan patriarch of a noble Italian family, whom he had appointed governor of the African province of Byzacena in what is now Libya during 313. To him Constantine explains "that when his own confession or a clear and well substantiated investigation has determined through proofs and arguments that a person is a murderer, an adulterer, an evil-doer, or poisoner, which are atrocious crimes," that person should not make endless appeals unless he can obtain support for his view from "witnesses and examination under torture," and can make a case that he has been wrongly convicted through the influence of his accuser. Concern that a person could be overwhelmed through the power of his adversary rather than the truth will recur throughout Constantine's reign as he seeks to protect his subjects from oppression at the hands of those more powerful than they.[9]

In a similar vein, in the next year, 314, he would write to Aelianus, telling him that people named in anonymous denunciations should "flourish, free from fear, with security," and be warned only that they make sure that no one should suspect them of the crimes for which they have been denounced. If a person thinks that there is a case against someone, he should prove it openly.[10] The point he was making was relevant to an inquiry that Aelianus had diligently conducted in the previous year. The case abounded in forged documents and was connected with a Christian controversy raging in his province. It also seems that he was a pagan, making it appear that Constantine's Christianity was not so all-encompassing as to eclipse his belief in public order or his willingness to entrust delicate matters in the Christian community to the judgment of a non-Christian.[11]

The efficiency of the legal system was intimately related to another great passion of Constantine's: maintaining the stability of the family unit. At about this time another experienced official, the *vicarius* Domitius Celsus, the man in overall charge of the African provinces, would hear from Constantine on a matter involving kidnapping; Constantine would tell him that those who "inflict pitiable childlessness" on parents should be sentenced to well-known punishments. Free men should be sent to the mines, from which they should never be released (conditions in the mines were notoriously brutal) while a slave or a freedman would be thrown to the beasts as soon as possible, though a freedman might be placed in a gladiatorial *ludus* [training facility] "on this condition that before he is able to do anything by which he could defend himself, he should be consumed by the sword."[12]

This message sent on August 1 reiterates that Constantine was quite willing to use the traditional penalties that had been routinely inflicted upon Christians. In February of 320 he would write to Valerius Maximus Basilius, then prefect of the city (and a member of another wealthy Italian family), about the law on treason. Charges of treason were especially unpleasant since the accused, even holding a social status that would usually render him immune from such a fate, could be questioned under torture. On this point Constantine reiterates Galerius' edict on accusations ordering that the accuser can be tortured as well. If a slave or freedman should bring a false charge (a very nasty way of getting back at a hated master) "the declaration of such outrageous audacity will be suppressed immediately at the beginning of the action, through the sentence of the judge, and the guilty party shall be crucified without a hearing."[13] It seems likely that this response, which reproduces Galerius' regulation, was produced because Maximus had asked what the law was on this point. Even if Constantine had no fondness for him, Galerius was still a legitimate emperor, and, for Constantine, that mattered more than personal likes or dislikes even if this also meant imposing a penalty—crucifixion—that made Christians especially squeamish.

In a similarly traditional vein Constantine had written, two years before, to the new *vicarius* of Africa, Locrius Verinus, a senator from Etruria who would become an important member of the governing circle when entrusted with the prefecture of the city during the critical mid-320s; Constantine would tell him that if a person was guilty of parricide—either attempted or successful— he "will be subjected neither to the sword nor the flames nor any other such penalty, but he shall be inserted in a sack, and confined within the fierce narrows he shall be mixed with the escort serpents, such as the nature of the region provides, or he shall be thrown into a nearby sea or river, so that while alive he shall begin to lose the enjoyment of the elements so that the heavens will be taken away from him while alive and the earth from him when dead."[14] This grisly penalty, known simply as "the sack," dated back to the earliest period of Roman history and was intimately related with pagan notions of the way that one dealt with extreme impurity. The one deviation from the use of traditional penalties appears in an order given to Eumelius, Verinus' predecessor as *vicarius* of Africa, telling him not to tattoo notice of conviction on the face of a man condemned to hard labor or to a ludus, "since the penalty of the conviction may equally be tattooed on his hands or on his legs so that the face, which is made in the form of celestial beauty will be minimally damaged."[15]

As a man, Constantine might be interested in new ways of defining his relationship to the divine as he needed to establish his place vis-à-vis his predecessors. The pattern that is revealed in these texts applies to both spheres. His approach to religious issues during this decade is to take certain actions that could be read as overtly favorable to Christians, while continuing policies in accord either with earlier tradition or with his own previous practice.

Most notable in this regard is the regularization of the bronze coinage between 313 and 319 in that most of the output during these years bore a portrait on one side and the image of "Invincible Sun the Companion" on the reverse (see figure 19.1).[16] This can be read as a sign that Constantine wished to advertise the continuing assistance of the god of his father, whose contribution to the victory at the Milvian Bridge was so prominently promoted in his current propaganda.[17] Otherwise it might be read, perhaps more subtly, as occluding the traditional gods of Rome from the picture.[18] The meaning may even have been in the eye of the beholder. But the one thing that "Invincible Sun the Companion" is self-evidently not is the Christian God—unless again you had heard Constantine speak of the shining God who appeared in the watchpost of heaven, were accustomed to associating solar imagery with Christ, and/or

(a)   (b)

(c)

FIGURE 19.1

(a) Constantine and the Invincible Sun on a coin minted at Trier between 313 and 315. The image of Invincible Sun (b) clearly echoes the image that began to be publicized in the reign of Aurelian seen on this coin of Aurelian (c), minted in 274. Source: Courtesy of the author.

saw significance in the fact that the day of the Sun with which each week began was celebrated by Christians as the Lord's Day. That was certainly the conclusion that an official in the Egyptian city of Oxyrhynchus would draw when he announced in 325 that court would not be in session on "The Lords Day."

The decision of the Oxyrhynchite presumably resulted from the extension of the practice recommended to Helpidius, the *vicarius* of Rome on July 3, 321, in a rescript stating that Sundays should not "be occupied with the altercations, quarrels and contentions of litigants," though people should be able to engage in legal actions that would be regarded as joyful such as the emancipation of a child from the authority of a father or the freeing of a slave. Then too he noted that while people in cities should take the day off, "rural folk should freely engage at will in agriculture since it often happens that on no other day is it more convenient to sow grain in furrows or place vines in trenches" so that the opportunity afforded by the "heavenly" gift of good weather should not be missed.[19]

In other matters, Constantine's decisions show a desire to combine innovation with tradition—tradition that seems now well embedded in his administrative repertoire. An important case in point was a law of January 1, 320, governing family relationships, which concerned marriages between women and "fiscal slaves" (probably an extension of earlier rulings that had made some unions between free women and "higher-class" slaves less impermissible than others), forfeitures, the violence of tax collectors, inheritance law, and the abolition of one of the more onerous provisions of marriage law instituted in the time of Augustus. This last imposed penalties on those who had no offspring, or those who had chosen not to remarry once an earlier marriage had ended with fewer than three children.[20] In Constantine's revision: "Those who were considered celibates according to the ancient law are freed from the imminent terrors of the laws and so shall live as if amongst those supported by the bonds of matrimony and there should be to each one equal opportunity for taking what is due," though he retains a penalty for married persons who have no children, a situation that he attributes solely to the wife. It seems that his view is then that if people do not happen to have children by the time a marriage ends, that is to be put up to their misfortune, but the normal result of a marriage should be children. If there are none, the implication here is that the woman is using contraception (which was at best rudimentary and readily conflated with an early term abortion) against her husband's wishes.[21]

Taken out of context, as it is by Eusebius, who lauds it as a sign of Constantine's devout Christianity, the ruling does indeed appear quite radical.[22] In the context of the law as a whole, while it is not impossible to attribute it to Constantine's new faith, the new ruling appears to be part of a program designed to reduce what he saw as socially disruptive litigation and abusive practices, for it is also stated that people who are having trouble paying their taxes should not fear that they will be thrown into prison or beaten with the plumbum (a dangerous leaded whip). If such a person continues to refuse to pay he should be taken into the less stringent military custody while his estates are turned over to his fellow citizens so that they pay what is owed (taxes were assessed on communities so that a person who failed to pay his fair share was imposing a burden on his fellows).[23]

As with the abolition of penalties for the celibate, Constantine evidently fears that there will be those who stretch the limits of his generosity too far. Elsewhere his laws seek to limit the circumstances under which people can challenge a will, suggesting that his primary concern was to protect property rights. Two years later the panegyrist Nazarius would suggest that because Constantine was very keen on traditional morality, laws that strengthened marriage and subdued vice, marriage legislation might have ideological as well as practical purposes. Just as Diocletian saw proper matrimonial customs as definitionally Roman in his edict on close-kin marriage, so too Nazarius suggests that legislation regarding good marriage could signal that the emperor was keen on the proper order of society, for which successful marriage and family stability were a metaphor. Constantine would much later let slip that he was aware that the actual effect of legislation on domestic matters might be no more than slight.[24]

Another area in which innovation joined with tradition was divination. In 320, Constantine wrote to Maximus (the one we've already encountered in his role as prefect of the city) stating that no one should consult a *haruspex* in private and that if anyone came forward with information about someone who had done so, he should not be treated as an informer. If people wish to consult diviners in public, they are free to do so. *Haruspex* in this sense means "private diviner," and bans on private divination or asking questions about the health of one's neighbors, damaging their property, and so forth go back to the middle of the fifth century BC. In the case that Maximus is asking him about, Constantine orders that the diviner be burned at the stake and the individual consulting him be exiled to an island, the assumption being that the latter is rich since he has a house large enough to accommodate a secret consultation.[25] The instructions to Maximus on this point reiterate and refine the terms of an edict issued the year before in which Constantine had said:

> We prohibit *haruspices* and priests and those who are accustomed to minister to such ceremony to approach a private house or, under the pretext of friendship enter the doorway of another person. The penalty is set against them if they violate the law. Those of you who want to do this for yourselves, go to the public altars and temples of your custom and celebrate the rites for we do not prohibit the practice of long custom under the open light of day.[26]

In his inquiry Maximus seems to be pointing out that some definition of the "penalty set" would be a good idea, and it's worth noting that the somewhat neutral "those who want to do this for themselves" of the edict becomes in the letter to Maximus, himself a pagan, "those wishing to serve their superstition."

In February 320, Maximus appears to have notified Constantine that the Colosseum had been struck by lightning. Given the seriousness of the matter, it is not surprising that Maximus went immediately to the official order of the *haruspices*—established long ago by the emperor Claudius I to preserve what he feared would be a dying art—to find out what this meant. Constantine replies:

> If it is established that some part of our palace or other public work is struck by lightning, retaining the custom of ancient observation, it shall be inquired of the *haruspices* what it portends, and the written opinions, having been diligently assembled, should be referred to our learning, and permission shall be given to others of making use of this practice so long as they abstain from private sacrifices, which are specifically prohibited.[27]

A particularly interesting addition to this ruling is that "others may [make use] of this practice," suggesting that while consulting the official *haruspices*—whom, unlike the praetorian guard, he did not disband after defeating Maxentius—is generally limited to matters concerning emperors, other people too may have legitimate reason to worry about natural signs and require the reassurance available via competent divination. He also allowed a priest to be created in the name of his family, a *sacredos gentis Flaviae,* to oversee the imperial cult in North Africa, allowed the construction of a temple for his family there, and, at Rome, allowed the establishment of college of priests in honor of his family.[28]

In his dealings with divination and the imperial cult, Constantine appears to be at some pains to change nothing with respect to traditional practice, at the same time advancing the status of his co-religionists. The first thing he did— and perhaps the least surprising given the linkage between status and immunity—almost immediately after the battle of the Milvian Bridge, was to grant Christian clerics immunity from civic *munera*. Constantine would emend this when it was pointed out to him that people were becoming clerics just to avoid *munera*; he would later state that such people *could not* become clerics, and that people who became clerics to avoid *munera* should be restored to their town councils. The initial gesture toward the clergy may presage a massive grant of immunity that Constantine issued for members of his staff later in the year, presumably to reward them for their service in the campaign against Maxentius.[29]

It was in 318 that Constantine came to one of his most important decisions in connection with the standing of the church, issued in what was probably an edict. It allowed litigants to transfer cases from civic courts to courts adminis-tered by a bishop.[30]

In such a case Constantine envisages a situation in which an individual decides that he wants the bishop to hear the matter—only civil cases are involved—after he has brought an action before a civil court. The situation is analogous to decisions to seek arbitration—also unavailable in criminal cases—which likewise were heard outside a regular court and in which the decision of the arbitrator was binding upon both parties. The point of arbitration proce-dures was to provide an alternative to courts that seem to have been crowded, slow, and subject to a seemingly endless cycle of appeals.

Christians had long favored episcopal arbitration within their own com-munity. In the Gospel of Matthew they were told that they should settle their disputes themselves, while in his first letter to the Corinthians, Paul tells the congregation that Christians make better judges than others. A second to third-century text, the Testament of the Twelve Apostles, laid down strict rules for the moral conduct of bishops, making it clear that they needed to be impar-tial arbiters to heal divisions within the community.[31] The main problem with Constantine's decision, from a Christian perspective, was that Christians tra-ditionally had a very different understanding of the role their bishop ought to play: ideally he was a person who aimed at restoring a damaged community, unlike the judge or arbitrator of the pagan world who was supposed to hold for one side against the other. From what he says here, one might wonder whether Constantine was aware of the difference.[32]

The power of the bishop as a civic authority is asserted within the next few years in two other rulings, both concerned with the right to conduct the cere-mony resulting in the freeing of a slave within the confines of a church. The most important of these is a ruling, reflected in a rescript of 321 to Ossius of Cordoba, one of the most important Christians in Constantine's entourage, stating that people "of religious mind" can free their slaves in "the bosom of the Church." Ordinary parishioners have to do this with the bishop present, while clerics can do this themselves "in the sight of the church and of religious people," and have their action recognized as legitimate on the day that they do so.[33]

The issue of the manumission of slaves was profoundly complex as slaves who had been freed would ordinarily become Roman citizens. In this case, bishops and priests are being given permission to create Roman citizens out of slaves on the spot, though it appears that Constantine wants to limit such grants of full citizenship under this process to occasions when there would be plenty of witnesses. Two years later he would write to a bishop named Protogenes (probably in Serdica):

> It has for a long time been permitted that masters could manumit their slaves in a Catholic church if they did so in sight of the people and in the presence of the bishops of the Christians, so that for the purpose of having a memorial of the act, as a record thereof, some sort of writing should be drawn up which they [the bishops] should sign as witnesses. Hence freedom may be given or bequeathed by you in whatever manner any of you may desire, provided that clear evidence of our wishes appears.[34]

The assertion that for a long time masters have been permitted to free their slaves in a church if they do so in sight of the bishop and the congregation is plainly not a reference to the rescript that Ossius received, but very likely to a third law (now lost) that is mentioned by the fifth-century historian Sozomon. The response to Protogenes is not unlike those to be found in other documents in which Constantine refers an official to an earlier decision or edict. His concern that there be a permanent record is in line with a concern expressed elsewhere that a person's status be incontestable, as well as with his evident distress when it was not. These rules certainly improve the position of Christians, and they don't self-evidently make things worse for non-Christians, unless Constantine was assuming that a bishop would automatically favor a Christian in a legal dispute—unprovable at this distance one way or the other; and it would certainly violate what was already an important tenet of episcopal integrity (a quality perhaps more often ideal than real, but in this case Constantine is dealing with the ideal). It is reasonable to conclude from all this that the new rules promoted the integration of the church's structures into broader civil society.

The rulings of these years reveal Constantine's desire to create a unified regime of Christians and non-Christians, of both his former supporters and those who had stood, at least for a while, with Maxentius. They reveal eclecticism in matters of religion—a willingness to assert that bishops are locally important people to be treated as having the same rights as a pagan priest or a local magistrate. Constantine is plainly willing to tweak a senior official whose religious views he doesn't share but is also willing to appoint pagan officials to investigate quarrels within the church and have them torture Christians if they feel it is necessary.

20.

MAXIMUS AND BASSUS

THE GENERAL TENOR OF Constantine's administrative acts in the decade after the battle of the Milvian Bridge reveals his attention to detail, a general desire for his empire to run properly, and even when changing things, a desire to respect precedent. The preserved record of his dealings with two officials in particular—the urban prefects Valerius Maximus Basilius (prefect from 319 to 321) and his predecessor, Septimius Bassus who had been consul in 317, and prefect from May 15 that year until September 1, 319—enables us to go further. The ample documentation of his dealings with these men, who were essentially his deputies in Rome, allows us to see how Constantine understood his role as emperor.

The framework within which Constantine's interaction with Maximus and Bassus takes place is most often provided by the Roman legal system, especially that of civil procedure. The system of civil procedure comprised essentially four kinds of action: a "personal action" brought by someone claiming that a service had not been performed; a "real action" brought by someone laying claim to some object; an "action for restitution" in which a claim could be made both for the recovery of an object and the infliction of a penalty upon the person who had withheld it or inflicted damage; and an "action in law," claiming that an individual had violated a ruling set out in a statute.[1] Once an action was brought before a magistrate, he would set a time limit within which the two sides would produce the witnesses and documents they needed to prove their cases—this could include a rush by both parties to acquire private rescripts from the emperor. One or the other litigant might have to produce a bond to ensure that he would show up for the hearing or to be confiscated as a penalty for bringing a bogus action. The hearing would take place before a single judge, who, after consulting with his advisers, would render a written decision. The loser could then appeal the decision.

In cases of inheritance, the law was based on the concept of universal succession whereby an heir would take on the risks and duties of the deceased as a whole. Liability for inheritance was determined through relationship to a *paterfamilias*, the head of the family group or *familia*. The *paterfamilias* could leave property to whomever he wished, but if he died without making a will, the property would be allotted according to strict principles of biological relationship, and if he did make a will, it was generally assumed that he would leave the bulk of his property to immediate relatives. When it came to determining who had the best claim, those in the first class, the "privileged heirs" or *sui heredes*, were those who had been subject to the power, *potestas*, of the *paterfamilias* at the time of his death, and who thereby became independent (*sui iuris* or "of their legal power"). Unless, according to an extremely archaic formula, the wife of the *paterfamilias* had married in such a way that she passed under his *potestas*, she was not seen as part of the *familia*. She had remained under the authority of her own *paterfamilias*, even when married, and would inherit "in her own legal right" from her father, at which point she would have the right to dispose of her property as she saw fit (most often to her children, even children by a failed marriage).

If there were no "privileged heirs," the dead person's estate would pass to his kin, or "agnates," those most closely related through the male line.[2] A woman, for instance, who died without making a will would have her estate taken up by her brothers or other male relatives, even if she had children, for the simple reason that those children were not deemed to be part of her *familia*.

Children were always regarded as belonging to the *familia* of their father, and if they were underage when their father died they would be placed under the care of a tutor responsible for managing their property until they came of age (twelve for girls, fourteen for boys). In ideal circumstances, a dying father would nominate tutors for his children; if he died intestate, it would be up to the local authorities to do this. And given that being an honest tutor was a potentially time- and therefore resource-consumptive activity, service as a tutor was classified as a personal *munus*. Once a child came of age and until the age of eighteen for a girl or twenty for a boy, he or she would usually be assigned a *curator* or adviser to prevent irresponsible behavior vis-à-vis the estate (a *curator* was also appointed for someone thought to be insane or a spendthrift).[3]

The first surviving relevant communication with Bassus is Constantine's statement that if a litigant showed up with a rescript that was valid on the point of law that it addressed when it was issued, it would still have force even if the law had been changed by a subsequent edict; whereas if a rescript was issued after the edict and asserted a point of earlier law, it would *not* be valid, since rescripts should accord with the public law and "it is fitting and right that only We [the emperor always uses the plural when speaking in his own voice] shall investigate an interpretation that has been interposed between equity and statute." The point is an important one because it asserts that the emperor alone is the source of law.[4] Although Constantine's response to Bassus might seem logical, a ruling like that could cause problems in a world where people were intent on obtaining private rescripts to support their positions, and where those rescripts were not always consistent.

Much that appears in this correspondence gets down to fine issues of procedure, suggesting that Constantine was taking a very personal interest in the way the legal system ran, and that even very senior officials felt that they needed to clear such issues at court. So it was that on March 18, 318, Constantine ordered that judges provide sufficient explanations when issuing decisions in important cases. Evidently there were judges who, either uncertain of their opinions or all too certain of their wisdom, might choose to occlude their reasoning through extreme brevity or feel that they were above the need for explanation. On May 19, he stated that a new time limit must be set in cases where one litigant has died so that his heirs can understand the issue, or in the case of an intestate estate, an agnate could decide whether it is worth accepting an inheritance burdened with litigation.[5] On October 7, Constantine states that in accord with a ruling of "the divine Antoninus" (Antoninus Pius, reigned 138–161), "an emperor most learned in the law," gifts between parents and children would remain valid even if the child had not been emancipated (and was thus still in his father's *potestas* and not able to own property) and even if the gift has not been delivered. A third-century BC law, the Cincian Law, which allowed certain kinds of gifts only if elaborate formulae were correctly recited, was changed so that gifts would be valid even if the formulae were incorrectly recited. The final surviving provision—that this ruling will be valid for all pending litigation—may well have been necessary either because Bassus had pointed out that people had received rescripts stating the opposite, or because, in Constantine's view, Pius' law made any subsequent ruling invalid.[6] A few days later Constantine wrote to Bassus telling him that no young person should appear in court unless he had a curator, which is essentially a statement of the point for having one in the first place.[7] The last thing we know that Bassus received from Constantine was a lengthy set of instructions about the time limits for children who had inherited as minors to bring a suit for the restitution of property that they felt had been taken from them in their younger years.[8]

Constantine's correspondence with Maximus on civil and procedural matters is very similar to that with Bassus. In one typical case he issued an immensely long ruling on the subject of gifts between spouses and relatives, expanding on the ruling on gifts under the *lex Cincia* that Bassus had received. The aim here is to restrict suits that seek to damage the outcomes of affectionate relationships and generally to restrict causes of litigation by setting out cleanly what would count as a legal gift and what would not.[9]

In 319, four years before his ruling on spousal gifts, Constantine issued one on betrothal gifts, expressing his displeasure with "the practice of the ancients" according to which people did not have to return betrothal gifts when a couple broke up. The ruling effectively puts the burden of proof that gifts should be returned on the party breaking off the engagement. Unless one of the betrothed had died, in which case gifts should be returned to the heirs or, in the event of the recipient's death, to the giver, what counted was that the person who had broken off the engagement should make restitution. This was important because it meant that claims about the personal conduct of one or the other party as the cause of the breakup would not be allowed. As young girls were more likely to be the victims of a broken engagement, the measure reveals a marked desire to assist the weaker party.[10] In 316 Constantine had written to Octavianus, the commander of the troops in the Spanish provinces, telling him that if a man of high rank raped a young girl, invaded the property of another, or was caught committing any other crime he should be tried where he was accused and that "accusation excludes all privilege of rank when a criminal case rather than a civil or monetary matter is brought."[11]

Although Constantine might have an interest in protecting the weaker party against persecution by the more powerful, his attitude toward slavery was deeply ambivalent. There was, it seems, in his view, no worse state. He abhorred the possibility that a person could be unfairly condemned to that status, a sentence that he saw as the emblematic act of a tyrant. In seeking to prevent people from being unfairly enslaved, he asserted the importance of a person's birth status in determining his status as an adult. On the other hand, he did little to alleviate the condition of those who were already slaves, and deplored the notion that a free person could associate with a slave on an equal basis. In all of this, Constantine's attitudes are harsher than those of earlier generations and probably reflect changes in the course of the third century. For earlier periods, the issue of slave status was complicated because a very great many slaves were freed by their masters, usually in their twenties or thirties (or so it seems; the statistical basis for this assertion is less than ideal). As a temporary status, slavery, while "staining" the character of those subjected to it, was a status out of which a person could mature into full personhood. It was thus even possible for slaves to have relationships with free people without necessarily reducing their partner to their own status. For Constantine, the dividing line was sharper and the "stain" of slavery deeper.[12]

Constantine's attitude, however, does not mean that he wished to make things worse. One of the actions that his government took on behalf of slaves whose status was not questionable was to prevent their families from being broken up when imperial estates were rented out. That this move is contained in a missive to a mid-level manager and might not have been thought important enough for Constantine's attention reflects a general apprehension that slaves who were treated abominably might revolt.[13]

Constantine's concerns about birth status also figure in documents sent to other officials; among them is a powerful missive to Menander, then most likely the *vicarius* of Africa, in which he registers his horror that starving parents are selling their children into slavery. He orders Menander to tell the provincial officials that they "should grant necessary sustenance to all whom they find to be in a wretched poverty, and from the storehouse they should immediately give adequate food. It is abhorrent to our ways that we should allow anyone to be overcome by hunger or to commit an evil deed."[14]

"Freedom was of such great importance to our ancestors that it was not possible to take it away from fathers to whom the power of life and death over sons had been given"—thus wrote Constantine in 324 to Maximus even though it is clear from the context that he deplored the use of that freedom to sell one's children into slavery. The upshot was to make it easier for free people who had been sold to reclaim their freedom, in particular alleviating the situation of those who, raised in the house of another as if they were slaves, had agreed to be sold, while minors, because they were unaware of their true status. The other crucial factor here is that birth status should remain inviolate: if a person was of free birth, that birthright could not be taken away, even by a parent. And once legally freed—even if the individual didn't know it—he would always be free.[15]

In dealing with issues of status, intent and knowledge on the part of the litigant were particularly important to Constantine. Similarly, in his ruling on marriages involving freeborn women who married fiscal slaves without knowing their status, they would not have to give up their freedom, but their children could not be full citizens. He notes: "If an unforeseen error or simple ignorance or lapse due to infirm age drove [them] into these nets of cohabitation, these shall be exempted from our sanctions." By implication, if people could be expected to know what they were about, they would have a harder time regaining free status, an issue that may be related to Constantine's view that citizens should be respectable people.[16]

The question of intent is also operative in a couple of other rulings on the topic of unions between slaves (other than fiscal) and free persons. If people were aware of what they were doing, they were going to be in trouble. So it was that in 317 Constantine had stated that any woman who married a slave, if she had been warned in advance that she was doing so, would be enslaved herself, while in 318 he took on the issue of people who had the status of town councillors (decurions) who resided with slave women who did not belong to them as if they were legally married. In a case like this, the woman would be sent to the mines and the man would be exiled to an island, losing all his property, which, if he had no heirs, would be handed over to the city in which he was a decurion. The point here was to prevent people from entering into unions with slaves just so they would no longer have to undertake *munera*—since the outcome of such a liaison would be that they would be turfed out of their town council in disgrace. The way Constantine saw it, the offender went but the property remained to support civic activities. If the slave's owner's agents realized what was going on and turned a blind eye, they too would be heading for exile, and if the owner himself wittingly allowed it to happen, he would lose his property.[17]

Constantine's understanding of propriety governs other decisions with respect to status during these years. In another letter to Maximus he states that if a slave who has been freed insults his patron or commits a crime, he (the text assumes a male slave) can be reenslaved. Roman citizenship can only be restored to him if he proves himself worthy after punishment and if his masters petition the emperor. The measure restated a point of law that had been established for more than a century, though probably somewhat more harshly than under Diocletian.[18]

In another case, however, he extends the rights of people (assuming they are of good character) whom others are trying to enslave. In such a case the accused was supposed to appeal to a patron who would prove his claim to freedom, but if no such patron could be found he might look for a sponsor by posting a written notice "so that a person's claim will not be ignored through silence or proclaimed in an absurd manner so that those persons who learn of it may be willing to undertake to defend his free status." If no sponsor materialized, the individual would be handed over to the claimant as a slave. But if a sponsor could be found later (even years later), the "claim of freedom was not destroyed" and the slave could go to court with the newly found sponsor and have his freedom restored. If someone died in slavery and his or her heirs were then able to prove wrongful enslavement, the family responsible for it would pay a fine; furthermore those who defended claims to freedom would be exempt from fines. In the end, his concern is once again that those too weak to defend themselves will be victims of a pitiless system wherein "the domination of victory takes freedom away from defeated enemies" and that the laws should only inflict penalties on those who hurt others.[19]

Behind these lines lies the cruel procedure for reclaiming a fugitive slave—or as the case might be, the procedure that could allow a person to claim as a slave a person who was free. The full horror and humiliation of the practice strikes us most clearly not from the pages of any legal text, but rather from the pages of Apuleius' *Golden Ass*, in a sequence where the Goddess Venus is seeking Psyche, her son Cupid's girlfriend. Venus is appalled that Cupid has been seeing Psyche, of whom she disapproved, and, when she cannot find the girl—who she claims is her servant simply on the grounds that she is human—she summons the god Mercury to find her. She tells him that he must "as a herald make a public proclamation of a reward for tracking her down ... clearly indicate the marks by which she can be recognized, so that if anyone is charged with unlawfully concealing her, he cannot defend himself on the plea of ignorance." Mercury sped around the world appearing before gatherings of every community and as instructed performed the duty of making proclamation: If anyone can retrieve from her flight the runaway daughter of the king, the maidservant of Venus called Psyche, or indicate her hidden whereabouts, he should meet with the herald Mercury ... whoever does this will obtain as a reward from Venus herself seven sweet kisses, and a particularly honeyed one imparted with the thrust of her caressing tongue. In this case Psyche turns herself in, but the proclamation of Mercury illustrates, as Apuleius intended it, the horrific injustice of such cases where the power imbalances between the two sides were so great, and it is just that sort of injustice with which Constantine is here concerned.[20]

Concerned as he no doubt was about preventing people from becoming slaves who ought not to be, and about freeing the unjustly enslaved, Constantine was much less solicitous of those who actually were slaves, as we have seen. In 319 he wrote to Bassus:

> If a master should beat a slave with rods or lashes or throw him into chains for the sake of restraint, putting aside all consideration of days or legal interpretation, he will sustain no fear of a criminal charge if the slave should die. But he should not use his right immoderately, for then he will be accused of homicide, or if he voluntarily kills him either with the blow of a club or of a stone or inflicts a lethal wound using an actual weapon, or orders that the slave be suspended by a noose, or commands by a vile order that he should be cast down or that the virus of a poison be poured into him or lacerates his body with public punishments, tearing his sides with the claws of wild beasts or burning his limbs by moving fire close or, with the savagery of inhuman barbarians he should force bodies weakening and flowing with dark blood mixed with gore to surrender life in the midst of tortures.

The issue of brutality to slaves had a very long history in the Roman world. The general feeling was that good men did not torture slaves or punish them without reason; but a master could still be brutal and might not care if people found his behavior despicable. In the second century, Antoninus Pius had taken a stronger line against master-slave violence than Constantine did in this case. The second century is also the time when *The Life of Aesop* assumed the form in which it has come down to us. *The Life* is a wonderful work of fiction containing the collective wisdom of slaves (albeit only male ones); it makes clear that slaves routinely feared beatings and suspected their masters of plotting to justify flogging them, while the wealthy tended to fear their slaves as well as their own tempers. In taking a less compassionate line than Pius, Constantine acknowledges that people will beat their slaves and that there is nothing that he can (or would wish) to do to stop it; but he is nonetheless inclined to limit the brutality of masters by preventing them from employing the dreadful tortures available to agents of the imperial government or that their own creative imaginations prompt them to use.[21]

Whatever the subject, one thing that is crystal clear in the administrative acts of these years, as it will be in later years, is that Constantine expected his officials to do their jobs properly, and it seems that he had no qualms about calling them out if he felt they were underperforming. In 319 he wrote Bassus pointing out that officials would be fined if they were slow in preparing the documentation necessary to judge an appeal, or if they were not ensuring that judges were following the law as the emperor decreed it.[22] It cannot have been the unguided hand of an imperial secretary who wrote as follows to Maximus in 321:

> All judges, and especially your sublimity, who represent us in trials, must do this [follow the law as decreed]. 1. Complaint also arises from litigants, because you, who have received the right to act in place of the emperor, deny their appeals. It is necessary to prevent such a practice. For what is harsher and more unworthy than that a person endowed with power should grow so insolent through its exercise that he should despise the right of appeal, that he should refuse to issue a report and deny the possibility of rebuttal as if appeals were devised for the purpose of slandering judges, and not as a privilege of a litigant, or as if in this matter the equity of the judge should be considered, but rather the need of the litigant.[23]

The message was taken, and Maximus continued for several more years in high office. It is through his correspondence with Maximus that the personality of

Constantine the administrator emerges most clearly. He is willing to rebuke, and to forgive; to chide Maximus for his religious beliefs while appreciating his value as someone to whom he can safely delegate responsibility. It is not always a smooth relationship, but it seems to have been one that worked. Also these documents show something of Constantine's view of his role as emperor. From the often long (and almost invariably turgid) screeds that emerge from his chancery, we get the impression that for him the imperial palace is the font of all wisdom. It is his job as emperor to instruct his subjects in the law and to make sure that they follow it. He is no radical reformer, but neither is he wedded to the past. He sees himself as an enlightened ruler working within a tradition to make his empire a better place.

21.

THE DONATIST CONTROVERSY

A S PEEVED AS CONSTANTINE might have been from time to time with
Maximus, there was no aspect of governing during these years that tried
his patience so unremittingly as did the controversy that was tearing the church
in Africa apart even as he was taking power in Britain.[1]

Carthage, which was the focal point of the dispute, had produced a number
of notable Christian writers in the previous century—and for many of them the
issue of the way a Christian should behave in time of persecution was of crucial
importance. One of the most eloquent of these authors was a young woman
named Vibia Perpetua, whose diaries, written in Greek in the days leading up to
her execution on March 3, 207 AD, were joined with two other accounts of the
day and rapidly translated into Latin, becoming a model for later African persecution narrative. Perpetua was crystal clear on the point that in dying she was
following the path set out for her by God, a view confirmed by a series of visions
she experienced while in prison. These caused her to abandon her newborn
child and to reject the desperate pleas of her mother and father that she relent
from her path. For Perpetua, martyrdom, death giving witness to her faith, was
central to her sense of what it was to be a Christian. It is quite likely that she knew
her immensely eloquent contemporary, Tertullian, who memorably asserted that
the blood of martyrs was seed for the church and that persecution, coming as it
did from God, could not be escaped (oddly he never experienced martyrdom
himself). Very different was the view of Cyprian, bishop of Carthage at the time
of Decius' edict on sacrifices (250) and during the persecution of Valerian (257–
60), to which he fell victim. Cyprian, while condemning those who collaborated
with the persecuting authorities either by sacrificing as the edict demanded, or
by purchasing a fake certificate of sacrifice, saw no reason to put himself in the

way of the persecuting authorities. He went into hiding and would later claim that the fact that a crowd in the amphitheater called for his execution was a sort of virtual martyrdom that was more than good enough. What he found deeply troubling was the group of "confessors," people who publicly refused to sacrifice as the edict required but were not punished (though they may have been threatened), who allied with actual martyrs, a category which now included people who had been tortured but survived as well as those who had died to undermine his authority as bishop. Cyprian's response was to redefine the position of martyrs, who in the past had been thought to have special power to intercede with God independently of the Church so that they could only exercise this power with the approval of the bishop. The obvious evidence of suffering at the hands of the authorities, such as scars, were no longer a sufficient condition to claim the authority of a martyr. One had to have the significance of one's experience confirmed by the bishop![2]

When Valerian's edict was promulgated, Cyprian could no longer hide. He was arrested and held on a private estate until the order came for his execution. As a man of high status he was spared the gross indignity of death in the amphitheater and simply beheaded in a garden. It is perhaps ironic that his own death at the hands of the persecuting authority gave his views the authority of a martyr, and possibly significance in later generations that they might not otherwise have had. One of those views—one very different from that of a Tertullian or Perpetua—was that persecution was God's punishment for the sins of his community and that one should learn from the experience and become a better person. This would remain one view among many. Lactantius, for instance, took a somewhat different tack as he saw persecution as stemming from the action of the Devil through evil men and believed that it was wrong to provoke the imperial authorities.

If Lactantius had been living in North Africa in 313 he would probably have found himself aligned with a man named Caecilian, who claimed the position of bishop of Carthage, and could assert that his position on persecution and martyrdom aligned with that of Cyprian. He would have been opposed to a man named Donatus, who would soon be claiming the position of bishop of Carthage in succession to a man named Majorian. Both Donatus and Majorian asserted that Caecilian was a traitor to their faith who had performed abominable deeds during 303 when Diocletian's persecution edict was promulgated in

North Africa. Although the story of the quarrel involved many subsidiary factors, the roots of their dispute lay in the very different understandings of persecution represented in the works of Cyprian and Tertullian or Perpetua. The great church that Caecilian occupied as bishop contained the relics of Perpetua and her companions, a powerful statement of the centrality of martyrdom to Christian self-definition in the North African Church.

In looking at the dispute from Caecilian's perspective, we have the benefit of a book by Optatus of Milevis, a later fourth-century Christian. According to Optatus, Caecilian's supporters attributed the outbreak of the quarrel not to the persecution edict but rather to a dispute of a somewhat earlier date between the then archdeacon Caecilian and a woman named Lucilla, whom Caecilian had reprimanded for kissing a relic before taking communion.[3] As this version of the story has it, Lucilla would become the leader of a faction that would try to prevent Caecilian from becoming bishop of Carthage after the death of his patron, the bishop Mensurius of Carthage, who had died in the course of a principled stand against imperial authority. According to this story, a man named Felix who had written a slanderous letter about "the tyrant emperor" is said to have taken refuge with Mensurius, and when Mensurius refused to turn him over, an imperial order arrived stating that if he did not surrender Felix, he would be arrested. Mensurius realized that he would have to go, but he worried a great deal about what would happen in his absence to the mass of gold and silver that was in his church. So before departing, he handed the treasure over to the elders of the community and left an inventory with an old woman who was instructed, in the event that he did not return, to hand it over to the next bishop.[4] The identity of the emperor to whom Mensurius was ordered to plead his case is unknown, but since the original offense concerned Maximian—who is described as a "tyrant emperor," and Maxentius is later mentioned by name, it is likely that the unnamed emperor in this passage is a third figure. That would most likely be Severus.

Mensurius died before he could return home, and the nearby bishops of Numidia, acting in concert with their senior bishop, Secundus, overturned the election of a man called Donatus (not to be confused with the Donatist's later champion) in favor of another cleric, Silvanus, in return for a large bribe. As his rivals alleged in later years, Silvanus was an avowed *traditor*—guilty of having handed over Scripture in the persecution and thus of collaboration with the persecuting authorities—so his election undermined any moral force that

Secundus possessed because of his strong stand against Diocletian's persecution edict of 303 and his assertion that there was something morally wrong with Mensurius' less extreme position.[5]

When news came of the accession of the emperor Maxentius in 306, two senior members of the Carthaginian Church, Botrus and Celestius, who were allegedly withholding the church plate that Mensurius had placed in their care, summoned a synod of the neighboring bishops in the hope that they might secure the election of one of themselves. But the will of the people thwarted their dastardly plot, proclaiming Caecilian as their bishop.

Bishop Felix of Abthungi then consecrated Caecilian. Summoned to produce an account of the treasures that had been left with them, Botrus and Celestius broke communion with the church, allied themselves with Lucilla, and summoned Secundus with his gang of corrupt Numidian bishops to their aid. The Numidians tried to invalidate the election of Caecilian, and, failing that, elected one Majorian as bishop, "and that was the cause of the schism."[6] To further damage Caecilian's claim to the episcopal seat, they accused Felix of Abthungi of having been a *traditor*. And so the situation remained until, after his defeat of Maxentius, Constantine ordered the return of church property. The result of the order to restore property was that both Majorian and Caecilian showed up before the governor, claiming everything for themselves and asserting that their rivals had no standing.

The position of Caecilian's party appears unassailable in the narrative of Optatus of Milevis. Sadly, Optatus' selective collection of documents completely ignores the position of their rivals. Instead of trying to refute the powerful charges against them, the supporters of the Caecilianist position simply tried to quietly bury those charges.

The Donatist position had virtually nothing to do with the issues adduced by Caecilian's party and reveals a very much more sinister pattern of behavior. The thrust of the case against Caecilian was not simply that he associated with a *traditor* named Felix but that he had collaborated with the persecuting authorities and was a murderer. The real story, from their point of view, involved a level of brutality on Caecilian's part that may explain the dogged determination of the Donatists to have nothing to do with him.

The essence of the Donatist position emerges from an exchange of letters that they produced at a council held at Carthage in 411, along with a text known as the *Acts of the Abitinian Martyrs*. According to the Donatists, Mensurius had written to Secundus telling him that he had refused to hand scriptures over to the persecuting authorities; instead, he had hidden them in his house, leaving some heretical works (why he kept such things lying around is a mystery) in his church to be discovered by the people sent to find the sacred books. The authorities at Carthage had actually complained that bishop Mensurius had not turned over the relevant works, but the governor, who had his own reasons for not believing that Mensurius was a problem, declined to investigate. Mensurius went on to point out in his letter that some disreputable "debtors" had gotten themselves thrown into prison, so that as martyrs they could wash away their sins and receive the continuing support of the Christian community. His view on this matter seems to follow Cyprian's that people could only be regarded as martyrs if the bishop approved their status, and in this case Mensurius was crystal clear that these people should not gain that status.

Secundus responded, in what was described as a collegial tone, by describing the behavior of the persecutors in his own province, giving a list of people who had been killed or tortured and recommending that these people be honored as martyrs. When the local *curator* (mayor) and town council had sent a centurion along with a *beneficiarius* (police officer) to see him, he went on, he had told them he was a Christian bishop, not a *traditor*, and that when they had asked him for something to take away he had declined to give them anything for he would neither lie nor provide an example of lying to others.[7] The thrust of this exchange, which both sides later admitted was not overtly hostile, was that Mensurius was unsympathetic to martyrs. It might also be read as a confession to the acts with which he would be charged in the *Acts of the Abitinian Martyrs*.

The Abitinian martyrs—very likely the people about whom Mensurius had written so disparaginingly to Secundus—were a group of Christians who had been arrested for openly defying Diocletian's edict by celebrating the Eucharist.[8] They were brought before Anullinus, who subjected them to severe torture to make them recant. When they refused, he ordered them to be imprisoned under harsh conditions. According a passage, retained in only one of the six manuscripts preserving a copy of the text, the origins of the schism are to be found in their incarceration. In this version, Mensurius, "polluted by his recent handing over of the Scriptures," ordered Caecilian to stand guard with a collection of thugs before the prison to beat anyone trying to bring food to the martyrs within. The account ends with the words "for this reason the holy Church follows the martyrs and detests the treason of Mensurius."[9]

The fact that Caecilian's faction avoided the issue of Mensurius' conduct lends credence to the tale told by his adversaries, and later generations of anti-Donatists would attempt to dissociate their cause from that of Mensurius.[10] Unfortunately for the Donatists, Mensurius' behavior as they described it also made it very difficult to assail him before a Roman magistrate: few, if any, imperial officials would agree that a man who had supported the action of one of their own had acted incorrectly. The Donatist case against Caecilian stems from his having been elected illegally according to the laws of the church rather than for assisting the persecuting authorities, a situation that can be attributed to the imperial government's willingness to allow the church to establish its own rules for episcopal succession. If it could be shown that Caecilian had not been elected according to the rules of the church, that would cause his removal, while a claim, years after the fact, that he had attacked some of his fellow Christians who were thought by the imperial government to be criminals and on the orders of his bishop, was unlikely to gain any traction.[11]

Constantine's preference for Caecilian's cause can first be traced in a letter he sent to Anullinus—possibly the son of the Anullinus just mentioned, persecutor of the Abitinian martyrs and now urban prefect at Rome—at the end of 312 or early in 313 stating that properties that had once belonged to "the Universal [Catholic] Church of the Christians" should be restored to them. Caecilian asserted that he was the representative of the "Universal Church," and he had stolen a march on his adversaries by contacting Ossius the bishop of Cordoba who had been with Constantine during the campaign against Maxentius. Ossius plainly helped him, for in a separate letter to Caecilian, dispatched at about the same time as the letter to Anullinus, Constantine ordered the *rationalis* (chief financial official) of Africa to give money to priests loyal to Caecilian.[12]

The letter to Caecilian was followed shortly afterward by another to Anullinus in which Constantine ordered that all priests loyal to Caecilian should receive immunity from civic liturgies, which simply seems to be a restatement of his decision earlier in the year (and perhaps occasioned by a query from Anullinus as to whether all clerics should have immunity or merely some).[13] At this point he may not have grasped how serious the situation was. He would soon find out

as Majorian, the bishop of the anti-Caecilianist faction came forward, presenting a powerful refutation of his rival's position in April 313.

Majorian's case was based on two documents, one being a sealed denunciation of Caecilian as a person, the other an open statement that he was not the
legal bishop in terms of church custom. Majorian petitioned Constantine to
appoint a church council in Gaul to decide the case, naming the bishops he
would like to hear it. Constantine granted his appeal, writing to Miltiades, the
bishop of Rome, asking him to sit with the three bishops from Gaul. Miltiades
was a holdover from the time of Maxentius, creating a difficult political situation; compounding the difficulty was Miltiades' interest in not having the Italian
hierarchy coopted by Gallic bishops. Constantine seems to have recognized the
delicacy of the situation and felt it politically important to let Miltiades have
his way, allowing him to pack the council with an additional fifteen bishops of
his own choosing. Constantine was adhering to imperial precedent in that his
choice of bishops recalled Aurelian's, when, in a comparable circumstance he
called for a council of Italian bishops; Miltiades' role was that of a *iudex vice
Caesaris* (judge in the place of Caesar), and the issue was to be dealt with as one
of civil law. But at some point in the months leading up to the council, Majorian
died. So it was that on September 30, 313, the Donatus who would give his name
to the anti-Caecilianist movement presented the case.[14]

The council of Rome was a diplomatic disaster, in large part because
Miltiades took the council as an opportunity to gain control of the African
church by making it clear that Caecilian owed his survival to Miltiades' own
patronage. In order to do this, the bishops sidestepped the main issues and simply condemned Caecilian's opponents for insisting on the rebaptism of people
who had been communicants of Caecilian—a completely unrelated issue that
recalled the conduct of African schismatics condemned in the wake of Decius'
edict on sacrifices in the mid-third century. In failing to address the main issues
and or recognize that Donatus needed to be able to take away something that
would please his supporters if there were to be any chance of settlement, the
council guaranteed that the trouble would continue. Indeed, the first thing that
Donatus did was to accuse Miltiades himself of having been a *traditor*; and he
urged members of his party to resist Miltiades' attempt to unify the church by
suggesting that Caecilian recognize all the bishops who had been appointed by
Majorian. Constantine accepted the council's advice to forbid Donatus' return

to Carthage. It may not have helped Donatus' position that three Gallic bishops who had accompanied Constantine on the campaign of 312 were at the council, and that the Donatists had earlier cast aspersions on the integrity of Ossius, who had also been on that expedition.[15]

From Constantine's actions after the council of Rome we can deduce that he realized things had not gone well and that he wished to be seen favoring compromise and consensus rather than having to resort to the use of force. In 314 he allowed a second council to be convened to hear further charges against the Caecilianist faction.[16]

That council convened at Arles on August 1, with Constantine sitting as a layman in the audience. Among the rules that it issued were three directly concerning the controversy in Africa. One was the statement that clerics who can be proven on the basis of public documents to have turned over scripture, communion vessels, or the names of fellow Christians to the authorities would be removed from their positions, but that any ordinations they had performed would not be invalid. They recognized the situation had become so poisonous that "there are many who seem to oppose the church, and through bribed witnesses think that they should be allowed to bring accusations." The bishops reiterated their view that such charges should not be allowed unless there is documentary support.[17] Implicit here is a fundamental distrust of the Donatist way of doing business, and the ruling that ordinations could not be invalidated even if performed by proven traditores looks like a plea to both sides to allow bygones to be bygones; and it paralleled their decision regarding rebaptism (the second of the three relevant rulings), asserting, as they did, that it didn't matter who had baptized an individual so long as that person proved that he or she was an orthodox believer.[18] In the third, the bishops at the council held that "those who falsely accuse their brethren...are not to communicate [take holy communion] until the day of their death." This reiterated the view taken by the bishops who had convened at Elvira (in present day Spain) in or around 305.[19] The council did not so much defend Caecilian as it demanded that people act respectably.

So the verdict of the council of Arles was that whatever merit there might have been to the Donatist case had been invalidated by their representatives' rebarbative conduct and evidence for violation, on Donatist's part, of standing church practice.[20] Most important, it established that the matter remained entirely within the church. Constantine was present, but he affected nothing. The independence of the church from imperial control was formally maintained. This was underscored by the formal letter from the council to the emperor informing him of its decision, to which Constantine responded at length, equally formally and supporting the bishops against the appeal that the Donatists lodged with him immediately afterward.[21] The language with which he describes the Donatists is notable for its ferocity of expression, and equally notable is the openness with which the emperor asserts his own faith—this is the same letter in which Constantine revealed his encounter with the God who sits at the watchpost of heaven and identified that God as the Christian God:

> In very truth it was not without good cause that the mercy of Christ withdrew from these, in whom it is clear as day that their madness is of such a kind that we find them abhorrent even to the heavenly dispensation; so great a madness persists in them when, with incredible arrogance, they persuade themselves of things that it is not right either to say or hear, repudiating the equitable judgment that had been given by the will of heaven.... They demand my judgment, when I myself await the judgment of heaven.[22]

Does the emperor's vehemence of expression in this letter hint at the possibility that one of the weaknesses he admits to recognizing in himself was a ferociously bad temper? Perhaps he was impatient with those who didn't see the world his way—a trait that certainly appears in his correspondence with Maximus, despite his obvious respect for the man. Marcus Aurelius once had written to himself that it was crucially important for an emperor to control his emotions. Constantine seems to have striven toward the same goal, and his dealings with Donatus would prove a mighty test.[23]

Constantine had a good deal to say on his own account about the outcome of the council, writing letters (of which two have been preserved) condemning the Donatists.[24] And there the matter would have remained if the Donatists had not returned with fresh complaints at the beginning of 315, producing documents, as the bishops assembled at Arles said they must, to prove that Felix of Abthungi, the man who had ordained Caecilian, was a *traditor*. When the governor of Africa heard the case, he found that the evidence against Felix was forged.[25] This did not stop the Donatists. They lodged yet another complaint with Constantine, who equivocated, first allowing the Donatist bishops who had been held in Gaul to return to Africa, then changing his mind and summoning them to a fresh hearing at which Caecilian would be present.

The business dragged on into the fall of 315, when Constantine, now at Milan, and with much else to concern him (not least, the birth of a son to his brother-in-law Licinius), again pronounced in favor of Caecilian. The Donatists accepted his decision with the same grace that they had shown in response to all previous decisions, continuing to spark riots at Carthage as they had throughout the year. Constantine finally lost patience. On November 10, 316, having left Cibalae in Croatia at that point in pursuit of Licinius' army, he wrote to the *vicarius* of Africa outlining the history of the dispute and, possibly, ordering Donatist churches to be confiscated.[26] In 319, he would write to the Etruscan senator Verinus, telling him that when slanderous pamphlets turn up, the person slandered should suffer no harm, but, rather, the slanderer should be apprehended and made to prove his case in court. The ruling would have applied to the Donatists, for Constantine now banished the controversy from the realm of religion and placed it in the remit of civil and criminal law.[27] This could explain how it came about that on March 12, 317, imperial troops burst into a Donatist church at Carthage and slaughtered the congregation.[28] For the Donatists, they would be martyrs. For Constantine, they were people engaging in an illegal assembly.

The direct assault on the Donatists lasted until 321, when Constantine suddenly relented, ordering the *vicarius* of Africa to restore Donatist exiles and writing to the bishops of Africa: "When vengeance is left to God, a harsher penalty is exacted from one's enemies."[29] Both he and the Donatists appear to have learned from the experience. Donatus had learned that direct provocation of the imperial government didn't work; and after the return of the exiled bishops, which signaled that Constantine might be content to live and let live, he flourished. By 337, Caecilian appears to have dwindled into insignificance, while Donatus was able to assemble a council at Carthage that included no fewer than 270 bishops.[30] Constantine had shown that although he could defeat any opponent on the battlefield, he now understood that attempting to defeat an opponent whose cause was conscience-driven was an altogether different undertaking.

The foundational tale of the Donatist movement, one of courage in the face of oppression, murder, and persecution, was a far more compelling tale than the Caecilianist story of theft and corruption. The Donatist narrative appealed to a basic sense of justice in ways that the opposition's, which asserted the worst about human nature, did not. Perhaps, in the end, Constantine too had come to believe this. Perhaps he also reflected on the lessons of his youth, not least that sweeping efforts to compel conformity were unlikely to work.

VII

TRIUMPH AND TRAGEDY

22.

THE DEFEAT OF LICINIUS

LICINIUS, EMPEROR OF THE EAST, projected the image of a cheery soul. His beefy portraits looked to the tradition of Diocletian and Maximian—he was of military bearing, energetic-looking, bearded (see figure 22.1).[1] Constantine's portraits are beardless, youthful, displaying the serenity that appears in the panegyrics; his style echoes that of Augustus and, way before him, Alexander the Great, whose military skill he emulated. In their physical appearance, as their subjects would have been able to witness in works of art great and small, the two men could not have been more different. Licinius represented stability, continuity with the ways of Diocletian; Constantine represented a return to the glory of days long past, inspiring a new vision of the future. Despite the continuing prominence of Constantius in Constantine's propaganda, his self-presentation was decidedly unlike that of his father or his sainted ancestor Claudius. Beyond the world of appearances, there was less to separate the two men than might meet the eye.

Although the legislative record of Licinius would be formally abolished in December 324 after his defeat by Constantine, some of his enactments survived, absorbed into the body of legal documentation just as he and Constantine had absorbed Galerius' Edict on False Accusations into their own practice. Indeed, Licinius himself, although ruthless in dealing with the human remainder of his predecessor Maximinus' regime, had left intact a ruling granting immunity from capitation tax to people registered as urban citizens (as opposed to peasants who lived outside a city), which itself confirmed an earlier decision by Diocletian.[2]

The search for utterances from Licinius himself turns up a ruling that women who knowingly marry slaves will become slaves—they remain free if

FIGURE 22.1
Licinius. Source: Courtesy of the author.

unaware of their spouse's status, but the children take the husband's status as slaves—a rather more sweeping statement than any Constantine issued. It may be part of a longer set of rulings that included the statement that if slaves were caught fleeing to the barbarians they should have their feet mutilated and be sent to the mines.[3] Even more certainly his is a series of quotations from a text issued to the people of Bithynia on the status of people who served the court. Nicomedia, which Licinius adopted as his principal residence, was in Bithynia. These statements reflect Licinius' attempt to sort out problems arising from the court's presence in the area. Thus he rules that minor bureaucrats should not be admitted to court rank until they have finished their service and proved themselves honest; those workers in the mints should retain their status. People who have earned their rank and fulfilled their municipal obligations should enjoy the privileges due them, whereas those who have acquired rank through acts of venal patronage should be stripped of all privileges and sent home to perform their obligatory *munera*. Overall these rulings demonstrate a much closer association between the palace bureaucracy and the local governing classes than Constantine seems to have achieved. In his part of the empire, as we noted earlier, high office in the civil service was dominated by the Italian aristocracy.

Devoted as both men may have been to efficient civilian government, the most important institution to either was the army. For both men it's hard to find out anything in our sources about military administration. All we can know on that score is that Constantine's general staff was dominated by officers of German extraction—which virtually replicated the situation in the decades after Gallienus when recently prominent Balkan officers shared power with the senatorial nobility.[4] We are better informed about the conditions under which their soldiers served. It is from this area that the longest and most indisputably Licinian document has come down to us. It is a text composed almost immediately after the death of Galerius, no doubt with the prospect of war with Maximinus clearly in view. The text that survives in two copies on bronze tablets reveals that in Licinius' army, soldiers did very well. They received exemption for themselves and four other "heads" (capita), the basic unit for calculating taxation, both while in service and upon retirement after the full term of twenty-five years' service; soldiers who took an honorable discharge after twenty years retained an exemption for two "heads"; soldiers who retired because they were wounded also retained the exemption for two heads. Soldiers who did not receive an honorable discharge received no benefits since people obtaining these generous grants needed to show a "habit of good life." Military commanders were told that they needed to provide discharge papers themselves, presumably because papers with their seals were less likely to be challenged than documents that came from the unit's clerk, and they were told that they should inscribe the emperor's new regulations on bronze tablets in all the camps under their command.[5]

The change from the practice of Diocletian is quite noticeable. Under him a soldier who had served in the regular army after twenty years of service and the receipt of either a medical or honorary discharge could have received immunity from personal and civic *munera*. Men who received honorary discharges without having served the full time were denied exemption, as were those who served in auxiliary units.[6] The vastly more generous terms of Licinius' grant essentially removed retired soldiers and their families from the census roles and all that implied as far as taxation was concerned, wherever they might settle.[7] Constantine's soldiers were not nearly so well recompensed for their efforts. The emperor would be forced to address the issue a few years after his first victory over Licinius, when he would have troops stationed in places where Licinius' had been and who might have learned about the terms under which their rivals had been employed.[8]

The document recording Constantine's meeting with some plainly angry veterans in 320 provides us with one of the clearest available pictures of his style.

Preserved through records kept by Constantine himself, it appears to follow a bout of negotiation with the troops. It begins with the emperor's carefully stage-managed entrance:

> When he entered into the headquarters and was saluted by the prefects, tribunes and the most eminent men, it was acclaimed: Constantine Augustus, Gods preserve you, your safety is our safety, we speak truly, we speak justly.
>
> The assembled veterans acclaimed: Constantine Augustus, why have we been made veterans, if we have no privilege?
>
> Constantine Augustus said: I ought always to augment the happiness of my fellow veterans than to diminish it.
>
> Victorinus the veteran said: We should not be assigned to compulsory public services and burdens in any locations.
>
> Constantine Augustus: Tell me more clearly, what are the compulsory public services that more seriously irritate you.
>
> All the veterans acclaimed: Surely you yourself see.[9]

Constantine had of course seen, and the rest of the document contains a far more lucid summary of veterans' benefits than Licinius' chancery had been able to produce. Notable as well here is the troops' greeting "Gods preserve you," as he entered the room. Although he was a Christian, his veterans were not, and the notion that the forthcoming war with Licinius was to be some sort of religious crusade to protect the Christians of the east from Licinius' persecution would presumably have been lost on the men serving in the front ranks.

It is Eusebius, in his biography of Constantine, who asserts that Licinius' persecution of his co-religionists drove the western emperor into action. Sadly, the extent of this persecution and its date seem to be confused in Eusebius' mind, as he places it before the war at Cibalae and elides the years between. In his *History of the Church*, the last version of which followed immediately upon that final conflict, he indicates that the persecution extended only to a ban on bishops assembling. In fact, the ban may have had nothing to do with Constantine, and a great deal to do with a controversy that was even then dividing the church. The bone of contention was the nature of God and his relationship with Christ—were they the same divine essence or were they similar?—a debate initiated some years past at Alexandria. Licinius' wife Constantia remained devoutly Christian and appears to have been close to another Eusebius, the bishop of Nicomedia, who exploited his proximity to the palace in his relations with the other bishops.

The conversation that Eusebius says Licinius had with his closest intimates—about the importance of defeating Constantine so as to preserve the worship of the traditional Roman gods—does not fit very obviously into this context. Neither do certain facts. The forthcoming war was in prospect before Nazarius rose to deliver his panegyric in 321. War would have seemed imminent when, that same year, Constantine ceased to recognize the joint consulship of Licinius and his son. It had been a condition of the treaty that ended the previous war in 317 that for each year there would be only one set of consuls for the whole empire. As of the summer of 321, there were two sets. In 323 Constantine pursued a band of Gothic raiders into Licinius' lands, implying that Licinius was responsible for an attack on his territory, and he began to assemble a powerful fleet at Piraeus.

Major naval operations had been noticeably absent from the annals of Roman warfare since the year 31 BC when the emperor Augustus defeated Mark Antony at the battle of Actium. Since then the only naval operations involving fleets had been Aurelian's reconquest of Egypt and the war waged by Maximian and Constantius against the former commander of the Rhine frontier, Carausius, in the 280s and 290s. In the Mediterranean, the Roman naval forces were maintained essentially to patrol against pirates or to transport troops from the western and Syrian garrisons. Their pathetic state of readiness was amply demonstrated during the mid-third century by their failure to contain troublesome raiders, whether Black Sea tribesmen who ravaged the Aegean coastline in the time of Valerian and Gallienus or adventurous Franks looting the western Mediterranean during Probus' reign. Any substantial Mediterranean fleet would be a departure from what existed, and Constantine's preparations at Piraeus indicated that he was planning a war that would carry his forces into the heart of Licinius' realm, assisted by a greatly enlarged fleet.

With the legacy of his father's invasion of Britain still fresh in his mind as well as Maxentius' more recent invasion of Africa, he may also have felt that he could draw from a reservoir of naval experience that his opponent would be hard-pressed to match. Given the record of hostility between the two regimes, surprise was not an appropriate tactic; massive advance planning was therefore the order of the day. Constantine was not a man to underestimate potential obstacles or to fail to take what he saw as the necessary steps to meet them. News that a fleet was building would give Licinius something to worry about. Was the plan for a direct assault or was it to land troops somewhere in the rear of his army? Anything that would inject a degree of uncertainty into Licinius' deliberations would be useful—he had shown himself rather too competent when it came to a straight-up confrontation.

Constantine's invasion of the east began in the summer of 324. Meanwhile the empire still had to be governed, and it was to men like Locrius Verinus—last seen dealing with Donatists as *vicarius* of Africa and now prefect of Rome—that Constantine turned. One task that he allotted to an official named Dalmatius was to set down the ages at which young people would be considered mature; and Constantine himself sent an important missive to Severus, probably praetorian prefect at the time, telling him that people who merely purchased their ranks at the palace should be booted out—it was "fitting that only those who are employed in the palace or work in the administration should be selected for the bestowal of honors."[10] The measure looks like a house-cleaning operation ahead of what would predictably be the complex task of integrating survivors of Licinius' regime with his own people (Constantine appears to have been totally confident about the likely outcome of the campaign). The last communication on record as the campaign began is also to Verinus: it is a lengthy discussion on the subject of the appropriate rate of pay for swine-catchers.[11]

The same texts that show Constantine in action also reveal a novel feature of the regime: the extensive involvement of members of his immediate family in positions of very great responsibility. One praetorian prefect this year who was traveling with him was one Flavius Constantius. We have no information as to who he was, but the fact that he shared two elements of Constantine's name (the emperor was formally known as Flavius Valerius Constantinus) suggests that he was probably a blood relative. The Dalmatius mentioned in the preceding paragraph is likely Constantine's half-brother, and his son Crispus, now in his early twenties, was in command of the fleet.[12]

As Constantine and his family moved east with his entourage and troops, Licinius once again mustered his forces at Adrianople. On July 3, he was utterly defeated.[13] Constantine seems to have led the decisive attack himself, in the course of which he was wounded in the leg, while Licinius fled the field for the city of Byzantium.[14] There he appointed a general called Martianus to command his forces on the far side of the Bosporus (the straits dividing Europe from Asia).

The record of Constantine's wound reveals not only the continuing importance of the warrior ideology of the imperial position—it was just three years earlier that Nazarius had added Constantine's secret scouting mission to the story of the Italian campaign—but also further problematizes the narrative of Eusebius. In his *Life of Constantine* the bishop reports that Constantine went into battle with the aid of a miraculous battle standard. Evidently visualized as taking the form of the labarum first mentioned in relation to the battle of the Milvian Bridge, this standard had amazing power.[15] Carried into battle by fifty select guardsmen, it provided special protection for those around it: if the standard bearer should drop it in fear, the javelin coming his way would skewer him, while the man who then seized the standard was safe from all peril. The standard's staff acted like a magnet, attracting javelins to itself so that it came to resemble a giant pincushion. As with the story of the cross in the sky before the Milvian Bridge, Eusebius claims Constantine himself as the source for this information "much later."[16] If this was the case and since Eusebius seemed not to know about the standard or the vision until a year before Constantine's death when he wrote his speech celebrating the thirtieth anniversary of Constantine's accession, one might wonder if "much later" in *The Life of Constantine* means "more than a decade later." In 325 there seems to have been no need to Christianize this fast-moving narrative, or conceal the emperor's injury.

With Licinius in Byzantium, the next phase of the campaign took place at sea: the western fleet was unmatchable, as Licinius' admiral learned at his peril. Having lost control of the Bosporus, Licinius abandoned his men in Byzantium to take command of fresh forces near Chalcedon. Constantine landed his army without opposition north of Licinius' position, forcing him to fight, probably on September 18, at a place called Chrysoplis (modern Üsküdar in Turkey). The result was now a foregone conclusion as Licinius was plainly outmatched. He fled to Nicomedia, and the troops who had been left in Byzantium surrendered, the campaign all but over. On or just before December 16, 324, Constantia, assisted by Eusebius (bishop of Nicomedia, no relation to Constantine's biographer), negotiated the surrender of her husband.[17] He was sent into exile at

Thessalonica, where he was executed shortly afterward, allegedly for conspiring with barbarians.

Constantine was now sole ruler of the Roman Empire. He may have learned something of the art of government from his father, more perhaps from Diocletian. As we have seen, he knew how to govern: he guided his officials with a firm hand, and he understood his position as emperor within the tradition of imperial power that had developed over the centuries. But the victory of Constantine stemmed from more than just skill in the art of government, from more even than his extraordinary ability on the battlefield. Constantine's victory stemmed from his own toughness and determination, qualities honed in the train of Diocletian but perhaps instilled earlier in the palace at Trier, or as his mother grasped her dignity and self-respect in the wake of rejection. Constantine had learned that there would be no one upon whom he could rely as much as he relied upon himself, and this is reflected in his belief in the god who guided him. Constantine's god was still a very personal god, one whom he met on his own and who provided him guidance on an intensely personal basis; the god who Constantine believed to have guided him to victory was the god who had mercy upon him for his failings, and who protected him from evil.

23.

THE EASTERN EMPIRE

I N TAKING CONTROL OF Licinius' empire, Constantine confronted far greater challenges than those that had faced him after the defeat of Maxentius. In 312 there were well-established connections between his own court and Maxentius' senatorial aristocracy whose members appear to have moved seamlessly into his service. This situation may well have been eased by his father's long residence in the west and reasonable coordination between his court and Maximian's over the years. There were no such preexisting links with the governing classes of the eastern cities or with the senior echelons of Licinius' bureaucracy, yet these were the people Constantine would need to deal with if he was to find a way to survive after his conquest. It was also the case, as we have already seen regarding veterans' benefits, that practice in the east varied in some particulars from that in the west, and while some measure of the old regime might be tacitly accepted—hence the survival of Licinius' letter to the Bithynians in the *Theodosian Code*—pretty much everything would have to be reviewed, a point signaled on December 16, 324, when Constantine issued the edict, now de rigueur in cases of victory in civil war, invalidating all the "acts of the tyrant."[1] The next year promised to be immensely busy.

The earliest surviving text for 325 in the Theodosian Code reveals the difficulty of the task that Constantine faced, not least that symbolic gestures such as abolishing the "acts of the tyrant" could bring their own problems with them. On February 12, he issued an edict stating that "although the acts of the tyrant and his judges are invalidated, no one should wish through fraud to overturn what he did or what was legitimately done"—a wise move, as invalidating more than a decade of administrative regulation would have caused chaos.[2] It might have been read to mean that Constantine was trying to figure out what to do

FIGURE 23.1

This hexagonal pendant, which shows various figures from classical mythology, is one of five pieces that once formed a gold chain of such value that it was most likely given by Constantine to one of his most senior supporters; possibly, given the provenance of this piece in the Balkans, the praetorian prefect Flavius Constantius. Source: Stanze di Farraello, Vatican Palace. Scala/Art Resource, NY.

with his new territory. Among the many decisions that he would have to make were where he would live, how he would deal with Licinius' army, what agents of the old regime he could trust, and what eastern practices could be left in place.

Finding a way to integrate the eastern governing class into his own regime was going to be immensely problematic. And how would he handle the Italian aristocracy, upon whom his power depended, and the western general staff which had served him so well? There was no parallel in the east to the Roman Senate, and although there was a court infrastructure, it was far from obvious that he could simply graft Licinius' court onto his own. He knew from experience that he could not simply breeze in and fire the old guard if he wanted to build a stable regime.

The Christians were plainly high on Constantine's list of people to make contact with, and one of his early missives was addressed to the Christians of the east.[3] He begins by focusing on the difference between those devoted to the "most sacred cult of the Christians" and those who had treated them with contempt: it is plain for all to see that now the power of the great God has been clearly demonstrated through Constantine's victory.[4] Those who are mindful of "the most powerful" observed what was decent and right, while those who persecuted the followers of "the most powerful" had been utterly defeated: "many of their armies have been slaughtered, many have been turned in flight and their entire military establishment has fallen into disgraceful defeat."[5] War had arisen from persecution, and "the divinity" had sent forth a savior. Having examined Constantine's service, the Highest God determined that he was a worthy instrument. Beginning from the western sea around Britain, Constantine had righted wrongs, becoming convinced without a shadow of a doubt that he owed his success to "the greatest God."[6]

Then the emperor issued an order of restitution, freeing those who were imprisoned, restoring to their previous positions those who had lost them and returning property—though exempting martyrs from ordinary rules of inheritance. Their property was to go to the church.[7] Those, including the imperial treasury, who had taken such property would lose all claim to it and give it back to the rightful owners. The language here is redolent of that used in rulings over disputed inheritances, contested property, and status. A rescript sent in September 325 to an official named Helladius may indicate that these provisions were already in place. For Constantine tells him that "contrary to the rule of ancient law and the rescripts of former emperors," a petitioner in a property case, who traditionally had to produce evidence to support a claim, no longer needed to do so; and if the petitioner could not produce the evidence, the defendant had to prove his/her rightful possession of the property.[8]

The letter as a whole, without Constantine ever specifying who the "greatest God" is, offers an admirable statement of his devotion to the God who has guided him to success. A western Christian might well recognize the influence of Lactantius' *Concerning the Deaths of the Persecutors*, but the letter speaks not just to Christians but to all people about the importance of piety and justice—qualities that knew no ideological or religious boundaries. For Christians such as the magistrate at Oxyrhynchus—who within months of Licinius' defeat would use the term "the Lord's Day" when ordering the postponement of a hearing—the letter seemed an affirmation of the legitimacy of their faith. But, most important, there was nothing here to offend a pagan; the significance of the evils perpetrated by the persecutors of the church lay less in their own faith than in the fact that they did wrong by the Highest God, whose existence and power were now so widely accepted and variously understood, especially in Asia Minor.[9]

In this letter to the Christian community, Constantine shows no sign of being aware that different Christian groups might show up to claim confiscated property, though the absence of any reference to the "Catholic" Church—the standard term in earlier texts for those whom Constantine recognized as being in communion—may reflect his awareness that western and eastern Christianity could not necessarily be assumed to be as one. Certainly he soon realized that there were serious problems besetting the church, for he summoned a meeting of bishops at Antioch, probably thinking to attend, but then decided on a meeting later at Nicaea where he would be ready to settle his new subjects' outstanding issues.

In July at the latest, he reintroduced himself to all the peoples of the empire. Declaring that he was devoted to good government, he invited those who felt that a member of the imperial entourage or any other official had wronged them to present their case to himself in person. And if the claim were proved, he himself would take vengeance on whoever "has hitherto deceived us with simulated integrity." For it was only by approaching people in this way that Constantine could be assured that "the highest divinity" would "always be propitious" to him and keep him safe, "with the state flourishing and unharmed."[10] A few months later, probably in conjunction with this edict, he wrote to Flavius Constantius telling him that he had urged any subjects, displeased with the treatment they received when appealing cases to their own governors, to write directly to him.[11] In essence and in line with the earlier letter to the Christian community, Constantine was reaffirming his desire to make sure that justice was done. The consistency of his statements on the subject leaves little doubt of his sincerity; but Diocletian and Galerius had said the same, and no earlier Roman emperor on record, apparently, had thought otherwise. Whether expressed by a pagan or by a Christian, the government's value system remained intact—at least for now.

The challenge that every emperor faced was to ensure that he could carry out his essential tasks; control his officials' behavior; ensure that the infrastructure of the state functioned and that the army was under control. In the course of the year, Constantine had taken action on taxes and on integrating Licinius' troops with his own. On April 24, his court had issued a reminder that taxes could not be set by local magistrates because they would be tempted to shift the burden of payment from themselves to the poor. In June and July he was in repeated communication with Valerius Maximus (probably a relative of the Maximus we have already met as prefect of Rome), then serving as *vicarius* of the east.[12]

First, Constantine raised with Maximus the question of veterans' retirement benefits, apparently having decided to change the deal he'd agreed to in 320. Under the new rules, a soldier in a regular line unit whether in the field army (*comitatenses*) or in a frontier army (*riparenses*) would receive only four exemptions—one each for himself and his wife, his mother and his father; after retirement it would be reduced to just one exemption, for himself only, unless he left the service because he had been wounded. If not wounded, he would get the benefit so long as he didn't leave the service before completing twenty-five years' service. Soldiers who did not serve in regular line units (cavalry and auxiliary units) were awarded exemptions only for themselves while on active service, thereby maintaining the traditional distinction between these units. In an earlier edict he had maintained the status quo with respect to soldiers' wills: in their last testaments they could leave their property to whoever they wished and "if they note any wish by letters inscribed with blood on the sheath of their sword or on their shield, or if they write anything in the dust with their sword as they give up their lives during battle," those wishes too should be valid. The right of soldiers to make testamentary provisions outside the norm stemmed from the acknowledgment that their identities as soldiers might be stronger than any links with relatives whom they might not have seen in years, that they might have families configured in somewhat unconventional ways, or that they might die while their fathers were still alive.[13] Yet another edict on military matters stated that veterans would be given farms, money for equipment, a yoke of oxen and seed grain, or tax exemptions so that they could engage in business. The reason for this beneficence was that Constantine worried that veterans, left in idleness, would slip into poverty.[14]

Two later communications show his tendency to seek reconciliation wherever possible and to try to ensure that his wealthier subjects didn't cheat the less fortunate ones. First on the list was the old penalty by which criminals were sentenced to fight each other to the death in the arena (*damnatio ad ludum*, "condemnation to the gladiatorial training facility"); second was the behavior of property holders. As far as these last were concerned, we know that Constantine instructed Maximus about people who had the decurial status which would require service on a town council in two places: if they tried to evade the more irksome *munera* to which they would be subject in a larger city by declaring themselves residents in the smaller place, they should serve in both. And if landowners tried to exact more than the usual rents from tenant farmers, they should be stopped and forced to return the excess.[15] *Damnatio ad ludum*, while still employed in the west, had fallen out of common usage in the east; when Maximus asked whether he should use it, he was told to send offenders to the mines instead.

This ruling, like the earlier ones on veterans' benefits, shows that Constantine was concerned with more than simply applying western practices to the east. The same rule applied when it came to the issue of faith, as would become evident at the great council of bishops from all parts of the empire, which he convened at the city of Nicaea in May 325.

24.

CONSTANTINE SPEAKS TO THE BISHOPS

THE COUNCIL OF NICAEA, a watershed event in the history of Christianity, took place at a moment when Constantine was particularly concerned with reconciling eastern and western ways of doing business. It followed on his wide-reaching discussion of his own faith contained in his *Oration to the Saints*, which was probably written for a meeting of the clergy of Bithynia sometime around Easter of 325. It was an important moment for Constantine—there would have been some in the audience who would have remembered him as the young courtier of Diocletian many years earlier. He needed to set the record straight and show people who he had become.[1]

The *Oration* is known in English from the title it acquired in the manuscripts of Eusebius' *Life of Constantine*. Read out loud, the discussion would take about two hours, and it would appear to have been composed with a view to proving Constantine's intellectual credentials to his co-religionists.

His speech opens with an acclamation of Easter, an event seen as establishing the church and revealing the one true God to mortals—the God who was the creator of all, but who remained unworshipped despite all the indications given by the Holy Spirit. And it was unrighteousness that had prevented people from perceiving the truth. Christ had established the church, but the wickedness of nations had conspired to oust his works and reestablish their own superstition. Virtue, though, had now subdued that wickedness. Constantine declares that he will venture great things through the love of the divine, which has been implanted in him—he says later in the speech that he wishes that he had received the revelation of the true God long ago—and that God's help has enhanced his skills as a speaker. God, as Constantine understands him, in a discussion heavily influenced by Plato, is above all things, with no beginning and no birth. He also understands that it was not through any lesion of God's bowels that the Son had come into being, but it was through Providence that the Son became the governor of the sensible world and its inhabitants.

Constantine next describes the nature of creation at some length, then the folly of philosophers who have not understood the truth. At this point the emperor finds himself in deep water, seeming pretty clearly to contradict the understanding of God and his relationship with Christ that he expounded just minutes earlier.[2] The problem is Plato, the great Greek philosopher of the fourth century BC whose thought exercised enormous influence over intellectual life in the fourth century AD. In Constantine's view he

> excelled all others in gentleness and first accustomed human intellects to revert from the sensible to the intelligible and the things that are always thus, the one who taught us to look up to things above, did well when he postulated the god above being, then made a second subordinate to this one, dividing the two essences numerically, while both shared one perfection and the essence of the second god received its concrete existence from the first.[3]

The question of the precise relationship between God and Christ—whether they were identical, as Constantine suggests at the beginning of his speech, or of two essences—was at the heart of the debate between the church's two warring factions. Is it plausible that Constantine, who doesn't reveal himself in this document to be a profound philosophic thinker, did not grasp the problem? Extending this line of reasoning further, we might also presume that whoever helped him with the speech—emperors might write their own material, but it's unlikely that they issued major statements without checking with others first—was blind to the problem too. Neither view is especially plausible. If, as seems likely, the speech was delivered in the months preceding the council that was intended to resolve the issue, we might expect Constantine to have left clues that would encourage people from both camps to show up thinking that the matter had not been predetermined.

He had also written at about this time to the major protagonists in the quarrel over the nature of the Trinity, telling them that with the help of the Supreme Being he would be able to entrust the discussion to his devout listeners and shift them to a more reasonable position: there was no reason when the discord concerned a matter of importance why the same approach would not work that succeeded "when the issue constituting a general obstacle is small and utterly trivial."[4] Constantine may have been no great philosopher, but he was a very experienced administrator and only too aware from his experience with Donatus and his North African colleagues that appearing to have decided a question in advance was potentially catastrophic. Furthermore, the suggestion that Plato (whose doctrines he quotes as interpreted by an influential second-century AD disciple) understood the divine, albeit imperfectly, could be seen as a signal to the leading intellectuals of the east that he was willing to enter into a dialogue with them as well.

Constantine now moves on to the subject of his conversion, and the victories he says stem from his faith. He then returns to the marvel of creation, the inadvisability of sin, the incarnation, and the wisdom of living "according to God's command" so as to ensure that we "pass our lives in immortal and unchanging abodes, superior to all fate." The teachings of Christ figure next, then the prophecies of his coming; he recalls his own visits to Memphis and Babylon in earlier years. Then comes an idiosyncratic reading of the Book of Daniel, followed by comments from the Erythraean Sibyl, whose wisdom figured prominently in Lactantius' thinking, and Constantine adopts Lactantius' view that Virgil's Fourth Eclogue, a poem that might in fact have been influenced by Sibylline verses circulating in the first century BC, derived from a prophecy by the Cumaean Sibyl (a mythic being who lived near the Bay of Naples).[5]

In the last section of the speech Constantine attributes his victories to his piety:

> I ascribe to your goodwill all my good fortune and that of those who are mine. And the evidence is that everything has turned out according to my prayers—acts of courage, victories, trophies over my enemies. Even the great city is conscious of it and gives praise with reverence, while the people of the most dear city approve, even if it was deceived by unsafe hopes into choosing a champion, who was suddenly overtaken in a fitting manner worthy of his atrocities.[6]

The "great city" is plainly Rome; the "dear city" is Nicomedia, and the champion is Licinius. As if addressing Licinius in person, he remonstrates with him about his poor religious choices. He comments on the deaths of Decius, Valerian, and Aurelian (falsely enshrined by Lactantius as an aspirant persecutor). And for Diocletian he reserves considerable venom—he who "after the murder-lust of the persecution, having voted himself down, unwittingly renounced himself as one unworthy of power, and confessed the harmfulness of his folly." Constantine recognizes Diocletian's failures and those of his immediate predecessors on whom the judgment of God has fallen. This same God has awarded him his glorious victories. He, the best judge, the best guide to immortality and bestower of eternal life, "is an unconquerable ally and defender of the righteous."[7]

In this speech we see Constantine as he wished to be seen and heard. His God was both the God of creation and the God of battles. Although a soldier, he displays learning, both traditional and Christian, when announcing that posterity would not see him as yet another emperor in the tradition of Diocletian, and he gives promise of the necessary skill to deal with the problem that awaited him at Nicaea. In setting his own record straight he has made it clear that he will be no Diocletian, he will be no persecutor—that was an important message to get out just before a contentious meeting about the nature of God and in light of what people might have heard about the state of affairs in Africa. Eusebius' *History of the Church* is the source for a number of the surviving documents about the early years of the Donatist controversy. These were clearly circulating in the east by 324. Eusebius cites them as a sign of his new emperor's devotion to the church. Others who read them may have been less sanguine and would have wondered which emperor would show up at the meeting he had summoned. Would it be the man who had foresworn persecution, or would it be the man whose handling of the Donatist affairs could be seen as having been less than even-handed?

25.

THE ARIAN CONTROVERSY

BEFORE GOING WITH CONSTANTINE to Nicaea, now the city of Iznik in western Turkey, we must travel south to Alexandria in Egypt. Alexandria had long been one of the intellectual capitals of the Roman World. Founded by Alexander the Great in the 330s BC, the city had emerged as a major imperial capital in its own right in the decades after Alexander died in 323. It remained the capital of the Ptolemaic dynasty, which descended from one of Alexander's generals, until the last Ptolemy, the (in)famous Queen Cleopatra VII, surrendered to the emperor Augustus and committed suicide in 30 BC. Located at the western end of the Nile Delta, the ancient city was a massively important cultural center. Visitors could still marvel at the great lighthouse on the island of Pharos—138 meters tall, it was one of the seven wonders of the ancient world— visit the tomb of Alexander the Great; admire the old royal palaces, decked out with statues "borrowed" from earlier Egyptian monuments much as the arch of Constantine had been adorned by material taken from earlier imperial monuments; or visit the great library, the Mousaion, founded as a center for the preservation and extension of Greek learning. It was a city famous for its art and for its lively intellectual life, one whose security was crucial for the economic well-being of the empire. Its harbor was the principal port through which the wealth of Egypt and luxuries imported from India passed into the Mediterranean. Home to many significant pagan thinkers, it was also the place of many of the most important Christian thinkers of the previous century. It was this heritage that would be the cause of great concern as Constantine entered the debate over the relationship between the elements of the Christian Trinity—the Father, Son, and Holy Spirit.

A debate had arisen in the third century between those who believed that the Father, Son, and Holy Spirit were three different expressions of a single being, a view known as monarchianism, and those who held that the three elements of the Trinity were three *hypostaseis* or substances of the same being. The point of the second position was that the three elements of the Trinity had separate but equal form. One of the most important representatives of the anti-monarchian view at Alexandria was Origen, who taught there, castrated himself there, and moved off to Caesarea in Palestine where he died as a result of ill treatment in the wake of Decius' edict on sacrifices. Another supporter of this view and staunch opponent of extreme monarchian theology was Dionysius, a convert from paganism who was bishop for nearly thirty years from the 230s into the 260s.[1]

The anti-monarchian view, well articulated in Alexandria, was also important in Syria, where Antioch was a major cultural as well as administrative center. In Diocletian's time, the most important thinker in the Syrian church had been a teacher named Lucian, a man of immense courage who spent the last years of his life in prison at Nicomedia, before Maximinus beheaded him in 312. Among his pupils was Eusebius—not the biographer of Constantine but a relative of one of Licinius' most important officials—who served as bishop of Beirut in Lebanon (where there was a famous school of Roman law) before taking up the bishopric of Nicomedia. It was because he assumed this role that he had become close to Constantia and had been in a position to negotiate Licinius' surrender to Constantine.

Although Eusebius of Nicomedia will often seem to be the key figure in the debate over the Trinity, more because of his influence than his theological acumen, the debate takes its name from a charismatic priest named Arius, who is said to have been a skillful debater and an active preacher who had responsibility for a group of 700 holy virgins as well as his own church.[2] Arius had a background in Platonic philosophy and it seems that he had studied with Lucian at Antioch, where he may have made the acquaintance of Eusebius of Nicomedia, who would later support him in his struggles with the hierarchy at Alexandria.[3] These struggles arose because Arius preached a strongly anti-monarchian theology, and monarchian theology had become dominant at Alexandria in Diocletian's time.[4]

The controversy that would surround Arius' teaching would focus on basic questions regarding what constituted a proper Christian life in addition to pinpointing God's relationship to humanity. These were issues that bore on the question of what counted as martyrdom along with lifestyle choices that were becoming more prevalent among Christians in the sixty or so years before Diocletian issued his persecution edict in 303, when martyrdom had seemed more a theoretical than a real possibility. The lifestyle that Arius affected was the tip of an ascetic iceberg that was, even then, giving rise to a recognizably new form of Christian: the monk. Monastic self-mortification would replace the agony of martyrdom as a way of defining a place within the Christian hierarchy that lay outside the control of the bishops. The battle over Arius' teaching would also become a struggle to control this increasingly important development within the church.[5]

The fabric of the ecclesiastical hierarchy at Alexandria had been frayed by another controversy. Like the Donatist conflict, the quarrel between Peter of Alexandria and Meletius of Lycopolis in northern Egypt was a direct consequence of Diocletian's persecution edict. When news of the edict came, Peter fled the city, returning in 306 to take up his duties as the primate of Egypt and issue a decree setting out how to treat members of the faith who might be thought to have lapsed in some way. Not surprisingly, he thought that those Christians who had fled, as he had, had done the right thing. Those who, obeying the edict, had handed over scripture had done no wrong either. Only those who had publicly sacrificed were to be punished. Unfortunately for Peter, one person who fell into this latter category was allegedly Colluthus, who was replaced as bishop of Lycopolis by Meletius, in whose opinion those who had lapsed needed to seek forgiveness from those who had suffered; and if a priest had lapsed, he could never regain his position and would be readmitted to communion only after a period of penance.[6]

Peter's position, to judge from the canons of the Council of Ancyra (probably convened in 314), was more closely aligned with mainstream thought in the church:

> Priests who sacrificed, and then renewed the fight, not through some deceit, but in truth, neither arranging in advance or with deliberate purpose or persuading (some official) so that they should appear to be subjected to torture, which is applied in appearance and form, shall partake of the honor of their position, but they shall neither make the offering, or preach, or perform any of the functions of priestly offices.[7]

In other words, those who offered sacrifice under duress, having tried unsuccessfully to flee, should have no action taken against them. People who were not priests when they sacrificed under such circumstances could be "be ordained as having committed no fault in the persecution."[8] The key factor here was intent: if the individual had been distraught when participating in a sacrifice, then he would be treated leniently, but if he had participated willingly he would suffer penance.[9] The aim of the bishops in using intent in determining guilt was plainly to defuse controversies such as Meletius had inflamed. Unfortunately for those who thought this way, the issue could not simply be shoved under the ecclesiastical carpet. In Egypt particularly, strict enforcement of Diocletian's edict aggravated the division between the two camps.[10]

When Galerius issued his edict of persecution in 306, the recently returned Peter fled again and remained in hiding for some time. Meletius took the opportunity offered by Peter's departure to assume his duties as primate of Alexandria. An outraged Peter wrote his congregation ordering them to have nothing to do with Meletius until he could return and examine him, which he did—and determined that he should be excommunicated, a decision that couldn't have surprised anyone and was made all the easier to enforce by the fact that Meletius had been arrested and was at that moment incarcerated in a mine in Palestine.[11] Some of Peter's own supporters may well have regarded his conduct as equivocal, and this may be reflected in a later story according to which the schism between Peter and Meletius arose when the two of them were in prison together, separated only by a curtain hung across the middle of the cell![12] Fiction though this may be, its existence pinpoints a perceived weakness in Peter's case, at least until the time that he himself could gain the authority of a martyr for his doctrines. And become a martyr he did, when he was arrested and killed on the evening of November 25–26, 311. Peter's death took some of the wind out of Meletius' sails; one tradition has it that Arius had broken with Peter over his treatment of Meletius and had asked forgiveness of Peter's successor Achillas. Achillas died shortly after his accession and was succeeded in turn by Alexander, who may have defeated Arius in the election to the episcopal seat.[13]

Alexander tried to reconcile the different Christian groups, arriving at what seems to have been a watchful truce with the Meletians, permitting debate over doctrine.[14] Alexander himself may, at least at the beginning, have been willing to countenance a range of discussion at the seminars that he held on the nature of the Christian God. In doing so Alexander took a strong monarchian line in advocating that the Father and the Son were *homoousios*, "consubstantial." He might have had reasons for doing this that had nothing to do with Meletius; the monarchian position answered pagan claims that Christ was a person not unlike Apollonius of Tyana, the great pagan wonder worker of the first century, and thus in no way exceptional. Unfortunately for Alexander, the extreme position flew in the face of earlier teachings—including those of the revered Dionysius—and an effort to silence voices that had long had a place in discussions was bound to arouse antipathy, which is exactly what happened.[15] Still these seminars seem to have allowed for open discussion until the Meletians complained that Alexander was harboring a heretic in Arius. It was at this point that Alexander tried to silence his rival, and Arius looked for help from abroad.[16] This would be forthcoming, for even if there were differences of opinion among anti-monarchians as to how the Trinity should be understood—Eusebius of Nicomedia did not see eye-to-eye with Arius on all matters—most of the opposition could agree that the use of the word *homoousios* was obnoxious because to them it implied that the uncreated Father suffered bodily diminution in the creation of the Son.[17]

Perhaps the most significant aspect of the dispute between Arius and Alexander in 322 is that there was so little about it that was new. At least at the outset, it is arguable that the controversy between the two men had more to do with local autonomy and the structure of the church in Alexandria than with doctrine, since anyone licensed to preach in an Alexandrian church was allowed free rein on questions of doctrine. According to Alexander, the debate gathered strength when Arius urged a number of priests to see things his way and took advantage of his following among the virgins of Alexandria.[18] This version emphasized that the dispute was internal to the Alexandrian church and that Arius was doctrinally eccentric.

The real problem, especially as the powerful Eusebius took Arius' side, was that the dispute raised serious questions about Alexander's own qualification to be bishop, and this was intolerable when he still had to tread carefully around Meletians, who thought the same thing because he represented the party of Peter.[19] To defend his position, Alexander summoned a council of Egyptian bishops to condemn Arius and reassert his control in the eyes of the Christian community as a whole. The letter he sent to the churches of the east after the council voted to excommunicate Arius in 322 gives some sense of the two dimensions, personal and doctrinal, that the struggle had assumed. Indeed, Alexander opened with an attack not on Arius but on Eusebius of Nicomedia, who "thinks that the affairs of the Church are under his control because he deserted his charge at Beirut and cast longing glances at the church at Nicomedia (and he did this with impunity)." This is an interesting statement because Alexander is suggesting that Eusebius is using his position as bishop at the imperial capital to assert authority over his fellow Christians. If Alexander could think such a thing, it is highly unlikely that Licinius had been as hostile to the church as Eusebius of Caesarea would later claim. If an ambitious and well-connected man like Eusebius of Nicomedia had thought that Nicomedia was a potential lions' den, it is most unlikely that he would have left Beirut to go there. Indeed, Alexander said that Eusebius began to play the role of a prince of the church, putting "himself at the head of these apostates...daring even to send commendatory letters in all directions concerning them, if by any means he might inveigle some of the ignorant into this most base heresy which is hostile to Christ."[20] There is a sense here that by moving to Nicomedia, Eusebius was claiming primacy over other bishops, and Arius' doctrine was perhaps less urgent an issue than how one might deal with a court bishop as Eusebius may now have seemed to the Alexandrians.

Alexander's hostility to Eusebius was not entirely without justification. Eusebius had sent a letter supporting Arius' position to the bishops of the east, and the first thing that Arius appears to have done when the council was over was to write to Eusebius asking for his help.[21] And Eusebius was not Alexander's only problem. He complained, for instance, of numerous preachers in Alexandria and elsewhere being won over by Arius' eloquence.[22] In one letter, he lists prelates, including the bishops of Libya, who asserted the distinction between the Father and Son that was central to Arius' teaching, claiming (falsely) that it was a heresy of their own devising.[23]

Arius then wrote to Alexander and the clerics who supported him in 322 characterizing Alexander as being, among other things, a Manichaean—a member of the faith originating in Persia, to which Diocletian had so strongly objected as well. Arius even went so far as to claim that Alexander's doctrine tracked that of Mani, who had grown up as a member of a Jewish-Christian splinter group in what is now Iraq. Mani, so Arius said, held that the Son was a *homoousios meros tou patros* (consubstantial part of the Father).[24] This underscored the crucial theological point, for Arius held that the Son was created after the Father, and subordinate to him; and created so that he could mediate between his Father and the created world. In this formulation, the Father was the "true God" and the Son was entitled to divinity because he participated in the Father's "substance." If the Son was a creation of the Father, he could not be *homoousios*.[25]

Having returned to his church, Arius wrote to Eusebius and others asking for their support.[26] Since Eusebius maintained that the members of the Trinity were three essences of God, he clearly thought that Arius' teachings were closer to his own than Alexander's belief in a single essence comprising three Persons.[27]

Neither side gained the decisive advantage in Alexandria itself even though Arius tried to support his view by explaining in a poem entitled the *Thalia*, which clarified his claims to authority. It opened with the statement:

> According to the faith of the chosen of God and of those knowledgeable of God, of the holy children, of those who expound the word *God* correctly, receiving the Holy Spirit, I have learned these things from the participants of wisdom, from those who are pleasing [to God], and from those who are divinely taught in all things. I follow in their footsteps, the famous one, proceeding with correct learning, suffering much for the glory of God, learning from God, I know wisdom and knowledge.

Arius thus combines in his person the role of the inspired prophet and overtones of persecution.[28] The words just quoted reveal another layer of Arius' thought having to do with what is to us the still murky realm of popular culture, where ideas fused to be reshaped by teachers on street corners as well as in churches. Arius' ability to catch a different tone helped him withstand the assaults of the Alexandrian establishment and reach out to other leaders of the church.

And while he resisted his opponents in the streets, he also responded bitterly to the attacks on his thinking that reverberated in the higher echelons of the church. In a letter to Eusebius in 322 he complained that the bishops who supported him—including Eusebius of Caesarea, the biographer of

Constantine—had been excommunicated by their rivals, while others, who were "heretics and uncatechized" in his view, were retained in communion despite "saying that the Son is a belch, or that he is a projection, or that he is unbegotten."[29] Indeed, by this point the situation was so polarized that without recourse to direct imperial intervention—not Licinius' style in matters of the mind—there was no real way to resolve the dispute. This was the situation when Constantine emerged victorious from the final struggle with Licinius.

26.

NICAEA

A S HE LEARNED MORE about the dispute, Constantine seems to have decided that Antioch would be a bad place to meet. He therefore summoned a new council to a more neutral spot, choosing first Ancyra, and then Nicaea, which, being close to Nicomedia, would spare him a long trip into lands where supporters of the old regime might lurk. The reasons that he offered, however, were less sinister; he simply stated that the weather was nice, Nicaea was easier for western bishops to reach, and having the meeting there meant that "I may be present as a spectator and participator in those things which will be done."[1] In saying this he reiterated his desire that the church find its own unity, but he was not above giving the assembled bishops some added help in their deliberations. The presence of the western bishops would act as a counterbalance and lend the council an aura of—unprecedented—universality. He would also try to defuse the quarrel by suggesting that the doctrinal issue was of little importance, compared to other, far weightier, decisions that had to be made; by this he hoped to create common ground between the two parties and soften the blow of a defeat for one side or the other. In his letter to Arius and Alexander before they all met, he said that the disagreement between them was not of great moment in light of the fact that there was "one faith between us"—indeed, he hoped that they could reconcile even before the meeting. Furthermore, he did not say these things so as to force them "to come to an agreement on every aspect of this very silly question, whatever it actually is." It should be possible, he went on, for the dignity of the meeting to be preserved and "fellowship be kept generally, even though on detail some serious disagreement may arise between you over a tiny matter since we neither all agree among ourselves in wanting the same thing, nor does one single being and mind operate within us."[2]

The bishops arriving at Nicaea would have known that the way to their new emperor's heart was through compromise, and the meeting was evidently stage-managed to ensure that this point was made from the very start. It opened, probably under the presidency of Nicaea's bishop, Theognis, in early June. In his opening address, delivered in Latin with a simultaneous Greek translation—a courteous nod to his audience of Greek-speakers—Constantine said:

> It is the object of my prayers, my friends, to share in your company, and now that I have received this, I know I must express my gratitude to the King of all, because, in addition to everything else he has allowed me to see in this, which is better than any other good thing; I mean, to receive you all gathered together and to observe one unanimous opinion shared by all. Let no jealous enemy ruin our prosperity; now that the war of the tyrants against God has been swept away by the power of God the Savior, let no other malignant demon encompass the divine law with blasphemies by other means. For to me, internal division in the Church of God is graver than any war or fierce battle, and these things appear to cause more pain than secular affairs.[3]

When the opening formalities were completed, Eusebius of Caesarea opened the proceedings with a confession of faith that Constantine immediately declared to be in essential conformity with his own (it lacked only the word *homoousios*).[4] This was no doubt a well-arranged piece of political theater— and precisely the sort of thing that had been missing in Constantine's dealings with the Donatists. Eusebius had arrived under a ban of excommunication from the anti-Arian bishops, but Constantine's first act was to make a public display of reconciliation, indicating unequivocally that it was this rather than the award of total victory to one side or the other that was the order of the day. Just in case anyone had missed the point, it was reinforced when Eustathius of Antioch read out some work of Eusebius of Nicomedia that was regarded as heretical.[5] Then Constantine himself put forward his own version of what we now know as the Nicene Creed, composed, it is said, by a Cappadocian priest named Hermogenes and in terms that were very close to Eusebius of Caesarea's confession of faith.[6] This creed remains the best-known utterance by a Roman emperor in the modern world:

> We believe in one God, the Father Almighty, Maker of all things visible and invisible—and in one Lord Jesus Christ, the Son of God, the only begotten of the Father, who is of the same substance of the Father; God of God, Light of Light, true God of true God; begotten not made, consubstantial with the Father; by whom all things were made, both which are in heaven and on earth; who for the sake of us men, and on account of our salvation, descended, became incarnate, was made man, suffered, and rose again on the third day; he ascended into the heavens, and will come to judge the living and the dead. We also believe in the Holy Ghost. But those who say "There was a time when he was not" and "Before his generation he was not," and "he came to be from nothing," or those who pretend that the Son of God is "Of other hypostasis or substance," or "created" or "alterable" or "mutable," the universal and apostolic Church anathematizes.[7]

It is hard at this distance to grasp the extraordinary originality of what Constantine proposed to do; there had never been a universal creed, and bishops who were used to working with their own baptismal creeds are unlikely to have seen the need for such a statement.[8] The decision to issue a creed as a universal definition of the faith looks very much like the sort of thing that an experienced imperial administrator would have decided on. One of the many failures of the negotiations over the Donatist controversy was the absence of any statement that could provide a way forward. The Constantine who had so recently proclaimed his belief in the power of his god does not seem to have been remotely interested in watching the church tear itself apart arguing about the precise nature of the relationship between different elements of the Trinity. In Constantine's world power flowed from the top and it would be in heaven as it was on earth. In its original conception, the Nicene creed does not emerge through a theological process; it comes through an imperial legislative one. In issuing edicts, emperors might take advice from experts before issuing their own decrees, and so it was in this case that the emperor took advice from experts and arrived at a formulation that he regarded as reasonable.

The bishops adopted Constantine's creed on June 19, then set about their other business: defining church practice—also at the emperor's request—setting for the whole empire a standard date of Easter and attempting to reconcile the Meletians with the Alexandrian church. The reconciliation involved creating a structure within which they could reunite with their fellow Christians, something that had been lacking in the meetings held to sort out the North African situation—an especially telling point, as the issues were so similar to those that had divided the African Christians. According to the settlement, Meletius was confirmed as bishop of Lycopolis and his ordinations were accepted as valid, though he was forbidden to ordain any more priests, and his priests were to be subordinate to those ordained by Alexander. A Meletian priest who submitted to Alexander could have full clerical privileges; and if Alexander agreed to a congregation's request for a priest who had been of the Meletian persuasion, that priest could replace one of Alexander's priests when the former died.[9] It was a generous settlement underlining the message that all those present should have taken away with them: Constantine wanted a peaceful reunification of the church and favored compromise as the way of achieving that end.

The Easter question was rather different. In his speech at Nicomedia, Constantine had made it clear that in his understanding of Christianity great stress was placed on the resurrection; this he appears to have seen as prefiguring his own experience with God. God's willingness to forgive his earlier errors and show him the path to victory had become a critical fact of his life. So it was that the crucifixion and resurrection proved that God "has not availed himself of his great power to requite the insult, but has forgiven humans for their foolish thoughts, reckoning folly and error intrinsic to humanity, while himself abiding by his own decision and abating not a jot of his natural love of mankind."[10]

The problem was that there were two ways of calculating Easter, both linked with the celebration of Passover, which was celebrated in the month of Nisan, then the first month of the Jewish calendar, usually corresponding to March/April in the modern Gregorian calendar. Passover began with a feast on the fourteenth of Nisan followed by a festival week. In Christian tradition the resurrection was inextricably linked with the beginning of Passover, and Christians expected to mark the day by fasting. The problem was determining each year what the anniversary should be since the Jewish lunisolar calendar was (and is) inconsistent with the solar calendar used by Christians. This meant that commemoration of the resurrection, if linked with Passover, could not fall on the actual day. To solve this problem, one group within the church held that Easter should be celebrated on the Sunday following the first full moon after the spring equinox; another held that it should be celebrated on the date in the Greco-Roman calendar that corresponded to Nisan 14. Most western churches, along with communities in what is now Turkey, had also adopted the closest Sunday to Nisan 14 as the appropriate day. Churches in Syria, Palestine, and Egypt used Nisan 14. The verdict of the council was that Easter should be celebrated on a Sunday—which in effect meant that the side that had emerged victorious in the debate over the Trinity had lost in the one over the date of Easter.[11]

The reasoning that underlay Constantine's decision is, to modern sensibility, deeply troubling, for he said that "nothing should be held in common with that nation of liars and Christ-killers," after having declared it was "in the first place unworthy to observe that most sacred festival in accordance with the practice of the Jews; having sullied their own hands with a heinous crime, such blood-stained men are, as one might expect, mentally blind." The vehemence of this rhetoric did not, however, reflect actual behavior. Instead, it reflected the often bitter and inflated language of religious controversy as it had developed over the centuries. Pagans had accused Christians of incest and cannibalism (a reading of the Eucharist), of atheism and engaging in illicit secret meetings to the detriment of mankind. Jesus was a failed magician, and Christians were terminally foolish for following "undemonstrated truths." The anti-Jewish diatribes of the pagan world were equally vicious and of far longer standing, as pagans stated that Jews were members of a race of lepers expelled from Egypt; people whose dietary laws were bizarre; whose prophet, Moses, was a magician. Pagan attacks on Jewish communities in cities like Alexandria could be exceptionally violent, and in Egypt at least, there was a strand of viciously anti-Semitic literature that associated the practice of Judaism with Roman oppression! Jews saw Christians as fools who had abandoned the true faith in pursuit of a false prophet and, on occasion, had encouraged local pogroms against them.[12]

Vicious as the rhetoric might be, and vicious as the conduct was on occasion, most people managed to get along most of the time. As the history of Diocletian's persecution showed, most people preferred not to be drawn into violent quarrels with their neighbors; and if they felt their neighbors' religious practices were offensive, they were more likely simply to ignore them or refuse to associate with these people unless there was some external spark that might turn latent prejudice into violence. Changing the date of Easter was not such a spark, and the council at Nicaea did not greatly impact Jewish communities throughout the empire: the Jews retained their privileges (which included some limited immunity from *munera* for important leaders).[13] What the council did achieve, aside from standardizing the celebration of Easter, was to help bind the rival parties together in that each had given something up.

The outcome may have exceeded even Constantine's hopes. All but two bishops, both Libyan, subscribed to the canons of the council, including the creed. The two recalcitrants were excommunicated, as were Arius and some priests who continued to support him.[14] Shortly after, Constantine convicted Eusebius of Nicomedia of remaining in contact with Arius and removed him from his see. Both men were soon allowed back into communion when they publicly stated their accord with the Nicene creed.

Although Christological controversy would continue for centuries, for a while after the Council of Nicaea, a remarkable peace obtained. Constantine had shown that he had learned from earlier failures that compromise was the preferable path to peace. The Nicene creed did not depend upon any preexisting theological statement, which was perhaps one of its greatest strengths; it stated a view of God that would not be disagreeable to the majority present and made it clear that certain "errors" of Arius and his followers would not be acceptable. In so doing it had the coincidental effect of placing at the heart of subsequent Christian theology the notion that the Father was of the same essence as the Son—that they were indeed *homousios*.[15] It was precisely this point that would often seem to be a matter of grave controversy in the years that followed, but it is also the basic clarity and simplicity of the doctrine that has, in the twentieth century, made the creed a valued statement of faith in mainstream Christian traditions.[16] So it is that today the Nicene Creed is what Constantine intended it to be.

27.

CONSTANTINOPLE AND ROME

NICOMEDIA WAS A CITY with which Constantine had powerful associations. In his speech to the bishops he vividly recalls the demeanor of Diocletian on the day that his palace caught fire—the result of a lightning strike, he says—and it was very likely the city where his first wife Minervina died.[1] It was not a place that he could avoid as the physical infrastructure of administration had been built up there since the time of Diocletian: he needed a palace, a basilica, a mint, and a circus, all of which Nicomedia provided. What he did not need was a palace dominated by the staff of his predecessor, or a basilica and a circus redolent of earlier regimes. He needed a new place to live, and by the time of his decisive victory over Licinius at Chrysopolis he had already chosen it—a place that could also serve as a memorial to his triumph.

Having to choose a new residence doesn't mean that Constantine was permanently shifting his center of government: he had had his reasons for moving the court to Serdica after 317. The problem that he now faced was that Trier was too far to the west to be an effective seat of administrative power, while a return to Rome would mean leaving the east before he could be sure that it would be loyal to him. Serdica was a very useful base for an emperor who was planning a war against a foe located at the other end of the Balkans, but it had no harbor and was harder to get to than a place like Nicomedia.

At a pinch, of course, any of these places could serve, so long as the emperor was content to be constantly on the move, but that's something that Constantine, along with his immediate predecessors, appears to have been less keen on than Diocletian. So if he was uncomfortable with Nicomedia, where to settle? He considered a number of spots, including Ilium, Chalcedon, Thessalonica, and, finally, Byzantium. It is alleged that he was on the verge of deciding on Ilium when he was convinced by a divine vision that it would be wrong to found a new Rome on the site of a city so closely linked with the old (Ilium was the descendant of ancient Troy, birthplace of Aeneas who was one of the founders of Rome). The result was that he chose Byzantium instead, declaring that God ordered him to give the city his name.[2]

Byzantium—Constantinople as it would be known from now on—may have been, in Constantine's formulation, God's choice for him. It was also a reasonably obvious choice from a practical point of view. The city was, by this time, nearly as old as Rome itself, having been founded in the sixth century (Rome was a seventh-century foundation); it had long been an important stopping point for ships trading with the Black Sea, an important source of grain for the Mediterranean lands. As a result of its economic importance, it had always been powerfully defended, as Constantine knew from the recent war with Licinius, and many of the essentials for an imperial city were already in place there. Moreover, despite stories that he took an age to make up his mind about it, there is evidence he had identified the city as his future capital before Licinius' surrender.[3]

Byzantium had a record of supporting losers. It had the appearance of a major Roman city, rather than a Greek one, because it had chosen poorly in 193: in that year the city's council had decided to back Pescennius Niger when he contested the throne against Septimius Severus (and had continued to resist Severus for several years after Niger's defeat). When he finally captured Byzantium, Severus, a man not renowned for his merciful disposition, decided to punish not simply those who had defied him (they were executed) but the city itself, which he ordered to be burned and remodeled in a new Roman style that would efface its former Greek identity.

Severus' new city boasted colonnaded streets, a basilica, a massive new shrine to the emperors of Rome—which included a courtyard surrounded by four stoas, or Tetrastoön—plus a bathhouse and a circus. The Tetrastoön and the bathhouse stood opposite each other on the north and south sides of an avenue that fed into the Forum. The basilica was on the other side of the Forum and flanked a second new avenue running down from the north, beginning at a building known as the Strategeion, which appears to have included a training ground of some sort. A third avenue, the Mese, connected the Forum with the city wall in the west. The circus was to occupy the area to the south of the bathhouse. It was a good beginning even if it had been left incomplete at the time of Severus' death in 211.

In selecting Byzantium as his Constantinople, Constantine committed himself to providing the necessary buildings for the imperial government and to enhancing the city's overall appearance. In choosing a place with a quasi-imperial past he was also linking himself with the days preceding the reign of Valerian when a single emperor ran the empire. As he celebrated his victory he could feel confident that the spirit of Diocletian would no longer loom over him as it probably had when he entered the palace at Nicomedia.

What we do not know is how precisely Constantine carried out the city's refoundation, but certain things were supposed to take place when a new city came into being whether or not it was replacing an old one on the same site. The reason for this, in the Roman tradition, is that cities were by definition sacred spaces, and the establishment of a new city involved two religious ceremonies.

The first of these was the *limitatio* in which the city limits were set out, traditionally involving a procession during which a priest would plow a furrow to mark the new boundary. When the city was ready, the next ceremony would be the *inauguratio* in which the civic space was "liberated and pronounced to be designated," meaning that that space and its functions were freed from all divine constraints. According to Roman tradition, this could only be carried out when enough of the city had been built for the ceremony to be meaningful— but it was also Roman tradition that the ceremony should involve augurs, who belonged to one of the traditional Roman priesthoods charged with overseeing the relationship between the city and the gods (especially Jupiter) by observing signs, especially in the sky and, in particular, the flight of birds. Constantine appears to have participated in the rites (which may have involved the casting of a horoscope, possibly as a substitute for augury) on November 8, 324, before Licinius' surrender.[4] It is likely that he led the procession, and, if it was part of this ceremony, he may even have plowed the furrow (or part of it) himself, but there would have been no animal sacrifice: the ceremony would have been a Christian adaptation of an age-old tradition not unlike his entry into Rome in 312. Then, probably in the year after that, he began to make detailed plans, laying out the location of new churches and temples.

Even as the new capital was being made ready, Constantine was headed west to celebrate the twentieth anniversary of his accession on July 25, 326. He

FIGURE 27.1

The Great Cameo of Constantine and Fausta. The boy in front of Constantine in the chariot in this
scene is probably Crispus, and the date is most likely 315. The identity of the female figure behind
Constantine is problematic, but it could be Helena. Constantine assumes the role of Jupiter with
his thunderbolt. What is especially striking is the way the artist depicts the affectionate relationship
between Constantine and Fausta. Source: Courtesy of the GeldMuseum, Utrecht, The Netherlands.

determined to commemorate the event at Rome. This would be the last time
that he would see the city.

His wife, Fausta, who had been living with him in Serdica, had presumably
journeyed with him to Nicomedia, quite probably with the numerous offspring
that had resulted from what was plainly an intensely physical relationship: she
had produced her second son, Constantius, on August 7, 317, exactly a year after
the birth of Constantine, her first son; then her elder daughter, Constantina,
within a year or so of Constantius' birth, and shortly afterward a second daughter, Helena. Her fifth child, Constans, was born in 323.[5]

In 324, Fausta's role in guaranteeing a new generation of rulers began to be
widely advertised. In one series of gold medallions struck at Trier, Constantine
appears on the obverse (front); the reverse (back) depicts the two Caesars
Crispus and Constantine (II) standing with clasped hands on either side of
Fausta, whose hands are placed on their shoulders with the legend "fortunate
offspring of Constantine Augustus."[6] A second series has a bust of Fausta on the

obverse while the reverse depicts her with a nimbus of light around her head and facing a throne set on a platform decorated with garlands. She is holding a child and standing between two goddesses—Good Fortune (Felicitas) and Piety (Pietas)—and two lesser divinities stand on either side of the throne. This is a style that is repeated on two other gold series showing Fausta on the obverse with the legend "Piety of the Empress." Coins of the kind that would circulate far more widely—and probably represent miniature versions of larger paintings— depict her on the obverse carrying two children, with the legend "Hope of the State" and Optatianus, the poetically inclined future prefect of Rome, offers a rather poor pun on her name in a poem describing Constantine as triumph- ing throughout *faustis saeculis* ("the fortunate centuries"). At the same time, Constantine's mother Helena also appears on coins, perhaps to remind people of the importance that both generations of women played in perpetuating the imperial line.[7] It is worth noting that Fausta had assumed the role of Crispus' mother—possibly an ideological gesture, but one that might have struck people as odd as she was only about four years his senior. Her relationship with him would have been formed many years earlier during their joint childhood in Trier, at which point her role was likely that of older sister.

The one person who would not be traveling west with the imperial party was Crispus, who had returned to Trier—the city served as his headquarters while Constantine was in Serdica—where he presumably had played an important symbolic role as the "family presence" in the area. A contemporary poet, writing about the anniversary of Constantine's accession, praises Crispus for protecting the Rhine and the Rhône while handing out harsh laws to the Franks. He is the "sacred boy, rightly the hope of such great peace."[8] He was not the only member of the family to stay in the west; Constantine's half-brother Julius Constantius had taken up residence in Etruria where his wife had further augmented the imperial clan by giving birth to a son named Gallus. Gallus would briefly hold the position of Caesar to Constantius II in the 350s, and it is his fate in that role that offers the only legitimate clue to Crispus' death in the spring of 326.

In 350, Constantine II was long dead after a quarrel with the court of his brother Constans, and Constans was recently dead as the result of an uprising in Gaul led by a German general named Magnentius. In order to reassert con- trol over the west, Constantius II felt that he needed to leave a family member in charge of the east, which he had ruled since Constantine's death thirteen years earlier—and he had for this but two choices: the sons of his cousin Constantius, Julian and Gallus. Gallus, being the eldest, was the natural choice and was duly married to Constantine's daughter Constantina, just as a few years later Julian would be chosen for the same job and would be married to Helena.

As Constantius took his army west for what proved a highly successful, if bloody, campaign, Gallus was sent to Antioch. The problem with Gallus is that he seems to have had a very poor understanding of his role, which allowed him very limited authority. When Gallus tried to claim greater authority fights broke out with senior bureaucrats, one of whom was murdered in a riot that Gallus fomented at Antioch. When Constantius ordered his cousin to leave the city, Gallus stopped off at Constantinople, where he further offended Constantius by taking his seat in the imperial box to enjoy a day of chariot racing. On his way to Pola (modern Pula in Croatia) where he was taken next, Constantina died. At Pola, members of Constantius' court interrogated him about his behavior in Antioch. Gallus tried to blame Constantia, at which point the proceedings were reported to Constantius who ordered the immediate execution of Gallus, along with three of his close associates. We are also told that this is where Crispus had been executed many years before.[9]

The relevance of Gallus' story to Crispus' stems both from Constantius' evident interest in imitating his own father and from the nature of the position that both held. Constantine's conception of the role of Caesar seems to have been very different from that of Diocletian or, indeed, from that of Licinius, whose two short-lived appointees to that post had both been experienced generals. Constantine, who appointed his infant son Constantine to the post at birth, and did the same for Constantius a few years later, seems to have reverted to an earlier definition whereby the holder of the post, as successor designate, possessed only as much authority as the emperor deemed fitting. When Constantius appointed Gallus, then Julian to the position, he seems to have been doing so according to his father's notion that a Caesar was essentially to be seen but not heard.

Junius Bassus, a member (most likely pagan) of the Roman aristocracy had been in office as praetorian prefect in the western provinces since 318; it is significant that he remained in office. Did he have a hand in Crispus' downfall? It's hard to imagine that so senior an official would not have been consulted on a matter of such importance. One of the consuls of 325, Valerius Proculus, was removed from office in disgrace. Was there a falling-out between Constantine and elements of the Italian aristocracy? Had Crispus gotten himself involved in a fight on the other side of his father? If none of this can fully explain what happened to Crispus, it does suggest that everything might not have been well in the western empire.[10]

We will never know what happened to Crispus, or why he plummeted, in the space of just over a year—we can date his death to the first half of 326—from glorious heir apparent to the chopping block. It is likely that he was summoned to his death from Trier and it is possible that Constantine could not bear to be present for the trial, if we are right to read Constantius' conduct here as an imitation of his father's.

A few months later, Fausta vanishes from public view. Again we cannot know why, but one source tells us that she died in 328. Her sudden disappearance from the imperial record makes it very tempting now, as at the time, to link her exit from public life with that of Crispus. The fact that her actual death may have taken place a couple of years later suggests that she was sent into internal exile.[11] Another piece of evidence may confirm that Fausta's removal was the result of a severe disagreement with which it might be possible for others to sympathize: both Helena, Constantine's mother, and Eutropia, Fausta's mother, stepped into the role of empress while Fausta was evidently still alive. It is also telling that Eusebius never mentions her in his *Life of Constantine*.

The story as we have it from the most reliable sources was substantially expanded over time. Aurelius Victor, who completed his *Book Concerning the Caesars* in 361, says simply that Constantine had ordered his eldest son killed for some unknown reason.[12]

It is Eutropius, writing in 369 (under a regime that would not be as chary of mentioning embarrassing events of the previous dynasty), who gives much more precise information: "Constantine, through insolence born of success, changed somewhat from his pleasant mildness of spirit. First he assailed his relatives, killing his son, an excellent man, then the son of his sister, a youth of agreeable nature, and after that, his wife, and then many friends."[13] The fact that Eutropius would be able to come up with this information reveals that there was some sort of narrative tradition, now lost to us, that preserved the memory of events that were otherwise obscured. What is particularly interesting about Eutropius' version—aside from the fact that he interposes the death of the younger Licinius between the deaths of Crispus and Fausta (a some-what unlikely proposition considering that Licinius' father was killed a year earlier)—is that he sees their deaths as resulting from a change in Constantine's behavior rather than from their own misconduct. He seems unaware of the story that Fausta caused Crispus' fall—a story that doesn't appear in the record for another generation.

The first extant report that Fausta was responsible for the death of Crispus, and that Constantine was then convinced by a grieving Helena to kill Fausta in a hot bath, is in the anonymous *Short History Concerning the Caesars*, written shortly after the death of Theodosius I in 395: "Constantine, having obtained the whole Roman empire, and ruling through great good fortune in war, on the suggestion of his wife, Fausta, so they say, ordered his son Crispus to be killed. Then he killed his wife Fausta, throwing her into blazing hot baths, when his mother Helena assailed him in intense grief for her grandson."[14] It is only later that we are told that Fausta had tried to seduce Crispus, and that when she failed she persuaded Constantine to kill him. Then according to the fifth-century historian Philostorgius, Constantine found that she had commit-ted adultery with a *cursor* (scout) and had her eunuchs cast her into the bath-house. The significance of this version is the timing: while the fall of Crispus is attributed to Fausta, her own demise is put at some later time and not seen as directly linked with his. Philostorgius is a notoriously independent witness to political events of the fourth century, and we might reasonably see in his account a reflection of the very nasty stories that were circulated about Fausta after the end of the Constantinian dynasty.[15] Certainly his account is not the same as that known to the anonymous epitomator, and it is not the one known to our final late witness, the sixth-century pagan Zosimus who derives what he has here from late fourth-century historian Eunapius.[16] His version goes as follows:

> When he arrived at Rome, full of arrogance, he found it necessary to initiate his career of impiety in his own household, for Crispus, his son who, as I have already said, was judged worthy of the rank of Caesar, came under suspicion of having an affair with his step-mother, Fausta, and was executed without regard to the laws of nature; when Helena, the mother of Constantine was upset by the violence, and unable to accept the young man's execution, Constantine,

to console her, piled a greater evil upon that evil, ordering a bath to be super-heated, and that Fausta be placed in it until she died.[17]

He goes on to say that Constantine converted to Christianity because he could find no one else to forgive him for the killings, and founded Constantinople because he could no longer bear to be in Rome.[18] Both these observations are plainly wrong and simply confirm the impression that later authors were dealing with a sufficiently fluid tradition, stemming from lack of real information, that their accounts are fantasies.

Later stories do nothing to illuminate the situation in 326. All we can know is that Crispus was executed upon his father's orders, and that Fausta was ousted from public life. Constantine may have been ever after profoundly sorry for what had happened. Even years later, when he felt that the imperial college could be expanded to include more than Fausta's three sons, he did not remarry, and there is no suggestion that he contracted any other significant relationship with a woman. This doesn't at all fit the pattern of his earlier conduct, or that of other emperors, for whom prolonged bachelorhood seems not to have been an option. Constantine's self-imposed celibacy leaves us one final impression. However serious their quarrel, and serious it must have been, he seems never to have ceased loving his wife.

VIII

RULER OF THE WORLD

———————————

28.

CONSTANTINE'S GOVERNMENT

ALTHOUGH THE MOST DRAMATIC events of the year AD 326 resist definitive reconstruction, there is a great deal of evidence for Constantine's
ongoing efforts to forge a new empire-wide government. With the foundation of
Constantinople, a new order began to take shape as he realized what Diocletian
had long ago known: one man could not govern the empire from one place.
Constantine had recently learned, to his bitter cost, that neither could it be governed by young men who did not understand their place in the greater system.
Thus, while his surviving sons would be showcased as fine examples of dynastic continuity and his mother and mother-in-law would emerge as important
dynastic banner carriers in the absence of an empress, the actual business of
government was carried on by Constantine with highly experienced civilian
and military officials.

With Crispus dead, the government of the west was now in the hands of Junius
Bassus. As praetorian prefect, he filled a part of the administrative role that under
Diocletian's system had been held by a Caesar. In 331 the superior position of the
prefects was recognized when Constantine issued an edict describing them as individuals "who alone are known to be representatives of our sacred self." These men
were remembered as possessing power that was virtually imperial in scope. The
military duties of a Caesar would presumably have been performed by the commanders of the field armies, the *magistri peditum* (masters of foot) and the *magistri
equitum* (masters of cavalry), who are attested in the records of Roman government
after Constantine's death in such a way as to make it plain that these posts existed
while Constantine was on the throne.

One of Constantine's officers, whom we encounter briefly, is the Frankish
general Bonitus, who is said to have done important service in the war with

Licinius, while Bonosus, a very senior officer in the 340s, and Magnentius (mentioned earlier) were busy climbing the ladder of promotion during Constantine's lifetime. Magnentius would seize the throne thirteen years after Constantine's death, wearing his devotion to the Christian faith on his sleeve. In the east it is likely that Ursicinus, who would command the cavalry forces along the Persian frontier for many years, was already established. He too was a westerner, as was the German Barbatio, whose career probably began before Constantine's death since he was commanding Gallus' guards in 350. Arbitio, who seems to have risen from very humble origins—it is alleged that he entered the imperial service as a common soldier—is described as one of Constantine's generals. When we meet him in the 350s he is disagreeable and old; in the 360s, when he played an important role in a civil war, he is positively ancient.

On the civilian side, where the highest office remained the praetorian prefecture, officials who were making their presence felt were Aemilianus, known only through a single document that shows he was a praetorian prefect at Rome in 328; Valerius Maximus, soon to be praetorian prefect; Flavius Constantius and Evagrius, then praetorian prefects, who stayed in the east and in the Balkans while Constantine went west in 326. Then there was Flavius Ablabius, even then en route to the praetorian prefecture that he would occupy throughout the 330s; Lucius Papius Pacatianus would serve in the same office primarily in Italy, from 332 to 337; and Felix was praetorian prefect in the African provinces. Ablabius was a devout Christian, allegedly from a very humble background; while Evagrius' birthplace, Megara, a smallish place in mainland Greece, suggests that he too was not a product of the imperial upper crust; other evidence suggests he was a pagan.[1]

The nature of the regime is further indicated by the list of consuls in the 330s, which is dominated by the praetorian prefects and members of the highest (western) aristocracy. The consuls for 331 were Junius Bassus and Maximus; Papius Pacatianus was consul in 332 along with a future prefect of the city named Hilarianus. Dalmatius, Constantine's half-brother, makes an appearance in 333 (a moment of some significance for Constantine's succession-planning) along with Zenophilus, a long-term servant of the regime best known to us now for his investigation of Donatists. Optatus, consul in 334, was a powerful courtier who had made his mark as a rhetorician, even though he was not of aristocratic birth; it was said that he owed his influence to his wife's willingness to put herself forward to obtain favors. He was the first man to be awarded the status of patrician; an ancient term, once the designation only of an elite group within the Senate at Rome, it now came to indicate a person specially favored by the emperor. There could be no question about the background of his colleague Anicius Paulinus, a member of an immensely powerful Italian clan, who was heading for the prefecture of the city the next year. The consuls of 335 included Julius Constantius, Constantine's other half-brother, along with Ceionius Rufius Albinus whose background was similar to that of Paulinus. The only consuls of this period about whose families we have limited or no information are Facundus (336) and Felicianus (337). We do know, though, that their colleagues were, respectively, Nepotianus, a brother-in-law of the emperor, and Titianus, a future urban then praetorian prefect. One of the striking features of the post-Licinian regime as it took shape is that the soldiers, many of whom entered the imperial service from outside the empire, appear to have been more routinely Christian than the civil officials, recruited as they were from the upper echelons of urban society. The other point that emerges is that, while marginally less uniformly a collection of Italian multi-millionaires than it had been before 324, Constantine's inner circle remained very western.[2]

Although he brought that inner circle with him, he continued to reach out to his new subjects, issuing orders both ideological and practical. On January 5, 326, for instance, while at Heraclea near Constantinople, Constantine wrote to Evagrius saying that if a person caught committing a crime worthy of "prison barriers and the squalor of custody" confessed the deed so that there was a public record, that confession could be used in court to restrain a judge's "intemperate rage." His point was that with a confession in hand, there was no need to torture the defendant. On March 8, possibly about the time the action against Crispus was under way, Constantine wrote to Bassus telling him that lawyers who "by their criminal bargains despoil and denude those who are in need of their resources" and take on cases simply to see if they can acquire the best of their clients' property "ought to be separated from the company of honest men and the sight of judges." In September he wrote to Evagrius to the effect that if a man sold anything under duress to any imperial official (even a minor one), both the property and the money paid for it should be returned to the seller— and that the same penalty would hold if the official extorted the property in the name of a relative.

The next month he addressed Acilius Severus, prefect of Rome: judges should exert themselves, he told him, to protect the property of absentees so that those who were abroad for some reason need not fear that whoever was looking after their property might lack adequate instructions; Constantine granted additional time for filing recovery suits. The people covered by this law are unlikely to have been the poor and downtrodden—rather, the scenario envisioned fits better those who had been in the imperial entourage during the war years and this may reflect the tensions between east and west we find elsewhere. Likewise it reflects Constantine's strongly held view that things like this shouldn't happen in his empire. On a very different note, but one mirroring these same tensions, he wrote to Evagrius on August 11, that year:

> Veterans to whom there is a good mind should work the fields or make money in the most respectable occupations or engage in trade. Capital punishment shall soon rise against those who neither cultivate fields nor display a useful life in worthy trades. Those through whom public quiet is disturbed ought to be stripped of all privileges so that if they should do wrong in the least way they may be subjected to all punishments.[3]

It is perhaps ironic in light of Constantine's own marital situation by the end of 326 that the early months of the year involved him in a number of significant decisions concerning marriage, all evidently governed by the principle that good marriages made for a good empire and that women needed to be, to some degree, protected from nasty gossip.

The first of these rulings, on February 3, was issued to an official named Africanus, a man possibly not of sufficiently high status that the emperor would ordinarily have seen correspondence regarding him. In this case the topic is adultery, and the ruling states that with women who work in taverns, account must be taken of the role that they play there. If a woman is a tavern keeper and is charged with adultery, a judge should hear the case. If, however, the woman is a server, she should be excused from the charge because of her low status—not because she might be forced through poverty to have sex with her customers but rather because "such persons, because of the poverty of their lives are not considered worthy of the consideration of the law." Scarcely an attitude that strikes the modern ear as enlightened, but not one likely to have bothered the average Roman. The class bias of the Roman world regarded the working poor as quite simply beyond the bounds of polite society.[4]

Of the next three surviving rulings of 326, one is an edict and the other two are embedded in correspondence with Evagrius. All of them raise the issue of class in the context of sexual misconduct and, thus, behavior that Constantine expected of people he sees as members of the class of persons who should set an example of reputable behavior for others to follow. The first of these documents is an edict, issued on April 4, taking on what seems to have been the not uncommon practice of "abduction marriage." Today it is a complex practice that in some cultures might be employed by consenting adults trying to avoid the economic penalties—dowry for the woman, bride price for the male—of traditional marriage customs; alternatively, it could be an act of extreme violence to compel a woman into a relationship she does not want. In Constantine's view the practice was wholly wrong no matter what anyone wished. In his view, even if the girl were to acquiesce in her abduction, her wishes should not be considered and she should be punished along with her abductor. If the "abduction" turned out to be elopement, it might be assumed that the girl had made the necessary arrangements through her nurse. In that case, "punishment shall first threaten the nurse whose service is proved to be detestable and whose discourse was bought so that her mouth and throat, which brought forth nefarious encouragements, will be blocked with the ingestion of molten lead." Even if the case was genuinely one of forcible abduction that the girl had tried to resist, doing "everything to protect herself with every effort and seeking the aid of neighbors," she would be punished by disinheritance. Slaves who produced information about such goings-on were to be rewarded, and parents who refused to prosecute were to be exiled. The punishment for the abductor, for any assistants, and, by implication, an unresisting abductee, was to be burned at the stake.

To judge from the envisaged participants in the cases just outlined—nurses, thugs, slaves, and suchlike—it is clear that Constantine was looking at instances involving members of the "respectable classes" and that he was demanding what he considered "respectable conduct" from them, which is probably why girls, who might more reasonably be seen as victims, were punished; he seemed to think that "respectable girls" did not get themselves into situations where they could be abducted. Insofar as Constantine might see these situations as typically involving the invasion of upper-class "territory" by the lower class, the ruling is in keeping with his wish to keep members of the different social classes in their places. In any event, members of the lower classes (and any others, for that matter) wishing to avoid dowries or bride prices could, under Roman law, simply cohabit for a year and a day to be recognized as a married couple. Interestingly as well, while some might be able to appeal to the biblical precedent whereby the "children of Benjamin" in the Book of Judges stole the "daughters of Shiloh," or the Roman story of the rape of the Sabine women in which Romulus, the founder of the city, had stocked his heavily male environment with women stolen from his neighbors at a festival, Constantine would have none of it.

When it came to governing the empire, what mattered to Constantine was reputable tradition, not the Bible. The view of "the ancients" that girls (by which he plainly meant teenagers) could not give testimony in court or conduct a lawsuit supported his view that even if a girl claimed that she was happy with the outcome of the abduction, she should be punished.[5] Since the victims of bride-kidnapping were then, as now, overwhelmingly teenagers, the effort to end the practice protected their interests by making it clear that they should resist any arrangement that was not completely above-board, or so Constantine appears to have thought. If so, it is consistent with his earlier measure on the return of betrothal presents, and with another one, issued to Bassus three days later, in which he concerns himself with the welfare of upper-class girls who might be coerced into having sex with their guardians or tutors when they wished to marry. In such a case, he pointed out that when a girl comes of age and wishes to marry, her tutor is responsible for "determining that her virginity is intact." Clearly, some tutors were willing to make this declaration if the girl had lost her virginity to them. Constantine noted that a man like that should be deported to an island and his property confiscated, a punishment he regarded as moderate since elsewhere he suggested that this kind of person should be burned at the stake. That, however, was not a typical punishment for people of high status, which by definition included tutors.[6]

The subject of adultery cropped up again in April 326 when Constantine wrote to Evagrius on the subject. He noted that since adultery as it now stood was a public crime (a legacy of Augustan marriage legislation), anyone who wished to do so could bring a charge. From now on, however, the right of denunciation should no longer be permitted to "those wishing to defile marriages": in future, only "the nearest and closest kin"—in particular the father, the cousin, and especially the brother—"whom truth or anger drives to accusation" could bring a charge. Most of all, he said, it was up to the husband "to be the avenger of the marital couch, for the ancient emperors in the past granted to him the right to accuse on the grounds of suspicion and not to be constrained within a certain period of declaration." By excluding outsiders from bringing accusations of adultery, Constantine again appears to be protecting the interests of the "polite classes" from outsiders.[7] The new rule is also consistent with Constantine's dislike of nasty gossip.

That June Constantine issued another edict on the subject, from which only one bit survives: "that no one shall be permitted to have a concubine while married." This refers to the situation in which a man of some standing entered into a long-term relationship with a woman of lower status. This was typical of men on either side of marriage, the most famous instance being Bishop Augustine of Hippo, who had an extended relationship with a concubine before his conversion. Older men tended to enter into such relationships after divorce or the death of their spouse when they didn't want any more heirs. With younger men it was because they wanted sex and companionship before marriage. Constantine's aim here is most likely to discourage people from maintaining any ongoing relationships with lower-status women when they marry.[8]

From the surviving marriage legislation in April 326 we can deduce why the compilers of the Theodosian Code a century later did not feel it necessary to include post-Constantinian texts in their work. The documents produced during Constantine's time were regarded as good enough to determine later practice, which was what that emperor intended. The concentration of rulings, evocative of moments such as Hadrian's ruling on the entertainment industry 200 years earlier, may also suggest that Constantine decided this was the time to issue a set of his own rules. It is perhaps significant that the primary beneficiaries of his new policies were envisioned as young girls or women of good families, while the ruling on concubines demonstrates an interest in the welfare of wives since the ban would enable them to divorce their spouses and retrieve their dowries. By moving to assist those who were most disadvantaged under current law, Constantine may have been trying to advertise his interest in fair deals for all— or at least for those who were regarded as existing in the eyes of the law.

Just as his regime diverged from Licinius' on retirement plans for soldiers, it also deviated concerning other members of the imperial service. Now that a new court was being established, it was important that new rules be established that would apply to imperial service in all parts of the empire. We find the first sign that something was brewing in a couple of rescripts issued the previous year. In one, sent to Valerius Maximus in July 325 and dealing with those reappointed to official positions, Constantine asks him to make sure that these people are not evading their curial duties, while also asserting that those already approved for imperial service are protected by their oaths and by patronage.

Three months later he decreed that people who deserted their town councils for imperial service without having obtained a moderately senior rank should be compelled to carry out their municipal duties. In April 326 he wrote to Constantius that "since the most unjust tyrant" (Licinius) had ruled that magisterial assistants in the imperial service who had earned an honorable discharge were subject to those same municipal services, he should make sure that the practice stopped. In May he wrote to Evagrius that "town councils are being deserted by those who are linked to them by birth" and that places in the imperial service were being obtained through patronage: he wished all councils to know that if these deserters were caught, provided they had spent less than twenty years in the imperial service, they would be recalled to fulfill their duties. Given that Evagrius, like Constantius, was operating in the east, the problem was plainly to do with people employed under Licinius and Maximinus.

In case Constantine's efforts to sort these matters out should be seen to threaten the status of members of his entourage, he issued about now a ruling that any who had acquired property were allowed to keep it since they had without doubt earned it: after all, "they are not strangers to the dust and labor of the camps who accompany our standards, who are always present at our official acts, and whom the difficulties of expeditions and the multiplicity of journeys exercise even though they are intent on their erudite studies."[9]

Despite the turmoil in his personal life, Constantine continued to do his job as he saw fit, to communicate his values to his subordinates, and to try to ensure what, by his lights, was decent government for his people. The instability within the palace is balanced by stability among the senior officers of the administration who ensured that the complex transition from a divided to a united empire continued to run as smoothly as possible. Whatever he felt in private, Constantine tried to show his public the face of an emperor who knew his job.

29.

CONSTANTINOPLE

GOD, THE ARMY, MARRIAGE, and the bureaucracy: the matters that figure so prominently in Constantine's legislation during the two years following his defeat of Licinius represent the four pillars upon which he felt his
regime stood. God had brought him victory; along with his army, he needed
the imperial bureaucracy to govern; and he wished to rule an ordered society in
which people knew their place and the vulnerable were protected. In addition,
he had committed himself to constructing a new capital; as it was being named
for him, it was clearly envisaged as a grander place than the cities of his predecessors. Constantinople was not seen to be Rome's replacement, but it would
excel all other cities and be the focal point for those who aspired to a place in
his service. In Constantine's city would reside an aristocracy whose authority
depended on their relationship with him.

A city that was to be home to a great emperor needed to look the part. It was
funded by the money liberated from Licinius' treasury and by a special tax,
and as it took shape, there was no doubt that the city was going to be spectacular. The emperor himself may have carried out a second foundation ceremony
in which he marked out the city's boundaries on November 26, 328 (allegedly guided by the Christian God as he did so).[1] According to theories of civic
design current at the time, there was great interest in both civic *kosmos* (layout)
and *kallos* (appearance). The city's *kosmos* as a capital depended heavily on the
development of the governmental district, while its *kallos* was enhanced by the
display of public art, much of it ancient.

Constantine's city centered on the embellishment of the Severan additions—
the two *emboloi*, or colonnaded streets, which intersected near the baths of
Zeuxippus, the Tetrastoön and the basilica; and the remodeled circus, or

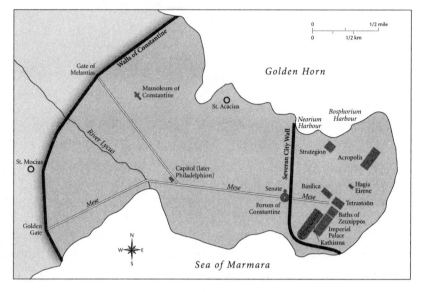

FIGURE 29.1
Plan of Constantinople. Source: After A. Tayfun Öner.

hippodrome, now fronting the imperial palace. The intersection of the *emboloi* was now marked with a massive tetrapylon (four-way arch) known as the Milion, a title that echoed the golden milestone in the Roman forum. The Tetrastoön was rededicated in honor of Helena, who had died in 328; she was buried in a mausoleum on the Via Labicana in a sarcophagus that may once have been intended to hold Constantine himself as it is decorated with images of soldiers defeating barbarians. The massive sarcophagus and the grand mausoleum (figure 29.2) are testimony—as is the commemoration of Helena in the new city—of the role she had played in her son's life.

On the northwest side of the Milion, the old basilica was transformed into a square court surrounded by porticoes (a peristyle) to house several institutions including a library and two small shrines. One shrine was to the goddess Rhea, the mother of Zeus, identified here with the Magna Mater or Great Mother, one of the most prominent goddesses in western Turkey and worshipped as the mother of the gods. The other was to the Tyche (Fortune) of Constantinople, in the shape of a new goddess named Anthousa (in Latin, Flora; in English, Flowering) whom Constantine had brought in to replace Keroë, the old city goddess of Byzantium.[2]

FIGURE 29.2
The sarcophagus of Helena shows Helena on the right. The martial imagery on this monument suggests
that it may originally have been designed to hold an emperor—surely Constantine himself. Source:
Courtesy of the author.

The imperial palace rose to the south of the Tetrastoön, with its great entrance,
the Chalke Gate, acting as the terminus for the *embolos* that ran south from
the Strategeion. Its western edge was marked by the much-enhanced circus, to
which it was joined through the Kathisma, or imperial box; the Bosporus and
the Sea of Marmara formed the palace's southern and eastern limits as it spread
out in numerous terraced pavilions and gardens.

The circus, on the model of the Circus Maximus in Rome, was transformed
into a victory monument. Included in its decoration were statues of the ass and
its keeper, evoking Eutyches and Nikon (Prosper and Victory), who had wan-
dered into Augustus' camp before the battle of Actium; these were imported
from Nicopolis, the city founded by Augustus on the site of his victory. Other
victory monuments were the Serpent Column, erected at Delphi after the
Greek victory over the Persians at Plataea in 479 BC, and an image of an eagle
defeating a snake. This last image appears on coins issued in conjunction with
Licinius' defeat. The close proximity of the Licinian victory monument and

the monuments to two of the defining military contests of the ancient world stressed Constantine's place as history's ultimate victor.

Other sculptures included famous figures of the past—Alexander the Great, Caesar, Augustus, and Diocletian—as well as statues sent by other cities to strengthen their ties with the new capital. Miletus, for instance, sent a statue of its citizen Theophanes (an intimate of Gnaeus Pompey, Caesar's rival for power) whose fellow citizens had voted him divine honors. From Rome came an image of the she-wolf suckling Romulus and Remus; and there were also representations of wild animals, of Zeus, and two statues of Hercules. There was a giant masonry obelisk, which still stands on the site of the circus' central barrier in modern Istanbul though its bronze covering has long since disappeared. It was placed there as a substitute: an authentic Egyptian obelisk like the one Augustus had put in the circus maximus at Rome, an object that Constantine had hoped to have, could not be transported in time.[3]

The great palace loomed behind the circus, and it is illustrative of the division between the public and private aspects of government that we do not know where, within this vast complex, the emperor had his private quarters, or where the individual bureaus of state were housed. All we know is that somewhere behind the great entrance was a house for Hormisdas, a Persian prince who had sought refuge with Constantine, and that some 6,500 people were employed within its walls.[4]

As the Mese, the city's central east-west artery, passed through the old city wall it intersected with another forum, this one round and centered on a massive porphyry column from Egypt supporting a gigantic statue of Constantine (figure 29.3). This newer forum, known as the Forum of Constantine, marked the exact center of the city, and on its northwest side arose a new building to house the city council—in grand style. If the Forum of Constantine symbolized the linkage between the emperor and the governing class, a plaza a bit farther to the west along the Mese, known as the Philadelphion, commemorated Constantine's family, perhaps with a bit of borrowed statuary since the famous porphyry image of the tetrarchs, now built into St. Mark's Cathedral in Venice, was originally housed here.[5] One final monument of note, rising in the city's northwest side near the new city wall, was a mausoleum. Intended as the future resting place of Constantine himself, this was a potent indication that there would be no abdication: clearly Constantine was not planning on leaving the city to molder away in some retirement palace destined to serve as his tomb.

The building program is emblematic of Constantine's approach to government. He shows himself fully aware and appreciative of the traditions of the past while seeking to set those traditions in a fresh context. The displays of famous statues stressed the new capital's appreciation of the traditions of other cities of the empire. The use of covered porticoes, emulating the cityscapes of Syria, showed that Constantinople was no imitation of Rome; indeed it may suggest that as Constantine traveled those lands in the train of Diocletian in his youth, they had made a powerful impression on him. The appearance of Diocletian in the circus and the porphyry representation of him with his three colleagues in the Philadelphion may also have indicated a new take on the old regime. In victory, Constantine could at last make peace with Diocletian's ghost and proclaim his own regime as its legitimate successor.

Work on the city seems to have proceeded at a tremendous pace, so that by May 11, 330, it was ready for its dedication. We don't know exactly what took place, but it appears that the festivities unrolled in two parts over two days. First there was a procession from the Philadelphion to the Forum of Constantine, which culminated in the placing of the great statue of the emperor on top of the porphyry column; the late sources mention prayers being said—not inherently unlikely, and so long as they were sacrifice-free, quite possibly inclusive enough to satisfy an audience used to acclamations of "the highest god." The statue of Constantine was itself confessionally neutral as it was still a statue of Apollo, but with the head, displaying a radiant crown emblematic of the sun, now possessing Constantine's features. In one hand it held a spear, in the other a globe supporting an eagle.

On the next day there was a procession in the circus, and the first chariot race was run in the revamped facility. Constantine wore a diadem set with pearls and other precious gems, recalling the words of Psalm 20: "You placed on his head a crown of precious stones." He ordered that the baths of Zeuxippus be opened and evidently opened the palace to the public. An image of Constantine had been made in gilded wood, holding a statuette of Anthousa, the new city goddess, in its right hand. This statue was presented to the crowd in the circus and he ordered that on every anniversary of the city's dedication it should be carried into the circus in a vehicle escorted by candle-bearing soldiers wearing cloaks

FIGURE 29.3

The image on the top is the great column of Constantine as it is today; the image on the bottom shows us what it would have looked like when complete and offers an image of Anthousa, the city goddess of Constantinople. Sources: (a) ©Shutterstock; (b) ©ONB Bildarchiv, Wien.

and boots; after they had rounded the turning post at the far end of the track, the statue would be presented to the reigning emperor in his box. The focus this day was not on God but on the One (in the words of a contemporary poet) "whom god loves"—Constantine. It was his intention that it would remain that way.[6]

Although Eusebius would later depict the foundation of Constantinople as a thoroughly Christian undertaking and the shipping of statuary from around the empire as a deliberate insult to the gods, the opening-day ceremonies (which he does not describe) paint a different picture. Constantine's regime was still largely non-Christian, and the active participation of non-Christians in shaping the city was clearly welcomed. Indeed, one non-Christian, Nicagoras, who prided himself on his role as the high priest of the ancient Mysteries at Eleusis, the immensely important rites that had been celebrated for more than a millennium in the vicinity of Athens, secured the porphyry column that played such a prominent role on May 11. We get a sense of his personality from two graffiti he left in Egypt's Valley of the Kings while on his antiquity hunt: "The Hierophant of the most holy mysteries at Eleusis, the son of Minucianus, an Athenian, examined the burial vaults many years after the divine Plato from Athens, admiring them and gave thanks to the Gods and to the most pious emperor Constantine for giving me the opportunity." Then on the wall opposite, he wrote: "In the seventh consulship of Constantine Augustus and the first consulship of Constantius Caesar. The Hierophant of the Eleusinian (Mysteries), Nicagoras, the son of Minucianus, an Athenian, examined the divine burial vaults, and admired them."[7]

Given that one of Constantine's aims was to unite his subjects at court, it would have been deeply unwise for him to let religion drive a wedge between them. Although the highest offices of state continued to be dominated by his traditional coterie, the court was now the prime instrument of political integration for those who, having (in theory) fulfilled their curial obligations, wished to climb the political ladder. So long as the aspiring official was of good moral character, he was welcome to join the imperial administration. Since the court would now be centered in the east where there were not many senators, Constantine would have to equate ranks in different parts of the service without making a man's birth status a determining factor in his career.

In the new system, the praetorian prefects retained the rank of "most eminent man" (*vir eminentissimus*). Senior equestrian officials of the next rank, such as the *praefectus annonae* at Rome and the *vicarii*, attained the title of "most famous man" (*vir clarissimus*), once reserved for senators.[8] Provincial governors, provincial military commanders, diocesan and provincial fiscal officials and the like retained the rank of "most perfect man" (*vir perfectissimus*).

At about the same time, Constantine regularized the position of imperial "companions," or *comites*. The title of *comes* (the singular form of *comites*) had a very long history before Constantine's time, with all manner of persons claiming or being awarded that title as a mark of status equivalent to the equally loosely applied title of imperial "friend" (*amicus*). At some point after Licinius' defeat, Constantine formalized the order of *comites*, dividing it into three grades depending on level of service. This distinction was ultimately reflected in the transformation of senior titles such as *magister rei privatae* to *comes rei privatae*, which indicated that the actual power structure of the empire was court based.[9]

Restructuring his aristocracy, Constantine created a new sort of senate, a point lost on many later commentators such as a fifth-century ecclesiastical historian who wrote "he founded a great council and assigned to it the same offices and festivals as the old one at Rome." In Constantine's own time, one writer contrasted the old capital (advantageously as he saw it) with the new city on the grounds that Rome "has a very great senate, composed of rich men"; and the *Descent of the Emperor Constantine* states that "he even created a senate of the second rank there [in Constantinople], and called its members the '*clari*' (famous)."[10] The "senate" referred to here appears to be the city council of Byzantium, now enlarged and housed opposite the great porphyry column, whose members were eligible to hold a special praetorship so that they might join the *clarissimi* (most famous).[11] Constantine further rewarded members of the Senate who chose to live in his city with houses and other privileges, in the same way that he rewarded important courtiers who resided in his company. The new body had the potential to develop into something more splendid, which it did, while offering no direct challenge to the ancient body at Rome. The contemporary poet Optatianus, ever adept at promulgating the official line, emphasized that Constantinople was the "second Rome" or "Rome's sister."[12]

The technical aspects of the creation of the new Senate, indicative of Constantine's thinking, are less significant than the social and domestic implications. For instance, the new imperial residence adopted what must already have been the well-established pattern of shipping foodstuffs that had once been sent exclusively to Rome to other imperial seats. Also, the creation of a new power center in the east kept eastern dignitaries closer to home while also perpetuating a concentration of power in the senatorial aristocracy of the west. This represented a continuation of a pattern evident during the years after Diocletian's abdication, when the hostility among his successors precluded movement from one court to another.[13] Now the stress was (in theory) on ability and moral rectitude, qualities that Constantine was willing to reward with generosity. Eusebius wrote:

> One who sought favor of the Emperor could not fail to obtain his request, nor was anyone who hoped for generous treatment disappointed in his expectations. Some received money in abundance, others goods; some acquired posts as prefects, others senatorial rank, others that of consuls; very many were designated governors; some were appointed *comites* of the first order, others of the second, others of the third. Similarly many thousands more shared honors as *clarissimi* or with a wide range of other titles; for in order to promote more persons the Emperor contrived different distinctions.

Those who later expressed contempt for Constantine told a very similar tale. Zosimus, writing in the sixth century, notes the impressive houses that he built for the senators who accompanied him to Constantinople, and others would complain of his excessive generosity to his supporters. The centrality of Constantine's beneficence finds no better witness than in Julian's panegyric for Constantius II, reflecting what was then the official line:

> He [Constantine] showed such goodwill to his subjects that the soldiers remember his gifts and great-hearted generosity so that they worship him like a god.... When he became lord of the whole empire, there was a great lack of money, like a drought, stemming from the greed of the tyrant, and there was an enormous quantity of wealth collected in the corners of the palace, he ordered the doors unlocked, flooding the land with wealth.[14]

A contemporary voice, that of the poet Palladas, notes the connection between the shipments of statuary to the capital, the circulation of coin, and the luxurious surroundings of the imperial elite—was it to join them that he had come to Constantinople? Palladas writes in one poem: "The owners of Olympian houses, becoming Christian, dwell within unharmed, for the pot that makes life-giving *folles* [bronze coins] will not put them in the fire." In another, writing in the persona of goddesses: "We Victories come, laughing maidens, bringing triumphs to the Christ-loving city. The ones who love the city created us, stamping figures appropriate to victories." Here Palladas is probably referring to coinage that began to be issued in the 330s commemorating the inauguration of Constantinople. Both extracts appear to comment on the social world that was emerging in the new capital, one where new mixed with old and where a professional curmudgeon, as Palladas presented himself, could find much upon which to hold forth.[15]

The public statue collections at Constantinople could barely have begun to accommodate the mass of material that would have accumulated if all the cities of the eastern empire (and some few of the west) had shipped just a couple of treasures to the city. The best work went on exhibit. The less famous could perhaps be sought out in private settings, while other pieces went into the melting pot, as Palladas suggests. Somehow Constantine acquired enough gold, as a somewhat bilious critic of his expenditures implies, to mint vast quantities of gold coin, which would become the standard medium of exchange for major transactions over the next several centuries. The economic thinking, however, underlying his decision to do so does not seem to have been profound. What Constantine knew was that if he rewarded his followers lavishly, they would love him. And so, it seems, they did.

Constantine did not found Constantinople as a replacement for Rome but rather as a replacement for Nicomedia. His mother was buried in state outside of Rome; members of his extended family continued to live there, and Rome would be very important for his son Constans when he was emperor. Still, in the fullness of time, Constantinople would efface Rome as the political center of the Roman world and as the preeminent Christian city in the world until its capture by the Ottoman Turks in 1453. It is perhaps fitting that before this happened, a city whose foundation combined so overtly the symbols of the pagan past with the Christian future should be the primary vehicle for the preservation of Greek classical literature and classical civilization as we know it in the modern world.

30.

AN ORDERED SOCIETY

I N HIS *LIFE OF CONSTANTINE*, Eusebius implies that the emperor devoted himself to ending pagan practices and advancing Christianity through legislation heavily influenced by his faith. "Having attached himself to God over all," he claims the emperor would consider from dawn to dusk who should benefit from his largesse and how to be "fair to all and impartial in those benefits." Eusebius considerably overstates the role of Constantine's faith in determining his relationship with his subjects. Although clear about his own beliefs, the emperor remained deeply concerned with the welfare of *all* his subjects and devoted to the notion that he ruled a well-regulated society where people knew their place, Christians included.[1]

One of the salient issues in the legislation of the 330s continued to be preserving the fiscal health of town councils. Typical of his legislation is a rescript to Evagrius in 336 telling him that when decurions or the sons of decurions flee their civic responsibilities for positions in the imperial administration they should be sent home. In 334, Constantine had written to the praetorian prefect Pacatianus expressing deep concern about the situation of public swine collectors at Rome, ordering that they "appear before the Roman people at a meeting," so that the people can make sure they are doing their job. (It's hard to say which is more significant here, the swine threat or the fact that this is the only subject thought worth addressing by a meeting of the Roman people in any of Constantine's legislation.) Later in the same year he told the praetorian prefect Felix that a shortage of architects in Africa meant that fathers who allowed sons older than eighteen to train in that subject would earn immunity from civic *munera* for both themselves and their offspring.

It was also important, especially in light of Constantine's renowned generosity, to make sure that people who did not belong there didn't try to slip into the imperial service. Ablabius was told in 333 that imperial officials' sons who were physically or morally incapable of following their fathers into the imperial service should not do so, and that officers should not accept "the useless son of a veteran" into the service. This last provision looks a bit like a scam—a boy might be placed on a duty roster to keep him off the civic rolls. Similarly, in 331, Constantine told Evagrius that people who sneaked into the imperial service through the operation of illicit patronage should be dismissed.

Constantine continued to be concerned that his earlier ruling granting immunity to clerics encouraged people to flee civic responsibility. In 329, Constantine had told both Ablabius and Bassus that people were not to claim exemption from public services by becoming clerics, and if they were found to have done so they should be sent packing. If one wished to be exempt from all civic *munera*, it was far better to be a ship captain. In 334, Constantine wrote to the ship captains who worked "for the assistance of the city which we endowed with the eternal name on the order of God" saying that they had been granted immunities from civic *munera* and should not have to take up civic offices that could be disadvantageous. They could not be compelled to be tutors, and they were immune from the Augustan marriage laws, which still, Constantine evidently felt, governed the lives of his subjects who did not live as "celibates," for whom immunity from these laws was established years before. The result of these generous grants is that the ship captains "expending almost nothing from their own resources, should engage in maritime trade with their own initiative."[2]

The dividing line between slave and free continued to be an issue that particularly exercised the emperor. Probably in 329 he set out the punishments for a woman who "secretly" married a slave: both were to be executed. If the union had taken place before the edict was issued they would be exiled and their children would remain free but would be stripped of the right to inherit. However, any children of an earlier, legitimate, marriage could inherit following the rules for intestate inheritance—that is, they would be given the first option on any property; if they took it up, the next heirs would be the woman's male relatives. Only if both the woman and her lover died before the passage of the law would their children be allowed to inherit as free persons.

The situation envisaged here appears to be anything but new: inscriptions attest to marriages between women and former slaves. A rescript to a woman named Theodora in AD 290 makes it plain that Diocletian was no more likely to be sympathetic to such a case than was Constantine. Indeed, the fact that the edict was thought to be needed at all might indicate that Constantine was doing no more than repeating a law that was already on the books—or, more likely, one that had just been wiped off the books when Licinius' legislation was declared invalid in 324. A wide-ranging action of 336 prevented upper-class men from having their children by slaves or other "women of ill-repute" declared legitimate. What is particularly interesting in this case is that the definition of "upper-class" might be taken to describe people who were eligible, or potentially eligible, to join the court: senators, *perfectissimi*, or people who had already held significant positions in their cities; mayors (*duumviri*), priests, either local or provincial, of the imperial cult.[3]

Unwilling as Constantine was for the children of slaves to enter the upper class, he certainly did not want the children of free people, constrained by poverty, to be sold into slavery. It appears, though, that an economic crisis (famine in Italy?) forced him to reconsider his earlier views. Two texts of 329 provide the evidence. The first is a rescript to Ablabius in which Constantine states that no one should be forced to sell a child into slavery because of poverty, and orders that the state should provide food and clothing for newborns without delay. Later in the year, however, perhaps because the situation was getting out of hand, he wrote, in an edict "to the Italians" that "according to the rulings of earlier emperors," a person who purchased a child from its parents could hold that child in whatever status he or she pleased, and anyone who later contested the person's right to the child would have to provide a substitute or pay the going rate for a slave. This was a contradiction to his decree of 315, when he had forbidden freeborn children to be sold into slavery, and that of 323, when he had written that parents were not to take away their children's liberty. The problem with these laws had been that if people could not enslave foundlings they were less likely to take them on, and impoverished parents might well find themselves incapable of rearing their child. In 331, he restated the new policy to Ablabius, reminding him that a person who took up a foundling could raise that child in whatever status he wished—either slave or free—and that people who once abandoned a child could not institute a suit for recovery at some later date.[4]

Constantine continued to view the ability of an owner to abuse a slave with an equanimity that might have given birth to his desire to help children avoid this status. In the same year, he (or a member of his staff) reiterated the earlier ruling that masters could not be prosecuted for murder if their slaves happened to die while being beaten. A year later he wrote to the *vicarius* Valerianus on the subject of runaway slaves. If a man deliberately harbored another man's slave, then he should return that property and also pay a fine; if he did it repeatedly, he would have to hand over additional slaves. Only if he could not have known the slave was a runaway would he not have to pay, but to support that claim the slave would have to give evidence under torture. Slaves were unlikely to flee if their master treated them decently. It is arguable that this text validates cruelty.[5]

Harsh as his rulings were toward slaves, Constantine continued to show genuine concern for the least advantaged members of the classes whom he thought the law should protect. In December 328 he told the younger Maximus (now praetorian prefect) that he needed to look into complaints about the behavior of certain governors who knuckled under to local bigwigs. To stop this from happening, the prefect should tell these governors to refer the cases to him "and thus will provision be made for public discipline and counsel be taken for the abused lower classes." Earlier that year he told Aemilianus, also a praetorian prefect, to make sure that the wealthier members of town councils were not allowed to assign *munera* to the weaker members of the community (this should be done by governors to ensure fairness). In 329 he told another official that rescripts granting immunity from *munera* were invalid.[6]

The problem was not always at the local level. In 334 he ordered that secretaries working for governors found to be engaging in corruption would lose the protection of their high status and be liable to judicial torture; and that people who had been compelled to sell things to minor imperial officials could bring actions for recovery. Then in one of the last surviving texts addressed to Felix as praetorian prefect: "If there should be a complaint of our provincials concerning the greed of the collectors of taxes and it should be proved that they have demanded something beyond ancient custom and the limits of our orders, those accused of such a crime should be punished with perpetual exile." At moments like these he seems to have been consciously at war with his own government, which he feared was hopelessly corrupt and biased in favor of the wealthy, and needed ways to be more open. In an edict of 331 he had stated that he would investigate the content of public acclamations to determine whether governors were doing their jobs since those who were loudly praised should be promoted while those who were censured should be fired. Senior officials should make sure that they looked into what was said by the crowds.[7]

Just as he worried about disadvantaged adults, so too Constantine continued to worry about children who were subject to abusive adults. In 330, for instance, he told Valerianus that although the law usually did not assist women just because they were ignorant of it, there was an exception for girls who married when they were underage: if they divorced, they could retain property given them by their former husbands even if the gift had not been registered in the public records office. Two years later, he stated that if a girl had been betrothed for two years and the marriage had not taken place, the engagement could be broken off with no discredit to the girl; and although anyone—such as a girl's parent or tutor—who broke off her engagement to a soldier before two years had elapsed should be deported to one of the islands of exile that were ubiquitous to the legislation of these years, after the two years, the parent or tutor was entitled to break the engagement. On June 17, 334, an official received an order telling him that if an action was brought against "pupils, widows or those worn out by illness and physically incapacitated at the court of Our Leniency," they could not be forced to testify in person and that if those "who are wretched from the injury of fortune should appeal to the court of our Serenity, especially when they fear the power of another, their adversaries will be compelled to appear at our investigation."[8]

Although aware that things could go wrong in families, Constantine hoped that people would treat each other decently. Two rulings of the 330s underscore this. In one, he expresses disgust at the thought that emancipated sons could be abusive toward their fathers. Indeed, if they behaved that way, their independent status should be voided and they should be returned to their father's authority. On the other hand, he was also concerned that parents do the right thing by their children, declaring that men who remarried were responsible for the upkeep of the property that children from a first marriage inherited from their mothers. This property would still be the children's and the father had the same responsibility for the property as he would have if he were appointed to be a legal guardian of another person's offspring.[9] Both rulings are clearly based on considerations of popular morality—they reflect what a reasonable person would think was just.

The senior officials changed over the years, of course, but the general tenor of Constantine's correspondence remains remarkably consistent in its concern for status, for the protection of the worthy weak, for its harshness to slaves and against corruption, and in its dislike for inefficiency. At times emotional, often harsh in his judgments, Constantine retains firm moral principles; none of these can be directly related to his faith but can be seen to descend naturally from his office—hence his frequent citation of the example of earlier emperors, as he understood it. These values are more or less in tune with the value system of the Roman world generally. Whether pagan or Christian, people were concerned with fairness, with the stability of their marriages, and with their standing in the world. As Constantine saw it, it was his job to nurture a moral climate in which his officials could govern. To men he felt he could trust—Bassus, the two Maximi, Felix, Evagrius, and Ablabius, for instance—he was willing to delegate great authority over long periods of time; he even brought Ablabius into his family as guardian of one son and father-in-law to another. He could do this because he was confident that they shared his own values.[10]

31.

CHRISTIANS, PAGANS, AND JEWS

A STATUE OF THE RECENTLY deceased Helena was erected in Constantinople when the city was dedicated on May 11, 330; three years earlier her hometown of Drepanum in what is now Turkey had been renamed in her honor when, in her early sixties, she had undertaken an important mission on behalf of her son.[1] Helena's role, in which Eutropia, Constantine's mother-in-law, briefly joined her, underscored the problem that Constantine faced after the tragedies of 326. Even though there was now no imperial prince of the right age and no empress to carry the dynastic banner, the imperial family needed to show its concern for its subjects across the entire empire. Demonstrations of concern required personal appearances.

Helena was experienced in the ways of the court and she had evidently become a devout Christian. This was important in the aftermath of the Council of Nicaea, and her proposed journey into the heart of the lands that had supported Arius would reaffirm the concern of the imperial house for the unity of the Christian community. In making this appearance, she could not, and would not, be seen as an agent of doctrinal orthodoxy; rather, she would be responding to requests from the bishop of Jerusalem that Constantine create a new Holy Land for all Christians, to complement his new capital for all Romans. Palestine—removed from the areas that still clung to the Classical past, areas like Athens or the Troad which were virtual museums of pagan antiquity—was an appropriate choice: it was home to scriptural narratives, and places of worship constructed there would not threaten the great shrines of the Greco-Roman past or be seen to conflict with them. And this would conform with the message trumpeted by people like Optatianus, some of whose poems celebrated Christ, as well as Constantine's devotion to the Highest God.[2]

One thing that Constantine had tended to avoid was open insult to the temples of the gods. Three on the acropolis of Byzantium were still open on Constantinople's inauguration day—which may have reassured the pagans not only in Constantine's entourage but those who were just visiting the city. In Jerusalem, however, he had given permission to bishop Macarius to destroy a temple of Aphrodite that had evidently been constructed over a cave identified as Christ's tomb.[3] Constantine would do the same thing in regard to another site, Mamre, where three angels allegedly visited Abraham. Here too there was a pagan shrine, and here too the shrine would be destroyed to allow the "true" historical significance of the site to be restored. Constantine's language in this case represents the essence of his policy: "In these circumstances it is right, so it seems to me, that by our provision this site should be kept clear of every defilement and restored to its ancient holy state, so that no other activity goes on there except the performance of the cult appropriate to God the Almighty, our savior and the Lord of the Universe."[4]

The action that Constantine took at Jerusalem provided a model for other initiatives involving individual temples that Eusebius attempted later to describe as reflecting an imperial policy of eradicating pagan worship. Eusebius says the emperor destroyed three temples in the east: one was to Asclepius at Aegeae; two were temples of Aphrodite—one at Aphaca and the other at Heliopolis (roughly thirty miles apart in what is now Lebanon).[5] The temple at Aegeae was famous both as an oracular site and as a home to the first-century AD holy-man Apollonius of Tyana, whose supporters had claimed that he was taken up into heaven after a career of wonder working on earth.[6] The rites at both temples of Aphrodite included sacred prostitution, the grounds on which Constantine had them demolished.

Action against individual temples was nothing new, especially those thought to threaten social cohesion. There is no reason to think that the destruction of any of these shrines was an act inspired solely by Christian doctrine. Eusebius' statement in recounting the destruction of Aphaca, that Constantine "had observed these things himself with imperial forethought," echoes the language of an imperial rescript, and the "personal letter" Eusebius says Constantine sent to Heliopolis, urging the people to give up their "atrocious habits," is likewise pretty clearly a reference to a specific request. Similarly his suppression of an Egyptian priesthood on the grounds of immorality owes more to imperial tradition than to Christian doctrine, and as in the case of Heliopolis, it is his response to a specific complaint. The most serious "pagan scandal" at Constantinople of which record has survived appears to have been a one-time event. Here a philosopher named Sopater, whom Constantine had invited to the capital, tried to harness the winds, using magic, so that the grain fleet would not reach the city. Both using magic and interfering with the grain were treasonable, so it's hardly surprising that he was executed.[7]

Back in Jerusalem, once the temple that stood on top of the tomb of Jesus was destroyed, the spot could be excavated. Eusebius notes: "Thus after its descent into darkness it came forth again to the light and enabled those who came as visitors to see plainly the story of the wonders wrought there, testifying by facts louder than any voice to the resurrection of the Savior."[8] Constantine's letter to Macarius instructing him to build reflects his evolving conception of the way the church and the court could work together, offering all the material support that Macarius needed to realize his vision since "it is right that the world's most miraculous place should be worthily embellished."

The church that was built was no ordinary one, either in size or design, for within its courtyard it contained both the alleged hill of Golgotha and the tomb (see figure 31.1).[9] It is also worth noting that it was the only building begun before Helena's arrival, perhaps because the site was already known and had been the object of controversy. The church itself, the ancestor of the modern Church of the Holy Sepulchre, stood into the eleventh century, when an angry caliph destroyed it. The present church, which stands on the same site, is largely the work of the crusader kingdom in the twelfth century.

When Helena arrived, she was to initiate work on two more churches connected with the life cycle of Christ: one at Bethlehem, to mark his birthplace; the other on the Mount of Olives, to mark the place of his ascension. Work seems to have proceeded more slowly at these sites, for although both were consecrated in Helena's presence, neither may have been completed before Constantine died in 337.[10]

Constantine's new Holy Land gave Christians a physical center for their history, but in a quite particular way. Whereas pagan shrines were eliminated so as not to conflict with Christian history, a Christian history centered in Palestine did not conflict with those of other centers of Mediterranean civilization. They might be thought to conflict with Jewish history, however, especially in the

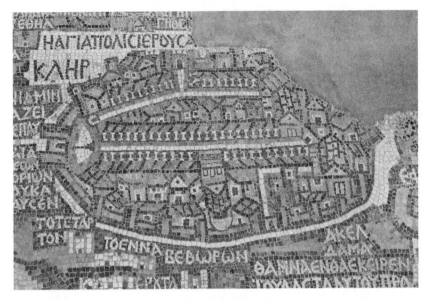

FIGURE 31.1

The original Church of the Holy Sepulcher, built on the orders of Constantine, was destroyed in the Middle Ages. Its descendant was built on the same site in the twelfth century. The form of Constantine's church appears on the image from the spectacular mosaic map of the Holy land discovered at Madaba in Jordan. Source: ©Shutterstock.

appropriation of Mamre (although in a sense Mamre had already been lost as a Jewish site). Since the reign of Hadrian, Jerusalem had been the Roman *colonia* of Aelia Capitolina and as such detached from its purely Jewish history. The new church was no more a challenge than the old shrine, so the status quo was maintained. There is no evidence that Constantine sought to appropriate any other biblical sites for purely Christian purposes.

His attitude to the vast majority of Jewish sites in Palestine is significant in light of the harsh language used of Judaism in the ruling about Easter at the Council of Nicaea. The record of his decisions on issues connected with Judaism suggests that, while hardly friendly, he was also unwilling to end long-established practices. We also have to bear in mind that Judaism had a long and vexed history with Rome well before Constantine took the throne. Jews might see Roman practice as a threat to their religious traditions, while Romans were deeply suspicious of a people who had rebelled three times between the 60s and 130s AD; these rebellions had led to ghastly reprisals by Vespasian and Hadrian, including, most famously, the destruction of the temple at Jerusalem in AD 70.

Also—and this was a major factor in sparking the revolt of the 130s—the Romans were culturally hostile to circumcision, which they viewed as a form of castration and Hadrian had banned.

After the revolt of the 130s, Roman attitudes toward Jewish practice ameliorated somewhat: Antoninus Pius (reigned 138–161) modified Hadrian's ban on circumcision so that fathers could circumcise their sons; and Jews were exempted from performing actions in the course of civic liturgies that violated the tenets of their faith.[11] In Judea, it appears that the Jewish patriarch had the authority to act as a judge in civil actions that pitted Jews against each other, or in matters of religious law.[12] Roman governors could, and did, act in support of the decisions of these courts. Additionally, Jewish priests were granted exemptions from all civic liturgies, and the patriarch was entitled to receive an annual tax from the Jewish communities that had spread throughout the Mediterranean world in the previous several centuries.[13]

The one area where the imperial government imposed restrictions on the practice of Judaism was in the conversion of non-Jews. A full convert to Judaism would have to be circumcised, and this ban remained in place, possibly leading to the growth of the class of *Theosebeis* (god-fearers) within the synagogue. Indeed, it was in the late third century that the jurist Paul wrote: "Roman citizens who allow themselves or their slaves to be circumcised according to the Jewish rite shall, with their property being confiscated, be relegated to an island in perpetuity. The doctors will endure capital punishment. If Jews circumcise slaves bought from another nation, they will either be deported or executed."[14]

Constantine's record in dealing with the Jewish community is mixed, but not out of keeping with standard imperial practice. His first statement, in a rescript to the city council at Cologne, simply states that Jews who were previously exempt from civic *munera* can now be assigned them. He adds: "So that something may be left to them of the solace of the previous rule, we extend to two or three persons the privilege of not being summoned by any nomination," indicating that the Jews in question were probably priestly officials. In so doing he appears to be treating these men as teachers and according them the same sort of exemptions that were afforded other teachers. In 330 he is concerned with a different group—specifically, the leaders of the Jewish community in Palestine (whose noses might be thought to be somewhat out of joint after Helena's visit)—writing to Ablabius that its most important leaders should have immunity from personal and public *munera*, and that those who were, at the time of his writing, decurions, should not be assigned as escorts since they should not be forced to go on journeys. Those who were not already decurions should not be forced to take up that status. A year later he wrote that a number of leaders in synagogues should receive exemption from *munera corporalia* (services requiring physical labor). The dates of these two texts are significant in light of a document he sent to Evagrius in 329 stating that "the Jews, their elders and their patriarchs" should know that if, after the publication of this law, they should attack a person who had "fled their feral sect and turned to the worship of God" they will be burned at the stake and that if a person "should join their nefarious sect from the public and join in their associations at large, he will sustain the just penalty along with them."[15]

The language of Evagrius' text resembles that in the discussion of Easter at the Council of Nicaea, but it is also similar to the language Constantine used in writing to other Christians—including the Donatists and Arius (as well as others whose behavior he disliked, such as the unfortunate nurses of girls involved in abductions). Six years later he wrote to Felix that if a Jew purchased and circumcised a Christian slave, the slave would be freed. At the same time "if any Jew should unlock for himself the door of eternal life and deliver himself to the worshippers and choose to be a Christian," none of his fellow Jews are to molest him in any way, and if they do, they may be punished. It is Constantine's hope that "on account of the love of the divine providence we trust that such a person will be safe in the whole Roman world and that due reverence for ourselves will be maintained."[16] There is little that can be attributed to Constantine's Christianity, certainly nothing that is not equally attributable to his being a Roman magistrate. The roots of modern anti-Semitism and the holocaust do not, despite what some might think, rest here with Constantine; if one insists on seeking (no matter how improbable that search is) for the sources of modern evil in the ancient world, that search might more easily take one to Hadrian or Vespasian—emperors who slaughtered the Jewish population of Palestine in response to revolts brought about through Roman misgovernment—than to Constantine. In either case, it is troubling to think that every bad idea, careless statement, outburst of passion, or simple rhetorical excess of 2,000 years ago shapes behavior in the modern world. To take such a line is to seek to exculpate modern thinkers and modern politicians for grotesque deeds of their own, and that is fundamentally an absurd notion. It would not be until the end of the fourth century that the imperial government would surrender to the bigotry of some bishops (Ambrose of Milan takes pride of place in this company) in turning a blind eye to persecution of Jewish communities by Christians. At that time no one appealed to the example of Constantine, and for the very good reason that there was nothing there to which they might appeal.

In the case of the Jews, as with the pagans, Constantine didn't appear inclined to take coercive action unless it was in response to a specific complaint. He learned from Diocletian the lesson that state-generated acts of persecution were pointless. His actions in Palestine revealed instead his growing tendency to make life easier for Christians, but to do so within the framework of existing imperial practice. There may be no better example of the extension of this policy to other contexts than in the way he handled an appeal made by a place called Orcistus in central Turkey. At some point in the past, Orcistus had been a city; more recently it had been demoted to the rank of village and attached to the city of Nacolea. The Orcistians appealed to Constantine, through Ablabius, to restore its civic status, pointing to the many fine features of their city: it was at a crossroads, it had a forum, it had terrific bathing facilities drawing on fresh-water springs, it had watermills and a public post station. Constantine agreed that Orcistus should become a city once more, adding that "in addition to all these things it is a sort of blessing that all who live there say that they are followers of the most sacred religion." These last few words may be Ablabius' embellishment, but the comment sums up the essential point: people who behave decently can expect good things no matter who they are, but it would be very much appreciated if they would embrace the emperor's "most sacred religion."[17]

An important counterpoint to the Orcistus dossier is found in a request from the town of Hispellum in Italy that its priest no longer have to travel to Volsinii every year to celebrate a festival in honor of the emperor. If their wish was granted, the city said, they would build a new temple "of magnificent workmanship" in honor of Constantine's family; they pointed out that Hispellum was conveniently located on a major road (the Flaminian Way)—implying a distinction from Volsinii (modern Bolsena), which was reachable only via steep and nearly impassable mountains. In those days this was not an entirely unfair statement for people coming from Hispellum's direction.

Constantine granted the request, renaming the city in honor of his youngest son, Constans (who was designated to rule the region in the future). He was pleased that they and the people of Volsinii should continue to celebrate gladiatorial games. He offered but one restriction: "that no temple dedicated in our name shall be defiled by the deceptions of any contagious and unreasonable religious belief." That's to say that there was to be no animal sacrifice. He also expressed pleasure that his decisions would allow old custom to stay intact while the people of Hispellum could rejoice in having gained something new, and in enhancing the empire with a splendid new building and a festival. Although it is likely that their request got no closer to Constantine than the office of the praetorian prefect, Papius Pacatianus, the author of this response, sought to represent the emperor's thoughts in a way that the he felt was reasonable.[18]

Constantine's point in dealing with cities was that Christianity was entirely compatible with imperial government. What was *not* compatible was doctrinal strife among Christians. Sometimes his intervention against specific Christian bishops fit the pattern of his interventions against individual pagan temples, suggesting that in his view, common decency trumped claims to religious affinity.

Christians who were willing to abide by the settlement reached at Nicaea and keep the peace within the community had little to fear from him and some reason to expect that good things would come their way. So it was that a mere two years after Nicaea, both Arius and Eusebius of Nicomedia were reconciled to Constantine (people later claimed that Eusebius wormed his way back into power through the favor of the emperor's half-sister Constantia). It was certainly true that while Constantine over time restricted the scope of ordinary clerics, he moved toward increasing the influence of bishops (in keeping with his general tendency to strengthen the hands of those closest to himself). The strongest statement of his faith in the good character of bishops is to be found in a long document that he dispatched to Ablabius in 333, ordering that the opinions of bishops should be binding—there could be no appeal against them—and that the prefect should enforce those decisions. An individual could appeal to a bishop's court at any time during a hearing in a secular court, since the "authority of sacred religion" can investigate cases more fully, and statements of bishops must be accepted as true.[19]

Given the enormous potential power hereby delivered to bishops, it is little wonder that Constantine took very harsh action against those who didn't live up to his expectations. This may be one reason three powerful bishops who had attended the Council of Nicaea on the anti-Arian side (one in a junior role) soon found themselves in deep trouble with their emperor. These were Eustathius of Antioch, Marcellus of Ancyra, and Athanasius of Alexandria.

Eustathius' ally, Athanasius, claimed that Eustathius, falsely accused of rudeness to Helena while she was on her way to Palestine, was traduced by "those around Eusebius (of Nicomedia)." Athanasius appears to have been wrong on both counts. It is entirely probable that Eustathius was exiled before Eusebius returned to power, and quite possibly before Helena arrived in Palestine, and that the reason for his removal was personal misconduct.[20] A church council summoned to investigate Eustathius on charges of sexual immorality convicted him of having fathered a child out of wedlock.[21]

Eusebius of Nicomedia, as Athanasius' complaints make plain, and even Arius himself were doing rather better. The two men appeared at an ecclesiastical council at Nicomedia where Eusebius admitted his faults and Arius recanted his heresy. Given that Constantine had earlier written to Arius telling him that he had been subverted by the Devil and that his heresy had been predicted ages before by the Erythraean Sibyl, this signals either a remarkable change of heart or an indication that even Constantine's harshest rhetoric masked an ability to compromise—or both.[22]

The different issues confronting Athanasius and Marcellus during the next decade culminated in two very different outcomes: Marcellus was removed for entirely theological reasons, while Athanasius caused his own removal by his violent conduct. In Marcellus' case the eliminating agent was an ecclesiastical council held in conjunction with the celebration of the thirtieth anniversary of Constantine's accession. Marcellus was accused of teaching two things that Constantine did not believe—that Christ's existence began with Mary and that the world would end. In his speech before Nicaea, Constantine had made it abundantly clear that Christ's existence was eternal, as was his kingdom (which the emperor by now seemed to associate rather closely with his own, making Marcellus' statement potentially treasonable). Marcellus actually did hold both these beliefs and was sent to live in Illyricum.[23]

The case of Athanasius, a far more powerful bishop, was more complex, though here too unwillingness to think as the emperor thought seems to have been at the heart of the problem. The trouble began on the very first day of

Athanasius' tenure as bishop. It is quite likely that he was below the custom-ary age for a bishop, and it certainly seems to have been the case that local custom did not condone the consecration of a bishop behind the locked doors of a church (Athanasius was consecrated in this way). Athanasius' consecra-tion, at which only seven bishops were present, preempted a council, including fifty-four bishops from other parts of Egypt, evidently organized with the aim of selecting a candidate who might unite the church.[24]

Perceiving the need to strengthen his position, Athanasius took himself off to the desert, where increasing numbers of Christians were taking up residence as monks in more or less organized groups.[25] His desire to draw these groups into his entourage was spurred by his dislike for the Meletian faction, which set him at odds with the decrees of Nicaea. In 330, Athanasius withdrew from Alexandria, evidently to avoid assisting some Meletians with their tax obli-gations. He returned to the city and then set out on a journey through the Mareotis, a region of the Nile delta, where one of his colleagues assaulted a priest named Ischyras on the grounds that he was a heretic, smashing a chalice and overturning an altar.[26]

At the heart of it all was the fact that Athanasius refused to compromise with his rivals, and this Constantine took very seriously, even after those rivals disgraced themselves on more than one occasion by bringing patently false charges against him: in 334, for instance, Athanasius proved, before the council that had assembled to try him, that a man he was accused of having murdered was alive.[27] But by 335 the emperor's patience was finally at an end, and after a church council condemned Athanasius, he exiled the bishop to Gaul. Although many of the charges against Athanasius may have been questionable, there can be no doubt that he was violent toward his enemies.[28] His was the sort of behav-ior that Constantine was trying to end.

Unlike many of his rivals, chief among them Eusebius of Nicomedia, Athanasius seems to have missed the point, in that he was less in keeping with the spirit of Nicaea than were Arius and his former supporters who had later acknowledged their errors.[29] The broader significance of the careers of Eustathius, Marcellus, and Athanasius is that their treatment by Constantine mirrors his treatment of pagans who displeased him. His main concern was to promote religious peace and coexistence, and he would penalize any who caused strife.

32.

NEIGHBORS

THE VICTORY OVER LICINIUS at Chrysopolis in 324 did not bring peace on earth. Although details are scanty since they mostly come from changes in the list of victory titles that Constantine accumulated, we know that there was major trouble on both the Rhine and the Danube frontiers in 328–329. At this point Constantine built a massive stone bridge at Oescus (northwest of modern Pleven in Bulgaria) on the Danube, and he himself took the field along that river in 332, 334, and 336. On the first of these occasions he fought the Goths, who then dominated the eastern end of the region, and on the second he concentrated his attention on the Sarmatian peoples in the more westerly parts of the Danube basin. The campaign in 336 led to the proclamation of Constantine as Dacicus Maximus, a title deriving from the name of a people that no longer existed, the Dacians, and commemorated instead some territorial conquest north of the Danube in the area that Aurelian had abandoned in 271.[1]

Although he was chary about imposing his personal religious preferences on his domestic subjects, Constantine was far less reticent in dealing with his neighbors. So it was that when, in 336, the Goths elected to make peace, he agreed to the traditional terms—that the Goths send men to serve in the Roman army, and that the Romans would dispatch gifts to Gothic chieftains who demonstrated loyalty to the empire. Constantine would also take the opportunity to promote Christianity in their lands. To assist him in this he appointed a man named Ulfilas as bishop to their people. The descendant of people taken captive during the raids along the Black Sea coast of Turkey in the 250s and 260s, Ulfilas created a written form of the Gothic language into which he could translate scripture. In so doing, he planted in the minds of some Goths the notion that they (or their neighbors) might participate in Roman culture through religion rather than by the more traditional means through service in the Roman army. It is perhaps testimony to his success that Goths who did not themselves convert recognized in Christianity a threat to their traditional existence. And, although Ulfilas was driven into exile after Constantine's death and ended his life ministering to a Gothic community within the empire, he left behind other Christians in the Gothic homeland.[2]

In the kingdoms of Armenia, Aksum (Ethiopia), and Iberia (roughly the eastern zone of the modern Republic of Georgia), Christian missionaries achieved more significant successes.[3] Of these perhaps the most spectacular was that of the king of Aksum. Two boys, so the story goes, once slaves of a philosopher named Meropius, were the prime movers. One of them, Frumentarius, became the king's chief adviser and gave Christian merchants particular trading privileges, which hastened the process of converting the young ruler. In time Frumentarius made contact with Athanasius and was ordained, while his companion returned to Roman territory where he too was ordained, becoming a priest at Tyre.[4]

The conversion of Armenia took place even before 324, when its king, Tiridates III, led the way by converting under the influence of the Cappadocian bishop Gregory the Illuminator in 313 or 314.[5] Iberia, which stretched along the northern border of both the Roman and Persian empires, converted in the 330s, with the king leading the way under the influence of a rather mysterious woman whose faith enabled her to conduct miraculous cures.[6] It was this woman's activities that brought the church to the attention of the king, who converted, it was related, when he was rescued from a darkness that enveloped him in a forest while hunting. By the mid-330s Constantine was showing interest in the prospect of dealing a knockout blow to the Persian Empire, and appears to have been very pleased by these developments, sending aid for the construction of churches. For the king of Iberia, whose realm contained hitherto many Zoroastrians, the new faith was a powerful symbol of a new political affiliation. It may be that in this case religion proved a rather more successful vehicle for diplomacy than among the Goths, since the more organized society of the Iberians could be converted from the top down once the king himself had converted.

Constantine's plans for Persia were aggressively pursued from the moment of his victory over Licinius. Optatianus suggests in some poems of the 320s that the Persians would soon be delighting in the rule of the western emperor; and it is quite likely that it was Constantine himself who sent a carefully crafted letter to Sapor II (a descendant of the victor over Valerian), who in 309 had acceded to the Persian throne while still in his mother's womb.

Written at about the same time as his oration to the bishops, the letter combines contemporary propaganda with little touches aimed at a Zoroastrian audience. Knowing that Zoroastrians saw themselves as representing the forces of truth against darkness, Constantine began by proclaiming that, led by the light of truth, he had recognized the divine faith. His God was alone responsible for his present state of magnificence, having led him over land and sea to defeat tyrants, and bringing salvation to all people. "Him," he wrote, "I call upon on bended knee, shunning all abominable blood and foul hateful odors, refusing all earthly splendor." He is the God of the Universe who takes pleasure in "works of kindliness and gentleness, befriending the meek, hating the violent, loving faithfulness, punishing unfaithfulness." He is also the God who "values highly the righteous empire," strengthening it and protecting the imperial peace of mind.[7]

Having established what a friend he had in his God, Constantine moved on to the offensive. Those who, "seduced by insane errors," attempted to deny the righteousness of his God had now been overwhelmingly punished—among them "that one, who was driven from these parts by divine wrath ... and was left in yours, where he caused the victory on your side to be very famous because of the shame he suffered." Hearing this variant, a Persian familiar with the usual imperial complaint about Valerian could not fail to note that it deprived Sapor of credit for the victory and attributed it all to Constantine's God. He might also have noted how the memory of the year 260 still lived on in the Roman consciousness: the capture of Valerian and his ignominious treatment by the Persians was something that could never be forgotten—and if it could never be forgotten, could it ever be fully avenged? Moreover, Constantine pointed out, in his own day the punishment of those who persecuted his God was notorious, so Sapor would be well advised to make sure Christians were well treated in his lands. That would make the Lord of the Universe ever so happy.[8]

Constantine's kindly thoughts carry a threat on two levels. One plainly is that the Christian God is a very fine god of battles, as recently proven by his own experience, and if the Persians don't recognize this they are going to be in deep

(a) (b)

(c) (d)

(e)

FIGURE 32.1
Constantine's vision for the future. The Caesars of 335 AD: Constantine II (a), Constantius II (b),
Constans (c), Dalmatius (d), and Hannibalianus (e). Source: Courtesy of the American Numismatic
Society.

trouble. The second, more mundane, point is that because Christians have, at times, been subject to persecution by the Zoroastrian authorities, the emperor is now alert to the welfare of a particular class of Persian subject in a way no Roman emperor had ever been before. Constantine's concern for Christians beyond the empire and his conviction that he has the very best God on his side are both consonant with his views expressed elsewhere, and it was most likely only pressing need on other fronts that kept him from taking action earlier.

War with Persia was important for the succession plans that Constantine had come to envision in 335. His praetorian prefects' long careers show him rewarding loyalty with loyalty. His half-brother, Dalmatius, who had shown loyalty to Constantine as well as considerable ability, had spent most of the reign in Toulouse before being promoted to the consulship in 332, then to a senior command on the eastern frontier. In 334 he had crushed a revolt on coastal Cilicia, then on Cyprus. In 335 Constantine named Dalmatius' two sons, Flavius Julius Dalmatius and Flavius Julius Hannibalianus, as Caesars on a par with his own sons by Fausta (see figure 32.1). After that, the younger Dalmatius appears to have been based in the Balkans while Hannibalianus was married to Constantina, Constantine's older daughter with whom he appears to have resided in Constantinople.

The appointment by Constantine of his nephew/son-in-law to the title King of Kings and king of the Pontic Peoples was a virtual declaration of war (certainly, it would have been read as a declaration of intent), for the title "King of Kings" was the title of the king of Persia. The story circulating that Constantine had been misled by a lying merchant who told him that treasures entrusted to him for the emperor by an Indian king had been stolen by Sapor may have been invented to conceal the degree of advance planning. Be that as it may, the war that would now ensue would ultimately go nowhere from the Roman perspective and would result in years of bloody conflict, largely on Roman territory.[9]

33.

END TIMES

A S THE YEAR 337 opened, Constantine's preparations were nearly complete. He was at Constantinople, along with his friend and loyal henchman
Evagrius, and would be there until the early spring. Gaius Annius Tiberianus,
who had been climbing the administrative ranks for some time—we first meet
him as an official in Africa during the mid-320s—was praetorian prefect in
Gaul; also living in Gaul was Constantine, Constantine and Fausta's eldest
son, now in his early twenties. In Africa a man called Gregorius now held the
prefecture long occupied by Felix, Maximus was in Illyricum with Dalmatius,
and Ablabius accompanied Constantius at Antioch.[1] The Christian community
in Persia, especially those living in present-day Iraq, appears to have heard a
rumor that the Roman emperor was coming. Sapor was mustering his forces.

Constantine had made sure that, should he not survive, the plan of succession
was clearly laid out. There would again be four emperors, each with an experienced adviser as his prefect to ensure an orderly transfer of power. The man
with whom he now chose to spend his time was Evagrius, and this attention
may have lent him—by far the most senior of the prefects—a certain authority
over the others. In Constantinople, the mausoleum built for Constantine himself was finished, though at this point, the emperor had no inkling how very
soon he would be resting within it.

Sometime around Easter (April 3, in that year), a Persian embassy had
appeared in Constantinople, which the emperor had promptly dismissed. The
moment for diplomacy was long past.

Shortly after leaving the city Constantine fell seriously ill. Alarmed, his
entourage persuaded him to make a detour to the baths of Pythia Therma, near
Helenopolis. His condition worsened. He proceeded to Helenopolis where he

worshipped at the shrine of the martyr Lucian, to whom his mother had been devoted, and from there to the environs of Nicomedia. He was now fading fast, and, according to Eusebius, it was at this point that he summoned an assembly of bishops, telling them that although he had wished to be baptized in the waters of the Jordan like Christ himself, that was no longer possible:

> God who knows what is good for us judges us worthy of these things here and now. So let there be no delay. If the Lord of life and death should wish us to live again here, even so it is once and for all decided that I am hereafter numbered among the people of God, and that I meet and join in the prayers with them all together. I shall now set for myself rules of life which befit God.[2]

Constantine spent the last six days of his life at Achyron, an imperial estate a little way from Nicomedia. As he felt death approaching, Eusebius of Nicomedia baptized him. No members of his immediate family were present, but he was surrounded by the vast extended family with which he had spent so much of his life, the imperial court. It is hard to imagine that Evagrius was not in the room when he died; and the presence of both the Christian bishop and the pagan prefect at his deathbed—if they were both there—expressed Constantine's dual aim during the last several decades of his life: namely, to worship the god who brought him victory and to fulfill his destiny as emperor in a way to equal, even exceed, the achievements of those who had gone before him.

Around noon, on May 22, 337, Constantine breathed his last.

EPILOGUE

I N WRITING OF THE deaths of Crispus and Fausta, the British historian Edward Gibbon observed that certainty about what had happened increased with the passage of time. That might be said of virtually everything connected with Constantine as he moved from the realm of mortality to that of memory. Of all Roman emperors he has kept the longest and most persistent presence in the consciousness of later generations; though, except for the Nicene Creed, very little of what he is remembered for has much to do with what he set out to do, while his authority has at times been invoked to support the most improbable assertions.

Given the complexity of Constantine's legacy, it is no wonder that confusion surrounds even the most basic detail connected with his passing: the location of his body. According to Eusebius, he was laid to rest in a building surrounded by twelve containers that would ideally hold relics of the twelve apostles, which in practice proved hard to locate: only the bones of Saints Timothy and Luke, neither an actual member of the original group, seem to have been procured before his death. It appears to have been Constantine's intent to lie in the company of the apostles in a building constructed in the style of a standard imperial tomb—uniting for all time his Christian and imperial aspects. His body was placed in a porphyry sarcophagus. About twenty years later, a bishop of Constantinople moved the sarcophagus to a church; however, on the orders of an infuriated Constantius, it was removed to be placed, probably, in the Church of the Twelve Apostles, which Constantius was even then completing (it appears that the containers for the apostles' relics were shifted to this church as well). In 370, probably, the sarcophagus was moved again, this time back to the east end of the mausoleum facing the entrance, where it remained for the better part of the next millennium if not longer, until the Turkish sack of Constantinople, which finally ended the direct line of succession from Augustus Caesar and

Constantine in 1453. Certainly the mausoleum was leveled at that point, as was the Church of the Twelve Apostles. The porphyry sarcophagus has not been seen since the sack of the city. A late tradition held that the bodies of Helena and Fausta were placed in the sarcophagus. Were husband and wife reunited in death? It is not impossible that Constantine would have wished it to be so.[1]

Even as Constantine's body was first laid to rest, the process of reconstructing his legacy was beginning. The first stage is reflected in what is probably the most egregious of Eusebius' assertions—that Constantine intended to leave the empire to his three sons. Those three sons did end up running the empire, at least in name, but that came about because in September 337 there was a coup d'état in which Dalmatius, Hannibalianus, and Julius Constantius, the last surviving son of Constantius I, were either executed through rigged judicial processes—in the case of Dalmatius, charged with poisoning Constantine—or murdered on the orders of Constantius II. We cannot now know how the events were orchestrated or who was the mastermind, since Constantine II and Constantius II, aged twenty-one and twenty, respectively, are unlikely to have been the prime movers (Constantine II seems to have been told what was happening after the event and to have subsequently had rather frosty relations with his brother). Just as significant, however, as the elimination of the imperial kin was the radical shift in the upper echelons of the eastern administration. By the end of 337, Evagrius and Maximus appear to have retired (possibly "were retired" would be more appropriate), and Ablabius was cashiered, then murdered by agents of Constantius at the Bithynian farm where he lived.[2]

The delay of some six months in carrying out these changes may be attributed to Constantine's most distressing legacy to his heirs—the war with Persia. Sapor attacked the empire shortly after Constantine died and the war would continue, with no clear advantage to either side until 363, when Constantine's nephew, Julian the Apostate, invaded Iraq. Julian botched his campaign and died in battle well inside Persian territory; his successor avoided the fate of Valerian only by signing a treaty with Sapor that gave up the provinces Diocletian had gained and surrendered the powerful border fortress city of Nisibis (modern Nusaybin in eastern Turkey) in addition.

The picture of Constantine that emerged in the reign of Constantius, who spent much of his time fighting Sapor, showed a much less complex figure than the one who had died in 337, one far less tolerant. That Constantine was, of course, the subject of *The Life of Constantine* by Eusebius of Caesarea, a figure whose influence would be inescapable for later generations of church historians. The mid-fourth century saw the beginnings of the actively hostile tradition associated with Julian the Apostate and his associates, painting a picture of a man given to luxury who disparaged the efforts of his most noble predecessors. This Constantine was the bastard child of the low-born Helena. He seized the throne as a usurper and only became a Christian to assuage the guilt he felt for having murdered Fausta and Crispus—the final acts in a career spent slaying his own family. He destroyed tradition, bankrupted the state, and started the war with Persia because he was a greedy fool.[3] It did not help that the Persian war really was a failure.

The hostile versions of Constantine's life have the advantage of some grounding in the political discourse of the day. Around AD 500 these versions were joined by an astonishing new story, which would give rise to one of the most important forgeries in European history, "The Donation of Constantine."

This addition to the canon concerned Constantine's conversion and his relationship with Sylvester, who succeeded Miltiades as bishop of Rome in 314. According to this story, allegedly written by a Greek at Rome named Eusebius, Constantine was much preoccupied with persecuting the Christians of Rome when he was smitten with leprosy. The emperor summoned whoever he could think of who might know of a cure and was told—by the priests of Jupiter on the Capitoline in some versions, by Magi and Jews in others—that he could be cured only if he bathed in the blood of freshly slaughtered infants. On his way to do just that, Constantine felt a surge of remorse for what he was about to do and ordered the children to be returned to their parents.

Saints Peter and Paul then appeared to him in a vision, telling him that if he summoned the bishop Sylvester he could be cured. Sylvester, who was in hiding with his clergy on Mt. Soracte (about twenty miles from Rome), duly appeared before the emperor who asked whether Peter and Paul were his gods. They were the servants of his God, Sylvester replied, and informed Constantine that he should prepare for baptism. Constantine did as he was told, and emerging some time later (on an Easter Sunday) from the baths of the Lateran palace, baptism accomplished, he found that he had indeed been cured. Thereafter he became a devout Christian, promoting the faith with vigor.[4]

This new account of Constantine's conversion spread with disturbing rapidity—disturbing, at least, to anyone thinking that people should be able to recognize nonsense when they hear it. It was known in Greek and Syriac versions by the mid-fifth century and rapidly became the most popular conversion story. By the ninth century it had taken on fresh significance as the inspiration for an "official document" that conferred great authority on the pope. "The Constitution of Constantine" as we now have it appears to have been produced in France, possibly in the Abbey of St. Denis near Paris or that at Corbie in the vicinity of Amiens, during the early ninth century.[5] The text is in the form of an edict of Constantine, reciting his experiences with Sylvester and then announcing that since Sylvester was the "vicar of the Son of God on earth," he and all popes after him (the bishop of Rome began to be routinely called "the pope" in the course of the fifth century) should have "primacy over the four distinguished sees of Antioch, Alexandria, Constantinople, and Jerusalem as well as over all churches of God" throughout the world since he is the leader of all priests and generally in charge of everything to do with the stability of the Christian faith.[6]

The "Constitution" was included in the *Decretum Gratiani*, a collection of texts for the study of canon law produced in the twelfth century by Gratian, an authority on the subject hailing from the great legal center of Bologna.

Despite its seemingly helpful content "The Donation" proved to be something of a double-edged sword, tending to remain in the background of disputes between the papacy and representatives of royal or imperial authority. It was all well and good for the pope to be given authority over Western Europe, but unfortunately it was an emperor who granted that authority, and what one emperor could give surely his descendant as the Holy Roman Emperor could take away. The Holy Roman Emperor Karl IV (1316–1378), for instance, appears to have carried the notion that he was Constantine's heir to the point of equipping himself as a "new" Constantine. This view of an emperor's role was not dissimilar to one that had evolved much farther east in the emergent Kievan state of Russia, where contact with Constantinople had introduced its rulers to images of Constantine and Helena, who now came to prefigure important figures in the history of the royal house.

Back in the west, the problem of imperial control meant suggestions that the donation was a fraud were not squelched as thoroughly as they might have been by papal authorities, and Pope Eugenius, not otherwise a supporter, seems not to have minded the Italian humanist Lorenzo Valla's demolition of the document's authenticity in 1440.[7]

By the mid-sixteenth century, with the rediscovery of antiquity (a popular scholarly pursuit) well under way, there was more than enough ancient information about Constantine to satisfy the curious. At this time the quaint image deployed on Roman mosaics of the twelfth and thirteenth centuries, in which Constantine kneels before Sylvester handing him the papal crown or serves him as a scout gave way to images of the visionary emperor channeling the power of God in battle—the ideal anti-Reformation emperor for the wars of religion. In Rome, for instance, Pope Leo X, in the midst of his conflict with Martin Luther, commissioned Raphael to produce frescoes combining the Eusebian Constantine with the medieval one, showing the vision of the cross, the battle of the Milvian Bridge, Constantine's baptism, and the Donation. A spectacular "Constantine cabinet" now in the Kunsthistorisches Museum at Vienna, dating to the 1660s, contains twelve images of the ruler based on different paintings. Depictions of the donation and Constantine's baptism by Sylvester are included, while others stress his role as a warrior and Eusebius' story of the cross in the sky.[8]

With the coming of the Enlightenment came new Constantines. Gibbon seems frankly puzzled by him and largely accepted Zosimus' picture of a great man who went bad after the events of 326, while one of the most influential works of the nineteenth century, Jacob Burckhardt's *The Age of Constantine the Great*, sees his spiritual life as of nugatory importance. In Burckhardt's formulation,

> attempts have often been made to penetrate into the religious consciousness of Constantine and to reconstruct a hypothetical picture of changes in his religious conviction. Such efforts are futile. In a genius driven without surcease by ambition and love for power there can be no question of Christianity and paganism, of conscious religiosity or irreligiosity; such a man is essentially unreligious, even if he pictures himself standing in the midst of a churchly community.[9]

In the twentieth century, however, in the popular imagination Constantine has tended to remain in the public eye precisely *because* of his Christianity, and to be presented in the context of a specific author's understanding of the history of the Church. John Carroll's study of the history of anti-Semitism in the Church, for example, sees it beginning with Constantine, in obvious contradiction to the evidence of Constantine's own actions. On an even grander scale (amplified in the movie version) is the notion that Constantine hijacked Christianity, burying the human nature of Christ and the feminine side of the faith for political reasons. The high priest of this Constantine is Dan Brown, who, in a memorable passage of his *Da Vinci Code*, has his villain explain:

> In Constantine's day, Rome's official religion was sun worship—the cult of Sol Invictus, or the Invincible Sun—and Constantine was its head priest. Unfortunately for him, a growing religious turmoil was gripping Rome. Three centuries after the crucifixion of Jesus Christ, Christ's followers had multiplied exponentially. Christians and pagans began warring, and the conflict grew to such proportions that it threatened to rend Rome in two. In 325 AD, he decided to unify Rome under a single religion. Christianity.... Historians still marvel at the brilliance with which Constantine converted the sun-worshipping pagans to Christianity. By fusing pagan symbols, dates, and rituals into the growing Christian tradition, he created a kind of hybrid religion that was acceptable to both parties.[10]

As with every modern version of Constantine, the urge to draw reductive conclusions is a strong one, and the religious question in a world where religious affiliation is still for so many a crucial aspect of their identity makes this both a reasonable and perhaps inevitable choice. Constantine may have been the most influential Christian after Paul of Tarsus, but a teleological view does scant justice to the complexity of the role that he played and to the complexity of the man himself.

The Constantine who emerges in the preceding pages shares characteristics with many of the Constantines who have gone before, with Burkhardt's Constantine, certainly, and even with the Constantine imagined in "The Donation of Constantine", for the author of the "Donation" understood religious conviction. Constantine was bold, willing to take great risk—and risks whose potential costs or benefits he understood full well.

To seize the throne was one of those great risks, but he knew that the consequence of inaction was to be death. And he understood that the acclamations of the army at York were inadequate to guarantee success as he raced against time to secure Trier and the Alpine passes ahead of Severus. The invasion of Italy, he knew, was a task at which many had failed. He approached the adventure with trepidation, drafting a plan of campaign that would take advantage of a foe's predictable reactions, while drawing on all his mental and physical resources in a mighty attempt to achieve the seemingly impossible. Against Licinius he again took great risks, but when Licinius took advantage of Constantine's tendency to recklessness, he knew to cut his losses and withdraw. Next time, he attacked in overwhelming force.

The qualities that Constantine esteemed were loyalty, efficiency, and hard work. He valued what he understood to be justice, he feared the power of the rich to oppress the weak, and he saw it as his role to provide his subjects with an ordered society. He was not a man to venture beyond the conventional morality of his time—he did not question the right of the rich to be rich, or suggest that the slave should be free, or that there might be anything wrong with the coercive power of the state. He shared these traits with those closest to him. He knew how to deal with people who were very different from himself, be they German generals or the descendants of Italian aristocrats with genealogies far longer than his own. The value of loyalty he may have learned from his father, who had not tossed him out of the palace in search of his own advancement; and it was a quality he shared with his mother Helena, who seems to have been an active presence during all the years of his ascent and into the years of victory.

Constantine was a man of great passion. His relationship with Helena was a potent force that informed his life, as was his early relationship with Minervina, whose son he cherished. He loved Fausta, whose well-being he protected in their early years together and from whom he seems to have been well nigh inseparable in their last decade as a couple. Passionate too was his relationship with the God he discovered as he searched for answers before the invasion of Italy. This God loved him, he firmly believed, and looked after him, and Constantine thanked and worshipped him for the guidance that he gave. But he also believed that to honor this God was not to dishonor other gods, or the traditions of the imperial office that he had imbibed in his youth and that guided him into old age.

Passion was also Constantine's undoing. We will never know why he ordered Crispus' death, or why he and Fausta parted ways—we can't even be sure that he didn't bear the responsibility for her death. We may sense his powerful, overwhelming temper. We may also sense his great remorse. There would not be another empress, and if the behavior of his son Constantius, a man of noted chastity, was modeled on his own, there was no bevy of concubines to fill the palace in his later years. He seems to have spent that time alone, perhaps in atonement for what he had done.

Even as he gave vent to his passions, he could understand that he was wrong to do so. In his youth he had seen another emperor act like this, an emperor with whom he would feel himself contending all his life. Diocletian too had been a man of great passion and energy, but when he ordered the great persecution he had acted like a sick fool. But he had not always been so. It was Diocletian's empire that influenced Constantine's conception of his own in later years. And he drew strength from the wisdom of his subjects even as he would devise ever more elaborate rituals to keep them at arm's length. For it was only from an Olympian height that the emperor could see all and reach out like a god to right the wrongs that he perceived.

Constantine changed the world not because he sought to, but because in seeking the power that was once Diocletian's he understood the limits of that power. And the impact of this most influential figure in the history of Christianity was profound precisely because he did not try to force his religious beliefs on others. He would welcome fellow worshippers with open arms, help others see things his way, but he would not compel them. That too he had learned from Diocletian's example—for it had become only too clear during that emperor's reign that bigotry and persecution made for bad government and betrayed the standards to which the ruler must aspire. The Roman people knew what was fair and what was not, and this emperor knew that he must always respect the values of the ruled and act accordingly. To the best of his ability, not always wisely, not always successfully, but with consistency, this is what Constantine did. It was that consistency, and the amazing energy that enabled him to carry out his vision of uniting the empire, that made Constantine not only one of the most successful emperors of Rome, but one of history's most influential leaders.

APPENDIX: FINDING CONSTANTINE

The narrative accounts of Constantine's reign come from very short Latin histories written some time after his death by people with little interest in religious issues so that they passed over his conversion in silence; from the pens of Christians, both contemporary and later; and from works dependent upon a history written at the end of the fourth century by a man called Eunapius.[1]

Eunapius was a committed pagan who thought that through his conversion to Christianity Constantine had set the empire on the path to destruction. Eunapius' history is largely known via quotations in later authors—especially the sixth-century pagan Zosimus, who shared his views of the Christian Church, and Christian authors of the fifth century who were at pains to denounce his words, especially his eccentric account of Constantine's conversion. Indeed, it is the desire to denounce Eunapius' account that seems to have lent far greater importance to what he had to say—depending as it does upon an alleged scandal involving Constantine's eldest son and his wife—than it actually merits.[2] The one exception to the general handling of the story of Constantine's life is a very short work entitled *The Descent of the Emperor Constantine*, which contains important information deriving from documents composed in Constantine's lifetime, while Eunapius' history (prior to the conversion) appears to have derived partly from a historian deeply interested in military operations and completely uninterested in religion. This individual's account appears to have ended around AD 324 when Constantine finally achieved the reunification of the empire; its sundry divisions in the course of his life detained us earlier in the book and was of considerable importance for understanding his career.[3]

From the Christian perspective, the primary narratives for Constantine's life include a short book by a North African Christian, Caecilius Lactantius, and three works by Bishop Eusebius of Caesarea, the last of which, *The Life of Constantine*, was completed after the ruler's death.

Lactantius lived from the 260s into the 320s and at various points in his life was quite close to Constantine, his influence on the emperor's thought being especially strong in the early 320s when he was employed as the tutor to Constantine's eldest son Crispus. For the period of Constantine's youth and reign down to 313, Lactantius' *Concerning the Deaths of the Persecutors*, probably completed toward the end of that year, offers a vigorous, and violently prejudiced, account. His principal villain was Galerius, who he sees as the dominant personality in Diocletian's later years on the throne and the driving force behind the great persecution. Despite (and, in part because of) his outright partisanship, Lactantius' work is of immense value not so much for the factual information that he provides—some of what he believed to be true seems not to have been, and he often appears ignorant of things that would have been germane to his cause—but rather because it reflects the public discourse of the era. So much of what we have from this period comes in the form of speeches of praise for the emperors—especially nine panegyrics surviving in Latin; on the other hand, Lactantius' stance as the author of what often seems to be an anti-panegyric in which the language of the regime is turned on its head offers insight into what ordinary people might have been thinking. It is unlikely that Lactantius was the only person who enjoyed scenes like his description of Galerius dying from an intestinal disorder, his decaying body stuffed with foul-smelling worms and polluting the air for miles around.

Another important point is that of perspective. Although Lactantius was North African and would later become prominent at Constantine's court, he was neither in North Africa nor at court when he wrote his book. It appears that he was living in or around the city of Nicomedia where he was professor of Latin at least until 303; also living there was the man to whom he dedicates the work, a Christian named Donatus, who had been imprisoned and tortured during the persecutions of the Christian Church. Another crucial aspect of *Concerning the Deaths of the Persecutors* is that the theme is precisely what the title proclaims: it is about the deaths of emperors who persecuted the Christians, and not, strictly speaking, about Constantine.[4]

The other Christian who wrote ostensibly historical work in the time of Constantine—Eusebius, bishop of Caesarea—was a man of enormous energy and vast output ranging from exegesis of Scripture to three works of history. The first of these, simply entitled *The Martyrs of Palestine*, details the course of the persecutions begun in 303 in his home district. The second was his immensely influential *History of the Church*, a book that defined the subject for future generations. The version that has survived is the third edition. The first edition concluded with a vision of the peaceful coexistence of the Christian and pagan communities at the end of the third century. The second version, inspired by the traumatic events of Diocletian's persecutions, ends with the victories of Constantine and Licinius in 312 and 313, which Eusebius sees as acts of divine vengeance upon persecutors, especially Maximinus Daia, an avid foe of the Christians who ruled the eastern provinces under Galerius after 305. Our draft of the history was compiled after Constantine defeated Licinius in 324. Eusebius's third work was the four-volume *Life of Constantine*, arguably written as a sort of appendix to the *History of the Church*.[5] He also wrote a panegyric to celebrate the thirtieth year as emperor, which he may have delivered to Constantine in person.

Eusebius' Constantine was a committed Christian from the moment he saw the vision of the cross in the sky (a vision for which Eusebius is our primary source); he was a new Moses leading his people forth from the horrors of persecution to triumph, crushing the grotesque tyrants who had abused the faithful. In victory he devoted himself to promoting Christian values and eradicating pagan worship.

Clear and powerful in its message, *The Life of Constantine* is a deeply problematic book. Although he quotes a great number of documents—and we can now be sure, thanks to a papyrus first published in 1954, that these documents are authentic—there are times when he quotes out of context or misunderstands what he is citing.[6] That, however, is not a particularly significant problem and the same point could be made about virtually any historian of the ancient world. Nor is the biggest problem Eusebius' failure to mention important people—for instance, Constantine's wives and his eldest son—or projects, or even that Eusebius is capable of misrepresenting something as important as Constantine's plans for the succession.[7] The fundamental problem with Eusebius' history is that his picture of Constantine's struggle against paganism is wrong and that his understanding of Constantine's conversion is based on a fantasy.

Much of what both Lactantius and Eusebius have to say about the time in which they lived tends to reflect the verbose official discourse of the period, by far the best evidence for which is provided by the nine surviving Latin panegyrics.[8] Of these, two were delivered to Constantius I and two to Maximian—one on Maximian's birthday in 291, the other in 288 to commemorate his accession three years earlier. Four were delivered to Constantine in person, and one to the Senate at Rome in 321 as if Constantine were present (he was in fact in the Balkans at the time). The speeches delivered at court before the emperors tend, not surprisingly, to reflect the "official message" that the rulers wished people to receive about them, especially those regarding Constantine which are highly revealing as to his state of mind early in his career. Those delivered by people speaking on behalf of provincial communities reflect the projected image of the emperor as it was received in well-informed local society—one did not want to insult the emperor while thanking him for his beneficence. It is unfortunate that the panegyrics, whose narrative style reflects the contemporary mode and which appears to have influenced the surviving narratives of Constantine's wars, are spread unevenly across the reign (and that there are not more of them). On the other hand, the speeches also reflect the locus of power: after 312, Constantine was rarely in Gaul, where the collection was assembled, or in Rome, and after 326 he would never again be west of the Adriatic.

Luckily we are able to follow Constantine's wanderings via the record preserved in the Theodosian Code. The emperor Theodosius II (reigned AD 408 to 451) commissioned the Code in 429; it was finished in 437 and promulgated at a meeting of the Roman Senate on 25 December 438.[9] Although some sections of it are now lost, what we have consists of some 2,500 individual decisions on matters of law issued between 313 and 437 and divided into hundreds of *tituli* or topics. More than 350 of these constitutions date to the time of Constantine. In addition there are nearly sixty more extracts preserved in the sixth-century *Codex Justinianus* (the project of the emperor Justinian, compiled between AD 529 and 534).

The texts as they have come down to us in the two Codes are edited versions of the original texts. Although the editing in the *Codex Justinianus* sometimes misrepresents the original texts quite substantially, we are more fortunate with the Theodosian Code. The survival of the original version of a ruling on gift-giving in another collection of Latin legal texts shows that while the Code's editors pared down the rhetoric of the original—sometimes rendering their own versions somewhat opaque—they did not significantly alter the meaning.[10] Although most of the texts included in the Code were imperial rescripts—responses to inquiries—they are largely not "private rescripts," or responses to inquiries by potential litigants.[11] Rather, the rescripts are responding to questions from senior officials, while other documents are in the form of edicts or general instructions from the emperor. These texts connect us directly with the inner circles of Constantine's government.

Although it is unlikely that he would have drafted many, or perhaps any, of the surviving texts, it is also highly unlikely that someone would have written instructions to the most senior officials of his government—the praetorian prefects, or the prefects of Rome—without Constantine knowing what was said. The secretaries who composed these documents were employed to speak for the emperor, so their work, at least in the case of documents addressed to senior officials, was bound to represent views compatible with the emperor's own.[12]

But, invaluable as documents contained in the Theodosian Code are as an insight into Constantine's administrative style, they must represent only a very small proportion of the total number that once existed. The editors of the Theodosian Code were not trying to provide a summary of Constantine's administrative history, useful as that would be to the twenty-first-century reader; rather, they were seeking texts relevant to the topics for which they needed precedents. Since we have no idea what the original sample size would have been or what issues interested Constantine's officials as opposed to the later editors, we cannot hope to use the surviving extracts to reconstruct imperial "policy." What we can do is reconstruct a credible list of imperial concerns and ways of dealing with them. Read in this manner, the Code may not tell us everything we might want to know, but it *can* tell us something about the way Constantine wanted to be seen and the way his mind worked when confronted with the details of administration.

In addition to sources that have survived via manuscript traditions, important information, often crucial and otherwise unknowable, is to be found in inscriptions and papyri—the material made from the papyrus plant that served as the writing medium in many parts of the empire—as well as in the record of coins, buildings, and the other arts. Mosaics, for instance, can show how

Romans might have visualized hunts or gladiatorial fights, a meeting with an emperor, or two people making love. A monument such as the Arch of Constantine in Rome is not simply a victory monument: it is a statement of imperial values, as is the Arch of Galerius (once part of the entrance to his palace at Thessalonica). Similarly, the palace of Diocletian at Split offers us a glimpse of that emperor's ideal world—a fort with elaborate sleeping quarters and several temples, as befitted a man who constantly stressed his devotion to the gods—while Constantine's buildings show us a great deal about the way he thought he might share his private interests with his subjects.

Inscriptions containing imperial letters and orders—ranging from the numerous copies of Diocletian's effort to fix wages and prices throughout the empire to the permission issued in Constantine's name during the last year of his life for an Italian city to erect a temple in his honor (provided that the good people of that city did not engage in sacrifice)—all show us the government in action. Where our literary sources are absent or woefully incomplete, masses of humble records such as tombstones and census returns on papyri help us understand the empire's demographics or the ways in which a child might be raised. Such texts bring us out of the world of the governing class and into that of the average person (if there is such a being). And it is in the papyri that we can pick up something of the dialogue between local officials and the higher reaches of government, and that we sense the limits of the government's power.[13]

My point in this book has been to tell Constantine's story through the sources as they were written rather than reading backward from the end of his life. In writing about Constantine I have preferred to stress the kinds of evidence that I feel come closer to him than others. The panegyrics (or some of them) and the Theodosian Code show us the mind of Constantine at work as well as something of his personality in ways that other texts—Eusebius' *Life*, for instance—do not.[14] This is not to deny the great importance of a work like Eusebius' in shaping later understanding of Constantine, but the *Life* tells a different story.

TIMELINE

260: Sapor captures Valerian; Postumus establishes *imperium Galliarum.*

262: Gallienus appoints Odaenathus *corrector totius orientis*; issues rescript restoring Christian property seized during the persecution in the east.

268: Odaenathus murdered; Gallienus murdered; Claudius II proclaimed Augustus.

269: Claudius wins victory at Naissus; Zenobia claims Odaenathus' position.

270: Palmyrene conquest of Egypt; death of Claudius; Aurelian proclaimed Augustus; death of Sapor I

272: Aurelian captures Palmyra.

273: Aurelian reforms imperial silver coinage.

275: Aurelian murdered; Tacitus proclaimed Augustus.

276: Tacitus murdered; Probus becomes Augustus.

282: Probus murdered; Carus becomes Augustus, begins invasion of Persia; birth of Constantine on February 27 (?)

283: Carus dies (is murdered) in Mesopotamia; Numerian succeeds as co-Augustus with Carinus.

284: Numerian murdered, Diocletian proclaimed Augustus (November 20).

285: Diocletian defeats Carinus; Diocletian appoints Maximian Caesar.

286: Diocletian elevates Maximian to the rank of Augustus (April 1).

287: Revolt of Carausius begins in northern Gaul and Britain.

289: Marriage of Constantius and Theodora (before April 21 of that year).

293: Constantius and Galerius made Caesars; murder of Carausius; Allectus becomes ruler in Britain.

296: Constantius recovers Britain; outbreak of war between Rome and Persia.

298: Galerius defeats Persians.

299: Treaty between Rome and Persia; birth of Fausta (?)

303: Diocletian promulgates first persecution edict against Christians (February 24).

305: Diocletian and Maximian abdicate; Constantius and Galerius become Augusti; Severus and Maximinus Daia becomes Caesars.

306: Constantius dies at York (July 25); Constantine proclaimed Caesar by the army in Britain; Maxentius claims the imperial power at Rome (October 28).

307: Marriage of Constantine and Fausta; Constantine restores Christian property confiscated under the persecution edict in his part of the empire; Severus imprisoned by Maxentius; Galerius fails to suppress revolt of Maxentius; Severus murdered on orders of Maxentius.

308: Maximian is received by Constantine in Gaul; council at Carnuntum; Licinius appointed Augustus by Galerius.

310: Maximian rebels against Constantine, fails, and commits suicide.

311: Deaths of Galerius and Diocletian

312: Probable date for Constantine's conversion to Christianity; Constantine invades Italy, defeats Maxentius at the battle of the Milvian Bridge on October 28; Maximinus Daia ends persecution of Christians.

313: Licinius defeats Maximinus Daia; Licinius' "Edict of Nicomedia" confirms end of persecution of Christians in the east.

314: Council of Arles to discuss the Donatist Controversy.

316: Birth of Constantine II (August 7); Constantine attacks Licinius; battle of Cibalae (October 8).

317: Battle of Adrianople; Licinius surrenders two Balkan dioceses to Constantine; birth of Constantius II (August 7).

323: Birth of Constans

324: Constantine defeats and deposes Licinius; selects Byzantium (Constantinople) as the site for a new capital.

325: Council of Nicaea (June)

326: Execution of Crispus Caesar; Fausta removed from public life.

327: Helena makes trip to the Holy Land.

328: Death of Helena

330: Dedication of Constantinople (May 11–12)

337: Death of Constantine (May 22); Constantine II, Constans, and Constantius II become Augusti (September 9).

339: Death of Constantine II

350: Constans murdered; Magnentius becomes Augustus in the western empire (January 18).

351: Constantius appoints Gallus as Caesar (March 15).

353: Constantius reunites empire; Magnentius commits suicide (August 10).

354: Gallus executed.

355: Constantius appoints Julian Caesar in Gaul (November 6).

360: Julian proclaimed Augustus in Gaul without Constantius' permission.

361: Julian invades the eastern empire; death of Constantius II (November 3); Julian proclaims allegiance to traditional gods.

363: Julian dies in Persia (June 26).

DRAMATIS PERSONAE

ABLABIUS, FLAVIUS: praetorian prefect of the east 329–337; executed in 337 by Constantius II. A Christian who rose to prominence from a humble family; consul with Iunius Bassus in 331.

AEMILIANUS: praetorian prefect, known from a single text of 328, served in the west.

ALEMANNI: Germanic federation centered on the upper Rhine valley, first attested in the early third century, often fought by Constantius and Constantine. The name means "All Men," presumably reflecting the composition of the group as a confederation of existing tribes.

ALEXANDER: bishop of Alexandria 311–328; attacked by Arius.

ALLECTUS: usurper, murdered Carausius in 293 to become emperor in Britain; committed suicide in the face of Constantius I's invasion of 296.

ANASTASIA: half-sister of Constantine, daughter of Constantius and Theodora, briefly married to Bassianus.

ANULLINUS, ANNIUS (probably): praetorian prefect of Severus in 306.

ANULLINUS, C. ANNIUS: consul 295; proconsul of Africa 303–304; prefect of Rome 306–307; 312 probably father of the next Anullinus and brother of the preceding Anullinus.

ANULLINUS, ANNIUS (probably): governor of Africa in 313.

ARIUS: Christian priest; eponymous founder of the Arian movement that was condemned at the Council of Nicaea.

ATHANASIUS: bishop of Alexandria 328–373.

AUGUSTUS: first emperor of Rome 31 BC–AD 14; his name subsequently became the title of the senior ruler of the empire.

AURELIAN, MARCUS AURELIUS: emperor 270–275, reunified the empire; murdered by a cabal of officers in 275.

AURELIUS, MARCUS: the emperor Marcus Aurelius Antoninus, ruled 161–180; generally regarded in antiquity and now as one of Rome's best emperors.

BASSIANUS: Caesar 316, married Anastasia, Constantine's half-sister; executed for treason in 316.

BASSUS, JUNIUS: praetorian prefect in the west 318–331; consul with Ablabius in 331.

BASSUS, SEPTIMIUS: prefect of Rome 317–319.

CAECILIAN: bishop of Carthage, enemy of the Donatists.

CARAUSIUS: separatist emperor in northern Gaul and Britain 287 (?)–293; murdered by his former supporters.

CARUS, MARCUS AURELIUS: emperor 282–283.

CARINUS, MARCUS AURELIUS: emperor 283–285, son of Carus.

CHARISIUS, ARCADIUS: *magister libellorum* (master of petitions) for Maximian in 286–287, then under Diocletian in 290–291; author of a number of legal works.

CLAUDIUS, MARCUS AURELIUS: emperor 268–270, falsely identified as an ancestor of Constantine.

CONSTANTIA: half-sister of Constantine, daughter of Constantius I and Theodora, married to Licinius 313–324.

CONSTANTIUS I: Caesar 293–305, Augustus 305–306, father of Constantine.

CONSTANTIUS II: born 317; Caesar 324–337; Augustus 337–361, son of Constantine and Fausta.

CONSTANTIUS, FLAVIUS: praetorian prefect in the east 324–326, then in Italy in 327, consul in 327 with Valerius Maximus. Possibly related to Constantine.

CONSTANTIUS, JULIUS: half-brother to Constantine, son of Constantius I and Theodora, father of Gallus and Julian, consul in 335; murdered after Constantine's death in 337.

CRISPUS, FLAVIUS JULIUS: Caesar 317–326, son of Constantine and Minervina, probably born ca. 303; executed in 326.

DALMATIUS FLAVIUS JULIUS: Caesar 335–337; son of Flavius Dalmatius, grandson of Constantius I.

DALMATIUS, FLAVIUS: Consul 333; son of Constantius II and Theodora.

DECIUS, GAIUS QUINTUS MESSIUS TRAIANUS: emperor 249–251, issued edict ordering all Romans to sacrifice; killed by the Goths.

DIOCLETIAN: Augustus 284–305. His full name was Gaius Valerius Aurelius Diocletianus, though before his accession it may have been Gaius Valerius Diocles.

DONATUS: leader of a Christian movement in North Africa that rejected the authority of Bishop Caecilian after 313; the movement took its name from him even though he was not its original founder.

ELAGABALUS: the tutelary divinity of Emesa. Although originally a mountain god (in Aramaic the name is God Mountain), he was understood as a Sun God in the late third century and is identified under Aurelian as Sol Invictus.

EUSEBIUS OF CAESAREA: bishop and author of numerous works on Christian doctrine and history. His *Life of Constantine* is one of the most influential sources for Constantine (though not in this book).

EUSEBIUS OF NICOMEDIA: arguably the most influential bishop in the Eastern Empire; although exiled after the Council of Nicaea, he soon returned to his see. He baptized Constantine on his deathbed.

EVAGRIUS: praetorian prefect 326; 329–331; 336–337, usually in the east. He was probably a pagan.

FAUSTA, FLAVIA MAXIMA, wife of Constantine 307–328 (?), daughter of Maximian Herculius and Eutropia, she was probably born in 299. She disappears from public life in 326; her children include Constantine II (b. 316), Constantius II (b. 317), Constans (b. 323), Constantina, and Helena; there is no direct evidence for the birthdates of her daughters.

FELIX: praetorian prefect, serving largely in Africa, 333–336.

FRANKS: Germanic federation located along the lower Rhine, first attested in the late third century, ancestors of the Merovingian and Carolingian rulers of medieval France. The name means "Free Men."

GALERIUS: Caesar 293–305; Augustus 305–311. His full name was Gaius Galerius Valerius Maximianus.

GALLIENUS, PUBLIUS EGNATIUS: emperor 253–268, son of Valerian.

GREGORIUS: *magister libellorum* (master of petitions) under Carinus and Diocletian; compiled the *Codex Gregorianus*.

GOTHS: confederation of east German peoples, originally from Scandinavia that moved into the area of the middle Danube. In the later fourth and fifth centuries, Gothic groups played a major role in the breakup of the western Roman Empire. The Gothic language, first given written form in Constantine's time, was used into the eighth century when it was spoken in parts of Spain and Portugal.

HADRIAN, AELIUS: emperor 117–138.

HANNIBALIANUS (1): son of Constantius I and Theodora.

HANNIBALIANUS (2): son of Flavius Dalmatius, grandson of Constantius I.

HELENA, FLAVIA JULIA: mother of Constantine, first wife of Constantius I. The year of her birth is uncertain; she died in 328.

HERMOGENIANUS: *magister libellorum* (master of petitions) for Diocletian in 295–298, afterward praetorian prefect until 302; compiled the *Codex Hermogenianus*.

LACTANTIUS, L. CAECILIUS FIRMIANUS: Christian teacher and theologian who lived from the 260s into the 320s; held chair in Latin at Nicomedia before the great persecution; later served as tutor to Constantine's son Crispus; author of *On the Deaths of the Persecutors* (among other works).

LICINIUS, VALERIUS LICINIANUS: Augustus 308–324; married Constantia in 313; executed in 325.

MAJORIAN: schismatic bishop of Carthage, hostile to Caecilian, succeeded by Donatus.

MAXENTIUS, MARCUS AURELIUS VALERIUS: separatist emperor in Italy and Africa 306–312, son of Maximian Herculius and Eutropia, brother of Fausta; died at the battle of the Milvian Bridge.

MAXIMIAN HERCULIUS, MARCUS AURELIUS VALERIUS: Caesar 285–286, Augustus, 286–305; stepfather of Theodora, wife of Constantius I, father of Maxentius and Fausta; committed suicide in 310.

MAXIMINUS DAIA, GALERIUS VALERIUS: Caesar 306–309; Augustus 309–311, nephew of Galerius; committed suicide in 313.

MAXIMUS, VALERIUS: prefect of Rome 319–323.

MAXIMUS, VALERIUS: *vicarius* of the east in 325; attested as praetorian prefect in 327–328, 332–323, and 337. He was consul in 327 with Flavius Constantius and probably related to the preceding Maximus.

MELETIUS: leader of rigorist Christian movement in Egypt (of which he was the eponymous founder) after the great persecution.

MENSURIUS: bishop of Carthage, died (probably) in 307. He was succeeded by Caecilian.

MILTIADES: bishop of Rome 310–314.

MINERVINA: first wife of Constantine, mother of Crispus, presumably deceased by 305.

NUMERIAN, MARCUS AURELIUS: Augustus 283–284, son of Carus, murdered in 284.

OPTATIANUS PORPHYRIANUS, PUBLILIUS: prefect of Rome 329; 33 (on both occasions very briefly); wrote poetry in Latin.

OSSIUS OF CORDOBA: bishop before the Council of Elvira (ca. 305) at which he participated; he was in Constantine's entourage before 313, played a role in the Donatist controversy, and presided at the Council of Nicaea.

PALLADAS: Greek epigrammatist, originally from Alexandria, later resident at Constantinople; some of his poetry comments on events of the reign of Constantine.

PAPIUS PACATIANUS: praetorian prefect 332–337, consul 332, served in the west.

PETER: bishop of Alexandria 300–311; opponent of Meletius, executed on the order of Maximinus Daia.

SAPOR I: king of Persia 240–270.

SAPOR II: king of Persia: 309/10–379.

SECUNDUS OF TIGISIS: bishop of Numidia at the time of Diocletian's persecution; adopted rigorist line and quarreled with Mensurius, one of the founders of the movement that would become Donatism.

SEVERUS, LUCIUS SEPTIMIUS: emperor 193–211.

SEVERUS , FLAVIUS VALERIUS: Caesar 305–306, then Augustus; surrendered to Maximian in the spring of 307 at Ravenna; was executed in the late summer by Maxentius.

THEODORA: daughter of Maximian Herculius, wife of Constantius I, mother of Flavius Dalmatius, Julius Constantius, Hannibalianus, Anastasia, Constantia, and Eutropia. She died ca. 327.

VALERIAN, P. LICINIUS CORNELIUS EGNATIUS: emperor 253–260; died in Persian captivity.

VALENS, AURELIUS VALERIUS: Augustus as colleague of Licinius in 316; executed in 316.

VOLUSIANUS, GAIUS CEIONIUS RUFIUS: praetorian prefect (of Maxentius) in 309–310; consul 311 and 314; prefect of Rome 313–315; exiled 315.

NOTES

INTRODUCTION

1. For this object, see the excellent publication in Deppert-Lippitz (1996); other elements of this object are in the collections at Dumbarton Oaks (2 pieces), the British Museum, and the Louvre.

1. THE CRISIS OF AD 260

1. For the events of 260 see Potter (1990): 31–46; for the continuing impact of Valerian's capture see E. K. Fowden (2006): 382.

2. Potter (2004): 257–62 for the events of these years, though, for a slightly different take on the role of Odaenathus, see Millar (1993): 157–70.

3. D. 50.4.18.1 (Charisius, fundamental for the time of Diocletian); for earlier periods see the lucid and important discussion in Neesen (1981) and Millar (1983); Millar (2004): 336–71.

4. See, in general, Potter (2004): 257–8; on location-specific definitions of wealth, see Dorotheos Didaskalia 2.6.

5. Potter (2004): 241–4 for a somewhat different view, see Rives (1999): 135–54; for more recent discussion, see Brent (2010): 193–223.

6. For the early evidence of hostility see P.Oxy 3035 with Parsons (2007): 203; for the edict in general, see Potter (2004): 255; for the importance of the edict of restoration, see Millar (1992a): 571–2.

7. See, for example, P. Cornelius Saecularis and G. Julius Donatus, consuls of 260 along with Destricius Juba, Flavius Antiochianus, Sallustius Saturninus, Nummius Albinus, and Cocceius Rufinus, on whom see Christol (1986): 188–9; 101; 189; 193; 200–203; 214–18; 187–8.

8. IGBR 3.2.1568 (Heraclianus); IGBR 3.2.1570 for Mucianus with Christol (1977); AE 1965 no. 114 with Gerov (1965).

9. Zos. 1.40.2.

10. PIR² P 572, possibly to be identified with PIR² D 159a.

11. For this view of Claudius, see Potter (2004): 263–8; for a different take on the end of Odaenathus' regime, see Hartmann (2001): 218–30 suggesting more agency on the part of Gallienus; for detailed discussion of the chronology of the years after 260, see Hartmann (2001): 231–41.

2. THE RENEWAL OF THE ROMAN EMPIRE

1. For the themes of the generals' school, see Syme (1971): 208–20. For the consuls of 270 and 271, both aristocrats see Christol (1986): 109–10, who is cautiously agnostic on the identification of the

Paternus of 269 with the consul of 267 and 268. For Bassus in 271 see Christol (1986): 111, and for Lupus, another very important player, see Christol (1986): 263–70.

2. *HA Aurelian* 25. 4–6; see also Halsberghe (1972): 132; 138–55.

3. Berrens (2004): 89–126.

4. Potter (2004): 267–72; Hartmann (2001): 300–8 for the cultural life of the Palmyrene court.

5. For the significance of the wall, see Esmonde Cleary (2003); for the wall at Rome, see esp. Dey (2011): 120.

6. Christol (1986): 111–14.

7. Potter (2004): 273.

8. For the "divine intelligence of Decius," see *SB* 5.7696 with Parsons (2007): 173; for refusal to accept imperial coin see *P.Oxy.* 1411 (the issue might have been that it was coinage of Macrianus and Quietus); for the economic impact of the feeding of Rome, see Aldrete and Mattingly (2010); for an overall survey of the Roman economy, see Goldsmith (1987): 34–59, whose methods and conclusions may be seen to be confirmed by Scheidel and Freisen (2009).

9. Potter (2004): 273–6.

10. Sauer (1998).

11. Zon. 12.30, saying that he captured Seleuceia and Ctesiphon (see also George 724 [Mosshammer, 472]:); Eutrop. *Brev.* 9.14.1; Festus, *Brev.* 24 with Bleckmann (1992): 133–35. The *HA Cari, Carini et Num.* 8.1 reports instead: *Mesopotamiam Carus cepit et Ctesifontem usque pervenit.* See also Aur. Vict. *De Caes.* 38.3; [Aur. Vict.] *Epit. de Caes.* 38.2, both asserting (as they would on the basis of their shared source) that he did not take Ctesiphon. For other sources, see the useful compilation in Dodgeon and Lieu (1991):112–19.

12. For the events of Numerian's reign see *CJ* 5.52.2 with Halfmann (1986): 242; Webb (1933) Numerian no. 462. The issue may be prospective, and its meaning is complicated by a similar issue of *adventus* coins for Carinus; see Webb (1933) Carinus no. 317; *HA V. Cari, Carini et Num.* 12.1–2; Aur. Vict. *Caes.* 38.7–8; [Aur. Vict.] *Epit.* 38.4–5; Eutrop. *Brev.* 18.2.

13. Cambi (2004): 39–40.

14. The place of Constantine's birth is secured by Firm. Mat. *Math.* 1.10.13; for the day, see *CIL* 1³: 255; 258; 259; the year of Constantine's birth is highly contentious. For the view that he was born ca. 285 see the excellent exposition in König (1987), 64 (282 seems to me preferable given the attested dates of his presence at the court of Diocletian). The case for putting the year of his birth around a decade earlier is made by Barnes (1982): 39–40. The crucial point is the date at which his eldest son, Crispus, was born, which was ca. 303, and the reference in *Pan.* 7.4.1 to Constantine's age at the time of his marriage to Minervina (i.e., *primo ingressu adulecentiae formares animum maritalem* and *iuvenis uxorius*) which, to my mind, invalidates the calculation made by Barnes; for the birth of Crispus see chapter 9 n. 4. For the nature of Constantius' relationship with Helena, arguing that she was a concubine, see Drijvers (1992), 16–19; Leadbetter (1998). These discussions do not place sufficient weight on Procop. *Aed.* 5.2.5 testifying to her birth at Drepanum (contra Barnes [2011]: 37–8 who would discount this). The epigraphic evidence for her marriage to Constantius from the 320s (e.g., *CIL* 10, nos. 678, 517 [*ILS* 708]) probably should not be discounted either, supporting the correct view of Barnes (2011): 33–6 that the marriage was legitimate—though the fact that I think the evidence supports her birth at Drepanum dissuades belief in the fantasy of Ambrose favored by Barnes (2011): 30–3; I am in complete concurrence with Barnes (1982): 36.

3. THE NEW EMPEROR

1. For the early career of Maximian, see *Pan.* 10.2.5–6 and Kuhoff (2001): 34–5 on the chronology.

2. For the Gallic rebels see Potter (2004): 281–2; for the view taken here; see also Kuhoff (2001): 35–9; 58 on the campaigns of these years with *Pan.* 11. 16–17; 10.6–7; for the role of the praetorian

prefect, see *D* 1.11.1 (Carisius); for the mysterious senior official, see *Pan.* 10.11.4 with Nixon and Rodgers (1994): 70 n. 38. For Constantius' military achievements see *Pan.* 8.1.6–2.1 with the excellent discussion in Nixon and Rodgers (1994): 110. For a different view on Constantius' role, see Kuhoff (2001): 119–120 with thorough citation of earlier scholarship.

4. EMPERORS AND SUBJECTS

1. *Pan.* 10.3.3–4 with the thorough discussion of scholarship in Kuhoff (2001): 329–70.

2. For a useful summary of the bibliography see Kuhoff (2001): 327–36 noting, as is appropriate that *praeses* appears still to have been the standard term for a civilian governor, except in Italy where the title for the administrator of one of the regions into which the peninsula had been divided was *corrector*.

3. *Pan.* 10. 7.5 on events with Bahram with further discussion in Dignas and Winter (2007): 27; Potter (2004): 290–2 and Fowden (1993): 32–4 on the significance of imperial proselytism.

4. For the texts mentioned in this paragraph, see Cooley (2009) (Augustus' autobiography); Potter and Damon (1999) (the events of AD 19–20); Oliver (1989): n. 184 (Marcus Aurelius and the Athenians); Potter and Mattingly (2010): 351–71 (for translations of the inscriptions relating to gladiators and the entertainment system with references to earlier publication). The classic study of the petition and response system is Millar (1992a); for the imperial "value system," see Noreña (2011): 62–100.

5. Corcoran (2000a): 85–91 on the careers of these jurists.

6. For the Praetor's Edict see Buckland (1975): 10–11; for the Diocletianic projects, see Connelly (2010a); Corcoran (2000a): 25–42.

7. *Pan.* 10.12.1–2.

8. Ver. *Aen.* 6.851–3 (Anchises); *ILS* 212 (Claudius' speech); Dio 60.17 (Messalina); Acts 22: 24–29 (Paul); Plin. *Ep.* 10.11 (relatives of his doctor); Fronto *Ant* 9.2 (p. 162 van den Hout) (Appian) see in general Woolf (2000); Dench (2005); Ando (2000); Mattingly (2010) for important recent work on the Roman concept of Romanness. For specific issues with citizenship see Dench (2005): 136–43.

9. Tac. *Agr.* 21.

10. For Trier in the imperial period, see Wrightman (1970): 92–123; for Ephesus, see Scherrer (2000); for Byzantium, see p. 240 below; for Caracalla see Oliver (1989) n. 260.

11. *CJ* 4.31.12 (Lucius Cornelianus); 8.41.7 (Zoilus); 8.13.23 (Macedonus); 10.32.8 (Platonianus); 10.32.6 (illiterates); 10.59.1 (*infames*).

12. *CJ* 10.58.1 (Lucillus); 10.42.6 (Polymnestor).

13. *CJ* 4.7.5 with Connolly (2010a): 117.

14. *CJ* 1.19.1; 7.13.1 with Corcoran (2000a): 108; *CJ* 2.19.9; 2.20.6; 2.31.2; 4.44.8 (Euodia) with Connolly (2010a): 114–7; *CJ* 9.1.12 (approach the governor); *CJ* 2.12.18 (male duty) with Corcoran (2000a): 106.

15. Morgan (2007): 107 with, for the *Life of Aesop*, see Hopkins (1993). I am indebted to Catherine Stockrahm for pointing out the gendered aspect of the *Life* to me.

16. Hopkins (1993): 6–10 on storytelling; Parsons (2007): 123–32 on letter writing, on which see also Malherbe (1988): 4–7 and the edition of *P. Bon.* 5 on his pp. 44–57.

17. Cribbiore (1985) on the quality of the hand; Morgan (2007): 98 on wealth (she discusses the school text on p. 97).

18. *Babr. Fab.*97 with Morgan (2007): 69.

19. *PSI* 2.120; *P.Oxy* 2661.10 with Morgan (2007): 99.

20. Morgan (2007): 193–199; for Hadrian and his secretary, see Hopkins (1993): 7.

21. J. Nollé (2007): 190.

5. A NEW LOOK

1. Lact. *DMP* 7.9–10; the discussion that follows is heavily influenced by von Hesberg (2004); see also Kuhoff (2001): 716–83 for an important survey, and pp. 718–9 on Nicomedia, in particular, pp. 719–20 on Antioch and pp. 720–21 on Milan; see also Mayer (2002): 28–31 (Nicomedia); 31–4 (Milan); 34–9 (Trier).

2. *ILS* 640 with discussion in Kuhoff (2001): 210 n. 572, note that Severus' name was chiseled out; for Titus, see Jos. *BJ* 7.96; for Trajan, see von Hesburg (2004): 143.

3. Suet. *Jul.* 37; Herod. 3.9.12; 4.3.7 with Potter (2005): 87 (pictures as a source); 7.2.8; Eunap. Fr 68 (Blockley) (hand of God); Priscus Fr. 22.3 (Blockley); for maps in this context, see esp. Talbert (2010): 136–57.

4. Aur. Vict. *De Caes.* 39.2; 4; Eutrop. *Brev.* 9.26 with Jones (1964): 1:40.

5. Sutherland and Carson (1967): 88–93 suggesting that the uniformity of style is connected with the control exercised over the whole empire by the finance department of Diocletian; for the portraits, see their discussion on p. 109.

6. Sporn (2004) esp. 393–7.

6. PERSIA AND THE CAESARS

1. The reconstruction of the British regime accepted here is that of Casey (1994): 47–8; for other options, which include a very short reign for Allectus, see Kuhoff (2001): 157–8; for the events in Egypt see Kuhoff (2001): 187–97.

2. The problem is well reflected in the contemporary poem published as *Select Papyri* 135; it is not a completely unproblematic text—on the issue of the date, see Barnes (1976b): 183, and Kuhoff (2001): 201 on the imperial villa in Spain where Maximian may have resided.

3. Aurel. Vict. *Caes.* 39.34 (stressing the difficulties Galerius faced in the first campaign); Eutrop. *Brev.* 9.24 (stressing Galerius' folly in the first campaign), Zon. 12.31 similar in tone to Jul. *Or.* 1. 18a-b; Festus *Brev.* 25 suggests that Victor and Eutropius give different takes on the same tradition, which is also reflected in Amm. 14.11.10; Oros. *Contra Pagan.* 7.25.9 similar to Theoph. *Chron.* A.M. 5793; for a powerful defense of the positive tradition, see Leadbetter (2009): 90–1. For the second campaign, see esp. Aurel Vict. *De Caes.* 39.35; Lact. *DMP* 9; Festus, *Brev.* 14; 25; Eutrop. 9. 25; Amm. 22.4.8; 23.5.11; Oros. *Contra Pagan.* 7.25.10–11; Jord. *Get.* 21; Mal. 13.306; 308; Theoph *Chron* AM 5793; Zon. 12.31; for the scouting expedition, see Eutrop. 9.25; Synesius *De regno* 17 with further discussion in Leadbetter (2009): 92 and p. 111 below.

4. For Galerius' outburst, see Pet. Patr. fr. 13 *FGH* 4, 189 trans. J. M. Lieu in Dodgeon and Lieu (1991): 132; the understanding of the treaty terms here depends on Dignas and Winter (2007): 124–30. For echoes of Valerian, see most notably *Pan.* 8. 10.4; Lact. *DMP* 9.6.

5. Fischer (2004): 123–8; Schmitt (2001) is excellent on internal changes in the legions in the second and third century and general developments of the late third century, as is Nicasie (1998): 13–42, who offers an excellent overview of earlier discussions on his pp. 1–11.

6. For Constantius' early life, see p. 27–8 above; for rebirth of the world, see *Pan.* 8.3.2 on the natural order and the need to revisit places too often; see 4.1 on the accord with the elements.

7. The passage cited is *Pan.* 8.10.1–3; see also *Pan.* 8.12–17 and Rees (2002): 123–4.

8. The discussion of the arch in this paragraph is heavily derivative from Pond Rothman (1977); see also Rees (1993): 186; for the palace, see Mayer (2002): 39–68.

9. Rees (1993): 196; Hekster (1999): 720.

10. *D.* 1.11.1–2.

11. *PLRE* Fl. Dalmatius 6 (p. 240–241); Julius Constantius (p. 226); Hannibalianus 1 (p. 407). *PLRE* Constantia I (p. 221); Anastasia 1 (p. 58); Eutropia 2 (p. 316); for Constantia, see also Pohlsander

(1993); for Anastasia, see Elliott (1996): 20–1, who takes this as evidence for Constantius' Christianity; for the alternative view see Grünewald (1990): 81–2.

12. Eutropia's birthdate is surmised by her marriage to Virius Nepotianus (*PLRE* Virius Nepotianus (p. 625)); he was consul in 335 and would thus have likely married in the first half of the 320s, at the latest. This would suggest that Eutropia was born after 300.

7. THE COURT OF DIOCLETIAN

1. Barnes (1982): 54–5 on the movements of Diocletian.

2. The discussion that follows owes a great deal to R. B. E. Smith (2007a); (2011).

3. Nicasie (1998): 47; Kuhoff (2001): 480–1.

4. Paul of Aegina 6.68 (I am indebted to Dr. Maud Gleason for bringing this to my attention). See also Hopkins (1978).

5. Jones (1964): 50–51; the post is that of the *magister memoriae*, the official in charge of foreign affairs.

6. Aurel. Vict. *De Caes.* 39.45; for the significance of Victor's commentary, see Kuhoff (2001): 544; Brandt (2004): 52.

7. *CJ* 10.48.2; for the *comites consistoriani*, see Schlinkert (1998): 140–2.

8. On behaviors in earlier centuries see Plin. *Ep.* 3.5.9; 6.31; Marc. Aurel. *Med.* 1.16; see in general Millar (1992a): 110–22; Wallace Hadrill (1982). For Lucian see Luc. *Nigr.* 21 with Avery (1940): 17; on the Diocletianic adventus the most accessible and important source here is *Pan.* 11.11.1–3 with Nixon and Rodgers (1994): 52 and their notes on the passage quoted.

9. For Eusebius' observation, see Eus. *VC* 1.19.1; for legislation dealing with members of the court, see p. 258 below; for displays of temper see p. 201; 283.

10. Pococke (1803): 59; 63.

11. Gagos and Potter (2006): 68–9; the *strategos*' name does not appear on the first roll (the one that primarily concerns us here) but there is good reason to think that he is the Apolinarius who is named on the second role; for cautious discussion see Skeat (1964): xxv.

12. *P. Panop. Beatty* 1.1–7; 10–11; 15–23.

13. For the silence about Domitianus, see Skeat (1964): xxii–xxiii; for the significance of noninterference, see Potter (2010a).

14. *P. Oxy.* 738 with Parsons (2007): 111 and Pococke (1803): 69; rice had been cultivated in the Nile valley for around two thousand years by the time of Constantine's visit.

15. Bagnall (1993): 27–32.

16. On the significance of boar hunting in particular, see Nollé (2005): 67.

17. For the issue of who owned the villa, see Wilson (1983): 86–99.

18. See now Gentili (1999) 3: 76–108; obviously the force of the message varies if India rather than Armenia is shown; otherwise the significance of the apses would modestly be the control of nature from the western to eastern border of the empire.

19. Gentili (1999) 3: 49–65.

20. The preceding discussion derives from Gordon (1990) and Scheid (2003): 79–86. The Pliny passage is *NH* 28.10.

21. Lact. *DMP* 10.1–2; see also Lact. *DI* 4.27, Barnes (1981): 18–19 gives the date of this purge as 299. His date privileges the plural in *DI* 4.27 over the account in *DMP*, which yields a date of 302 since Diocletian is alone in that version: *cum ageret in partibus orientis, ut erat pro timore scrutator rerum futurarum, immolabat pecudes et in iecoribus earum ventura quaerebat.* I take the plural in *DI* to be rhetorical in light of the emphasis on Diocletian alone in this passage and the fact that Lactantius is otherwise anything but loath to impute responsibility to Galerius. For Diocletian's presence in Syria

(indicated by in *partibus orientis*), see Barnes (1982): 55. For an effort to reconcile Lactantius' date for the persecution of the Christians in the army with Eusebius, see Woods (1992); but this is demonstrated to be incorrect by Burgess (1996), who shows that Eusebius evidently placed the persecution in 300. It might be possible to be more precise if there were independent evidence for the tenure of Veturius (see n. 25) mentioned by Eusebius as the mover of the persecution. But there is not. The version given in the text assumes that the account in *DMP* gives the best evidence, and that the time from the beginning of the "persecution in the army" was relatively short. It is possible to obtain some support for the date of 302 for the purge of the army from Drew-Bear (1979): 135, who argues that Gaius served under Galerius in 302 and Maximian in 303; in 299 he would have been under the command of Diocletian in Egypt, which would provide further evidence against Barnes' early date, if Drew-Bear's reconstruction can be accepted.

22. For the scene around Troy see Lane Fox (1986): 144–7; for records of oracles see Potter (1994): 37–40 and 55–7 on Christian critiques; Martin (2004): 125–225 is excellent on demons, both pagan and Christian. I am indebted to Professor E. Muehlberger for pointing this out to me.

23. Lact. *DMP* 10.2–4.

24. Jonkers (1954) 1. 2 (flamines who sacrifice after baptism); 3 (flamines who hold munera); 4 (catchumens as flamines); 56 (duumviri); 55 (civic priests continuing to wear crowns); 60 (martyrdom); see also, on related topics, 40 (people should not receive items offered in sacrifice as payment of debts); 41 (Christian masters should keep their slaves from sacrificing). For Lactantius on voluntary martyrdom, see *DMP* 13.2, and on this issue, see further de Ste. Croix (2006): 153–200; see also on the problem of the date of the Council of Elvira, which I take to be ca. 305 since a persecution has plainly taken place, and the Church seems to be living within the bounds set by pagan society; for discussion of this problem see J. Streeter in de Ste. Croix (2006): 99–104. For general discussion of Christian attitudes toward participation in pagan institutions, see Shean (2010): 71–104.

25. Eus. *HE* 8. 4.3; identified as Veturius in Jer. *Chron.* s.a. 301; *Chron. Prosper. Tir.* s.a. 298 with *PLRE* Veturius (p. 955); see also good discussion of earlier "soldier martyrs" unconnected with these events in Shean (2010): 194–205; see also Barnes (2010): 106–10.

26. For Christian attitudes toward martyrdom and suicide, see de Ste. Croix (2006) and Bowersock (1995).

8. IMPERIAL EDICTS AND MORAL CRUSADES

1. Lk 2:1; on edicts generally, see Millar (1992): 252–9.

2. *Coll.* 6.4 (*CJ* 5.4.17) with Corcoran (2000a): 173–4 on the context; Corcoran (2000b): 4–5 on the earlier text. The exact practice that is being legislated against is open to some question. Huebner (2007) offers a powerful argument to the effect that what appears as "close-kin" marriage is in fact marriage between a biological and adopted child—something was, as she notes on her p. 48, illegal as well under Roman law. Remijsen and Clarysse (2008) show that in Egypt, biological siblings were indeed marrying.

3. For the proper posture in listening to an imperial edict see Lieberman (1944): 6–9; for Syrian tax assessments see *AE* 1933 n. 145; for house-to-house census procedures see Bagnall and Frier (1994): 1–30.

4. *Coll.* 15.3 for the text; see also Corcoran (2000a): 135–6 for the context. For the spread of Manichaeism see Gardner and Lieu (2004): 73–93; 109–18 with translations of the relevant sources.

5. For the process of dividing provinces before the time of Diocletian, see Rouché (1981): 103–20; Potter (1998); for the Diocletianic divisions, see Kuhoff (2001): 336–70.

6. First published in Erim, Reynolds, and Crawford (1971) (with p. 175 on the nature of the text); see the text in Rouché (1989) no. 230; see also *PSI* 965; *P Ryl.* 4 no. 607; *P Oslo* 83 with Ruschenbusch (1977), reconciling the epigraphic and papyrological evidence; on the impact, Harl (1996): 152–3.

7. For the moment of promulgation, see Reynold's note in Rouché (1989) no. 231 (p. 268); for commentary, see Lact. *DMP* 7.6–7; for a summary of the scholarship on the issue and analysis of the terms, see Kuhoff (2001): 543–64.

8. *PE praef*, 5–6. For the text see Lauffer (1971).

9. *PE praef.* 7 (Lauffer).

10. *PE praef.* 9, 19 (Lauffer).

11. See Pliny *HN* 14.95 (price of wine in Italy in 89 BC); for local controls on the price of grain outside of Rome, see Garnsey (1988): 238–9. See in general the excellent discussion in Corcoran (2000a): 225–33.

12. For the price of wheat in Carthage in the 370s, ranging between 10 and 30 *modii* per solidus (equal to 1,000 denarii in the edict), see Amm. 28.1.18 with Corcoran (2000a): 226. For a survey of Egyptian prices versus those in the edict, see *P Oxy.* vol. 54, 233.

13. Lact. *DMP* 7.6–7.

14. Lact. *DMP* 7.7 with Corcoran (2000a): 232–33, contra Finhman (1991–92), with references to earlier works that argue that the edict was enforced, at least in the eastern part of the empire, until the victory of Licinius in 313.

15. P. 79 n. 21 above

16. See p. 111.

17. For the meeting between Galerius and Diocletian, see Lact. *DMP* 11.3–8, 18. The belief that Lactantius' picture, while obviously inflated by rhetoric, is substantially correct is central to the analysis in Barnes (1981): 14, 19; see also Seeck (1895–1920) 3:311, likewise following Lactantius, as does Stein (1959): 80–1, and, with circumspection, Jones (1964): 71. For actual promulgation of the edict, see Lact. *DMP* 11.7; Eus. *VC.* 2.51; with H. Grégoire (1913); for connection between the ideology of persecution and that on the price edict, see Kuhoff (2001): 278–9 and, for insistence on the singular importance of Diocletian in making the decision, see Const. *Orat.* 25 as well as Leadbetter (2009): 119–33.

18. Lact. *DMP* 12.1; Eus. *HE* 8.2.4; *MP* 1.1; *Acta Felicis* 1 with Duncan-Jones (1974).

19. See Lact. *DMP* 13.1, giving items 2, 3, and 4 on the list; Eus. *HE* 8.2.3–4, giving items 1, 2, 3, and 6. For brief discussion, see Corcoran (2000a): 179–81, though he gives only the items from Eusebius; Barnes (1981): 22–3. de Ste. Croix (2006): 35–78, remains fundamental, though see also Kuhoff (2001): 246–97.

20. For the fire, see Lact. *DMP* 14.2; Eus. *HE* 8.6.6; Const. *Orat.* 25 (an eyewitness account); for the defiance in Nicomedia, see Lact. *DMP* 13.2 (it cannot have helped that the person in question mocked the victory titles of the emperors in so doing; see also Eus. *HE* 8.5.1, who regarded it as a noteworthy act, as both Diocletian and Galerius were present); for the revolts, see Eus. *HE* 8.6.8–9 with Corcoran (2000a): 181, noting that the second edict does not appear to have been enforced in the west, and, on the revolt of Eugenius at Antioch, see Downey (1961): 330.

21. *P Oxy.* 2673 trans. Rea. For the text, see Rea (1979).

22. Optatus, *Tract.* App. 1.3–5=Maier (1987) no. 29.

23. Optatus, *Tract.* Appendix 1, p. 186; see also chapter 21.

24. The poem in question is Palladas 10.53; for the issue of the date, into discussion of which this poem has not been brought, see Wilkinson (2009); the crucial discussion of the paleographic evidence for the dating of P.CtYBR inv. 4000 is convincing, a point to which I am indebted to my colleague Richard Janko. For the Balkans, see R. Bratoz (2004): 209–51; for Palestine, see Potter (2010b): 604–7.

25. For the release, see Eus. *HE* 8.2.5, 6.10; Eus. *MP* 2 with Corcoran (2000a): 181–82.

26. For Constantine's place in the palace, I am indebted to Drake (forthcoming) for the observation that Constantine needed to reintroduce himself to Christians who would remember him as a courtier.

9. MINERVINA

1. The passage cited Apul. *Met.* 2.17 tr. Walsh; for the Trier ceiling, see Gaisser (2008): 26–9.

2. For life expectancy of women and ages at marriage, see Bagnall and Frier (1994): 84–90; 118–21, the evidence from Egyptian census returns upon which Bagnall and Frier base their analysis, provides the parameters within which such discussions must be conducted, but there are wide variations from the norm, and class can have an impact; see Evans Grubbs (1995): 54–102 for issues connected with marriage. For issues more specifically of ancient sexuality, see Richlin (2006).

3. The status of Constantine's relationship with Minervina has occasioned much debate; see Lucien-Brun (1970); there is no reason to imagine, with Barnes (2011): 48–9 that Minervina was a niece of Diocletian unless one wishes also to believe that Constantine was being considered for the succession at this point.

4. For discussion of views on the date of Crispus' birth see Pohlsander (1984): 81–87 with a thorough review of the scholarship. He favors a birthdate of c. 305, as does *PLRE* Crispus 4 (p. 233), which seems to me too late in light of the birth of Crispus' daughter Helena in 322 (*CTh* 9.38.1) and the suggestion that he was able to play some sort of role in military actions probably in 319 (*Pan.* 10. 17.2 with Nixon and Rodgers (1994): 346 n. 17; Barnes (1982): 83), an event said to fall with *pueriles anni*, which presume that he was not yet 18; for 303 see Palanque (1938): 245–46.

10. THE SUCCESSION

1. For Diocletian's meeting with Maximian see *Pan.* 7.9.2 with Nixon and Rodgers (1994): 188–90, pointing to the evidence of palatial construction as a sign that abdication was planned well in advance. Stein (1959): 68; 82 suggests that abdication was always planned, but that the final decision about when to do so was made by Diocletian only in 303. Seeck (1895–1920) 1:34–6 likewise argues that abdication was long planned, but that Constantine and Maxentius were the designated heirs until 303. For the argument that Galerius launched a thinly veiled coup, see Thomas (1973): 229–47; Barnes (1981): 25. For the *ludi saeculares*, see Zos. 2.7. Seston (1946): 210–21 suggests that the ideology of the regime bespoke opposition to biological succession, though noting that Maximian may still have had hopes for Maxentius; see also Leadbetter (2009): 134–46.

2. Lact. *DMP* 18.1–7; Const. *Orat* 25.

3. Aur. Vict. *De Caes.* 40.48, can be read as supporting Lactantius' view that the decision to abdicate was a sudden one. It is, however, unfortunate that Victor's tradition, which in this case depends upon a Latin history written at the end of Constantine's reign, can be shown to have been contaminated by Constantinian propaganda (see esp. *De Caes.* 40.2) and thus not representative of an independent polytheist tradition; see also Eutrop. *Brev.* 9.27.1; for the chronological manipulation, see Chastagnol (1967). On the numismatic point, see Kuhoff (2001): 784 with Sutherland and Carson (1967) n. 608; 612–14.

4. Lact. *DMP* 18.12–13. *Pan.* 10. 14.1, 8. 20.1 (see also *ILS* 629) with Seeck (1895–1920) 1:34, and pp. 456–7n on line 9. This evidence is more cogent than Lact. *DMP* 18.8. Seeck (1895–1920) 1:40, is entirely correct in stressing the fact that both Caesars were not in the top echelon of government at the time of their appointment. For what is known of their earlier careers, see Barnes (1982): 38–9.

5. Barnes (1982): 56 for Diocletian's movements and p. 60 for those of Maximian (Lact. *DMP* 18.1 for the meeting with Galerius).

6. Lact. *DMP* 19.2–6 is the source for the description in the text.

7. *ILS* 645 with Kuhoff (2001): 322; 786.

8. Eutrop. *Brev.* 9.27.2; Lact. *DMP* 26.10. Constantius' role in this ceremony is confirmed by *Pan.* 7. 5.3: *cuius tanta maturitas est ut, cum tibi pater imperium reliquisset, Caesaris tamen appellatione contentus exspectare malueris ut idem te qui illum declararet Augustum.*

11. THE NEW REGIME

1. Licinius, see *PLRE* p. 509 (Licinius 3); Pompeius Probus *PLRE* p. 740 (Probus 6); Andronicus *PLRE* p. 66 (Andronicus 6).

2. For Dionysius, see Chastagnol (1962): 34–6; Christol (1986): 139; *PLRE* Dionysius 12; for Paulinus, see Chastagnol (1962): 31–3; for Faustinus, see Chastagnol (1962): 33–4, for Nummius Tuscus, see Chastagnol (1962): 38–9; Christol (1986): 122; *PLRE* Tuscus 1; for Junius Tiberianus, who needs to be disentangled from his homonymous son, see Chastagnol (1962): 40–1; Christol (1986): 205–6 (for the disentanglement); for Aradius Rufinus, see Chastagnol (1962): 41; for Titianus, see Chastagnol (1962): 41–4 and Christol (1986): 239 on the family. Annius Anullinus is a complex figure; see Chastagnol (1962): 45–7, esp. p. 47, on the suggestion that the Anullinus who appears as a praetorian prefect in 306 is his brother.

3. *AE* 1942–43 no. 81. For the terminology, compare Lact. *DMP* 7.4: *vicarii praefectorum* and the discussion of Cledonius (*GL* v.13): *saepe quaesitum est, utrum vicarius debeat etiam is cui magnificentissimi praefecti vices suas in speciali causa mandaverunt; nam vicarius dicitur is qui ordine codicillorum vices ait amplissimae praefecturae. Ille vero mandatur propter absentiam praefectorum, non vicarius, sed vice agens, non praefecturae, sed praefectorum dicitur tantum*, which appears to be attempting to draw a linguistic distinction that is fanciful.

4. *IRT* 464. For different views, see Noethlichs (1982): 72–5, who places the development later, and Arnheim (1970): 595, who sees *vicarii* as deputy prefects assigned to rule groups of provinces under Diocletian. He is obviously right on the first point, but the nature of the job appears to change under Constantius as suggested earlier; see also the discussion in Kuhoff (2001): 788–9.

5. Eus. *VC* 1.25.1, 26.

6. For the edict on accusations, see now Corcoran (2007); for the edict on taxation, see Lact. *DMP* 23.1–9 with Leadbetter (2009): 170–4 and Nicolson (1999): 12–13.

7. Corcoran (2000a): 182.

8. The issue of his health is asserted at *Pan.* 6.7.1; 8.1 and could anyway be surmised from the events.

9. *Or.* 2. For the perils of Galerius see p. 56; 111; for Constantius, see *Pan.* 6.6.3; Eutrop. 9.23; Zon. 12.33; the date is disputed, with 301 being possible on the basis of victory titles while a date a few years earlier would make sense in terms of Eutropius' narrative; see Barnes (1982): 61 and Rodgers's note at *Pan.* 6.6.3 for the possibilities; for the version in 310, see *Pan.* 6.7.5 with Rodgers's note, and for Lactantius, see *DMP* 24.5–8; for other proposals on the development of the story, see Kuhoff (2001): 793 n. 1574.

10. *Pan.* 6.8.1.

11. For the numismatic evidence, see Sutherland and Carson (1967) n. 40; 46; 52c (London, crucial for the terms of the initial proclamation); 622; 623; 651a; 652c; 654; 657c; 658b (Trier); 117 (Lyons) with Kuhoff (2001): 798.

12. The issue of Galerius' response was plainly behind the scene at Constantine's marriage to Fausta the next year; for the location of the wedding, see *Pan.* 7.10.2 *in istis partibus*, which works more reasonably as a reference to Trier than Arles, the other location that has been proposed.

12. MAXENTIUS AND FAUSTA

1. On the irritation of the guard, see Lact. *DMP* 26.3; Zos. 2.9.3. See also *Or.* 6; Aur. Vict. *De Caes.* 41.5; Eutrop. *Brev.* 10.2.3 and König (1987): 84–5. For the logic, see Seeck (1895–1920) 1:78, suggesting that Galerius believed that soldiers should serve on the frontier. See also Stein (1959): 83; Kuhoff (2001): 805–6. For Anullinus, see Chastagnol (1962): 46–7. For a different view, see Barnes (1982): 117, who accepts the existence of the Anullinus whom Zosimus makes praetorian prefect, separating him from the governor of North Africa who he allows was the prefect of the city in 306–307. He would also identify the former praetorian prefect as *praefectus urbis* in 312, but that man seems to be identical to the *praefectus urbis* of 306–307.

2. The effort to involve Diocletian at this stage may be gleaned from *Pan.* 7.12.6–8 where Jupiter tells Maximian to carry on.

3. *Pan.* 7.14.3 (Constantius); 6.1–3 (girl with helmet); 4.1 (first marriage).

4. *Pan.* 7.4.2; 6.10.2; 4.16.5–6; Eutrop. *Brev.* 10.3.21.

5. *Pan.* 7.1.1 (two emperors); 7.7.4 (gifts).

6. *Pan.* 7.8.3–6 (career).

7. *Pan.* 7.10.5; the *privatus princeps* is Maximian.

8. *Pan.* 7.10.5 (collapse of Rome); *Pan.* 7.14.1 (pinnacle); 5–7 (concluding vision); grandfather, see Grünewald (1990): 34 and his texts 36–64 on pp. 186–90.

9. Leadbetter (2009): 195–6.

10. For the exile of Maximian, see Lact. *DMP* 28.2; Zos. 2.11; Eutrop. *Brev.* 10.3.1; for the date, see Sutherland and Carson (1967): 29–30. For the reception in Gaul, see Sutherland and Carson (1967) London n. 85; 90; 91; 93; 96; 100; Trier n. 761; 762; 766; 767; 768; 769; 772b; Lyons n. 237; 246; 249; 253; 262; 276; 281; 288; 290; 292.

11. For events leading up to the conference, see Lact. *DMP* 29.1–2; Zos. 2.10.4–7; Aur. Vict. *De Caes.* 40.8; [Aur. Vict.] *Epit. de Caes.* 39.6; Eutrop. *Brev.* 10.4.1–2; Stein (1959): 85–6; Barnes (1981): 32. For the results see Eutrop. *Brev.* 10.4.2 (sons of the Augusti). Eutrop. *Brev.* 9.28; [Aur. Vict.] *Epit. de Caes.* 39.6 (Diocletian); Lact. *DMP* 29.3; for Maximian's oath see *Pan.* 6.16.1. For use of the title see Grünewald (1990): 41–5.

12. Lact. *DMP* 20.2–4.

13. Duval (1997): 148–51; Mayer (2002): 80–91.

13. THE END OF MAXIMIAN

1. *Pan.* 6.14.6 is important here, describing Maximian as being repudiated by Illyricum (a phrase that must refer to Carnuntum); for the numismatic evidence, see Sutherland and Carson (1967): 119–21; 158–62; 237–40.

2. Zos. 2.12 with other details accumulated in Barnes (1982): 14–15 and, on Volusianus, Lenski (2008): 209–10.

3. *Pan.* 6.15.1.

4. *Pan.* 6.16.1 on the moment of usurpation; 6.18.4 places the event at Arles; Lact. *DMP* 26.3–5 has Maximian play the role of an adviser; Eutrop. *Brev.* 3.2 and Aurel Vict. *De Caes.* 40.21–2 do not have details of the location and Zosimus 2.11 is confused.

5. *Pan.* 6. 14. 1 (nod); 14.5 (death).

6. Lact. *DMP* 30.2–5; see also a story in which Fausta reveals an unspecified plot at Eutrop. *Brev.* 3.2 before Marseilles; Zos. 2.11 mentions that Fausta revealed the plot. It is notable that the story also presumes that Fausta slept apart from Constantine at this point.

7. *Pan.* 6.2.1–4.

8. *Pan.* 6.4.1–2.

9. *Pan.* 6.3.1.

10. *Pan.* 6.21.4–5

11. This reading of the vision is essentially in concord with Rodgers (1980), who offers a thorough survey of other opinions at the time of her writing, concerning the divinity seen in the vision (including the possibility that it is Sol or a Celtic version of Apollo). I am simply incapable of understanding how it is that Girardet (2010): 35–6 derives the vision described in Eusebius from this; see p. 150 n.1.

12. The position taken here is on the extreme end of views connected with this passage in asserting that the emperor did actually have a vision, but it seems to me that he did have visions. For a survey of opinion, see Grünewald (1990): 52–3.

13. Sutherland and Carson (1967): 42–3.

14. THE GATHERING STORM

1. *CIL* 6. 1696. The reading *praepositus fabricae* [*muri et portarum*] while plausible is obviously beyond proof at this point, see esp. Dey (2011): 43 n. 59. I read *formidine* for *industria* (which seems a deeply improbable restoration) in l. 8. See also Chastagnol (1960): 34–6; Christol (1986): 48–50; *PLRE* Tertullus 6 (pp. 883–4).

2. Chastagnol (1962): 50–8. For Hermogenes, see also *PLRE* Hermogenes 8 (p. 424).

3. *PLRE* Pompeianus 8 (p. 713).

4. Responses to such threats included riots in the circus, burning the offices of senior officials, and stoning people thought to be responsible; for a summary, see Virvoulet (1985): 73–4.

5. Cullhead (1994): 49–57; Hekster (1999): 725; on the Temple of Romulus, see (2011): 213; for some sensible skepticism about the extent of the Maxentian additions to the wall, see Dey (2011): 43–5; 285–91.

6. There can be no certainty about the date of Romulus' birth save that his father was not yet Augustus when he was born; see the discussion at *PLRE* Romulus 6 (p. 772). It might also be tempting to see the selection of this name as a subtle reference to Galerius' mother Romula—the notion that the name could represent a Roman ideology and inheritance need not be mutually exclusive; see Hekster (1999): 726.

7. *ILS* 8935 with Hekster (1999): 726–7.

8. Cullhead (1994): 57–9 (villa), 46 (coins).

9. Sutherland and Carson (1967): 346–7; 381–2 (Rome) 397; 403–4 (Ostia); 307; 275–6; 293–4 (Constantine at Ticinum); 324 (Constantine at Aquileia); 377 (Constantine at Rome) on coins; Cullhead (1994): 73 on religion.

10. Lact. *DMP* 34.1–5.

11. Hunt (2011) on Christians at the court of Constantine before 312; Barnes (1982): 66 on the movements of Maximinus. For the negotiations of 311, see Zos. 2.14.1, 17.2; Lact. *DMP* 43.2–3; Seeck (1895–1920): 1: 114–16; Stein (1959): 90; Barnes (1981): 41. It is hard to tell if an account in Zosimus of a projected alliance between Maxentius and Licinius against Constantine may be a reflection of these negotiations, a tale leaked by Licinius to encourage Constantine; see also Cullhead (1994): 82–5.

12. For the date, see *Pan.* 5.13.2 with Nixon and Rodgers (1994): 255–6.

13. *Pan.* 5.2.5; 4.2.

14. *Pan.* 5.10.1.

15. *Pan.* 5.10.2.

16. *Pan.* 5.14.4; see Nixon and Rodgers (1994): 286 n. 61 noting both the possibility that the reference is to Sol Invictus and otherwise that it is a reference to Crispus, which seems profoundly unlikely as Crispus is unmentioned in the panegyrics of either 310 or 313.

15. THE BATTLE OF THE MILVIAN BRIDGE

1. *Pan.* 12.5.2. For a discussion of the forces available to both sides, see Kuhoff (2001): 897 n. 1672 and the very sensible discussion in Cullhead (1994): 70.

2. On the possibility that Maxentius' forces were concentrated in the east because of fear of Licinius, see Kuhoff (2001): 899–900; Barnes (2011): 81 suggests that Constantine was afraid that Licinius would conquer Italy and isolate him in Gaul.

3. *Pan* 12.5.6; 4.21.4.

4. *Pan.* 12.6.1–2 compares the sack of Segusio with the sack of Gomphi by Caesar in 48 BC as an act of psychological warfare; 4.22.1.

5. *Pan.* 12.6.2–5; compare *Pan.* 4.22–24 stressing that the bulk of the Maxentian force consisted of mailed cavalry, a point which, at this distance, is impossible to affirm and seems rather dubious given its omission from the earlier speech. For the history of Roman mailed cavalry, see Eadie (1967); on the nature of infantry combat, see Keegan (1976) (especially on walls of bodies and units breaking from the rear); see also Matthews (2007): 279–303; Elton (1996): 108–16 on equipment.

6. *Pan.* 12.7.5–8.

7. *Pan.* 4.26.3–5 (scout).

8. *Pan.* 12.16.2; Lact. *DMP* 44.7; Pan. 4.27.6. Lactantius' statement that Constantine suffered reverses in the early stages of the campaign is unrelated to any other source and would seem to be the product of his desire to stress the importance of the vision that he wrongly places in the immediate context of the battle of the Milvian Bridge at *DMP* 44.5. His otherwise profound ignorance of the circumstances of the campaign might reasonably call into question his statement about the demonstration in the circus.

9. For this understanding of the dream, see Harris (2009): 41–2; 115–16.

10. *Pan.* 12.17.2; see also *Pan.* 12.30.1.

16. FREEDOM OF WORSHIP

1. Zos. 2. 17.2

2. Barnes (1982): 71.

3. Lact. *DMP* 45.1. It is likely that Licinius issued a restitution edict for Christians in his territory; see Lact. *DMP* 48.1; Euseb. *HE* 10.5.4 with Barnes (1981): 62 n. 4; see also Stein (1959): 92.

4. On Theotecnus' oracle, see Eus. *HE* 9.3; for methods of making statues speak and surviving examples of drilled statues, see Poulsen (1945). For the *Acts of Pilate*, see Eus. *HE* 9.5.1.

5. *TAM* 2.3.785; *AE* 1989 no. 1046 with Mitchell (1988): 108.

6. For the historical value of the acts of Theodotus, see Grégoire and Orgels (1951); Mitchell (1982), with important qualifications in Barnes (2010): 155–9, esp. with reference to the events in *M. Theod.* 20–31. For the nature of the community, see Elm (1994), 54–9. For Athenogenes, see Maraval (1990), 15–19. For the arrest, see *P. Ath.* 22–6, 31–6, and Barnes (2010): 147–8; for Eugenius, see *MAMA* 1.270; for events at Nicomedia, see Eus. *HE* 9.9a 1–12; Lact. *DMP* 37.1 with Mitchell (1988): 114–15.

7. For Maximinus' campaign, see Lact. *DMP* 45; Seeck (1895–1920) 1: 149–52; Stein (1959): 93; Barnes (1981): 63. For the vision of Licinius, see Lact. *DMP* 46.3–5; see, on Licinius' religiosity, Seeck (1895–1920) 1: 139; Weber (2000): 294–6. On the issue of numbers on both sides, which are arguably set to emphasize the importance of divine intervention, see Kuhoff (2001): 929. For the prayer, see Lact. *DMP* 46.6.

8. Anniversary, see Lact. *DMP* 46.7; negotiations, see Lact. *DMP* 46.12; suicide, see Lact. *DMP* 49.1–7; Eus. *HE* 9.10.14–15 (giving an alternative version in which Maximinus dies of disease).

9. Eus. *HE* 9.10.7–8 trans. Oulton, slightly adapted.

10. Eus. *HE* 10.5.1–14; Lact. *DMP* 48. For bibliography on the so-called Edict of Milan, see Corcoran (2000a): 158–60; Barnes (2011): 93–7.

11. Drake (2000): 193–8.

12. Lact. *DMP* 48.2–3, 11; Eus. *HE* 10.5.4–5.

13. The crucial contribution remains Seeck (1891); see Corcoran (2000a): 158–60 for a clear statement of technical aspects; Drake (2000): 194 is important on the broader significance, and Bardill (2012): 133 for more on the history of the question, though like Drake he may attribute more to Constantine's initiative than is strictly speaking necessary.

17. THE CONVERSION OF CONSTANTINE

1. There is perhaps no more robustly discussed issue connected with Constantine than the nature of the conversion and the nature of the visions connected with the conversion. The range of opinion is vast, extending from those who would prefer that Constantine actually saw something like what Eusebius says he saw to those who think the whole thing is an invention (only representative opinions are cited). For the argument that he saw something in the sky, see Baynes (1972): 9 with n. 31; Jones (1949): 96; Lane Fox (1986): 616; Liebeschuetz (1979): 178–9 (without actually admitting that this view depends upon the vision in the sky); Barnes (1985b) argues that Eusebius should be preferred to Lactantius, contra Seeck (1895–1920) 1:495n on p. 127 l. 27. Seeck, however, is correct in distinguishing the tradition of the dream from that of the vision of the cross. His view (1895–1920) 1:128 and that of MacMullen (1969): 81–96; Lane Fox (1986): 613; and Alföldi (1948): 19–23, that Constantine might have wished the Christian God to have power over polytheist divinities and thus been attracted to that view, is I think correct. Likewise, Baynes (1972): 60–2 properly distinguishes between vision and dream and canvasses a wide range of opinions; though not perhaps noting as strongly as might be stated that neither of the Christian versions of the conversion was publicized by the 320s, and neither is mentioned by Constantine himself in 325 (for the date of the *Oratio ad Sanctos*, see p. 221 n. 1), something reflected in a further version of a vision had been produced in a non-Christian context, but only one vision (which I think is important); see *Pan.* 4 (10) 14.1–7. The problem of Nazarius' description is noted by Alföldi (1948): 72, though he suggests that the heavenly army sent by Constantius to aid his son was intended to obscure a Christianizing version. Since Nazarius' version is earlier than that of Eusebius, however, it might be seen as a reflection of a tradition concerning a vision for which there was, as yet, no fixed text. Nicolson (2000) provides a useful discussion of theological aspects of Eusebius' version of the vision. Since 2003, discussion of the conversion has been dominated by the English translation of a powerfully argued paper, Weiss (2003), first published in German in 1993, which identifies the decisive vision with that reported in *Pan* 6.21.4–5 and agrees with the view first promulgated in Baynes and Jones that the phenomenon was a solar halo. See, for instance, Girardet (2010): 33–52, though it will be obvious from what follows that I disagree with the approach taken here; I continue to feel that one must read the sources in the order that they were written and one cannot read backward from 337 to 312, asserting that something not mentioned before 337 should have taken place in or before 312. I do think that Weiss and Girardet are absolutely correct in separating the decisive vision from the immediate circumstances of the battle of the Milvian Bridge. For further support of Weiss's view, see Barnes (2011): 74–5 though I should note that refusal to accept Weiss's view does not necessarily indicate an attachment to the Nazi party as is implied in his discussion. The discussion that follows is based on a paper that I delivered at the Langford Conference at Florida State University in 2010. The general approach—placing Constantine's experience in the context of other dream reports of emperors—owes much to Weber (2000).

2. *Pan.* 12.2.4–5.

3. Artem. *On.* 1.2 with the summary of his merits in Harris (2009): 273–7.

4. Rubin (1980): 24 is the source for this observation about dream narratives; see also Weber (2000): 202–10; 344–8; Harris (2009): 205.

5. For Marcus' dreams, see Marc. Aurel. *Med.* 2.17; 6.31; for the Rain Miracle, see the excellent treatment in Kovács (2009); for its reuse, see Rubin (1980).

6. Artem. *On.* 1.2.

7. Thessalus, *De virtutibus herbarum* (e cod. Matrit. Bibl. Nat. 4631) praef. 21–7.

8. Aristid. *Or.* 48.41.

9. Optatus, *Tract.* Appendix 5=Maier (1987) b. 21. For the significance of this passage, see also Baynes (1972): 13–14; Odahl (2010): 138–9, who seems to overstate the specifically Christian nature of phrases such as *Deus omnipotens in caeli specula residens*; Hunt (2011): 300.

10. Optatus, *Tract.* 1.23; on the significance of the appearance of these bishops with Miltiades at the first Donatist hearing, see Eck (2007): 77–8; Hunt (2011): 295; for the visions, see Weber (2000): 282–94 with an ample sampling of earlier discussions.

11. Eus. *VC* 1.30.1 see also *VC* 2.8.2 and p. 213. Barnes (2011): 76 argues that "much later" means at the council of Nicaea, but this would seem unlikely in light of the language of *VC* 2.8.2 since the victory over Licinius, with which the second event is linked was the year before the council.

12. Eus. *VC* 1. 27.2–3; Elliott (1996): 65–8 is good on the narrative inconsistencies, though I do not agree that Constantius was a Christian.

13. *Pan.* 7.14.3.

14. Eus. *VC* 1. 28.1.

15. *T.Theos.* 13.1; Lact. *DI* 1.7 with Robert (1971).

16. Eus. *VC* 1. 32.1–2.

17. On this point, see *LC* 9.12; I am indebted on this point to Drake (forthcoming); for the other event, see p. 213.

18. *Pan.* 4.7.3–4.

19. *Pan.* 4.14.1–2.

20. *Pan.* 4.29.2.

21. Lact. *DI* 2.9.5 tr. Bowen and Garnsey (2003): 148 on the sun; see also Eck (2007): 37; for the use of solar imagery in a Christian context, see Liebeschuetz (1979): 283–5; Brent (2010): 231–3; Stephenson (2010): 84–5; Shean (2010): 273–4, and, with further examples, Bardill (2012): 326–31.

18. REWORKING PAST AND FUTURE

1. Aurel Vict. *De Caes.* 40.26 with Marlowe (2011): 202; Curran (2000): 80–1.

2. Curran (2000): 93–6; 99–102; 109–14; Stephenson (2010):148–9.

3. See Torp (1953); Bowersock (2005); Barnes (2011): 88; Bardill (2012): 243.

4. The discussion in the text is a summary, with no pretense to originality, of Marlowe (2006): 223–34; see also Mayer (2002): 189–202, also good on the ideological implication is Bardill (2012): 222–30.

5. Pierce (1989): 389; Elsner (2000): 153–8.

6. See also Curran (2000): 86–90; Stephenson (2010): 153–6; see also Lenski (2008): 231–47.

7. Pierce (1989): 412–13; Grünewald (1990): 98–9.

8. The text is *ILS* 694; the discussion of *instinctus* derives entirely from Lenski (2008): 218–31.

9. Grünewald (1990): 71–3; 75–7.

10. Barnes (1975a): 186.

11. *Or.* 15 with Barnes (2011): 66; König (1987): 116–17.

12. *Or.* 15 with König (1987): 118 with *CTh.* 10.14.1; Mal. 12. 314 and Corcoran (1993): 108 on Licinius movements. On the Constantius in question—the future praetorian prefect (*PLRE* Constantius 5; also *PLRE* Constantius 1 [pp. 224–5]) rather than Constantine's half brother (*PLRE* Constantius 7 [p. 226])—there is no proof of the view taken in the text, merely my suspicion that such a mission would have involved a very senior official.

13. Zos. 2.18.2–4.

14. *Or.* 17; Zos. 2.19.2; for the rank of Augustus, see Barnes (1982): 19; König (1987): 126–7.

15. *Or.* 17 (for the location with König (1987): 128–9, on the text); Zos. 2.19.2–3.

16. *Or.* 18 (removal of Valens); Zos. 2.20.1; [Aur. Vict.] *Epit.* 40.9 (execution) with Barnes (2011): 103. For the peace terms, see *Or.* 19; Zos. 2.20.2 and Sutherland and Carson (1966): 67 for details of the settlement.

17. *Pan.* 4.9.3–4; see also p. 223 where the similarities between Maxentius and Licinius are suggested by Constantine himself at *Orat* 22.

18. *Pan.* 4.10.1–11.1.

19. For Fausta, see Sutherland and Carson (1966), 493–4; 504–5 n. 49; 51 (Fausta) n. 48; 50 (Fausta). For Maximian, see Sutherland and Carson (1966): 494; compare the treatment of Galeria Valeria, daughter of Diocletian and wife of Galerius see Sutherland and Carson (1967), 15; 499 n. 32–4; 500 n. 41–3; 560 n. 47; 562 n. 53; 57–8; 586 n. 46; 590 n. 71; 626–8 n. 80; 84; 91; 98; 631 n. 107; 637 n. 138; 639 n. 151; 673–5 n. 67; 74; 81; 680 n. 128; 129.

19. GOVERNING THE EMPIRE

1. *CTh* 13.10.1

2. *CTh* 10.10.1; 10.10. 2 with note 13 below where alternative explanations are discussed.

3. *CTh* 5.8.1.

4. *CJ* 13.5.1.

5. I owe this observation to the excellent paper that is Lenski (2011): 252.

6. *CTh* 10.8.1.

7. *CTh* 11.36.3 (Aelianus); 11.36.2 (Volusianus); 11.30,3 (Petronius); see also *PLRE* Petronius 3 (pp. 733–4) and Chastagnol (1962): 82–4. For the *navicularii* see *CTh.* 13.5.2-3 (315).

8. *CTh* 1.2.2.

9. *CTh* 11.36.1; for Aco Catullinus, whose son would be praetorian prefect in 341/2 and prefect of Rome in 342–4, see *PLRE* Catullinus 2 (p. 187).

10. *CTh* 9.34.2 with *PLRE* Aelianus 2 (p. 17).

11. Opt. *Tract.* App. 2.10=Maier (1987) n. 22.10; the confessional issue is evident in the statement: Constantine the greatest eternal Augustus and Licinius, the Caesars see fit to show piety to Christians who do not wish their doctrine to be corrupted, rather they wish that religion to be respected. Do not fool yourself that because you say you are a follower of God you cannot be tortured. You will be tortured so that you do not lie, something that seems to be foreign to Christians.

12. *CTh* 9.18, for Celsus see *PLRE* Celsus 8 (p. 195).

13. *CTh* 9.5.1 with Chastagnol (1962): 72–4 *PLRE* Maximus 48 (p. 590) on Maximus and Christol (1986): 250–2; Dietz (1980): 335 on the family in the third century. Aurel. Vict. *De Caes.* 41.4; Soz. *HE* 1.8.13 assert that Constantine abolished crucifixion, which is not implausible given the abolition of *damnatio ad ludum* in 325 and retention of reference to the penalty in *CTh.* 9.18; Barnes (2011): 136 and the excellent discussion in Harries (1999): 138–9. In the case of *CTh.* 10.10.2, the assumption in the text seems to me a more economical explanation than the view that the consular date in the Code is deeply corrupt, though see the important discussion of Corcoran (2007): 242–3 which

takes the opposite view; Barnes (1976a): 275-7 suggests that the text is Licinian; Seeck (1919): 50-51; 160 suggests the date as December 312 noting that it is mentioned in *Pan.* 12.4.4; for a more agnostic discussion of the way that the text came into the Code, see Matthews (2000): 268-9. It is with some considerable hesitation that I disagree with Corcoran, without whose excellent work our knowledge of this material would be very much diminished.

14. *CTh* 9. 15.1 with Chastagnol (1962): 74-6; *PLRE* Verinus 2 (p. 951)

15. *CTh* 9.40.2; for Eumelius, see *PLRE* Eumelius (p. 294).

16. Sutherland and Carson (1966): 98-106 (London); 122-6 (Lyons); 168-70; 172-7 (Trier, showing a greater variety of types); 235-53 (Arles); 296; 297-303; 307; 309 (Rome); 360-2; 366; 368; 370-1 (Ticinum, also with a wider variety of types); 392-3 (Aquileia); 426-8 (Siscia); note some post 320 issues at Sirmium on pp. 461, 467 and Bruun (1958): 15-37; for more recent discussions, see Wallraff (2001): 126-43; Berrens (2004): 15-62; Bardill (2012): 131-2 though the confessional explanation for the end of this coinage is unlikely in light of the near-simultaneous declaration of the *dies solis* as a holiday.

17. P. 165-8.

18. Sutherland and Carson (1966): 48.

19. *CTh* 2.8.1; *CJ* 3.12.2; the individual who took "The Lords Day" off appears on *P.Oxy.* 3759.

20. *CTh* 3.2.1 (forfeiture); 4.12.3 (marriages between women and fiscal slaves); for the Senatus Consultum Claudianum, which seems to influence this text, Evans Grubbs (1993a): 128, 141; and Buckland (1908): 324-6 on the specific category of slaves involved contra Harper (2011): 436-7, whose view that the category includes all slaves owned by the emperor is implausible in light of the evidence gathered in Buckland; see also Corcoran (2007): 236; 8.16.1 (abolition of disabilities for *caelibes*); 11.7.3 (no imprisonment for tax defaulters); *CJ* 6.9.9 (formulas in making wills); 6.23.15 (formulas for making wills); 6.37.21 (formulas in making wills) with, on these last two passages, Tate (2008): 240-8 and Matthews (2000): 236-40; on the legislation in general, see the useful summary in Corcoran (2000a): 71-72.

21. *CTh* 8.16.1.

22. Eus. *VC* 4.26.2-4; Soz. *HE* 1.9 with Eus. *HE* 10.8.12; *VC* 1.55.1-3; where what is arguably a similar measure by Licinius at this period is attacked, see Corcoran (1993): 102.

23. *CTh* 11.7.3.

24. See also the discussion in Evans Grubbs (1993b) 123-6 adducing as well *Pan.* 4.35.3; 38.4-5. For the suggestion that people might ignore the proscriptions of the law, see *CTh.* 8.12.5 with the useful discussion in Humphress (2006): 221.

25. *CTh* 9.16.1 with Potter (1994): 173-81 on the context; for the date and *CTh* 9.16.2, see Seeck (1919): 18.

26. *CTh* 9.16.2; note the contrast between *qui vero id vobis existimatis conducere, adite aras publicas adque delubra et consuetudinis vestrae celebrate sollemnia* here and *superstitioni enim suae servire cupientes poterunt publice ritum proprium exercere* in *CTh* 9.16.1.

27. *CTh* 16.10.1.

28. Aur. Vict. *De Caes.* 40. 28 (undated but in the immediate context of the defeat of Maxentius so probably 313); *CIL* 6. 1690; 1691; 1694; on the temple, also placed by Victor in the immediate aftermath of the Milvian Bridge, see Aur. Vict. *De Caes.* 40.26; on the problem of the temple's location, see Girardet (2010): 100.

29. For the date, see Eus. *HE* 10.7=Maier (1987) no. 13 with Seeck (1919): 151 with *CTh* 16.2.2; 3; Gaudemet (1947): 27-32; see also Piganol (1932): 102 associating this action with *CTh* 6.35.1, which removes the general action to the fall and would make the ruling in North Africa a precedent, which seems unlikely though attractive. The reconstruction offered here is admittedly not without difficulty as the consular date in the manuscripts for *CTh* 16.2.2 is 319, but Eus. *HE* 10.7 seems to me to

presuppose an earlier statement about which Anullinus is seeking clarification. The earlier document may be the *lex* referred to in Opt. *Tract.* App. 10 and *CTh* 16.2.7. For the restoration of clerics who were evading *munera* to councils, see *CTh* 16.2.3.

30. *CTh* 1.27 1 with Seeck (1919): 57 on the text (and date) with further discussion in Corcoran (2000a), 284–6; for a different view see Barnes (2011) 134.

31. On the role of the bishop as an arbitrator rather than a judge in the early church and the relationship between Christian practices and arbitration, see Gaudemet (1947): 35; for the earliest evidence, see Matt. 18.15–17; 1 Cor. 6.1–6; for the importance of the *Didascalia,* see Harries (1999): 192.

32. Harries (1999): 193–5; see also Rapp (2005): 245.

33. *CTh* 4.7.1; this is not the initial decision on this subject since Constantine did not make imperial policy through rescripts to bishops; *CTh* 1.13.1, which is dated to the consulship of Sabinus and Rufinus; the consuls of 316 should be dated to the consulship of Severus and Rufinus in 323 since it refers to an earlier decision; for this point, see Seeck (1919): 88. For the suggestion that the problem Seeck saw here is nonexistent because Sozomon *HE* 1.9 says that there were three laws and that the reference to a past law in this text may be to the earlier (now lost) law, see Bellen (1967): 320 followed by Langenfeld (1977): 27–8. While I think that Bellen is correct that the law referred to in *CJ* 1.13.1 is the lost law of Sozomon, the view that this text belongs in 316 requires the assumption that Constantine would be writing to the bishop of Serdica while that city was firmly under the control of Licinius; see also Harper (2011): 477–8 on the date, attempting to preserve 316 for *CTh* 1.13.1 including the suggestion that the first war was in 314 (suggesting that a real date can be obtained on the basis of arguing that something that did not happen happened). For aspects of the procedure, see also Buckland (1908): 449–51. Since the extant texts are rescripts rather than edicts, it is possible that we are in fact missing a good deal of the evidence known to Sozomon.

34. *CJ* 1.13.1.

20. MAXIMUS AND BASSUS

1. Gaius, *Institutes* 4.1–12; see also Buckland (1908): 674–95; the discussion in the text is perforce highly schematic since the actions possible under law were infinitely variable.

2. For the clearest explication of these principles, see Frier and McGinn (2004): 323–5; 342–3.

3. Frier and McGinn (2004): 424–7; for the age at which there would be curators, see *CTh* 2.17.1.

4. *CTh* 1.2.3; *CJ* 1.14.1.

5. *CJ* 7.57.7 (decisions); *CJ* 3.36.26; *CTh* 2.6.3; 11. 35.1 (time limits) with Seeck (1919): 62 on the linkage between the texts (*CTh* 2.6.3 has a subscription to 321); and showing that the correct date in Licinio A. V et Crispo C. conss. it is possible that this ruling was issued in December rather than May.

6. *CTh* 8.12.4.

7. *CTh* 3.17.1

8. *CTh* 2.16.2.

9. *Frag Vat.* 249; *CTh* 3.30.2; 8.12.1; *Consult.* 9.13 with Seeck (1919): 172.

10. *CTh* 3.5.2 with Evans Grubbs (1995): 156–71; and Apul. *Apol.* 92.

11. *CTh* 9.1.1.

12. For a splendid discussion of the issue of slave status in the earlier empire, see Mouritsen (2011): 10–35.

13. *CTh* 2.25 with good discussion in Harper (2011): 271–2 and background in Mouritsen (2011): 285–6.

14. *CTh* 11.27.2 with *PLRE* Menander 2 (pp. 595–6) and Harper (2011): 401; see also p. 271 below.

15. *CTh* 4.8.6; on the date, see Seeck (1919): 172 usefully discussed in Lenski (2011): 257–9; Harper (2011): 402–3 though the argument that there is a specific case of Balkan origin underlying this ruling is problematic in light of the fact that the addressee was in Rome.

16. *CTh* 4.12.3, on the connection with the law on marriage, see Corcoran (2000a): 194, and on the underlying theory, see Evans Grubbs (1993a): 141.

17. *CTh* 12.1.6.

18. *CJ* 6.7.2; for Severan precedent, see *D.* 25.3.6.1 (Modestinus); *CJ* 6.3.2; see, for Diocletian, *CJ* 6.3.12; 7.16.30 with discussion in Buckland (1908): 422–4; for the earlier empire see Mouritsen (2011): 55–7.

19. *CTh* 4.8.5.

20. Apul. *Met.* 6.7–8.

21. *CTh* 9.12.1, and *Coll.* 3.3.5 for Pius with useful discussion in Harper (2011): 232–3; Hopkins (1993). Harper (2011): 225–38 is especially good in forms of violence used by masters against slaves.

22. *CTh* 11.30.8 see also *CTh* 11.30.7.

23. *CTh* 11.30.11; the passage in question is illustrative of issues that arise in rendering these documents into English. The phrase translated "the right to act in place of the emperor" is *imaginem principalis disceptationis* which literally means "the form of imperial judgment," though *imago* would in this case seem to convey the "image in the eye of the beholder." In the next clause I alter a passive construction *a vobis . . . , appellationum adminicula respuuntur* to active for the sake of readability. Similar choices are made throughout in handling these texts.

21. THE DONATIST CONTROVERSY

1. In what follows, I essentially follow the views adumbrated in Potter (2004): 402–10.

2. For Pepetua see the excellent edition of Amait (1996), who argues for the primacy of the Latin text; a view supported by the majority of scholars, most recently Barnes (2010): 66–74 (offering a wide ranging summary of the scholarship). The view that the Greek text has priority stems from Robert (1982); Robert's view is supported, in my view, by narrative inconcinnities in the Latin version that do not exist in the Greek. For Tertullian see Barnes (1971). For Cyprian and persecution see Brent (2010): 250–89 which is extremely perceptive; for the politics of the situation see also Potter (1993) and Barnes (2010): 77–85 on the management of Cyprian's memory.

3. Opt. *Tract.* 1. 16.1. For the history of the text, see Labrousse (1995), 12–14, 32–56, and the lucid summary in Edwards (1997), xi–xxix. As for the kissing of relics in this story, see the important discussion of Wiśniewski (2011) arguing that the narrative is invented at a point when the handling of relics was controversial—in the mid-fourth century. See otherwise Lockwood (1989): 168–9.

4. Opt. *Tract.* 17. The issue of who the emperor is connected with the discussion of the chronology of the dispute. I follow Barnes' "early chronology"; for arguments in favor of a "late" chronology, see Lancel (1991) 4: 1553–7, who places the election of Secundus in 309. Since the *tyrannus imperator* of Opt. *Tract.* 1.17 must be an emperor on the throne during the persecution, this can only be Maximian. The most likely explanation for Mensurius' release is that Constantius had succeeded Maximian in the interim, meaning that the election of Caecilian cannot reasonably be pushed back further than early 307.

5. Opt. *Tract.* App. 1.13–16; App. 1.3–6.

6. Opt. *Tract.* 1.18.2–19.4 and App 1.6 (for the words quoted here).

7. Aug. *Breviculus* 13.25. Opt. *Tract.* 14.2 implies that it was well known that Secundus had been released from jail because he had agreed to hand over books of Scripture. For the situation in Numidia, see Frend (1952): 8. For Catholic discomfort with the martyrs of this period, see Lockwood (1989): 170.

8. *Act. Ab.* 3. For another martyrology evidently deriving from the Donatist tradition, see Chiesa (1996).

9. *Act. Ab.* 20.881–917, 21.957–60=Maier (1987) n. 4, pp. 86–87, 89); see also Aug. *Breviculus* 18.32–3.

10. The point was taken by Seeck (1895–1920) 3:509n on p. 322, l. 12. Frend (1952): 17, doubts the charges, but the essence of the case seems to be admitted in Mensurius' denunciation of the martyrs. The difference between Frend's approach, which places great stress on the history of division in North Africa over the subject of martyrdom (1952: 125–40), and that which is taken here, is that I believe that the opposition to Caecilian stems from specific behaviors rather than from a generalized tradition of discord, a point that emerges from the summary of the Donatist case in *Gesta. Con. Carth.* 3. 343. The severity of the charge would appear to be confirmed by Augustine's account of efforts to prove that the report of Caecilian's conduct is a forgery (*Breviculus* 3.14.26). On this point see also Drake (2000): 214. For later efforts to dissociate the anti-Donatists from Caecilian, see Aug. *Breviculus* 3.16.28.

11. Drake (2000): 212–13.

12. Anullinus' letter is Eus. *HE* 10.5.15–17=Maier (1987) no. 11. For the relationship between the Anullini see p. 109. For the dealings of Ossius, see Eus. *HE* 10.6.1–5=Maier (1987): no. 12, pp. 140–2, with her discussion of the date on p. 140.

13. For these documents see chap. 21 n. 30, this volume.

14. For Majorian's case, see Aug. *Ep.* 88.2. For the composition of the council, see Opt. *Tract.* 1.22.2 (giving a faulty text); see also Aug. *Ep.* 88.2; *Breviculus* 3.12.4; *Acta concil. Carthg.* 3.315 with Labrousse's n. 3 on Opt. *Tract.* 1.22.2 (pp. 222–3 of her edition). On Miltiades, see Opt. *Tract.* 23–4. For the significance of the appeal as calling into question Ossius' standing as a reliable guide to Christian affairs, see Drake (2000): 217; for the role of Miltiades in expanding the council, see Eus. *HE* 10.5. 18–20=Maier (1987) n. 16; Opt. *Tract.* App. 3=Maier (1987) n. 18 on p.154 with Drake (2000): 218. For Donatist attacks on Ossius, see Aug. *C. litt. Petil.* 1.4.7, 1.5.10, 1.8.13. Compare Eus. *HE* 7.30.19 on Paul of Samosata; for Miltiades' role, see Eck (2007): 74. For Donatus, see *Ep.* 43.2.4; *Ad Donat.* 17.21; *Breviculus* 3.12.24, identifying Donatus as being from Casa Nigra; see Alexander (1980): 540–7: Donatus of Casa Nigra was Donatus of Carthage, contra Barnes (1975b): 16–17. On the date of Majorian's death, see Frend (1952): 148.

15. Opt. *Tract.* 24.1. For the earlier controversy, see Cypr. *Ep.* 69.7, 71.1.1–2, 4, 73.1, 3, 75.5–6, 17, 22–25. For Miltiades' initiative, see Aug. *Ep.* 43.7, 16; for Donatus' charge against Miltiades, see Aug. *C. Parm.* 1.5.10; for the conclusion, see Opt. *Tract.* App. 3=Maier (1987) no. 18 ll. 34–6 with Eck (2007): 75.

16. There was also some truth to the Donatist claim that Miltiades had changed the rules on them without warning when he had insisted that they present actual evidence in accord with Roman legal procedure. The procedural issue is well made by Drake (2000): 218–19.

17. Arles *can.* 14 [in Jonkers (1954): 26]=Maier (1987) n. 20.

18. Arles *can.* 9 [in Jonkers (1954): 25]; for the parallel, see Maier (1987): n. 23.

19. Arles *can.* 15 [in Jonkers (1954): 26]; compare Elvira *can.* 73 [in Jonkers (1954): 21].

20. See also Opt. *Tract.* App. 4=Maier (1987) no. 20, a letter from the council to Silvester, the bishop of Rome.

21. Opt. *Tract.* App. n. 5=Maier (1987) no. 21.

22. Opt. *Tract.* App. 5=Maier (1987) no. 21, trans. Edwards (1997).

23. For Marcus, see Brunt (1974): 1–20; specifically, see *Med.* 4.16; 9.34, 42, 11.18.4 on controlling anger; see also 4.38, 6.53, 7.4, 10.12 for the importance of listening; see 6.20, 6.50, 7.26, 7.62, 8.17, 9.16, 9.27, 11.9 tolerating those who disagree; 7.7, 8.16 accepting help; 6.27 people who are wrong; 8.49, 11.13 people who speak ill of him.

24. Opt. *Tract.* App. n. 3=Maier (1987) no. 18; Eus. *HE* 10.5.21–24= Maier (1987): no. 19.

25. Opt. *Tract.* App. n. 2=Maier (1987) no. 22.

26. Aug. *C. Cresc.* 3.71.82=Maier (1987) no. 27; see also Barnes (1981): 60.

27. *CTh* 9.34.1; for his relationship to Constantine, possibly of very great length, see Harries (2010): 84.

28. Maier (1987) no. 28. There is an English translation in Tilley (1996), 51–60.

29. For the letter to Verinus, see Aug. *Contra partem Donati post gesta* 31.54, 33.56; for the letter to the bishops see Opt. *Tract.* App. n. 10=Maier (1987) no. 30.

30. Aug. *Ep.* 93.43 with Frend (1952): 167–8.

22. THE DEFEAT OF LICINIUS

1. Smith, R. R. R. (1997): 193.

2. *CTh* 13.10.2=*CJ* 11.49.1 (in part) and *CJ* 11.55.1, with Seeck (1919): 159 and further discussion in Corcoran (1993): 118.

3. *CTh* 4.12.1; *CJ* 6.1.3 with Seeck (1919): 53; 162 with further discussion in Corcoran (1993): 114; both are addressed to the same official who appears to have been a close associate of Licinius. On the marriage issue, see Evans Grubbs (1993a): 140–1.

4. *CTh* 10.7.1; 20.1; 12.1.5 with Seeck (1919); for Constantine's generals see p. 252.

5. Text in van Berchem (1952): 78–9; for the second, less complete copy, see *AE* 2007 n. 1224.

6. *CJ* 7.64.9; 10.55.2; 55.3 with van Berchem (1952): 77–8.

7. van Berchem (1952): 83.

8. Mitchell (2007): 63–4 recognizes the connection between these texts. The clear reference to Licinian provisions invalidates efforts to date the text to the period before 312; for a survey of these options, see Connolly (2010b): 96 n.8; Corcoran (2000a): 257–9.

9. *CTh* 7.20.2; for the surrounding negotiations, see Connolly (2010b): 103–14.

10. *CTh* 12.17.1 (Dalmatius); *CTh* 6.22.1 (to Severus, on whom see Seeck [1919]: 143, better than *PLRE* Severus 3, p. 831). The caution on this point in Barnes (1982): 130 is not unreasonable, but the content of the law suggests a man of very high rank and connection to the palace, which inclines me to agree with Seeck and to think that this is a document that Constantine would have reviewed.

11. *CTh* 14.4.2.

12. For Flavius Constantius, see *CTh* 15.14.1 with *PLRE* Constantius 5 (p. 225); for the Dalmatius of *CTh.* 12.17.1, see *PLRE* Dalmatius 6 (pp. 240–1). For Crispus' role see *Or.* 23; 26.

13. Zos. 2. 22.3–7; *Or.* 24 with *CTh* 7.20.1.

14. Zos. 2.22.6 on Constantine's role in the battle; *Or.* 24.

15. For a good discussion of the evidence for the Labrarum, see Girardet (2010): 52–76.

16. Eus. *VC* 2.8.1–9.3.

17. Socr. *HE* 1.4.2–4 (providing the information about the charge upon which Licinius was executed); the date for the battle of Chrysopolis (September 18) is provided by Hyd. *Descriptio Consulum* s.a 324; the date for the final surrender comes from *CTh* 15.14.1; Barnes (2011): 106 implies a more compressed chronology. For the date of Licinius' execution (simply given as 325), see Hyd. *Descriptio Consulum* s.a. 325.

23. THE EASTERN EMPIRE

1. *CTh* 15.14.1.

2. *CTh* 15.14.2.

3. Eus. *VC* 2.24–42. I presume this to be early because it seems to be concerned solely with Constantine's victory, while the council of Antioch, summoned for Easter, suggests that he was aware

of the divisions within the church; for signs that he was aware of the trouble in this letter, see next note.

4. Eus. *VC* 2.24.1; understand *tên…Christanismou therapeian* to be a translation of *ritus Christianus*, the terminology in *CTh* 16.2.5 *ad ritum alienae superstitionis*; but see 2.31.2; here *therapeia* may translate *servientes* (compare *CTh* 16.4: *quoniam conperimus quosdam ecclesiaticos et ceteros catholicae sectae servientes* to *VC* 2.31.2: *hoi theou therapontes*); it is significant that he avoids *secta Catholica*, standard in *CTh* 16.2.1; 4; 5 which might imply doctrinal favoritism.

5. Eus. *VC* 2.26.2; *to kreitton* of *VC* 2.25.1; 26.1; 28.1; 29.1; 30.2 and *to theion* of *VC* 2.27.2; 28.1; 30.1 is manifestly the concept appearing as *summa divinitas*; see *CTh* 9.1.4: *Ita mihi summa divinitas semper propitia sit et me incolumem praestet.* See also Eus. *VC* 2.38 for *megistos theos* and 42 for *tou panta dunatou theou*.

6. Eus. *VC* 2.29.1.

7. Eus. *VC* 2.34–41.

8. *CTh* 11.39.1 with *PLRE* Helladius 5 (p. 412) with Seeck (1919): 9; 109 for the place of issue, correcting Naissus to Nassete, which is between Chalcedon and Nicomedia; if correct, which the location of other documents in these months suggests, it would also show that Helladius was governing in the former territory of Licinius and thus would likely be dealing with cases under the restitution edict which, given the lack of a time limit, might in fact go back to the period of the persecutions of Diocletian, Galerius, or Maximinus.

9. See Digeser (2000): 206–7 on the tone of this document; for the Highest God, see Mitchell (1999) and (2010).

10. *CTh* 9.1.4.

11. *CTh* 1.5.1.

12. *CTh* 11.16.3 (tax assessments); for Maximus see *PLRE* Maximus 49 (pp. 590–1) Seeck (1919): 118; he was probably related to the prefect of Rome from 319–323.

13. *CJ* 6.21.15 with explanation at *D* 29.1.1 (Ulpian) and significant precedents at *CJ* 6.21.2; 3; 5; 6; 7; 8 with Campbell (1984): 210–29; for the date, see Seeck (1919): 88–9 showing that Constantine was in the Balkans on the date given in the manuscript—*Optato et Paulino cons*, hence restoring *Paulino et Juliano cons* is correct; see also Harries (2010): 88–90.

14. *CTh* 7.20.4 (to Maximus); 7.20.3 (farm implements); *CTh* 7.20.4 (to Maximus); *CTh* 7.20.3 (farm implements).

15. *CTh* 15.12.1 (*damnati*) with Potter (2010b): 599–603; 12.1.12; *CJ* 11.50.1.

24. CONSTANTINE SPEAKS TO THE BISHOPS

1. For the connection between Constantine's speech to the bishops and the council at Antioch, see Lane Fox (1986): 627–56, a fundamental study that set the parameters of later discussion. Lane Fox's views have been challenged on a number of grounds. Edwards (1999): 254–62 has shown conclusively (to my mind) that the speech was written in Latin and that it was translated into Greek by someone other than Eusebius (though it is not clear that the translation could not have been contemporaneous with the composition). As for the date and location, Edwards' effort to place the speech at Rome fails in light of the fact that Constantine, although speaking in Latin, seems to presume a Greek audience as the bulk of his references are to Greek rather than Latin texts. Barnes (2001b) following Bleckmann (1997) (though showing that Bleckmann's preference for a date in 327 is not plausible) offers important support for Lane Fox's belief that the speech was written for an Easter event, though he and Bleckmann would place this at Nicomedia, which is not implausible on Lane Fox's model since Lane Fox holds that the speech is a letter sent to the bishops at Antioch. Barnes is also correct in pointing out that the emperor who took control of Diocletian's army in *Orat.* 25 must be Licinius (2001b): 28. The view of the

circumstances and the date accepted here derive entirely from Drake (forthcoming). Edwards (2003): 1–62 provides a good translation with valuable notes. For the view, accepted here, that the speech represents Constantine's own thinking, see Bleckmann (1997): 184 and Drake (forthcoming).

2. Const. *Orat.* 1–8 with 11 (Constantine's experience).

3. Const. *Orat.* 9.3 tr. Edwards (2003): 14–15, rightly seen by Barnes (2001a): 34–5 as being essentially in agreement with Arian theology, especially in the invocation of *ho deuteros Theos*, "the second God." For other problems in the theology of the speech, in Const. *Orat.* 11, see Davies (1991): 611, though his explanation, that the Arian sentiments are later Eusebian interventions, seems dubious.

4. Eus. *VC* 2.68.3 tr. Hall.

5. For philosophers, see esp. Const. *Orat.* 14 tr. Edwards (2003): 32–3 with his note 1 on the passage. For Memphis and Babylon see Const. *Orat.* 16.2; for prophecies Const. *Orat.* 16–21; on the potential Sibylline influence on Virgil, see Nisbet (1975): 59–78; on Sibyls more generally, see Potter (1994): 58–97.

6. Const. *Orat.* 22.1 tr. Edwards (2003): 52–4 mildly adapted; for the identification of the "champion" as Licinius, see Bleckmann (1997): 190.

7. Const. *Orat.* 24–5; the first section quoted here is from Const. *Orat.* 25 in Edwards (2003): 58; the second is Const. *Orat.* 26 from Edwards (2003): 62.

25. THE ARIAN CONTROVERSY

1. Seeck (1895–1920), 3: 388; Ritter (1978): 696; see also Edwards (2006): 616 for a clear exposition of the doctrines.

2. Williams (1987): 30 for his background.

3. The evidence is contained in the letter preserved in Theod. *HE* 1.5.4 (also in Opitz [1934a] no. 1.1–3; Brennecke, Heil, Stockhausen and Wintjes [2007] no. 15.1–3). That they were not always as one theologically appears as a result of Eusebius' objection to some of Arius' teachings; see Theod. *HE* 1.6.3; see the important review of all issues connected with Arius by Kannengiesser (1983): 456–75; Kannengiesser (1986): 208; Gwynn (2007) passim on the later historiography of the dispute. For the issue of their connection with Lucian, see Parvis (2006): 40–3.

4. For the Alexandrian background, see esp. Wiles (1962): 344; Kannengiesser (1990): 392, 398, 401–2.

5. For the appointment of Arius as a preacher by Alexander, see Soz. *HE* 1.15.2; Epiph. *Pan.* 68.4.2, 69.1.2 with Seeck (1895–1920), 3: 542n on p. 386, l. 8; Barnes (1981): 202; Ritter (1978): 698–99. The sources for the outbreak of the conflict had an unusually strong documentary background, as later accounts were based upon collections of documents made by both sides from a very early date; see Socr. *HE* 1.6.41; Ath. *De Synod.* 18 with the valuable discussion of Schwartz (1905b); see also the excellent discussion in Parmentier (1998): lxxiii–lxxvi. On Epiphanius, see Schwartz (1905b): 258. Theod. *HE* 1.4.7–9 (also in Opitz [1934a] no. 14; Brennecke, Heil, Stockhausen and Wintjes [2007] no. 17). For the significance of the virgins, see Elm (1994): 350–3; and more generally for his connection with ascetics, see Brakke (1995): 9–22; 64–5.

6. Schwartz (1905a): 166–75; Kettler (1936); Barnes (1981): 201 for Peter's position; Epiph. *Pan.* 68.2.1, 4; Ath. *Apol. contra Ar.* 71; Soz. *HE* 1.24.1; Seeck (1895–1920) 3: 382 for the Meletian side.

7. Ancyra *can.* 1; for the text, see Jonkers (1954): 28; for details of the acts, and discussion of the date, see Parvis (2000); Parvis (2006): 11–30.

8. Ancyra *can.* 3, Jonkers (1954): 29. Canon 2 relates to deacons in the same situation as priests with the provision that they might receive absolution from a bishop.

9. Ancyra *can.* 4–5; Jonkers (1954): 30.

10. Euseb. *HE* 8.9.5–8 (8.10.1–10 is a version of the *Acts of Phileas*, a voluntary martyr, for which see also Musurillo [1972] no. 26), *MP* 8.1, including ninety-seven from Palestine who attract Eusebius' particular attention.

11. A Latin translation of Peter's letter is preserved in *Codex Vaticanus* lx, discussed by Schwartz (1905a): 177–9. This was later regarded as the beginning of the schism, which Athanasius dated to the nineteenth year before the Council of Nicaea; see Ath. *Epist. ad ep. Aeg. et Lib.* 22 with Seeck (1895–1920) 3: 54n on p. 383, l. 24. For Meletius' fate, see Epiph. *Pan.* 68.3; Ath. *Hist. Ar.* 60; Seeck (1895–1920) 3: 383; Barnes (1981): 202.

12. Epiph. *Pan.* 68.1.4; 3.3.

13. For the death of Peter, see Barnes (1981): 202, with the evidence for the date collected in his n. 112; for later events, see Soz. *HE* 1.15.2 with Schwartz (1905a) 186–87. For the possibility that Arius was Alexander's rival in the election, see Phil. *HE* 1.3; 1.2.9 on the earlier relationship between the two men with Parvis (2006): 73.

14. Schwartz (1905a): 187–8.

15. Chadwick (1960): 179; Lang (2000): 79–80.

16. Soz. *HE* 1.15.4; Epiph. *Pan.* 68.4, 69.5.

17. Stead (1973): 86–7; Eusebius of Nicomedia adhered to the view that there was one member of the Trinity, the Father, who was uncreated, and that the Son, being generated by the Father, could not be of the same substance, or *ousia*, as him.

18. For the quarrel, see Theod. *HE.* 1.4.5–7 (also in Opitz [1934a], no. 14); the date here is that of Parvis (2006): 69–70 contra Opitz (1934b); for a starting date in 323, see Schwartz (1905b); Telfer (1946); for 321, see Williams (1987): 56; for a balanced review of the problem, see Brennecke, Heil, Stockhausen and Wintjes (2007): xix–xxxii.

19. For Arius as the agent of Eusebius, see Kannengiesser (1970): 350; for the view that Arius' attack on Alexander was convenient to Eusebius and others but not directly instigated by them, see Williams (1985): 19–21.

20. Socr. *HE* 1.6.5 (also Opitz [1934a], no. 4b.4; Brennecke, Heil, Stockhausen and Wintjes [2007] no. 2.2; trans. Stevenson [1987]: 323).

21. Theod. *HE* 1.5 (also in Opitz [1934a] no. 1; Brennecke, Heil, Stockhausen and Wintjes [2007]: no. 15); for the chronology, see Parvis (2006): 73.

22. Theod. *HE* 1.4.

23. Theod. *HE* 1.4.35–6 (also in Opitz [1934a] no. 14; Brennecke, Heil, Stockhausen and Wintjes [2007]: no.17).

24. Ath. *De synod.* 16.3 (also in Opitz [1934a] no. 6; Brennecke, Heil, Stockhausen and Wintjes [2007]: no. 1). He also compares Alexander's thinking with that of the Valentians and Sabellians.

25. Ritter (1978): 701; H. Chadwick (1998): 565.

26. Opitz (1934a) nos. 4b, 5, 14; Brennecke, Heil, Stockhausen and Wintjes (2007): nos. 2.2; 3; 17.

27. Ritter (1978): 695; Chadwick (1998): 565.

28. For this view of the *Thalia*, see Williams (1985); the text quoted here is Arius, *Thalia* 4–11. For the text, see Metzler and Simon (1991): 37. For the accuracy of Athanasius' quotation of these lines, see also Hall (1985). For the view of Arius' position, see Brakke (1995): 64–5.

29. Theod. *HE* 1.5.3 (also in Opitz [1934a] no. 1.3; Brennecke, Heil, Stockhausen and Wintjes [2007] no. 15.3). Theodotus was bishop of Laodicea (and the dedicatee of one of Eusebius's major apologetic works), Paulinus was bishop of Tyre (another friend of Eusebius of Caesarea), while Athanasius of Anazarbus was a pupil of Lucian. For Theodotus, see Eus. *HE* 7.32.23 with Barnes (1981): 178; for Paulinus, see Euseb. *HE* 10.4.1; for Athanasius, see Phil. *HE* 3.15. Gregory was Eusebius' successor as bishop of Beirut, and Aëtius was bishop of Lydda. Their opponents were, respectively, the bishops of Antioch, Tripoli, and Jerusalem.

26. NICAEA

1. Opitz (1934a) no. 20; Brennecke, Heil, Stockhausen and Wintjes (2007): no.22; trans. Stevenson (1987): 338.

2. Eus. *VC* 2.70.4–7; translations quoted in the text are by Hall with minimal adaptation.

3. Eus. *VC* 3.12.1–2 trans. Hall with Drake (2000): 253, for stress on this point; for the issue of the presiding bishop, either Theognis as in the text, or possibly Eusebius of Nicomedia, see Drake (2000): 252.

4. Theod. *HE* 1.12.1. For a sympathetic discussion of the position of the bishops previously opposed to Alexander of Alexandria, see Chadwick (1960): 170–9.

5. Theod. *HE* 1.8.2 with Stead (1973): 98–100.

6. Basil, *Ep.* 81 with Barnes (1981): 216.

7. Socr. *HE* 1.8.4 (also in Opitz [1934A] no. 22; Brennecke, Heil, Stockhausen and Wintjes [2007]: no. 24).

8. Ayres (2004): 85–6.

9. Opitz (1934a) no. 23, 6–10; Brennecke, Heil, Stockhausen and Wintjes (2007): no. 25.

10. Const. *Orat.* 11 tr. Edwards (2003): 22.

11. See Eus. *VC* 3.19.1 on pre-Nicene observation.

12. See, for example, Minucius Felix, *Octavius* 8–10 for a lively version of incest and cannibalism, first attested as a charge in the mid-second century; for atheism, see, for instance, Luc. *Alex.* 25 and Or. *C. Cels.* 2.55; 5.14 on the resurrection; for the problem with Christian teaching from parables, see Whittaker (1984): 186 (quoting Galen); for Jews as foes of Alexandrian Greeks in the *Acta Alexandrinorum,* see Harker (2008): 91–2; for Moses as a magician, see Apuleius *Ap.* 90; Or. *C. Cels.* 4.51; for other abuse, see Jos. *Apion* passim. Whittaker (1984) is generally a very useful compendium for discourse of this sort.

13. Eus. *VC* 3.19.1; 18.2 tr. Hall; on the issue of immunities, see p. 278–9 .

14. Phil. *HE* 1.9.

15. Ayres (2004): 95–6; 99.

16. Ayres (2004): 387–404.

27. CONSTANTINOPLE AND ROME

1. Const. *Orat.* 25.

2. Serdica: Anon. post Dionem, *FHG* 4.199; Zon. 13.3.1–4; Ilium: Soz. *HE* 2.3; Zos. 2.30; Zon. 13.3; Chalcedon: Zon. 13.3; Kedrenos, p. 496; Thessalonica: Kedrenos, p. 496 with Dagron (1974): 29 n. 3, who gives further references. For Ilium, see *Anth. Gr.* 14.115; Soz. *HE* 2.3.3 with Dagron (1974): 31–2. For assertions of revelation, see *CTh.* 13.5.7: *pro commoditate urbis, quam aeterno nomine iubente deo donavimus...*

3. Dagron (1974): 32; Alföldi (1947): 11.

4. Theoph. *Chron* s.a. 5816; Lathoud (1924): 289–96; Dagron (1974): 33; Cracco Ruggini (1980): 598–9; 603 suggesting that the *limitatio* of Phil. *HE* 2.3 was in 328, see p. 259.

5. For the dates of birth, see Barnes (1982): 43.

6. Sutherland and Carson (1966): 203 n. 442.

7. For details of these coinages, see Potter (2009): 143; for the bad pun, see P. Opt. Porph. 13b.4 and possibly 20a.14.

8. P. Opt. Porph. 4.32–4; see also 9.24–6; 10.23–6 with discussion in Van Dam (2007): 99.

9. For the career of Gallus, see Potter (2004): 472–6; for the significance of Pola, see Amm. 14.11.20.

10. For Proculus, see in Bagnall, Cameron, Schwartz, and Worp (1987): 184 with Barnes (1976a): 280; for Porphyrius, see Chastagnol (1962): 80–2; Barnes (1975a): 184; for Bassus, see *PLRE* Bassus 14

(p. 154–5) suggesting that he was a Christian as does Barnes (1994b): 7; for the contrary case, see von Haehling (1978): 289.

11. Jerome *Chron*, s.a. 328; for Julius Constantius, who may have been sent into internal exile in Narbonne at this point, see Aus. *Prof.* 16.9–12.

12. Aurel Vict. *De Caes.* 41.11; for these sources see also Pohlsander (1984): 99–102.

13. Eutrop. *Brev.* 10.6.3.

14. [Aur. Vict.] *Epit.* 41.11.

15. Phil. *HE* 2.4; the account is a composite from Photius' summary, the *Passio Artemii*, and the Byzantine *Vita Constantini*. The details are consistent, but none of the three offers a direct quotation. For other places where Philostorgius provides important information not available elsewhere, see Philost. *HE* 7.15; 8.8.

16. See, in general, Blockley (1981): 1–26.

17. Zos. 2.29.2.

18. There is no question but that the source for Zosimus is Eunapius, or that this account was known to Sozomon, who expressly rejects it (Soz. *HE* 1.5.1); more interesting is the connection between the deaths of Crispus and Fausta and the conversion of Constantine, already adumbrated by Julian, who might reasonably be seen as the propagator of this aspect of the tradition. For Julian, see Jul. *Caes.* 38. Zosimus' notion that Constantine was guided by visions that helped him to power before the murders looks like an oblique reference to Eus. *VC* 1.47; 2.12; 16. For this dating of the emergence of the story, see also Desnier (1987); Bleckmann (2010): 351–2.

28. CONSTANTINE'S GOVERNMENT

1. *CTh* 11.30.16 (no appeal from a decision by a praetorian prefect). For the power of the prefects, see also Eunap. *VP* 463 and discussion in Gutsfeld (1998): 88–96. The text in question with respect to the military command structure is *CTh* 8.7.5 dated by Seeck, (1919) 21; 177 to 326, but see Matthews (2000): 232–6 cast his views in serious (or terminal) doubt; but see *PLRE* Veturius (p. 955) identified in Jerome and Prosper Tiro, both translating Eusebius' *stratopedarchês* (the term used at *HE* 8.4.3) as *magister militiae* under Diocletian; for the standard account of this development see Kelly (2006): 187. For Bonitus, see *PLRE* Bonitus 1 (p. 163); for Flavius Bonosus, see *PLRE* Bonosus 4 (p. 164) with the important caveat in Bagnall, Cameron, Schwartz, and Worp (1987): 222; for Magnentius, see *PLRE* Magnentius (p. 532); for Ursicinus, see *PLRE* Ursicinus 2 (985–6) with 15.5.19 on his service under Constantine; for Arbitio, see *PLRE* Arbitio 2 (p. 94–5); the key pieces of evidence for his Constantinian career are Amm. 15.2.4; 16.6.1; 26.9.4. For Aemilianus, see *PLRE* Aemilianus 3 (p. 22). For Ablabius and Evagrius, see von Haehling (1978): 55–8. Though on Evagrius' religiosity add Robert (1948): 94–102 showing that his grandson made a dedication to Hera under Julian, which makes it more likely than not that his grandfather was also a pagan. For Felix, see *PLRE* Felix 2 (pp. 331–2); for Abablius' origins, see esp. Eunap. *VP* 463–4.

2. For the consuls, see Bagnall, Cameron, Schwartz, and Worp (1987): 196–209. For the career of Optatus, see Lib. *Or.* 42.26 with *PLRE* Optatus 3 (p. 650) and Kelley (2006): 197–8.

3. The texts quoted in this, and the preceding, paragraph are *CTh* 9.3.2 (Evagrius); *CTh* 2.10.4 (Bassus); the issue was also addressed in *CTh* 2.10.3 (possibly on 3/6/325); *CJ* 2.19.11 (Evagrius); *CTh* 4.22.1 (Severus); *CTh* 7.20.7 (to Evagrius about veteran brigandage).

4. *CTh* 9.7.1 with *PLRE* Africanus 1 (p. 26) see also Arjava (1996): 217; McGinn (1999): 61 on the context.

5. The text in question is *CTh* 9.24.1. The subject of abduction marriage and bride theft in the modern world is the object of a vast and mostly depressing bibliography which I do not claim to command. My understanding in this case is based upon McLaren (2001): 953–84 and Werner (2004): 59–89; see also Bates, Conant, and Kudat (1974) (this is an introduction to a special issue of the

journal on the topic). Although the conclusions here differ from those of Evans Grubbs (1989), that article remains of critical importance for stressing the need to read this law with the aid of comparative material; my main disagreement is plainly that I do not think that Constantine cared about what peasants did with each other. Arjava (1996): 235–7 notes that what Constantine wrote about the legal status of women is not true of Classical Roman jurists, but that seems to confuse the issue as the people in question here are not adults. See also Harper (2011): 110.

6. *CTh* 9.8.1 with Beaucamp (1990) 1: 136; Seeck (1919): 176.

7. *CTh* 9.7.2 with Beaucamp (1990) 1: 148–58.

8. *CJ* 5.26.1 with Beaucamp (1990): 1:172–3; Arjava (1996): 205–10.

9. *CTh* 12.1.10 (to Maximus); *CTh* 12.1.11 (*CJ* 11.68.1) (to a praetorian prefect); *CTh* 8.4.1 (to Constantius); *CTh* 12.1.13 (to Evagrius); *CTh* 6.36 (Severus).

29. CONSTANTINOPLE

1. Cracco Ruggini (1980): 605–7.

2. For city design, see Saradi (1995), esp. 40–5; see also the valuable summary in Holum (2005), esp. 89–90; on the center of Constantinople, see Bassett (2004): 22–6; for Anthousa, see Mal. 13.8 (p. 322 Dindorf) with Lathoud (1925): 180–9 and Ando (2008): 189–98; for Helena, see Drijvers (1992): 73; Bardill (2012): 184–6.

3. Stephenson (2010): 200–201 is excellent on this point though he should not be blamed for the interpretation of the symbolism offered in the text; see also, on the other statuary, Bassett (2004): 62–7 and the important discussion of Robert (1969). On the obelisk, see esp. Bardill (2012): 151–8.

4. For the palace itself, see Noethlichs (1998): 25 and esp. 28 for the number of people who worked there.

5. For the porphyry column, see Fowden: (1991); Bardill (2012): 28–36. For the Senate, see *Expositio totius mundi* 50: *Origo* 30: *ibi etiam senatum constituit secundi ordinis: claros vocavit*; see also Zos. 2.38.3–4; for the connection with the statue of the tetrarchs, see Stephenson (2010): 198–9.

6. See, in general, Dagron (1974): 37–41; Lathoud (1925):191–5 on the problem of a pagan element to the procession, though the horoscope would have been cast in 324. The passage quoted is Mal. 13.9 (p. 322 Dindorf); the poet is Palladas; see *AP* 10.90 with Wilkinson (2009): 43.

7. The texts are Baillet (1920–6) no. 1265, 1889; the significance of these texts is stressed in Fowden (1987): 51–2.

8. Eus. *VC* 67.1 trans. Hall.

9. Jones (1964): 104–6; R. B. E. Smith (2007a): 180–2; Schlinkert (1998): 144–7.

10. Soz. *HE* 2.3.6. For similar statements in post-Constantinian sources, see Dagron (1974): 120 n. 1. The material quoted here is from *Expositio totius mundi* 50: *Origo* 30; see also Zos. 2.38.3–4.

11. Dagron (1974): 123 with correction with regard to the praetorship by Chastagnol (1976); Heather (1998): 185–6.

12. P. Optat. Porph. 4.6; 18.34; Them. *Epist. Constantii ad senatum* 19b, 23b with Dagron (1974): 124–5; Seeck (1908): 279; Barnes (1975a): 179; see also Nicolson (1999) for an interesting perspective on Lactantius' thinking about Rome's place in the world, which would make it hard to "replace" rather than "supplement" Rome as the center of the empire.

13. *Chron. Pasch.* 531; Eunap. *VP* p. 462; *CTh.* 13.5.7 on shipping; Heather (1994): 11–33.

14. The first passage quoted here is Eus *VC* 4.1.1–2 trans. Hall; the second is Jul. *Or.* 1.8 a–b; see also Zos. 2.31.3 with Paschoud's note. For a more hostile view, see Anon. *De rebus bellicis* 2.1–2. See also Aur. Vict. *De Caes.* 41.15; *Epit.* 41.16; Amm. Marc. 16.8.12; Jul. *Caes.* 335b and the good discussion in Kelley (2006): 192–7.

15. The poems in question are *AP* 9.528; 16. 282 with discussion in Wilkinson (2009): 38; Wilkinson (2010): 138.

30. AN ORDERED SOCIETY

1. Eus. *VC* 4.23 (ban on sacrifice); 4.27.3 (imperial cogitations). The issue of the edict on sacrifices remains contentious, but I see no reason to alter the view I took in Potter (2004): 433–4 (with a sample of previous literature on both sides); the contrary position is stated by Barnes (2011): 109–10 (with further literature).

2. *CTh* 12.1.22 (Evagrius 336); *CTh* 14.4.1 (Pacatianus, feral swine); *CTh* 12.1.21 (Felix on flamines); *CTh* 13.4.1 (Felix, architects); *CTh* 7.22.5 (Ablabius, sons of officials); *CTh* 12.1.20 (Evagrius, expulsion of patronage beneficiaries); *CTh* 16.2.6 (Ablabius on clerics); *CTh* 16.2.3 (to Bassus on clerics) with Seeck (1919): 64; see also *CTh* 16.2.7 protecting clerics wrongly assigned to *curiae* by heretics and Ch p. 21 n.30; *CTh* 13.5.7 (ship captains, compare *CTh* 13.5.6).

3. *CTh* 9.9.1; for the date, see Seeck (1919): 64, which must be correct if the place of issue is to be accepted; an argument for the earlier date might be supported by the observations in the text. The Diocletianic text is *CJ* 7.20.1; see further the useful discussion in Evans Grubbs (1995): 273–7; *CTh* 4.12.4 seems to presuppose *CTh* 9.9.1.

4. *CTh* 11.27.1 (329); *Frag. Vat.* 34 (315); *CTh* 4.8.6 (323 with p. 187–8); *CTh* 5.10.1 (329 contra Seeck [1919]: 65 who would redate the law to 319 or 320), but it appears to look to the same situation as addressed in *CTh* 11.27.1; 5.9.1 (331); see also the discussion in Harper (2011): 398–409.

5. *CTh* 9.12.2 with Harper (2011): 232; *CJ* 6.1.4 with Seeck (1919): 89 on the date (arguing for a shift from the mss. date of 317 on the basis of location and the easy corruption of the consular date); if that is the case, then the addressee is most likely the vicarius of Africa who received *CTh* 3.5.3; see also *CJ* 6.1.6 making the same point in 332.

6. *CTh* 1.5.2 (Maximus); *CTh* 11.16.4 (Aemilianus); *CTh* 12.1.17 (Paternus; known only through this text; see *PLRE* Lucretius Paternus 7, p. 672).

7. *CTh* 8.1.4; 8.15.2 corrupt officials, sent to Veronicianus, *vicarius* of Asia, known only from these texts and *CTh*. 11.16.6; see *PLRE* Veronicianus 1 (p. 952); *CTh* 1.16.4 (powerful man); *CJ* 4.62.4 to Felix on corrupt tax collectors; *CTh* 1.16.6 on acclamations.

8. *CTh* 3.5.3 to Valerian the vicarius, known only from this and one other text if he is not to be identified with Paternus Valerianus, which would add a third on dotal gifts; see *PLRE* Valerianus 4; Paternus Valerianus 14 (pp. 938–9); *CTh* 3.5.4; 5 to Pacatianus as praetorian prefect (engagement); *CTh* 1.22.2 to Andronicus, known only from this document; see *PLRE* Andronicus 1 (p. 64) (pupils, widows etc).

9. *Frag Vat.* 248 (emancipated sons, no addressee); *CTh* 8.18.3 to Severus of Spain on whom see *PLRE* Severus 4 (p. 831).

10. Gutsfeld (1998): 96.

31. CHRISTIANS, PAGANS, AND JEWS

1. The only evidence for her age is Eus. *VC* 3.46.1, but the statement accords with Eusebius' inaccurate statements about Constantine's age and makes her about a decade older than she was.

2. For the style and content of his work, see esp. Seeck (1908): 274–7.

3. Eus. *VC* 3.26.4–6, 30.34

4. Eus. *VC* 3.53.3 trans. Hall with Hunt (1982): 13–15; the action at Mamre was set in motion after a visit by Eutropia.

5. Eus. *VC* 3.55–8; see also the discussion in Lee (2006): 174; Aphaca was attributed an anti-Palmyerene stance in 272; for that aspect, see Hartmann (2001): 307.

6. Lane Fox (1986): 671; Potter (1989): 309–10.

7. Eus. *VC* 4.25.2–3; for Sopater, see Eunap. *VP* 6.2; for a very good summary of Constantine's dealing with pagans and Jews with which the discussion here is in substantial agreement, see Digeser (2000): 125–33.

8. Eus. *VC* 28 trans. Hall.

9. Eus. *VC.* 31.2–3 trans. Hall with Hunt (1982): 12.

10. Eus. *VC.* 3.43.1–3; Hunt (1982): 12–13, noting that Eusebius describes neither.

11. *D.* 50.2.3.3 (Ulpian); *D.* 27.1.15 (Modestinus) with Langenfeld (1977): 43–50; Lindner (1987): 68–71.

12. Oppenheimer (1998): 181–91.

13. Lindner (1987): 71–3.

14. Paul, *Sent.* 5.22.3 with Lindner (1987): 117–20; on the *theosebeis*, see Mitchell (2010): 189–96.

15. *CTh* 16.8.1. For the date, see Lindner (1987): 125 contra Seeck (1919): 48 (date) grouping 16.8.1 with *CTh* 16.9.2; 16.8.6; and p. 106 (place); for the specific groups and terms of the legislation, see Langenfeld (1977): 61; Noy (2011), and, in general, Millar (1992b).

16. *Sirm.* 4 with Langenfeld (1977): 66–84.

17. *MAMA* no. 305 panel 1 lines 39–43; for the date, see Chastagnol (1981): 398; on Christianity in the area, see Van Dam (2007): 179–83. As for the actual amenities of the place, Constantine appears somewhat more demanding than Galerius, whose positive response to Heraclea Sintica in Macedonia is far less elaborate; see *AE* (2002) n. 1293.

18. The basic study of this text is now Gascou (1962).

19. *Sirm.* 1, see Piganiol (1932): 180 for the intriguing suggestion that most of the prose here could repeat an earlier document sent by Ablabius.

20. What follows is heavily derivative from Gwynn (2007): 140–2; Parvis (2006): 101–7. It is not beyond the realm of possibility that he did insult Helena (Ath. *Hist. Ar.* 4) in some way since she allegedly revered Lucian of Antioch; see Phil. *HE* 2.12 with Hunt (1982): 36.

21. Theod. *HE* 1.21 (woman, allegedly a bribed prostitute, produces her child by him in court, allegedly lying); Soz. *HE* 2.19 (claims he disgraced the priesthood); Phil. *HE* 2.7 (sexual immorality). For the alternative charge, that he was a Sabellian, see Socr. *HE* 1.23.8–24.1.

22. For Constantine's letter, see Opitz (1934a) 34=Brennecke, Heil, von Stockhausen and Wintjes (2007) n. 27; for the reconciliation at Nicomedia, see Parvis (2006): 102–4.

23. Parvis (2006): 130.

24. Ath. *Apol. contra Ar.* 6.5.6, denying the charge; but see also Soz. *HE* 2.17. Sozomen quotes a document by Apolinarius the Syrian that models the election of Athanasius on an imperial acclamation, stressing the *recusatio*; Soz. *HE* 2.17 describes the scene in the church.

25. Brakke (1995): 80–2, 113.

26. Ath. *Apol. contra Ar.* 60.1–2 with Barnes (2001a): 21 (refusal to help Meletians with tax obligations); Ath. *Apol. contra Ar.* 63.1–4 (assault).

27. Ath. *Apol. contra Ar.* 66–70 with Barnes (2001a): 28.

28. *P. London* 1914.

29. Drake (2000): 261–8.

32. NEIGHBORS

1. For Constantine's dealings with the Goths, see Heather (1991): 107–15.

2. Barnes (1990); Heather (1991): 104–5.

3. See in general Fowden (1993), 101–16.

4. Ruf. *HE* 10.9–10; Socr. *HE.* 1.19; Soz. *HE* 2.24; Theod. *HE* 1.23 (the latter three all depend on Rufinus).

5. Soz. *HE* 2.8; for a Christian community there in the mid–third century, see Euseb. *HE* 6.46.

6. Ruf. *HE* 1.10–11; Soz. *HE* 2.7 with Braund (1994), 251–2.

7. Publ. Optat. Porph. 5.5–6; 13; 14.13–26; for the date of the letter to Sapor, see Barnes (1985a): 131–2. The passages quoted in Hall's translation are Eus. *VC* 4.10.1; 3; 4.

8. The passage quoted directly in Hall's translation is Eus. *VC* 11.2.

9. For the handling of Dalmatius and Constantius, see Burgess (2008): 8–9, though on Calocaerus, see also Burgess (1999): 216. For the problematic natures of the sources, see the excellent treatment in Fowden (1994): 148–53.

33. END TIMES

1. For Gregorius, see *PLRE* Gregorius 3 (p. 403); he did not last the year and appears to have been offensive to the Donatists; for Tiberianus, possibly a poet, see *PLRE* Tiberianus 4 (p. 911). He would also be out of office within the year.

2. Eus. *VC* 4.62.2–3 tr. Hall; for the Persian embassy, see Burgess (1999): 230–1; the chronology and itinerary accepted here are derived from Burgess (1993; for the date and time of death, see Eus. *VC* 4.64.2).

EPILOGUE

1. The crucial evidence for the later placement of the porphyry sarcophagus comes from the description of the Church of the Twelve Apostles by Nikolas Mesarites in the twelfth century, on which see Downey (1957), esp. sec. 39 for the description of the mausoleum. For the reconstruction accepted here, see Downey (1951); Grierson, Mango, and Ševčenko (1962): 4–5; 20; 39–40; see also Bardill (2012): 367–84. The tradition about Fausta's inclusion, along with that of Helena is Kedr. 1. 519–20 with Grierson, Mango, and Ševčenko (1962): 40 (attributing the decision to Constantius II, but it is unlikely that he would have acted against the known wishes of his father). Helena's remains in fact stayed in Rome, which makes it likely that a second body in the sarcophagus would have been Fausta's. For Helena's remains, some of which reside in the Church of Santa Maria in Aracoeli, see Drijvers (1992): 75–6.

2. Eunap. *VP* 464 with Burgess (2008): 14–18; 42–3 for thorough discussion of the diverse traditions and a convincing reconstruction of events.

3. Bleckmann (2010); Fowden (1994).

4. See Lieu (1998): 136–49 for a concise summary of the issues.

5. Fried (2007): 107–9; Miethke (2008): 37–9; Pohlkamp (2007).

6. *Const. Constantini.* 11–12 tr. Bowersock (2007): 173–5.

7. Fried (2007): 26–7 on the problem; Mierau (2008) on Karl IV; Marti (2007) on the situation in Russia; Bowersock (2007): viii–x on the reception of Valla.

8. For the mosaics, see Fried (2007): 22 with plates 3–5; for the frescoes, see Van Dam (2011): 24–5; for the cabinet, see Quednau (2008).

9. Burkhardt (1940): 292.

10. Carroll (2001); the passage quote here is Brown (2003): 232.

APPENDIX

1. For the Latin Epitomators there is a very useful introduction in Rohrbacher (2002): 42–63.

2. Paschoud (1971): 334–53; the issue is properly contextualized in Bleckmann (2010): 351–2.

3. On the *Descent of the Emperor Constantine*, or the *Origo Constantini Imperatoris*, see König (1987). For Praxagoras, the likely source of Eunapius' account of Constantine before 324, see R. B. E. Smith (2007b); oddly there is no reference to this excellent paper in Barnes (2011): 195–7.

4. This view of Lactantius' career is essentially that of Heck (2009): 118–130 who makes a solid case that Lactantius arrived in Trier at the end of 313 or early in 314. For a radically different view, suggesting that Lactantius was in the west and at the court of Constantine in 311–312, see Barnes (2011): 176–8; this view is based on a demonstrably incorrect view of the date of Crispus' birth (p. 98) and fails to explain the wide discrepancies between Lactantius' account of the campaign of 312 and that in *Pan.* 12.

5. The basic treatment is now Cameron and Hall (1999): 1–46, though see also Barnes (1989) on diverse generic elements of the life; Barnes (1994c) on stages of composition and Barnes (2011): 9–12.

6. For the papyrological issue, see Jones and Skeat (1954). There is a useful summary of the resuscitation of Eusebius in Barnes (2011): 7; but see also Elliott (1991): 164–9 on Nicaea. For some specific issues, see Eus. *VC* 4.51; 4.68.3; Burgess (2008): 11–12 and p. 293 on the succession; the omissions are all the more striking given the inclusion of some of the actors in earlier works. For Crispus, see *HE* 10.9.4; 6 with discussion in Barnes (2011): 5 of the removal of Crispus' name from a late revision of the work; for Dalmatius see Eus. *LC* 3.4 also with Barnes (2011): 5; Seeck (1895–1920) 4: 45; the version of the succession in Eusebius was taken up in a somewhat different form in Jul. *Or.* 2.94c .

7. Curran (2000): 76–109; Eus. *VC* 1.40 on western buildings.

8. There is an excellent discussion of the collection as a whole in Rees (2002): 19–26 and in Nixon and Rodgers (1994): 3–10. It is emblematic of the approach in Barnes (2011) that he includes no discussion of the panegyrics in his introduction on documents for the reign of Constantine and relegates consideration of the corpus to a four page appendix (C) on his pages 181–4.

9. Matthews (2000): 1–10; 31.

10. See, in general, the excellent introduction to the issue in Evans Grubbs (1995): 43–7; and the important, detailed studies of Simon (1977): 84–120 and Matthews (2000): 200–53. The nature of these texts as bureaucratic memoranda rather than "laws" in the modern sense is well stated in Millar (2007): 7–8 showing that the methodological criticisms of Evans Grubbs' work in Shaw (1996), although trenchantly expressed, are not well taken.

11. For private rescripts see Connolly (2010a): 22–34.

12. On this point see Dörries (1954): 208.

13. For the role of coins in the dissemination of the imperial image see Noreña (2011): 190–218; for the arch of Galerius see p. 60–61 for the arch of Constantine, see p. 166–8; for the inscription at Hispellum, p. 281; for the palace of Diocletian, see Mayer (2002): 69–79.

14. For this approach see also Dörries (1954); Baynes (1972): 6.

BIBLIOGRAPHY

Aldrete G. and Mattingly, D. J. (2010). Feeding the City: The Organization, Operation and Scale of the Supply System for Rome. In Potter and Mattingly, 195–228.

Alexander, J. S. (1980). The Motive for a Distinction between Donatus of Carthage and Donatus of Casae Nigrae. *JTS* 31: 540–7.

Alföldi, A. (1947). On the Foundation of Constantinople: A Few Notes. *JRS* 37: 10–16.

Alföldi, A. (1948). *The Conversion of Constantine and Pagan Rome*. Oxford.

Amit. J. (1996). *Passion de Perpétue et de Félicité suivi des actes*. Sources Chrétiennes no. 417. Paris.

Ando, C. (2000). *Imperial Ideology and Provincial Loyalty in the Roman Empire*. Berkeley.

Ando, C. (2008). *The Matter of the Gods: Religion and the Roman Empire*. Berkeley.

Arjava, A. (1996). *Women and Law in Late Antiquity*. Oxford.

Arnheim, M. T. W. (1970). Vicars in the Later Roman Empire. *Historia* 19: 593–606.

Avery, W.T. 1940. The *Adoratio Purpurae* and the Importance of the Imperial Purple in the Fourth Century of the Christian Era. *MAAR* 17: 66–80.

Ayres, L. (2004). *Nicaea and Its Legacy: An Approach to Fourth Century Trinitarian Theology*. Oxford.

Bagnall, R. S. (1993). *Egypt in Late Antiquity*. Princeton.

Bagnall, R. S., Cameron, A., Schwartz S., and Worp, K. (1987). *Consuls of the Later Roman Empire*. Atlanta.

Bagnall, R.S. and Frier, B.W. (1994) *The Demography of Roman Egypt*. Cambridge.

Baillet, J. (1920–26). *Inscriptions grecques et latines des Tombeaux des Rois ou Syringes à Thèbes*. Cairo.

Bardill, J. (2012). *Constantine, Divine Emperor of the Christian Golden Age*. Cambridge.

Barnes, T.D. (1971). *Tertullian: A Literary and Historical Study*. Oxford.

Barnes T. D. (1975a). Publilius Optatianus Porfyrius. *AJP* 96: 173–86.

Barnes T. D. (1975b). The Beginnings of Donatism. *JTS* 26: 16–17.

Barnes T. D. (1976a). Three Imperial Edicts. *ZPE* 21: 275–81.

Barnes T. D. (1976b). Imperial Campaigns, A.D. 285–311. *Phoenix* 30: 174–93.

Barnes T. D. (1981). *Constantine and Eusebius*. Cambridge, MA.

Barnes T. D. (1982). *The New Empire of Diocletian and Constantine*. Cambridge, MA.

Barnes T. D. (1985a). Constantine and the Christians of Persia. *JRS* 75: 126–36.

Barnes T. D. (1985b). The Conversion of Constantine. *Échos du Monde Classique*, vol. 4, pp. 381–7; also in Barnes (1994a), chap. 3.

Barnes, T.D. (1989). "Panegyric, History and Hagiography in Eusebius' Life of Constantine." In Williams, R., ed., *The Making of Orthodoxy: Essays in Honor of Henry Chadwick*, pp. 94–123. Cambridge.

Barnes T. D. (1990). The Consecration of Ulfila. *JTS* 41: 541–55; also in Barnes (1994a) chap. 10.

Barnes T. D. (1994a). *From Eusebius to Augustine*. Brookfield.

Barnes T. D. (1994b). *The Religious Affiliation of Consuls and Prefects. In Barnes (1994a) chap. 7.

Barnes T. D. (1994c). *Two Drafts of Eusebius' Life of Constantine*. In Barnes (1994a) chap. 12.

Barnes T. D. (2001a). *Athanasius and Constantius: Theology and Politics in the Constantinian Empire.* Cambridge, MA.

Barnes T. D. (2001b). Constantine's Speech to the Assembly of the Saints: Place and Date of Delivery. *JTS* 52: 26–36.

Barnes T. D. (2010). *Early Christian Hagiography and Roman History*. Tübingen.

Barnes T. D. (2011). *Constantine: Dynasty, Religion and Power in the Later Roman Empire*. Oxford.

Bassett, S. (2004). *The Urban Image of Late Antique Constantinople*. Cambridge.

Bates, D. C., Conant, F., and Kudat, A. (1974). Introduction: Kidnapping and Elopement as Alternative Systems of Marriage. *Anthropological Quarterly* 47: 233–7.

Baynes, N. H. (1972). *Constantine the Great and the Christian Church*. London.

Beaucamp, J. (1990). *Le statut de la femme à Byzance (4e–7e siècle).* Traveaux et Mémoires du Centre de Recherche d'Histoire et Civilisation de Byzance n. 5. Paris.

Bellen, H. (1967). Review of F. Fabbrini, La Manumissio in Ecclesia. *Tijdschrift voor Rechtsgeschiedenis* 35: 319–23.

Berrens, S. (2004). *Sonnenkult und Kaisertum von den Severern bis zu Constantin I (193–337 n. Chr).* Historia Einzelschriften 185. Stuttgart.

Bleckmann, B. (1992). *Die Reichskrise des III. Jahrhunderts in der spätantiken und byzantinischen Geschichtsschreibung: Untersuchungen zu den nachdionischen Quellen der Chronik des Johannes Zonaras*. Munich.

Bleckmann, B. (1997). Ein Kaiser als Prediger: Zur Datierung der konstantinischen "Rede an die Versammlung der Heiligen." *Hermes* 125: 183–202.

Bleckmann, B. (2010). Constantinus Tyrannus: das negative Konstantinsbild in der paganen Historiographie und seine Nuancen. In Turner, A. J., Chong-Gossard, K-O, Vervaet, F. J., eds., *Private and Public Lies: The Discourse of Deceit in the Graeco-Roman World*. Pp. 343–54. Leiden.

Blockley, R. C. (1981). *The Fragmentary Classicising Historians of the Later Roman Empire: Eunapius, Olympiodorus, Priscus and Malchus*, vol. 1. Liverpool.

Boschung, D. and Eck, W. (2004). *Tetrarchie: ein neues Regierungssystem und seine mediale Präsentation*. Cologne.

Bowen, A. and Garnsey, P. (2003). *Lactantius: The Divine Institutes*. Liverpool.

Bowersock, G. W. (1995). *Martyrdom and Rome*. Cambridge.

Bowersock, G. W. (2005). Peter and Constantine. In Tronzo, W., ed., *St. Peter's in the Vatican*. Pp. 5–15. Cambridge.

Bowersock, G. W. (2007). *Valla on the Donation of Constantine*. Cambridge, MA.

Brakke, D. (1995). *Athanasius and the Politics of Asceticism*. Oxford.

Brandt, H. (2004). Erneute Überlegungen zum Preisedikt Diokletians. In Demandt, Goltz, and Schlange-Schöningen, eds., 47–55.

Bratoz, R. (2004). Die diokletianische Christenverfolgung in den Donau- und Balkan-provinzen. In Demandt, Goltz, and Schlange-Schöningen, eds., 209–5.

Braund, D. (1994). *Georgia in Antiquity: A History of Colchis and Transcaucasian Iberia, 550 BC–AD 562*. Oxford.

Brennecke, C., Heil, U., von Stockhausen, A. and Wintjes, A. (2007). *Athanasius Werke 3.1 Dokumente zur Geschichte des*

Brent, A. (2010). *Cyprian and Roman Carthage*. Cambridge.

Brown, D. (2003). *The Da Vinci Code*. New York.

Brunt, P. A. (1974). Marcus Aurelius in His *Meditations*. *JRS* 64: 1–20.

Bruun, P. (1958). The Disappearance of Sol from the Coins of Constantine. *Arctos; Acta Philologica Fennica*, n.s. 2: 15–37.

Buckland, W. W. (1908). *The Roman Law of Slavery:The Condition of the Slave in Private Law from Augustus to Justinian*. Cambridge.

Buckland, W. W. (1975). *A Textbook of Roman Law from Augustus to Justinian*. 3rd ed. Cambridge.

Burgess, R. (1993). *ΑΧΥΡΩΝ* or *ΠΡΟΑΣΤΕΙΟΝ* the Location and Circumstances of Constantine's Death. *JTS* 50: 151–61.

Burgess, R. (1996). The Date of the Persecution of Christians in the Army. *JTS* 47: 157–8.

Burgess, R. (1999). *Studies in Eusebian and Post-Eusebian Chronology*. Historia Einzelschriften 135. Stuttgart.

Burgess, R. (2008). Summer of Blood: The Great Massacre of 337 and the Promotion of the Sons of Constantine. *Dumbarton Oaks Papers* 62:5–51.

Burkhardt, J. (1940). *The Age of Constantine the Great*, tr. M. Hadas. New York.

Cambi, N. (2004) Tetrarchic Practice in Name Giving. In Demandt, Goltz, and Schlange-Schöningen, 38–46.

Cameron, A. and Hall, S. G. (1999). *Eusebius: The Life of Constantine*. Oxford.

Campbell, J. B. (1984). *The Emperor and the Roman Army*. Oxford.

Carroll, J. (2001). *Constantine's Sword: The Church and the Jews—A History*. New York.

Casey, P. J. (1994). *Carausius and Allectus: The British Usurpers*. London.

Chadwick, H. (1960). Faith and Order at the Council of Nicaea: A Note on the Background of the Sixth Canon. *HTR* 53: 171–95. also in *History and Thought of the Early Church* (London, 1982), chap. 12.

Chadwick, H. (1998). Orthodoxy and Heresy from the Death of Constantine to the Eve of the First Council of Ephesus. In Cameron, A. and Garnsey, P. D., eds., *The Cambridge Ancient History*, 2nd ed., vol. 13, pp. 561–600. Cambridge.

Chastagnol, A. (1962). *Les Fastes de la Préfecture de Rome au Bas-Empire*. Paris.

Chastagnol, A. (1967). Les années régnales de Maximien Hercule en Égypte et les fêtes vicennales du 20 Novembre 303, *Revue Numismatique*, 6th ser., 9: 54–81.

Chastagnol, A. (1976). Remarques sur les sénateurs orientaux au IVᵉ siècle. *Acta Antiqua* 24 (1976): 341–56.

Chastagnol, A. (1981). L'inscription constantinienne d'Orcistus. *MEFRA* 93: 381–416.

Chiesa, P. (1996). Un testo agiografico africano ad Aquileia: gli Acta di Gallonio e dei martiri di Timida Regia. *Analecta Bollandiana* 114: 241–68.

Christol, M. (1977). La carrière de Traianus Mucianus et l'origine des *protectors*. *Chiron* 7: 393–408.

Christol, M. (1986). *Essai sur l'évolution des carrièrres sénatoriales dans la 2ᵉ moitié du IIIᵉ s. ap. J-C*. Paris.

Connolly, S. (2010a). *Lives behind the Laws: The World of the* Codex Hermogenianus. Bloomington.

Connolly, S. (2010b). Constantine Answers the Veterans. In McGill, Sogno, and Watts, eds., 93–114.

Cooley, A. (2009). *Res Gestae Divi Augusti.*Cambridge.

Corcoran, S. (1993). Hidden from History: The Legislation of Licinius. In Harries and Wood, 97–119.

Corcoran, S. (2000a). *The Empire of the Tetrarchs: Imperial Pronouncements and Government AD 284–324*. Rev. ed. Oxford.

Corcoran, S. (2000b). The Sins of the Fathers. A Neglected Constitution of Diocletian on Incest. *Journal of Legal History* 21.2: 1–34

Corcoran, S. (2007). Galerius' Jigsaw Puzzle: The Caesariani Dossier. *Antiquité Tardive* 15: 221–50.

Cracco Ruggini, L. (1980). Vettio Agorio Pretestato e la fondazione sacra di Constantinopoli. In *Philias Charin. Miscellanea de studi classici in onore di Eugenio Manni*. Pp. 593–610. Rome.

Cribbiore, R. (1985). A Schooltablet from the Hearst Museum. *ZPE* 107: 263–70.

Cullhead, M. (1994). Conservator urbis suae: *Studies in the Politics and Propaganda of the Emperor Maxentius*. Acta Instituti Romani Regni Sueciae ser. 8 n. 20. Stockholm.

Curran, E. (2000). *Pagan City and Christian Capital: Rome in the Fourth Century*. Oxford.

Dagron, G. (1974). *Naissance d'une capitale: Constantinople et ses institutions de 330 à 451*. Paris.

Davies, P. S. (1991). Constantine's Editor. *JTS* 42: 610–18.

Demandt, A., Goltz, A., and Schlange-Schöningen, H., eds (2004). *Diokletian und die Tetrarchie: Aspekte einer Zeitenwende*. Berlin.

Dench, E. (2005). *Romulus' Asylum: Roman Identities from the Age of Alexander to the Age of Hadrian*. Oxford.

Deppert-Lippitz, B. (1996). Late Roman Splendor: Jewelry from the Age of Constantine. *Cleveland Studies in the History of Art* 1: 30–71.

Desnier, J. C. (1987). Zozime II.29 et la mort de Fausta. *Bulletin de l'Association Guillaume Budé*: 297–309.

Dey, H. W. (2011). *The Aurelian Wall and the Refashioning of Imperial Rome AD 271–855*. Cambridge.

Dietz, K. (1980). *Senatus contra principem: Untersuchungen zue senatorischen Opposition gegen Kaiser Maximinus Thrax*. Munich.

Digeser, E. D. (2000). *Lactantius and Rome: The Making of a Christian Empire*. Ithaca.

Dignas, B. and Winter, E. (2007). *Rome and Persia in Late Antiquity*. Cambridge.

Dodgeon, M. H. and Lieu, S. N. C. (1991). *The Roman Eastern Frontier and the Persian Wars AD 226–363*. London.

Dörries, H. (1954). *Das Selbstzeugnis Kaiser Konstantins*. Göttingen.

Downey, G. (1951). The Builder of the Original Church of the Apostles at Constantinople: A Contribution to the Criticism of the "Vita Constantini" Attributed to Eusebius. *Dumbarton Oaks Papers* 6: 51+53–80.

Downey, G. (1957). Nikolas Mesarites: Description of the Church of the Holy Apostles at Constantinople. *Transactions of the American Philosophical Society*. New Series 47 n. 6: 855–924.

Downey, G. (1961). *A History of Antioch in Syria*. Princeton.

Drake, H. A. (2000). *Constantine and the Bishops*. Baltimore.

Drake, H.A. (forthcoming). *The Orations of Constantine and Eusebius*. Berlin.

Drew-Bear, T. (1979). Les voyages d'Aurélius Gaius, soldat de Dioclétien. In Fahd, T., ed., *La géographie administrative et politique d'Alexandre à Mahomet: Actes du Colloque de Strasbourg 14–16 juin 1979*. Pp. 93–141. Strasbourg.

Drijvers, J. H. W. (1992). *Helena Augusta: The Mother of Constantine the Great and the Legend of Her Finding of the True Cross*. Leiden.

Duncan-Jones, R. P. (1974). An African Saint and His Interrogator. *JTS* 25: 106–10.

Duval, N. (1997). Les résidences impériales: Leur rapport avec les problèmes de légitimité, les partages de l'Empire et la combinaisons dynastiques. In Paschoud, F. and Szidat J., eds., *Usurpation in der Spätantike*, Historia Einzelschriften 111. Pp. 127–54. Stuttgart.

Eadie J. (1967). The Development of Roman Mailed Cavalry. *JRS* 57: 161–773.

Eck, W. (2007). Eine historische Zeitenwende: Kaiser Constantins Hinwendung zum Christentum und die gallischen Biscöfe. In Schuller, F. and Wolff H., eds., *Konstantin der Große: Kaiser und Epochenwende*. Pp. 69–94.

Edwards, M. J. (1997). *Optatus: Against the Donatists*. Liverpool.

Edwards, M. J. (1999). The Constantinian Circle and the *Oration to the Saints*. In Edwards, M., Goodman, M., and Price, S., *Apologetics in the Roman Empire: Pagans, Jews and Christians*. Pp. 250–75. Oxford.

Edwards, M. J. (2003). *Constantine and Christendom: The Oration to the Saints; The Greek and Latin Accounts of the Discovery of the Cross; The Edict of Constantine to Silvester*. Liverpool.

Edwards, M.J. (2006). Christian Thought. In Potter, 607–619.

Elliott, T. G. (1991). Eusebian Frauds in *Vita Constantini*. *Phoenix* 45: 162–71.

Elliott, T. G. (1996). *The Christianity of Constantine the Great*. Scranton.

Elm, S. (1994). *Virgins of God: The Making of Asceticism in Late Antiquity*. Oxford.

Elsner, J. (2000). From the Culture of Spolia to the Cult of Relics: The Arch of Constantine and the Genesis of Late Antique Forms. *PBSR* 68: 149–84.

Elton, H. (1996). *Warfare in Roman Europe AD 350–425*. Oxford.

Erim, K. T., Reynolds, J., and Crawford, M. H. (1971). Diocletian's Currency Reform: A New Inscription. *JRS* 61: 171–7.

Esmonde Cleary, S. (2003). Civil Defenses in the West under the High Empire. In P. Wilson, ed., *The Archaeology of Roman Towns. Studies in Honour of John S. Wacher*. Pp. 73–85. Oxford.

Evans Grubbs, J. (1989). Abduction Marriage in Antiquity: A Law of Constantine (CTh IX. 24. I) and Its Social Context. *JRS* 79: 59–83.

Evans Grubbs, J. (1993a). "Marriage More Shameful Than Adultery": Slave-Mistress Relationships, "Mixed Marriages," and Late Roman Law. *Phoenix* 47: 125–54.

Evans Grubbs, J. (1993b). Constantine and Imperial Legislation on the Family. In Harries and Wood, 120–42.

Evans Grubbs, J. (1995). *Law and Family in Late Antiquity: The Emperor Constantine's Marriage Legislation*. Oxford.

Finhman, I. F. (1991–1992). State and Prices in Byzantine Egypt. *Scripta Classica Israelica* 11: 139–48.

Fischer, T. (2004). Das römische Heer in Zeit der Tetrarchie. Eine Armee zwischen Innovation und Kontinuität? In Boschung and Eck, 103–32.

Fowden, E. K. (2006). Constantine and the Peoples of the Eastern Frontier. In Lenski, 377–98.

Fowden, G. (1987). Nicagoras of Athens and the Lateran Obelisk. *JHS* 107: 51–7.

Fowden, G. (1991). Constantine's Porphyry Column: The Earliest Literary Allusion. *JRS* 81: 119–31.

Fowden, G. (1993). *Empire to Commonwealth: Consequences of Monotheism in Late Antiquity*. Princeton.

Fowden, G. (1994). The Last Days of Constantine: Oppositional Versions and Their Influence. *JRS* 84: 146–70.

Frend, W. H. C. (1952). *The Donatist Church: A Movement of Protest in Roman North Africa*. Oxford.

Fried, J. (2007). Donation of Constantine *and* Constitutum Constantini. Berlin.

Frier, B. W. and McGinn, T. A. J. (2004). *A Casebook on Roman Family Law*. Oxford.

Gagos, T. and Potter, D. S. (2006). Documents. In Potter, 45–74.

Gaisser, J. H. (2008). *The Fortunes of Apuleius and the Golden Ass: A Study in Transmission and Reception*. Princeton.

Gardner, I. and Lieu, S. (2004). *Manichaean Texts from the Roman Empire*. Cambridge.

Garnsey, P. (1988). *Famine and Food Supply in the Greco-Roman World: Responses to Risk and Crisis*. Cambridge.

Gascous, J. (1967). Le rescript d'Hispellum. *MEFR* 79: 600–59.

Gaudemet, J. (1947). La législation religeuse de Constantin. *Revue d'histoire de l'Église de France* 122: 25–61.

Gentili, G. V. (1999). *La villa romana di Piazza Amerina Palazzo Erculio*. Osimo.

Gerov, B. (1965). La carriera di Marciano generale di Gallieno. *Athenaeum* 43: 333–54.

Girardet, K. M. (2007). *Kaiser Konstantine der Grosse: Historische Leistung und Rezeption in Europa*. Bonn.

Girardet, K. M. (2010). *Der Kaiser und sein Gott: das Christentum im Denken und in der reliionpolitik Konstnatins des Grossen*. Berlin.

Goldsmith, R. (1987). *Premodern Financial Systems: A Historical Comparative Study*. Cambridge.

Goltz, A. and Schlange-Schöningen, H. (2008). *Konstantin der Große: Das Bild des Kaisers im Wandel der Zeiten*. Vienna.

Gordon, A. E. (1990). The Veil of Power: Emperors, Sacrificers, and Benefactors. In M. Beard and K. North eds., *Pagan Priests*. Pp. 201–31. London.

Grégoire, H. (1913). Les chrétiens et l'oracle de Didymes. In *Mélanges Holleaux* 81–91. Paris.

Grégoire, H. and Orgels, P. (1951). La passion de S. Théodote d'Ancyre, oeuvre du pseudo-Nil, et son noyau montaniste. *BZ* 44: 165–84.

Grierson, P., Mango, C., and Ševčenko, I. (1962). The Tombs and Obits of the Byzantine Emperors (337–1042); with an Additional Note. *Dumbarton Oaks Papers* 16: 1+3–63.

Grünewald, T. (1990). *Constantinus Maximus Augustus: Heerschaftspropaganda in der zeitgenössischen Überlieferung*. Historia Einzelschiften 64. Stuttgart.

Gutsfeld, A. (1998). Der Prätorianerpräfekt und der kaiserliche Hof im 4 Jahrhundert n. Chr. In Winterling, 75–102.

Gwynn, D. M. (2007). *The Eusebians: The Polemic of Athanasius and the Construction of the "Arian Controversy."* Oxford.

Halfmann, H. (1986). *Itinera principum: Geschichte und Typologie der Kaiserreisen im Römischen Reich*. Weisbaden.

Hall, S. G. (1985). The *Thalia* in Athanasius' Accounts. In R. C. Gregg, ed., *Arianism: Historical and Theological Reassessments*. Pp. 37–58. Philadelphia.

Halsberghe, G. H. (1972). *The Cult of Sol Invictus*. Leide.

Harker, A. (2008). *Loyalty and Dissidence in Roman Egypt: The Case of the* Acta Alexandrinorum. Cambridge.

Harl, K. (1996). *Coinage in the Roman Economy*. Baltimore.

Harper, K. (2011). *Slavery in the Late Roman World AD 275–425*. Cambridge.

Harries, J. (1999). *Law and Empire in Late Antiquity*. Cambridge.

Harries, J. (2010). Constantine the Lawgiver. In McGill, Sogno, and Watts, 73–92.

Harries, J. and Wood, I., eds. (1993). *The Theodosian Code: Studies in the Imperial Law of Late Antiquity*. London.

Harris, W. V. (2009). *Dreams and Experience in Classical Antiquity*. Cambridge, MA.

Hartmann, U. (2001). *Das palmyrenische Teilreich*. Stuttgart.

Heather, P. (1991). *Goths and Romans, 332–489*. Oxford.

Heather, P. (1994). New Men for New Constantines. In Magdalino, P., ed., *New Constantines*. Pp. 11–33. Aldershot.

Heather, P. (1998). Senators and Senates. In Cameron, A. and Garnsey, P., eds., *The Cambridge Ancient History*, 2nd ed., vol. 13, pp. 184–210. Cambridge.

Heck, E. (2009). Constantin und Lactanz in Trier—Chronologisch. *Historia* 58: 118–30.

Hekster, O. (1999). The City of Rome in Late Imperial Ideology: The Tetrarchs, Maxentius and Constantine. *Mediterraneo Antico* 2: 717–48.

Holum, K. G. (2005). The Classical City in the Sixth Century: Survival and Transformation. In M. Maas, ed., *The Cambridge Companion to the Age of Justinian*. Pp. 87–112. Cambridge.

Hopkins, K. (1978). The Political Power of Eunuchs. In K. Hopkins, ed., *Conquerors and Slaves: Sociological Studies in Roman History,* vol. 1, pp., 172–96. Cambridge.

Hopkins, K. (1993). Novel Evidence for Roman Slavery. *Past and Present* 138: 3–27.

Huebner, S.R. (2007). "Brother-Sister Marriage" in Roman Egypt: A Curiosity of Humankind or a Widespread Family Strategy. *JRS* 97: 21–49

Humphress, C. (2006). Civil Law and Social Life. In Lenski, 205–25.

Hunt, E. D. (1982). *Holy Land Pilgrimage in the Later Roman Empire, AD 312–460.* Oxford.

Hunt, E. D. (2011). "Fellow Servants of God": Roman Emperor and Christian Bishop in the Age of Constantine. In Richardson and Santangelo, 291–311.

Jones, A. H. M. (1949). *Constantine and the Conversion of Europe.* London.

Jones, A. H. M. (1964). *The Later Roman Empire 284–602: A Social, Economic and Administrative Survey.* Oxford.

Jones, A. H. M. and Skeat, T. C. (1954). Notes on the Constantinian Documents in Eusebius' *Life of Constantine. JEH* 5: 196–200.

Jonkers, E. J. (1954). *Acta et symbola conciliorum quae saeculo quarto habita sunt.* Leiden.

Kannengiesser, C. (1970). Où et quand Arius composa-t-il la Thalie. *Kyriakon: Festschrift J. Quasten* 1 Pp. 346–51. Münster.

Kannengiesser, C. (1983). Arius and the Arians. *Theological Studies* 44: 456–75. Also in *Arius and Athanasius: Two Alexandrian Theologians* (Brookfield, Vt., 1991), chap. 2.

Kannengiesser, C. (1986). Athanasius of Alexandria vs. Arius: The Alexandrian Crisis. In Pearson, B. A. and Goehring, J. E. eds., *The Roots of Egyptian Christianity.* Pp. 204–15. Philadelphia. Also in *Arius and Athanasius: Two Alexandrian Theologians* (Brookfield, Vt., 1991), chap. 12.

Kannengiesser, C. (1990). Alexander and Arius of Alexandria: The Last Ante-Nicene Theologians. In *Miscelánea En Homenaje Al P. Antonio Orbe Compostellanum* 34, nos. 1–2, pp. 391–403. Santiago de Compestella, 1990; also in *Arius and Athanasius* (Brookfield, Vt., 1991), chap. 4.

Keegan, J. (1976). *The Face of Battle: A Study of Agincourt, Waterloo, and the Somme.* London.

Kelly, C. (2006). Bureaucracy and Government. In Lenski, 183–204.

Kettler, F. H. (1936). Die melitianische Streit in Ägypten. *Zeitschrift für die neutestamentliche Wissenschaft* 35: 155–93.

König, I. (1987). *Origo Constantini.* Trier.

Kovács, P. (2009). *Marcus Aurelius' Rain Miracle and the Marcomannic Wars.* Leiden.

Kuhoff, W. (2001) *Diokletian und die Epoche der Tetrarchie: Das römische Reich zwischen Krisenbewaltigung und Neuaufbau (284–313 n. Chr.).* Frankfurt.

Labrousse, M. (1995). *Optat de Milève, Traité contre les Donatistes,* vol. 1. Sources Chrétiennes no. 412. Paris.

Lancel, S. (1991). *Actes de la conférence de Carthage en 411,* vol. 4. Sources Chrétiennes no. 373. Paris.

Lane Fox, R. J. (1986). *Pagans and Christians.* London.

Lang, U. M. (2000). The Christological Controversy at the Synod of Antioch in 268/9. *JTS* 51: 54–80.

Langenfeld, H. (1977). *Christianisierungspolitik und Sklavengesetzgebung der römischen Kaiser non Konstantin bis Theodosius II.* Bonn.

Lathoud, D. (1924). La consecration et la dédicace de Constantinople I. *Echos D'Orient* 23: 289–314.

Lathoud, D. (1925). La consecration et la dédicace de Constantinople II. *Echos D'Orient* 24: 180–201.

Lauffer, S. (1971). *Diokletians Preisedikt.* Berlin.

Leadbetter, B. (1998). The Illegitimacy of Constantine and the Birth of the Tetrarchy. In Lieu, S. and Montserrat, D., eds., *Constantine: History, Historiography, and Legend.* Pp. 74–85. London.

Leadbetter, B. (2009). *Galerius and the Will of Diocletian*. London.

Lee, A. D. (2006). Traditional Religions. In Lenski, 159–78.

Lenski, N., ed. (2006). *The Cambridge Companion to the Age of Constantine*. Cambridge.

Lenski, N. (2008). Evoking the Pagan Past: *Instinctu Divinitatis* and Constantine's Capture of Rome. *JLA* 1: 204–57.

Lenski, N. (2011). Constantine and the Law of Slavery: *Libertas* and the Fusion of Roman and Christian Values. In G. Crifò, ed., *Atti dell'Accademia Romanistica Costantiniana XVIII 2007*. Pp. 253–60. Perugia.

Lieberman, S. (1944). Roman Legal Institutions in Early Rabbinics and in the *Acta Martyrum*. *JQR* 35: 1–57.

Liebeschuetz, W. (1979). *Continuity and Change in Roman Religion*. Oxford.

Lieu, S. (1998). From Legend to History: The Medieval and Byzantine Transformation of Constantine's *Vita*. In Lieu, S. and Montserrat, D. eds., *Constantine: History, Historiography and Legend*. Pp. 136–76. London.

Lindner, A. (1987). *The Jews in Roman Imperial Legislation*. Detroit.

Lockwood, R. (1989). Potens and Factiosa Femina: Women, Martyrs and Schism in Roman North Africa. *AugStud* 20: 165–82.

Lucien-Brun, X. (1970). Minervine, épouse ou concubine. *Bulletin de l'Association Guillaume Budé* 391–406.

MacMullen, R. (1969). Constantine and the Miraculous. *GRBS* 9: 81–96. Also in MacMullen, R. *Changes in the Roman Empire* (Princeton, 1990): 107–16.

Maier, J.-L. (1987). *Le dossier du donatisme*, vol. 1, *Des origines à la mort de Constance II (303–361)*, Texte und Untersuchungen zur Geschichte der alchristlichen Literatur 134. Berlin.

Malherbe, A. (1988). *Ancient Epistolary Theorists*. SBL Sources for Biblical Study 19. Atlanta.

Maraval, P. (1990). *La passion inédite de S. Athénogène de Pédachthoé en Cappadoce (BHG 197b)*, Subsidia Hagiographica 75. Brussels.

Marlowe, E. (2006). Framing the Sun: The Arch of Constantine and the Roman Cityscape. *Art Bulletin* 88: 223–42.

Marlowe, E. (2011). "*Liberator urbis suae*: Constantine and the Ghost of Maxentius." In Ewald, B. C. and Noreña, C. eds., *The Emperor and Rome: Space, Representation and Ritual*. Yale Classical Studies 35: 199–215. Cambridge.

Marti, R. (2007). Konstantin der Große in der orthodoxen slavischen Welt. In Girardet, 133–48.

Martin, D. (2004). *Inventing Superstition from the Hippocratics to the Christians*. Cambridge, MA.

Matthews, J. F. (2000). *Laying Down the Law: A Study of the Theodosian Code*. New Haven.

Matthews, J. F. (2007). *The Roman Empire of Ammianus*. Rpr. with a new introduction. Ann Arbor.

Mattingly, D. J. (2010). *Imperialism, Power, and Identity: Experiencing the Roman Empire* (Miriam S. Balmuth Lectures in Ancient History and Archaeology). Princeton.

Mayer, E. (2002). *Rom ist dort wo der Kaiser ist. Untersuchungen zu den Staatsdenkmälern des dezentralisierten Reiches von Diocletian bis zu Theodosius II*. Bonn.

McGill, S., Sogno, C., and Watts, E., eds. (2010). *From the Tetrarchs to the Theodosians: Later Roman History and Culture, 284–450 CE*. Yale Classical Studies 34. Cambridge.

McGinn, T. A. J. (1999). The Social Policy of Constantine in *CTh* 4.6.3. *Tijdschrift voor rechtsgeschiedenis* 67: 57–73.

McLaren, A. E. (2001). Marriage by Abduction in Twentieth Century China. *Modern Asian Studies* 35.4: 953–84.

Metzler, K. and Simon, F. (1991). *Ariana et Athanasiana: Studien zur Überlieferung und zu philologische Problemen der Werke des Athanasius von Alexandrien*, Abhandlungen der Rheinisch-Westfälischen Akademie der Wissenschaften 83. Opladen.

Mierau, H. J. (2008). Karl IV. Im Zeichen des "wahren" Kreuzes. Konstantin als Vorbild für einen spätmittelalterlichen Kaiser. In Goltz and Schlange-Schöningen, 109–38.

Miethke, J. (2008). Die "Konstantinische Schenkung" in der mittelalterlichen Diskussion. Ausgewälte Kapitel einer vershlungenen Rezeptionsgeschichte. In Goltz and Schlange-Schöningen, 35–108.

Millar F. (1983). Empire and City from Augustus to Julian: Obligations, Excuses and Status. *JRS* 73:76–96; also in Millar (2004): 336–71.

Millar F. (1992a). *The Emperor in the Roman World*. Rev. ed. London.

Millar F. (1992b). The Jews in the Greco-Roman Diaspora between Paganism and Christianity A.D. 312–438. In Lieu, J., North, J., and Rajak, T., *The Jews among Pagans and Christians in the Roman Empire*. Pp. 97–123. London; also in Millar (2006): 432–56.

Millar F. (1993). *The Roman Near East 31 BC–AD 337*. Cambridge, MA.

Millar F. (2004). *Rome, the Greek World and the East*, vol. 2: *Government Society and Culture in the Roman Empire*. Chapel Hill.

Millar F. (2006). *Rome, the Greek World and the East*, vol. 3: *The Greek World, the Jews and the East*. Chapel Hill.

Millar F. (2007). *A Greek Roman Empire: Power and Belief under Theodosius II (408–450)*. Berkeley.

Mitchell, S. (1982). The Life of Saint Theodotus of Ancyra. *AS* 35: 93–113.

Mitchell, S. (1988). Maximinus and the Christians in A.D. 312: A New Latin Inscription. *JRS* 78: 105–24.

Mitchell, S. (1999). The Cult of Theos Hypsistos between Pagans, Jews and Christians. In Athanassiadi, P. and Frede, M., eds., *Pagan Monotheism in Late Antiquity*. Pp. 81–148. Oxford.

Mitchell, S. (2007). *A History of the Later Roman Empire AD 284–261*. Oxford.

Mitchell, S. (2010). Further Thoughts on the Cult of Theos Hypsistos. In Mitchell, S. and Van Nuffelen, P., eds., *One God: Pagan Monotheism in the Roman Empire*. Pp. 167–208. Cambridge.

Morgan, T. (2007). *Popular Morality in the Early Roman Empire*. Cambridge.

Mouritsen, H. (2011). *The Freedman in the Roman World*. Cambridge.

Musurillo, H. (1972). *Acts of the Christian Martyrs*. Oxford.

Neesen, L. (1981). Die Entwicklung der Leistungen der Ämter (munera et honores) im römischen Kaiserreich des zweiten bis vierten Jahrhunderts. *Historia* 30: 203–35.

Nicasie. M. J. (1998). *Twilight of Empire: The Roman Army from the Reign of Diocletian until the Battle of Adrianople*. Amsterdam.

Nicolson, O. P. (1999). *Civitas Quae Adhuc Sustenat Omnia*: Lactantius and the City of Rome. In Klingshirn, W. E. and Vessey, M., eds., *The Limits of Ancient Christianity: Essays on Late Antique Thought and Culture in Honor of R.A. Markus*. Pp. 7–25. Ann Arbor.

Nicolson, O. P. (2000). Constantine's Vision of the Cross. *Vigiliae Christianae* 54: 309–23.

Nisbet, R. G. M. (1975). Virgil's Fourth Eclogue: Easterners and Westerners. *BICS* 22: 59–78; also in Nisbet, R. G. M., *Collected Papers on Latin Literature* (Oxford, 1995) (edited by S. J. Harrison): 47–75.

Nixon, C. E. V. and Rodgers, B. S. (1994). *In Praise of Later Roman Emperors*. Berkeley.

Noethlichs, K. L. (1982). Zur Entstehung der Diözesan als Mittelinstanz des spätrömischen Verwaltungssystems. *Historia* 31: 70–81.

Noethlichs, K. L. (1998). Strukturen und Funktionen des spätantiken Kaiserhofs. In Winterling, 13–49.

Nollé, J. (2005). Boars, Bears and Buds: Farming in Asia Minor and the Protection of Men, Animals and Crops. In Mitchell, S. and Katsari, C., eds., *Patterns in the Economy of Roman Asia Minor.* Pp. 53–82. Swansea.

Nollé, J. (2007). *Kleinasiatische Losorakel: Astragal- und Alphabetchresmologien der hochkaiserzeitlichen Orakelrenaissance.* Munich.

Noreña, C. F. (2011). *Imperial Ideals in the Roman West: Representation, Circulation, Power.* Cambridge.

Noy, D. (2011). Jewish Priests and Synagogue Officials in the Greco-Roman Diaspora of Late Antiquity. In Richardson and Santangelo, 313–32.

Odahl, C. M. (2010). *Constantine and the Christian Empire.* 2nd ed. London.

Oliver, J. H. (1989). *Greek Constitutions of Early Roman Emperors from Inscriptions and Papyri.* Memoirs of the American Philosophical Association n. 178. Philadelphia.

Opitz, H. G (1934a). *Athanasius Werke 2.2 Urkunden zur Geschichte des arianischen Streites 318–328.* Berlin, 1934.

Opitz, H. G. (1934b). Die Zeitfolge des arianischen Streites von den Anfängen bis zum Jahre 328. *Zeitschrift für die neutestamentliche Wissenschaft* 33: 131–59.

Oppenheimer, A. (1998). Jewish Penal Authority in Roman Judaea. In Goodman, M., ed., *Jews in a Greco-Roman World*, vol. 3, pt. 1., pp. 181–91. Oxford.

Palanque, J.-R. (1938). Chronologie Constantinienne. *REA* 40: 241–50.

Parmentier, L. (ed. Hansen, G.C.) (1998). Theodoret, *Kirchengeschichte,* GCS n.f. 5. Berlin.

Parsons, P. (2007). *City of the Sharp-Nosed Fish: Greek Papyri beneath the Egyptian Sand Reveal a Long-Lost World.* London.

Parvis, S. (2000). The Canons of Ancyra and Caesarea (314): Lebon's Thesis Revisited. *JTS* 52: 625–36.

Parvis, S. (2006). *Marcellus of Ancyra and the Lost Years of the Arian Controversy 325–345.* Oxford.

Paschoud, F. (1971). Zosime 2,29 et la version païenne de la conversion de Constantin. *Historia* 20: 334–53.

Pierce, P. (1989). The Arch of Constantine: Propaganda and Ideology in Late-Roman Art. *Art History* 12: 387–418.

Piganiol, A. (1932). *L'Empereur Constantine.* Paris.

Pococke, R. (1803). *Travels of Richard Pococke F.R.S. through Egypt Interspersed with Remarks and Observations by Captain Norden.* Philadelphia.

Pohlkamp, W. (2007). Konstantin der Große und die Stadt Rom im Speigel der römischen Silvester-Akten (Actus Silvestri). In Girardet, 87–112.

Pohlsander, H.A. (1984). Crispus: Brilliant Career and Tragic End. *Historia* 33: 79–106.

Pohlsander, H.A. (1993). Constantia. *Ancient Society* 24: 151–67.

Pond Rothman, M. S. (1977). The Thematic Organization of the Panel Reliefs on the Arch of Galerius. *AJA* 81: 174–93.

Potter, D. (1989). Recent Inscriptions from Flat Cilicia. *JRA* 2: 305–12.

Potter, D. (1990). *Prophecy and History in the Crisis of the Roman Empire: A Historical Commentary of the Thirteenth Sibylline Oracle.* Oxford.

Potter, D. (1993). Martyrdom as Spectacle. In Scodel, R. ed. *Theater and Society in the Classical World.* Pp. 53–88. Ann Arbor.

Potter, D. (1994). *Prophets and Emperors: Human and Divine Authority from Augustus to Theodosius.* Cambridge, MA.

Potter, D. (1998). Procurators in Asia and Dacia under Marcus Aurelius: A Case Study of Imperial Initiative in Government. *ZPE* 123: 270–4.

Potter, D. (2004). *The Roman Empire at Bay AD 180–395*. London.

Potter, D. (2005). *Literary Texts and the Roman Historian*. Rev. ed. London.

Potter, D. (2006). *A Companion to the Roman Empire*. Oxford.

Potter, D. (2009). Constantine and Fausta. In Harvey, P. and Conybeare, C. eds., *Maxima Debetur Magistro Reverentia: Essays on Rome and the Roman Tradition in Honor of Russell T. Scott*. Pp. 137–55. Como.

Potter, D. (2010a). The Unity of the Roman Empire. In McGill, Sogno, and Watts, 13–32.

Potter, D. (2010b). Constantine and the Gladiators. CQ 60: 596-606.

Potter, D. and Damon, C. (1999). The *Senatus Consultum de Cn. Pisone patre*. AJP 120: 14–41.

Potter, D. and Mattingly, D. J. (2010). *Life, Death and Entertainment in the Roman Empire*. Rev. ed. Ann Arbor.

Poulsen, F. (1945). Talking, Weeping and Bleeding Sculptures: A Chapter in the History of Religious Fraud. *Acta Archaeologica* 16: 178–95.

Quednau, R. (2008). Ein römischer Kabinettschrank mit Szenen Konstantins des Großen für Kaiser Leopold I. in Wein. In Goltz and Schlange-Schöningen, 161–210.

Rapp, C. (2005). *Holy Bishops in Late Antiquity: The Nature of Christian Leadership in an Age of Transition*. Berkeley.

Rea, J. (1979). P.Oxy. XXXIII 2673.2: πύλη to ὕλην. ZPE 35: 128.

Rees, R. (1993). Images and Image: A Re-examination of Tetrarchic Ideology. *Greece and Rome* 40: 181–200.

Rees, R. (2002). *Layers of Loyalty in Latin Panegyric AD 289–307*. Oxford.

Remijsen, S. and Clarysse, W. (2008). Incest or Adoption? Brother-Sister Marriage in Roman Egypt Revisited. *JRS* 98: 53–61.

Richardson, J. H. and Santangelo, F. (2011). *Priests and State in the Roman World*. Stuttgart.

Richlin, A. (2006). Sexuality in the Roman Empire. In Potter, 327–53.

Ritter, A. M. (1978). Arianismus. *Theologische Realenzyklopädie*, 3: 692–719. Berlin.

Rives, J. B. (1999). The Decree of Decius and the Religion of Empire. *JRS* 89: 135–54.

Robert, L. (1948). Épigrammes relatives a des gouverneurs *Hellenica* 4: 35–114. Paris.

Robert, L. (1969). Théophane de Mytilène à Constantinople. *CRAI* 42–64; also in *Opera Minora Selecta* 5: 561–83.

Robert, L. (1971). Une oracle grave à Oinoanda. *CRAI* 597–619; also in *Opera Minora Selecta* 5: 617–39.

Robert, L. (1982). Une Vision de Pérpetue Martyre. *CRAI*: 228–276; also in *Opera Minora Selecta* 5: 791–839.

Rodgers, B. S. (1980). Constantine's Pagan Vision. *Byzantion* 50: 259–78.

Rohrbacher, D. (2002). *The Historians of Late Antiquity*. London.

Rouché, C. (1981). Rome, Aphrodisias and the Third Century. *JRS* 71: 103–20.

Rouché, C. (1989). *Aphrodisias in Late Antiquity*. Journal of Roman Studies Monograph 5. London.

Rubin, Z. (1980). *Civil War Propaganda and Historiography*. Brussels.

Ruschenbusch, E. (1977). Diokletians Währungsreform vom 1.9.301. ZPE 26: 193–210.

Saradi, H. (1995). The Kallos of the Byzantine City: The Development of a Rhetorical Topos and Historical Reality. *Gesta* 34: 37–57.

Sauer, E. (1998). M. Annius Florianus: Ein Drei-Monate-Kaiser und die ihm zu Ehren aufgestellten Steinmonument (276 n. Chr.). *Historia* 47: 174–203.

Scheid, J. (2003). *An Introduction to Roman Religion*. Bloomington.

Scheidel W. and Freisen, S. J. (2009). The Size of the Economy and the Distribution of Income in the Roman Empire. *JRS* 99: 61–91.

Scherrer, P. (2000). *Ephesus; The New Guide*, tr. L. Bier and G. M. Luxon. Istanbul.

Schlinkert, D. (1998). Dem Kaiser folgen. Kaiser, Senatsadel und höfische Funktionselite (*comites consistoriani*) von der "Tetrarchie" Diokletians bis zum Ende der konstantinischen Dynastie. In Winterling, 133–59.

Schmitt, O. (2001). Stärke, Struktur und Genese des comitatensischen Infanterienumerus. *Bonner Jahrbücher* 201: 92–111.

Schwartz, E. (1905a). Die Quellen über den melitianischen Streit. *Nachrichten von der k. Gesellschaft der Wissenschaften zu Göttingen, phil.-hist. Klasse* (1905), 164–87; also in E. Schwartz, *Gesammelte Schriften*, vol. 3 (Berlin, 1959), 89–100.

Schwartz, E. (1905b). Die Dokumente des arianischen Streits bis 325. *Nachrichten von der k. Gesellschaft der Wissenschaften zu Göttingen, phil.-hist. Klasse* (1905), 257–99; also in E. Schwartz, *Gesammelte Schriften*, vol. 3 (Berlin, 1959), 117–68.

Schwartz, E.(1908). Das antiochenische Synoldalschreiben von 325. *Nachrichten von der k. Gesellschaft der Wissenschaften zu Göttingen, phil.-hist. Klasse*, 305–79; also in *Gesammelte Schriften*, vol. 3 (Berlin, 1959), 169–87 (reprinting pp. 354–59; 365–74).

Seeck, O. (1891). Die sogenannte Edikt von Mailand. *Zeitschrift für Kirchengeschichte* 12: 381–6.

Seeck, O. (1895–1920). *Geschichte des Untergangs der antiken Welt*. 6 vols. Berlin.

Seeck, O. (1908). Das Leben des Dichters Porphyrius. *RhM* 65: 267–82.

Seeck, O. (1919). *Regesten der Kaiser und Päpste*. Stuttgart.

Seston, W. (1946). *Dioclétien et la tétrarchie*. Paris.

Shaw, B. D. (1996). Review of J. Evans Grubbs, *Law and Family in Late Antiquity: The Emperor Constantine's Marriage Legislation*. *BMCR* 8: 12.

Shean, J. F. (2010). *Soldiering for God: Christianity and the Roman Army*. Leiden.

Simon, D. V. (1977). *Konstantinisches Kaiserrecht: Studien anhand der Reskriptenpraxis und des Schenkungsrechts*. Frankfurt.

Skeat, T.C. (1964). *Papyri from Panopolis in the Chester Beatty Library Dublin (Chester Beatty Monographs I)*. Dublin.

Smith, R. B. E. (2007a). The Imperial Court of the Late Roman Empire c. AD 300–c. AD 450. In A. J. S. Spawforth, ed., *The Court and Court Society in Ancient Monarchies*. Pp. 157–232. Cambridge.

Smith, R. B. E. (2007b). A Lost Historian of Alexander "Descended for Alexander" and Read by Julian? Praxagoras of Athens Reviewed in Light of Attic Epigraphy. *Historia* 56: 356–80.

Smith, R. B. E. (2011). "Measures of Difference: The Fourth Century Transformation of the Roman Imperial Court." In D. S. Potter and R. J. A. Talbert, eds., *Classical Courts and Courtiers (AJP Special Issue)*. *AJP* 132: 125–52.

Smith, R. R. R. (1997). The Public Image of Licinius I: Portrait Sculpture and Imperial Ideology in the Early Fourth Century. *JRS* 87: 187–94.

Sporn, K. (2004). Kaiserliche Selbstdarstellung ohne Resonanz? Zur Rezeption tetrarchischer Bildsprache in der zeitgenössischen Privatkunst. In Boschung and Eck (2004): 381–99.

Ste. Croix, G. E. M. de. (2006). *Christian Persecution, Martyrdom, Orthodoxy*. Whitby, M. and Streeter, J., eds. Oxford.

Stead, J. C. (1973). "Eusebius" and the Council of Nicaea. *JTS* 24: 83–100.

Stein, E. (1959). *Histoire du Bas-Empire*, vol. 1. Paris.

Stephenson, P. (2010). *Constantine: Roman Emperor. Christian Victor*. London.

Stevenson, J. (1987). *A New Eusebius: Documents Illustrating the History of the Church to A.D. 337*. 2nd rev. ed. London.

Sutherland, C. V. H. and Carson, R. A. G. (1966). *The Roman Imperial Coinage 7 Constantine and Licinius A.D. 313-337*. London.

Sutherland, C. V. H. and Carson, R. A. G. (1967). *The Roman Imperial Coinage 6 from Diocletian's Reform (A.D. 294) to the Death of Maximinus (A.D. 313)*. London.

Syme, R. (1971). *Emperors and Biography: Studies in the* Historia Augusta. Oxford.

Talbert, R. J. A. (2010). *Rome's World: The Peutinger Map Reconsidered*. Cambridge.

Tate, J. C. (2008). Codification of Late Roman Inheritance Laws: *Fideicommissa* in the Theodosian Code. *Tijdschrift voor Rechsgeschiednis* 76: 237-48.

Telfer, W. (1946). When Did the Arian Controversy Begin? *JTS* 47: 129-42.

Thomas, G. S. R. (1973). L'Abdication de Dioclétien. *Byzantion* 43: 229-47.

Tilley, M. A. (1996). *Donatist Martyr Stories: The Church in Conflict in Roman North Africa*. Liverpool.

Torp, H. (1953). The Vatican Excavations and the Cult of St. Peter. *Acta Archaeologica* 24: 27-66.

van Berchem, D. (1952). *L'armée de Dioclétien et la réforme constantinienne*. Paris.

Van Dam, R. (2007). *The Roman Revolution of Constantine*. Cambridge.

Van Dam, R. (2011). *Remembering Constantine at the Milvian Bridge*. Cambridge.

Virvoulet, C. (1985). *Famines et émeutes à Rome des origines de la Rèpublique à la mort de Néron*. Collection de l'Ecole francaise de Rome 87. Rome.

von Haehling, R. (1978). *Die Religionszugehörigkeit der hohen Amtsträger des Römischen Reiches seit Constantins I. Alleinherrschaft bis zum Ende der Theodosianischen Dynastie: (324-450 bzw. 455 n. Chr.)*. Bonn.

von Hesberg, H. (2004). Residenzstädte und ihre höfische Infrastruktur—traditionelle und neue Raumkonzepte. In Boschung and Eck, 133-67.

Wallace-Hadrill, A. (1982). *Civilis Princeps*: Between Citizen and King. *JRS* 72: 32-48.

Wallraff, M. (2001). *Christus verus sol: Sonnenverehrung und Christentum in der Spätantike*. Münster.

Webb, P. H. (1933). *The Roman Imperial Coinage 5.2*. London.

Weber, G. (2000). *Kaiser, Träume und Visionen in Prinzipat und Spätantike*. Historia Einzelschriften 143. Stuttgart.

Weiss, P. (2003). The Vision of Constantine. *JRA* 16: 237-59.

Werner, C. (2004). The Rise of Nonconsensual Bride Kidnapping in Post-Soviet Kazakhstan. In P. J. Luong, ed., *The Transformation of Central Asia: States and Societies from Soviet Rule to Independence*. Pp. 59-89. Ithaca.

Wilkinson, K.W. (2009). Palladas and the Age of Constantine. *JRS* 99: 36-60.

Wilkinson, K.W. (2010). Palladas and the Foundation of Constantinople. *JRS* 100: 179-94.

Whittaker, M. (1984). *Jews and Christians: Graeco-Roman Views*. Cambridge.

Wiles, M. (1962). In Defense of Arius. *JTS* 13: 339-47.

Williams, R. (1985). The Quest of the Historical *Thalia*. In R. C. Gregg, ed., *Arianism: Historical and Theological Reassessments*. Pp. 19-21. Philadelphia.

Williams, R. (1987). *Arius: Heresy and Tradition*. London.

Wilson, R. J. A. (1983). *Piazza Amerina*. London.

Winterling, A. (1998). Comitatus: *Beiträge zur Erforschung des spätantiken Kaiserhofes*. Berlin.

Wiśniewski, R. (2011). Lucilla and the Bone: Remarks on an Early Testimony to the Cult of Relics. *JLA* 4: 157-61.

Woof, G. (2000). *Becoming Roman: The Origins of Provincial Civilization in Gaul*. Cambridge.

Woods, D. (1992). Two Notes on the Great Persecution. *JTS* 43: 128-34.

Wrightman, E. M. (1970). *Roman Trier and the Treveri*. London.

INDEX